EARLY REVIEWS

Like *Roots, The Warmth of Other Suns*, and *The 1619 Project*, Lise Pearlman's book *Huey P. Newton's Family: Roots of a Revolutionary Suicide* traces the journey of a black family. The book chronicles this journey from South East Arkansas and North East Louisiana to the San Francisco Bay Area during WWII. Their engagement gave birth to the Black Panther Party and the rest is history. This book is a must read for those seeking to understand the struggle for social, political and economic justice.
  ELIHU M. HARRIS, ESQ.
  Former Oakland Mayor, Assemblymember and
  Chancellor of the Peralta Community College District

Huey P. Newton's Family: Roots of a Revolutionary Suicide is rich in Black history and the numerous challenges faced by families within the Black community. It demonstrates the incredible leadership within the Newton family and the inequities they experienced. The family was able to overcome pervasive problems while also demonstrating a commitment to humanitarianism. With this book, Lise Pearlman has expertly captured the essence of the Newton Family.
  ARIF KHATIB
  Author, filmmaker and founder of the
  Multi-Ethnic Sports Hall of Fame

Library of Congress Cataloging-in-Publication Data

Names: Pearlman, Lise A., 1949- author
Title: Huey P. Newton's family : roots of a revolutionary suicide / by Lise Pearlman.
Description: Berkeley, California : Regent Press, [2025] | Includes bibliographical references and index. | Summary: ""Huey P. Newton's Family: Roots of a Revolutionary Suicide" was undertaken by the author at the request of Prof. Emeritus Melvin Newton (older brother of Huey Newton), Melvin's daughter Tracy Newton and son David Lautaro Newton. The project involved extensive family interviews and research to cover the background of Melvin and Huey P. Newton's parents, Walter and Armelia Newton, the tribal nature of family interactions, the lives of their siblings and other close relatives, their seven children and the collective family impact on Walter and Armelia's youngest son, iconic Black militant Huey P. Newton, who co-founded the Black Panther Party. Newton wrote in his autobiography Revolutionary Suicide -- and testified to a captivated audience in his 1968 death penalty trial -- that an understanding of the treatment of African-Americans since colonial days was necessary to understand who he was and where he came from. That testimony had a profound impact on the jury that had Newton's life in their hands, particularly affecting middleclass Black banker David Harper, who became the jury's revolutionary choice for foreman. This book puts Huey P. Newton's experiences and those of his family into historical context. It starts with Walter Newton's heritage and his wife Armelia Johnson Newton's family background from their primarily African roots: to their Caucasian ancestors; to the slavery of their African-American ancestors; to their upbringing in the segregated South; their hard-scrabble adult lives in Arkansas and Louisiana in the early 20th century; their move West to Oakland as part of the Great Migration; the racism they faced in California; Huey and Melvin Newton's disparate school experiences; Huey's teenage years: his involvement in the Afro-American Association's informal studies of Black authors; Melvin's role in creating a pioneering ethnic studies program at Oakland's Merritt College; the formation of the Black Panther Party; the shootout with two Oakland police officers for which the Panther leader was arrested and that became the focus of international attention to the treatment of Black men by the American justice system; Huey Newton's historic 1968 death penalty trial; his Mafia phase; his subsequent Cuban exile; his frayed and reestablished family relationships: his death; the murder trial of his assailant; and Huey Newton's extraordinary lasting impact"-- Provided by publisher.
Identifiers: LCCN 2025031634 (print) | LCCN 2025031635 (ebook) | ISBN 9781587907098 paperback | ISBN 9781587907104 hardback | ISBN 9781587907296 e-book
Subjects: LCSH: Newton, Huey P. | Newton, Huey P.--Family | Newton family | Black Panther Party--Biography | African American political activists--Biography | Political activists--United States--Biography | African American families
Classification: LCC E185.97.N48 P43 2025 (print) | LCC E185.97.N48 (ebook)
LC record available at https://lccn.loc.gov/2025031634
LC ebook record available at https://lccn.loc.gov/2025031635

HUEY P. NEWTON'S FAMILY: ROOTS OF A REVOLUTIONARY SUICIDE

Lise Pearlman is also the acclaimed author of

THE SKY'S THE LIMIT:
People v. Newton, the REAL Trial of the 20th Century?
(2012)

AMERICAN JUSTICE ON TRIAL
People v. Newton
(2016)

WITH JUSTICE FOR SOME
Politically Charged Criminal Trials in the Early 20th Century That Helped Shape Today's America
(2017)

CALL ME PHAEDRA
The Life and Times of Movement Lawyer Fay Stender
(2018)

THE LINDBERGH KIDNAPPING
Suspect No. 1: The Man Who Got Away
(2020)

HUEY P. NEWTON'S FAMILY: ROOTS OF A REVOLUTIONARY SUICIDE

BY

LISE PEARLMAN

REGENT PRESS
Berkeley, California

Copyright © 2025 by Lise Pearlman

[Paperback]
ISBN 13: 978-1-58790-709-8
ISBN 10: 1-58790-709-7

[Hardback]
ISBN 13: 978-1-58790-710-4
ISBN 10: 1-58790-710-0

[E-Book]
ISBN 13: 978-1-58790-729-6
ISBN 10: 1-58790-729-1

Library of Congress Control Number: 2025031634

All rights reserved under International and Pan-American Copyright Conventions. No part of this book may be used or reproduced in any manner whatsoever without the written permission of the copyright holder, except in the case of brief quotations embodied in critical articles and reviews.

This book includes interviews conducted for *American Justice on Trial: People v. Newton*, an award-winning documentary released in 2022 by Open Eye Pictures (re-released June 2025 under the title *In the Crosshairs)*. www.justicemovie.com. Quotes from such interviews are published here with permission from Open Eye Pictures.

Newton family photos reprinted with permission of Melvin Newton, Tracy Newton, Maurice Newton, and David Lautaro Newton.

Photos and quotes from Huey Newton and Herman Blake, *Revolutionary Suicide* (New York: Harcourt, Brace & Jovanovich, 1973) reprinted with permission of Fredrika Newton, the Huey P. Newton Foundation, and David Lautaro Newton.

Every effort has been made to credit sources and obtain permission where appropriate. If we have inadvertently used or credited material or images inaccurately or without applicable consent and they do not qualify as Fair Use under the U.S. Copyright Act, or are not in the public domain, please contact the publisher so appropriate steps can be taken.

Printed in the U.S.A.
REGENT PRESS
Berkeley, California
www.regentpress.net

Contents

Dedication vi
Author's Note vii
Foreword ix
Members of the Newton Family Tree x

Introduction 1
I   Walter Newton's Heritage 9
II   Armelia Johnson's Background 33
III   Arkansas 51
IV   Back to Louisiana 61
V   Westward Bound 121
VI   The Push and Pull of Family 161
VII   A New Era 229
VIII   The Trial 283
IX   Freeing Huey 355
X   Frayed Relationships 391
XI   Homesickness and Fresh Starts 453
XII   Death and Rebirth Larger Than Life 489

Endnotes 529
Sources 589
Index 570
Acknowledgments 581

Dedication

This book is dedicated to my good friend Melvin Newton, who was kind enough to share with me over many delightful afternoons the remarkable story of his life and that of his extended family — and to encourage other family members to do the same. What qualities shine through most about Melvin are his wisdom, candor, insights and consummate humanity. Above all, Melvin exudes both fierce family pride and personal humility, a tribute to his upbringing.

Author's Note

Much has been written about black militant icon Huey Newton and the Black Panther Party he co-founded. Yet until now, there has never been a comprehensive, intimate look at the Newton family. This book aims to shed light on how the Newton family's ancestry and interrelationships helped shape Newton's thinking and life trajectory.

Director Stanley Nelson introduced his acclaimed 2015 documentary, "The Black Panthers: Vanguard of the Revolution," with the ancient Buddhist parable of the blind men and the elephant. Each had a different take on the strange animal they encountered, depending on the feature they touched. Nothing could be more apt to describe the many facets of both the Panther organization and its co-founder Huey Percy Newton — ranging from adulation by Black youths to condemnation by authorities as dangerous thugs.

What was it in his family background that propelled him to become an iconic proponent of Black empowerment and pride despite his serious flaws as a role model? My goal is to provide a different perspective on Huey Newton than any others to date by focusing on the unique relationships his parents and siblings had with the youngest child in the family.

Huey Newton never expected to live past thirty after joining forces with ex-felons to fight systemic racism in American society. Committed to what he and other Black Panthers called "the horse's brow," Huey's biggest challenge became avoiding the fate of so many inner-city victims of the drug culture. He considered their deaths "reactionary suicide." By that he meant the reactionary conditions in impoverished urban communities which precipitated what Huey's long-time friend and biographer David Hilliard called "self-murder."

Huey ended his life on the razor's edge between revolutionary and reactionary suicide. Here is my take on how that played out from the viewpoints of his close-knit family.

— LISE PEARLMAN
JUNE 2025

Foreword by Melvin Newton

The following story is a chronicle of an African American family's life and journey from the hopeless South to the disappointing West of the United States of America. It is the story of trials, tribulation, segregation, discrimination, and deprivation. An American story. More importantly, it is a story of defiance, self-respect, pride, dignity, hopes, dreams, and triumph. It is the story of the collective interplay within family, each member influencing the others in an organic manner under the leadership of a sweet, loving, humorous mother and an oak-tree-like father as wise as Solomon, as strong as Samson, as patient as Job, and as courageous as David.

— Melvin David Newton
June 2025

Members of the Newton Family Tree

All of the members of the Newton family named below are listed alphabetically in the index.

THE NEWTON FAMILY'S PATERNAL ANCESTRY

Alice Hilliard Newton Carter (1885-1973). Alice Hilliard, grandmother of Huey P. Newton, was raised in Uniontown, Alabama. She gave birth to her son Walter in 1903 when she was 17. She married Alabama farmer Ben Newton between 1910 and 1915. Ben was a widower with 10 children from his first marriage. Alice and Ben had two more children: Melvin Lee Newton in Alabama and Benjamin Newton in Arkansas. After Ben's death she married David Carter and moved to Chicago, Illinois.

Ben Newton (1863 or 1865 - 19??), Walter Newton's stepfather. widowed Alabama farmer, he had ten children from his first marriage before he married Alice Hilliard The couple moved to Arkansas with Walter sometime after the birth of their son Melvin Lee Newton in 1916. They had another son Benjamin in Arkansas. Ben Senior's death date was likely before World War II.

E.S. Newton (1906-2005) E.S. was Walter Newton's younger stepbrother, the youngest son of Ben Newton and his first wife Lucie. E.S. may have been born with the name Earl or Ennis Newton. He went by the initials E.S. but named two of his sons Earl by different mothers. In his 20s he lived with Walter and Armelia Newton's family in West Monroe, Louisiana.

Walter Hilliard Newton (1903-1974), father of Huey P. Newton, was the son of Alice Hilliard and, per DNA records, Solomon Simon. Walter was born in Uniontown, Alabama, and took the last name Newton when his mother married Ben Newton. The family moved to Arkansas sometime after the birth of his half-brother Melvin Lee Newton in 1916. Walter married Armelia Johnson in Arkansas in 1921.They had seven children (see Armelia Johnson Newton).

Solomon Simon (1883-1962). DNA evidence indicates he was Walter Hilliard 's father. He lived at the time with his family in Demopolis, Alabama, about 20 miles West of Uniontown where Alice Hilliard lived. His father was Joseph Simon (1853-1904), a mule trader born in Maryland, the youngest son of Elias and Caroline Simon, Jewish immigrants in 1845 from Hess-Darmstadt , Germany. Solomon had 7 siblings. He got a degree in chemistry, married in 1906 and moved to Georgia.

NEWTON FAMILY'S MATERNAL ANCESTRY – THE JOHNSON FAMILY

Isaac Burnett, the older brother of Estella McElroy Johnson, Huey and Melvin Newton's grandmother, was the son of Martha and Jordan Burnett, both of whom were likely born into slavery. Jordan Burnett's marriage certificate described him as mulatto (bi-racial). Isaac Burnett was married to Annie "Sissy" Burnett. He established in Monroe, Louisiana, a highly successful grocery store and café, where family members worked. The couple had no children of their own.

Estella McElroy Johnson O'Neal (1884-1970), Melvin and Huey's grandmother. The family called Estella "Mama Stella" or "Muzz." She was born in Oakwood, Texas, the daughter of Martha and Jordan Burnett. Unlike her brother Isaac, she took her stepfather Sam McElroy's last name when her mother remarried. Estella married John Johnson in 1905 in Monroe, Louisiana. The couple had four daughters: Armelia, born in 1906; twins Orell and Ozell, born in 1913; and Jessie Mae, born in 1915.

John Johnson (c.1880- 19??) was born in Carencro, Louisiana and moved to Monroe in his early 20s. He married Estella McElroy in Monroe in 1905. They had four daughters before they separated .He died in New Orleans.(see Estella Johnson).

Armelia Johnson Newton (1906-1985), Huey P. Newton's mother. Armelia was born in Monroe, Louisiana, the eldest daughter of John and Estella Johnson. She married Walter Newton in Parkdale, Arkansas in 1921. The couple had the first three of their seven children there: Lee Edward in 1923 named for his father's half-brother Melvin Lee Newton; Myrtle in 1925; and Leola in 1927. They moved to West Monroe where Walter, Jr. was born in 1929 and nicknamed "Sonny Man". The family then moved to Bastrop where Doris was born in 1930, followed by Melvin David Newton in 1937, also named for his father's half-brother. The family moved from there to Oak Grove, Louisiana ,where their last child, Huey Percy Newton, was born in 1942 and named for the late Louisiana Governor, Huey Pierce Long.

Jessie Mae Johnson Ento Smith (1915-82). Jessie was the youngest sister of Armelia Newton. Jessie Mae had a daughter Ruby Jewel Lawson in 1929 in Monroe, Louisiana who was raised by Estella Johnson. Jessie Mae moved to Chicago to work for several years before she married Eddie Ray Ento and moved to California in 1941 She divorced Eddie Ento in the early 1950s and later married again. Eddie and Jessie had a son Eddie Ray Ento, Jr. (1949-2025) whom Jessie Mae raised in Berkeley, California.

Ozell Johnson Ward (1913-55). Armelia's younger sister and twin of Orell Newton Wood. She married Jack Ward. The couple had three children: Jimmie, Opal Mae and Annie Mabel. Jimmie Ward (nicknamed "Big Jimmie") partnered with Melvin Newton to buy the Lamp Post in 1968.

Orell Johnson Woods (1913-63) Armelia's younger sister and twin of Ozell Newton. . She married Jake Woods. They had ten children: John, Roy Lee, Clyde, Glinda, Linda, Estella, Shirley, Edward Lee, Berniece and Jake, named for his father. Jake Jr. moved to the Bay area shortly after his mother died.

NEWTON SIBLINGS AND THEIR FAMILIES

Doris Burnice Newton Godfrey (1930-2023) married Glen Godfrey and had three children: son Glen (nicknamed Ricky); and daughters Debra Godfrey Gatling and Kathy Godfrey.

Huey Percy Newton (1942-1989), co-founder of the Black Panther Party, was the youngest of seven siblings (see Armelia Newton for their names and birth years). Huey was born in Oak Grove, Louisiana and raised in Oakland, California from the age of three.

He married twice and had three stepchildren. His first marriage was in 1974 to Gwen Fountaine who already had two children, Jessica and Ronnie. That marriage ended in divorce. Huey married Fredrika Slaughter in 1984, who already had a son, Kieron Slaughter.

Lee Edward Newton (1923-2007) ("Brotha"). Lee Edward was the oldest child of Walter and Armelia Newton. He had a daughter Ester Lee with Cleaster Simmons in 1943 who was adopted after her mother's death by Cleaster's Uncle and Aunt Arthur and Bertha Smith.. Years later, after moving to Oakland, California, Lee Edward married Katherine Jackson, who had been a neighbor of the Newton family back in Bastrop, Louisiana. Lee and Katherine had two children: Armelia and Lawrence Newton.

Armelia Newton, Lee Edward and Katherine Newton's daughter, had two sons, Antoine Newton and Lamont Newton.

Leola Newton Carr Johnson ("Nana") (1927-2011). Leola married James Carr. They had five children: William Carr, who died in infancy; James Dario Carr; Evoria Carr Hensen (1949-2006); Gwen Carr and DeAngela "Terrez" Carr. Leola divorced and married Milliard ("Mel") Johnson in 1981. Ten years Melvin's senior, Leola was given Melvin as a baby to look after. They developed a close lifelong bond. Among Leola's own Godchildren was Melvin's son Gregory.

Myrtle Newton Seymour (1925-2012) ("Sista"). Myrtle had three children: a son Jimmy in 1945; Patrick in 1947 with a different boyfriend, and then married James Seymour with whom she had a daughter Patricia in 1948 (see Patricia Seymour Johnson). Myrtle helped raise Huey and considered herself as a second mother to her youngest brother.

Patricia Seymour Johnson (1948-) daughter of James and Myrtle Johnson. Her daughter Kim Johnson accompanied grandmother Myrtle to Huey's retrials in 1971.

Melvin David Newton (1937-) Melvin was born in Bastrop, Louisiana and raised from the age of 7 in Oakland, California. He married twice. His first marriage in 1964-was to Joyce Thomas. They had two children, Gregory, born in 1965, and Tracy, born in 1969. After his divorce, Melvin married Barbarette Alcorn in 1975, who had a son Maurice Alcorn from her first marriage to Billy Maurice Alcorn. Melvin and Barbarette had two children, David Lautaro Newton, born in 1978 and Brianna Newton, born in 1986.

Walter Newton, Jr. ("Sonny Man") (1929-2007), Sonny Man was given his baby brother Huey to look after when born. He never married. He had four children: Demetrius Newton in 1963 with Alice Jackson; Myesha Newton in 1972 with Sara Frazee; and two children by Veronica Hernandez when he was in his sixties, Andre and Valencia Newton.

Esther Smith White (**1943-), Lee Edward's daughter who** added the "h" to her first name when she was raised by her maternal great uncle and aunt, Arthur and Bertha Smith. Esther married Lennon White and the couple had three children: Tony, Tonja and Trasean.

COUSINS MENTIONED IN THE BOOK

Eddie Ray Ento, Jr. (1949-2025), Aunt Jessie Mae and Eddie Ray Ento's son.

Earl Newton "Jake", E.S. Newton's second son named Earl Newton.

Jimmy Seymour ("Little Jimmy"), Myrtle's son who worked at the Lamp Post bar.

Lucy Newton Robinson, E.S. Newton's daughter

Jimmie Ward ("Big Jimmie"), Aunt Ozell's son who partnered with Melvin Newton to buy the Lamp Post bar in 1968.

Jake Wood, Aunt Orell's son.

Ruby Jewel Johnson, Aunt Jessie Mae's first born.

RELATIVES BY MARRIAGE TO THE NEWTONS

Steve Johnson, husband of Myrtle's daughter Patricia and father of Kim Johnson, He was one of the first recruits by Huey in the fall of 1966 to the Black Panther Party for Self-Defense as their driver following Oakland police around on their beat.

Barbarette Felicia Payton Alcorn Newton (1944-2014), second wife of Melvin Newton, mother of David Lautaro Newton and Brianna Newton and stepmother of Gregory and Tracy Newton. Barbarette's parents, Ezra and Evelyn Payton, had 6 children of whom Barbarette was the oldest. The Paytons divorced and remarried and had 8 more children between them. Mentioned in this book is Barbarette's sister Alfredetta ("Detta") Lindberg, who lived in Oakland until 1983.

Gwen Fountaine Newton, first wife of Huey Newton and mother of Jessica and Ronnie Newton

Fredrika Slaughter Newton, second wife of Huey Newton and mother of Kieron Slaughter.

Joyce Thomas Newton, first wife of Melvin Newton and mother of Gregory and Tracy Newton.

Lennon White, Esther Smith White's husband (Lee Edward Newton's daughter For children see Esther White). Huey recruited Lennon as one of the first members of the Black Panther Party for Self-Defense in the fall of 1966.

Huey Newton after his release from prison in 1970 in his penthouse apartment at 1200 Lakeshore Avenue, Oakland, focusing his telescope across Lake Merritt to the 10th floor of the Alameda County Courthouse where he had been jailed before and during his 1968 death penalty trial.

Introduction

AFTER his release from prison on August 5, 1970, 28-year-old Huey Newton, the co-founder of the Black Panther Party for Self-Defense, holed up in his new penthouse apartment overlooking Oakland's Lake Merritt. From his living room, he had a clear view of the Alameda County Courthouse where, in 1968, he had been held in isolation, likely headed for the gas chamber.

Now, unexpectedly on the outside, he set himself the task of completing his autobiography. Huey was free on bond pending retrial for manslaughter of an Oakland policeman. In late May 1970, the California Court of Appeal had surprised almost all observers by reversing his 1968 voluntary manslaughter conviction. That conviction itself had been widely viewed as quite lenient given that it resulted from a shootout on a West Oakland street with two policemen in which one officer died and another officer and Huey were both hospitalized with serious wounds.

The shootout occurred in the predawn of October 28, 1967. Later that same morning, as Huey lay in agony on a gurney on his way into life-saving surgery, he had been handcuffed and charged with the first-degree murder of Officer John Frey. When Huey went on trial in 1968, even his most ardent supporters considered the death penalty a foregone conclusion. They had never heard of a Black man accused of killing a White cop who did not himself wind up dead. That summer of 1968 the packed courthouse was surrounded each day by Black Panthers chanting "Revolution has come! Time to pick up the gun!" and "The Sky's the Limit!" Huey spent his days in the air-conditioned courtroom dressed like a professor in a turtleneck and suit or sport jacket, seated next to his attorneys. But, at night, back in his isolation cell on the tenth floor, he wore a jailhouse jumpsuit or stripped naked.

Huey's older siblings and his father came to the courthouse as often as they could to show their support, but the trial was too painful for his mother to bear. When it became Huey's turn to testify in his own defense, the courtroom was even more densely crammed with observers than usual. Many would-be spectators were left waiting in frustration among the huge crowd of demonstrators outside, eagerly awaiting updates on how their hero was faring inside the hall of justice.

Panther Chief of Staff David Hilliard was among those who obtained a coveted seat in the gallery that day, along with reporters from local, national and overseas news media, underground papers, Newton's family and a number of FBI and California undercover agents prepared for any disruption.

More than forty-five years later, Hilliard vividly recalled how bold and moving Huey was when his lawyer Charles Garry called him to the stand after veteran Judge Monroe Friedman surprisingly overruled prosecutor Lowell Jensen's vigorous objections. Jensen kept pointing out that the jury's job was to weigh the evidence presented by both sides regarding the circumstances in a predawn confrontation on October 28, 1967 that resulted in Frey's death and the wounding of his back-up officer. That evidence included conflicting accounts of witnesses for both sides. How did Newton react to being stopped by Officer Frey for outstanding tickets on the borrowed VW he was driving? Who fired a gun first, and where did the fatal shots come from? But there Huey was with his life on the line, given the green light by the judge to use the witness chair as a stage to lay out the 10-point political platform he and Seale had begun distributing two years earlier.

Huey spent less than five minutes answering questions about his encounter with Officers John Frey and Herbert "Cliff" Heanes before dawn on October 28, 1968. Then, with the court's permission, Huey turned the courtroom into a classroom in an attempt to provide a rich and compelling context not just for his confrontation with the police but with the circumstances leading up to it. Notably, Judge Friedman overruled vigorous objections to much of Huey's testimony in this highly political capital case. The judge made the unusual decision not to shut Huey down when he summed up his experiences from birth as a Black American, his understanding of the racism that permeated the nation's history from colonial days through the nation's development, how America's past shaped his own life, world view and behavior, and how it gave rise to the Black Panther Party.

As Hilliard recalled in awe decades later, Huey began "educating the jury about our movement . . . about how we got here . . . a history lesson in the oppression and economic subjugation of Black folks in America." On that fateful day in the courtroom in August 1968, Huey Newton — aside from fighting for his life —- was, in his view, using the spotlight to fill in the blanks of a censored history for an immense audience far beyond the courtroom. His bold lecture on embedded racism from colonial days and his argument for his innocence were inextricably intertwined.

Newton's advocacy in the courtroom that day echoed traditions of resistance to slavery that were emerging before the mid-19th century. Huey pivoted toward the jury and spoke in an earnest professorial tone as he explained that some more enlightened Whites had just come to understand the truth about American history that minorities always knew:

> "The younger Whites have suddenly discovered that their fathers said many beautiful things in letters and constitutions, but in the final analysis they were hypocrites and the whole façade that they put up was only to hide their hypocrisy while they talked about the rights of mankind and equality for all. At that very moment they were plundering the world and murdering and enslaving Black people right in this country."

Newton's riveting speech echoed the impassioned demands of Blacks and other minorities on college campuses at the time for courses on ethnic studies to counter the Eurocentric history that had always been taught. The judge seemed just as mesmerized as everyone else by the lecture Huey gave to the ground-breaking jury of seven women and five men — for this was a history lesson totally at odds with the reverence they were all taught in school to accord to the nation's founding fathers.

Hilliard believed that "nobody there had seen anything like that before. ... He used the courtroom as a forum to validate our just cause for freedom, equality and justice." The background that Huey painted for the jury undoubtedly had a significant impact on its deliberations. The panel had listened closely both to surviving officer Cliff Heanes and Huey as they described that fatal morning in the fall of 1967. Weighing their conflicting accounts in light of other evidence, the panel found Huey's version more credible. The jury then surprised everyone in the courtroom by declaring Huey innocent of the murder charge that could have prompted his execution. Yet the panel believed that after being shot, Huey overreacted, killing Frey with Frey's own gun, resulting in a verdict of voluntary manslaughter.

Sentenced to two to fifteen years' incarceration, Huey spent nearly two years in the Men's Colony in San Luis Obispo, California, while awaiting the appellate court decision. Though the prison was more than three hours' drive south of Oakland, to buoy his spirits, Huey received frequent visits from family and friends as well as his lawyers. That was when Huey began work on his autobiography with the assistance of co-author Professor Herman Blake, who was himself a regular visitor to the Men's Colony.

The chances Huey would soon be released were then dim. Yet here he was in the fall of 1970, improbably contemplating the view from a telescope he kept in his penthouse living room — the barred window of the tenth-floor cell in the courthouse across the lake that he had occupied from late 1967 through the early fall of 1968.

* * *

Revolutionary Suicide was published in 1973 after Huey and his lawyers successfully defended two more trials for the death of Officer Frey. Both took place in the same courthouse where he had been prosecuted in 1968. The back-to-back manslaughter retrials each resulted in hung juries. Ultimately, and with great reluctance, the district attorney dropped all charges pursuant to a statute permitting dismissal "in furtherance of justice."

Huey dedicated the book: "To my mother and father, who have given me strength and made me unafraid of death and therefore unafraid of life." Foremost among his acknowledgments was to his older brother Melvin, who helped Huey finalize the story of his life. *Revolutionary Suicide* revealed details of Huey's childhood as the youngest of Walter and Armelia Newton's seven children, and his experiences that he believed led him to become a revolutionary.

Huey's second wife, Fredrika, noted in her 2009 introduction to a reissue of Huey's book that he was raised in a devoutly religious household. In addition to Walter Newton's jobs – sometimes two or three at a time – Huey's father faithfully performed services as a part-time assistant minister. Since both of Huey's parents were still alive in 1973 when the book was first published, one can generally rely on what Huey recounted of his childhood experiences and the stories his parents told him about the family before he was born. His parents and Melvin were available to help fill gaps.

Yet Melvin, his older sister Doris Newton Godfrey, and other close relatives later had more memories to add and some different recollections that helped elucidate the Newton family dynamics. Most important to the family was their nuclear family and extended family, which Melvin describes as tribal in nature. Even as the Newton offspring grew to adulthood, the siblings, their spouses and their children regularly gathered with Walter and Armelia for family birthdays and holidays. They greatly enjoyed each other's company, and had each other's back when times got tough. Walter and Armelia were the patriarch and matriarch respected by all, including close friends who often got included at family gatherings. Next in importance came other families with whom the Newtons gathered regularly at church. Later, as with many families, stresses caused a few rifts.

Huey felt that understanding how African-Americans had been treated from colonial days was necessary to understand who he was and where he came from. So here is an effort to put his experiences and those of his family into historical context.

I.

Walter Newton's Heritage

Starting Out

HUEY NEWTON'S father, Walter Newton, was half-White and light-colored, a condition that stigmatized him in childhood and greatly affected his outlook on life. Knowledge of that White grandfather had a strong effect on Walter's youngest son Huey as well. Huey opens "Starting Out," the first chapter of *Revolutionary Suicide*, with the observation that "Life does not always begin at birth. My life was forged in the lives of my parents before I was born, and even earlier in the history of all Black people. It is of a piece. My father's father was a White rapist."

Huey's father objected to Huey writing this bold statement about the grandfather he never met. Walter considered his mother to bear responsibility for having a child out of wedlock. The claim she was raped was based on a story passed down through other members of the family that Walter's mother was assaulted at the age of 13 by a man several decades older than her. The family always understood that Walter's father was Jewish and that his last name was Simon. A Jewish father explained Walter Newton's bi-racial features inherited by Huey and some of his siblings. Yet the story about Walter's father that Alice Hilliard Newton told distorted the truth. So what can be determined about Walter Newton's ancestry?

Alice Hilliard was an unmarried teenager when she gave birth to her son Walter on March 28, 1903, in Uniontown, Alabama, where a large number of Hilliards lived. (Alice might have been a distant relative of David Hilliard, Huey Newton's good friend from middle school in Oakland. David Hilliard's father was raised in the next county West of Uniontown — Marengo County, Alabama.

David's mother was from Rockville, Alabama, 90 miles south of Uniontown where David was born.)

Uniontown occupies 15 square miles in West Central Alabama, nearly 150 miles almost due north of Mobile, Alabama's only port. Today, 90 percent of Uniontown's 2100 residents are Black. In 1900, three years before Walter Hilliard was born, the population of Uniontown had risen to just over 1,000, about half of whom were Black.

By the turn of the century, the industry of Uniontown included cotton gins, warehouses and a cotton mill. It was also an early location for electricity and telephone services. We can bet that neither of those services were available to the Hilliards. Blacks remained at the bottom of the economic totem pole in neighborhoods often deprived of community services available to Whites. The Panthers' 10-point program recognized the continuing impact through the 1960s of disparities in housing, good-paying jobs and public services:

> "We want land, bread, housing, education, clothing, justice, peace and people's community control of technology."

We do not know anything about Alice's parents, but her grandparents were of the generation of nearly half a million slaves in Alabama freed in 1865 by the Thirteenth Amendment to the Constitution. Alice Hilliard's grandparents may have voted during Reconstruction but, by March 1903, when teen-aged Alice gave birth to her son Walter, none of the adults in her family likely maintained voting rights. African-Americans and some poor Whites had been deprived of the vote by revisions to the Alabama Constitution in 1901 that instituted a poll tax and other voting restrictions designed to ensure White supremacy.

The African Roots of the Newtons

HUEY saw his family history as having been forged in the history of all Black people. Melvin Newton reports that DNA testing of the Newton family indicates that most of their ancestors came from African countries. One-quarter of Melvin and Huey's ancestors came from Nigeria where slavery had endured from time immemorial in one form or another. Twelve percent came from the empire of Mali, where enslavement was also practiced for centuries. Nine percent of their ancestral genes originated in the Ivory Coast and Ghana, from which Louisiana in the late 1700s imported up to 3500 slaves per year.

Seven percent of Melvin and Huey Newtons' ancestors originated in Senegal which, from the fourteenth century through the nineteenth century, enslaved up to a third of its population. Another seven percent came from Benin and Togo, major sources of slave trading from the sixteenth through the nineteenth century. Two percent came from Cameroon, whose population, like that of Senegal, dates back to prehistory. Another two percent of their ancestors were from the Congo and Western Bantu people who originated in the border area between Nigeria and Cameroon. These were also significant sources of slaves traded to the Americas. Historian Jill Lepore describes the long global history of slavery, which mostly resulted from victors in battle exploiting the labor of the conquered:

"Slavery had been practiced in many parts of the world for centuries. [P]risoners of war . . . tended to be people of different faiths. Christians enslaved Jews; Muslims enslaved Christians; Christians enslaved Muslims. Since the Middle Ages, Muslim traders from North Africa had traded in Africans from below the Sahara, where slavery was widespread. . ... People captured in African wars were bought and sold in large markets by merchants and local officials and kings and, beginning in the 1450s, by Portuguese sea captains.

Christopher Columbus had engaged in the Portuguese slave trade before he ever set out to find a Western route to the Far East. Instead, he landed in what Europeans called the West Indies where he launched a Spanish colony bent on enslaving the native population of Haiti. The first documented slave trade in the British colonies occurred in Jamestown, Virginia in 1619. Where Huey's African ancestors first landed is unknown but daily existence for the family of Walter's mother Alice was in some ways just as arduous as the life of her ancestors in slavery times.

The Legacy of Slavery

WHEN Walter Hilliard was born in 1903, he and his family faced entrenched racism from Alabama's long history of slavery since white settlers first arrived in the territory in 1818. Desperate to find a viable place to grow crops outside the farmed-out original colonies, these settlers found arable land in Alabama which required intensive labor to produce profitable crops. With the importation of field slaves, Woodville — which was where Alice Hillard would be raised — quickly included far more Black residents than White. Almost all of those Blacks were considered to be property.

By the 1830s, abolitionist newspapers in the North had become greatly emboldened. When the American Anti-Slavery Society of New York started a mailing crusade to Southern targets in 1835, President Andrew Jackson backed the decision of his Postmaster General to halt distribution of all such highly provocative pamphlets. Some Southern legislatures had already banned them.

Until the mid-1830s, Congress had a practice of reading aloud all constituent petitions and assigning them to a committee for further action. Members of the American Anti-Slavery Society began flooding Congress with petitions. In response, in 1836, pro-slavery Congressmen had enough votes to institute a "gag rule" that prohibited consideration of any bill or petition relating "in any way, or to any extent whatsoever, to the subject of slavery or the abolition of slavery." In the meantime, mobs throughout the South made bonfires of abolitionist literature and burned in effigy some of the most famous proponents.

In November of 1837, a mob in Missouri went much further. They murdered minister Elijah Parish Lovejoy for publishing an abolitionist newspaper. The lynching made Lovejoy an instant martyr in the North.

Banning overtly abolitionist literature was just the start of political efforts to counter criticism of slavery. Southern slave owners remained concerned about shaping their children's attitude toward slave ownership. Historian Donald Yacovone notes that by the 1850s, those bent on preserving the South's slave-based economy turned to attacking schoolbooks.

Up until then, textbooks were mostly written by New Englanders whom many Southerners feared were educating their children with a "Yankee-centric" perspective on slavery. These Southerners wanted to replace history books with new texts "specifically designed for Southern students and readers." *New York Times* columnist Jamelle Bouie recently noted parallels with modern-day censorship: "Just as Governor Ron De Santos of Florida and other elected state officials have begun outlawing the teaching of critical race theory, similar efforts were launched in the antebellum South."

Prof. Yacovone summed up one proponent's argument for tossing all textbooks that did not endorse slavery: "Books that did not praise the 'doctrines' that 'we now believe' should be banned and never come within the range of juvenile reading.' . . . [They flew] the 'Black practical ensign of abolitionism.' Continued use of such works would only corrupt the minds of youth and 'spread dangerous heresies among us.' Even spelling books could not be trusted, as they contained covert condemnations of 'our peculiar institutions.'"

When Huey was born in World War II there were history books that still taught that "the slaves loved the people of the plantation and stood by them even after slavery was ended." *New York Times* present-day columnist Jamelle Bouie points out: "Southern slaveholders had moved from the regretful acceptance of slavery that characterized earlier generations of slaveholding elites to an embrace of slavery as a 'positive good' . . . and the only basis on which to build a functional and prosperous society.

In his early twenties, Huey joined an informal study group focused on Black History while Black churches and homes of civil rights activists in the Deep South in the early 1960s were being bombed, and peaceful marchers targeted by snipers and attacked by police dogs. Yet official history books still circulated in American classrooms touting the bondage endured by ancestors of African-Americans as what "made it possible for Negroes to come to America and to make contacts with civilized life." Historian David Blight recognized the purpose served by perpetuation of myths about America's slave-holding past: "A [still] segregated society demanded a segregated historical memory."

Prof. Yacovone studied hundreds of history textbooks to analyze their spin on slavery: "Until the mid-1960s, American history instruction from grammar school to the university relentlessly characterized slavery as a benevolent institution . . . and a gift to those Africans who had been lucky enough to be brought to the United States." What happened in the 1960s to challenge that benign view were pioneering efforts by activists, including Huey Newton and Bobby Seale. The pair launched the Black Panther Party in October of 1966 with a 10-point program listing education as a key priority:

5. We Want Education for Our People That Exposes the True Nature of This Decadent American Society. We Want Education That Teaches Us Our True History and Our Role in the Present-Day Society.

We believe in an educational system that will give to our people a knowledge of self. If a man does not have knowledge of himself and his position in society and the world then he has little chance to relate to anything else.

Historian Edward Ball, author of *Slaves in the Family,* acknowledges the truth about his own ancestors' source of enormous wealth: "cotton, rice, sugar and tobacco plantations were in many ways like prison camps, with their owners in the role of commandants."

Under Huey Newton's and Bobby Seale's leadership, the Panthers were determined to play a major role in exposing slavery's horrors by prompting the adoption of ethnic studies programs in institutions of higher learning across the country as well as successful pushes for the hiring of more minority faculty members. Feminists like Gloria Steinem, in turn, credit these ethnic studies programs as the model for hiring more women on college faculties and creating women's studies programs and gay and lesbian curricula at colleges across the country starting in the 1970s. Many more female and minority historians have since contributed their scholarship to view American history from their own perspective rather than accepting the White male lens through which our nation's history has traditionally been told.

Most highly publicized among these works was the

1619 Project launched in August of 2019, the 400th anniversary of the first African slaves to arrive in Jamestown, Virginia. In January 2024, the Huey P. Newton Foundation created a museum housing papers showing the role played by the Panther Party he co-founded more than half a century ago, planting the seeds for efforts like the 1619 Project to counterbalance the benign account of slavery in official narratives of American history.

Growing Up Outside Constitutional Protection

ONE of the biggest lessons absorbed by young Walter Newton growing up in the era of Jim Crow was the need for a gun for self-protection. Just over a decade before Walter was born, educator and civil rights advocate Ida B. Wells published a pamphlet of race crimes she had investigated as a journalist — *Southern Horrors: Lynch Law in All Its Phases*. Ida was born a slave with one White grandfather on her father's side. She was freed as a toddler by the Thirteenth Amendment. Her father, James Wells, became an ardent Republican during Reconstruction and a trustee of an all-Black college, now known as Rust College, where Ida later enrolled.

Ida came to the conclusion that all African-Americans who remained in the South needed to protect themselves from potential attack by White terrorists. She urged every Black household to have a Winchester rifle at hand. In her pamphlet *Southern Horrors: Lynch Law in all its Phases,* she observed: "The only times an Afro-American who was assaulted got away has been when he had a gun and used it in self-defense." In 2022, Clemson University confirmed Wells' statement: "... rates of Black lynching decreased with greater Black firearm access..." Famed orator Frederick Douglass had earlier expressed a similar need to back up demands for equal rights with access to guns: "A man's rights rest in three boxes: the ballot box, the jury box, and the cartridge box." Douglas's sons volunteered for the Union cause in the Civil War.

Ida was prepared to defend her own life against any

death threats, figuring she could take out at least one of her attackers. She wrote: "One had better die fighting against injustice than to die like a dog or a rat in a trap." Walter Newton had a similar attitude. That was how Huey came to feel, too. He did not expect to live beyond thirty and found it thrilling to seek out confrontations.

This cartoon was published in the Tuscaloosa, Alabama Independent Monitor *in 1869. The KKK not only terrorized freed slaves but also "carpetbaggers" from the North — in this case, Ohio. Tuscaloosa was just fifty miles north of where Walter Newton's presumed paternal ancestor would settle less than fifteen years later.*

Walter's White Father

WALTER'S MOTHER Alice Hilliard was five-foot-two and dark-skinned. Her father may well have been a sharecropper on a plantation on the outskirts of Uniontown. Alice gave birth to Walter on March 28, 1903. The teenage mother later told her children and others in the family she was just thirteen at the time, which would pinpoint her birth to 1889. But the most reliable record indicates she was born on September 1, 1885, and was just over seventeen-and-a-half on March 28, 1903.

The apocryphal story passed down through some members of the family to explain Walter's light skin was that Alice was a slave working on a plantation and was raped by her master. But Alice was born more than twenty years after the Civil War ended slavery. Walter's father had to have known Alice in the summer of 1902.

Alice and her baby stayed with her parents until Alice married Ben Newton sometime between 1910 and 1915. Ben, a widowed African-American farmer, was a generation older than his new wife. He was born in Dallas County, Alabama, just over 30 miles East of Uniontown, either in 1863 (per two censuses) or 1865 (per his first marriage license). Ben's parents were also both born in Alabama, presumably into slavery.

Ben married his first wife, Lucie, in 1886 when he was 21. Lucie, who was two years older, was born into slavery; Ben may have been as well. They had ten children, the oldest of whom helped their parents farm their property. Lucie likely died giving birth to her youngest child in 1906. Maternal death rates in the United States at the turn of the century were many multiples of their frequency today. Black women had little access to medical care and died at a far higher rate than White women, as is true in America even today.

Ben and Lucie's youngest son's name on the census was listed as "Ennis" but more than one family member later believed his birth name was likely Earl. As an adult, he would simply go by the initials "E.S." Three years younger than Walter, E.S. would become the sibling Walter got to know best. Alice and Ben Newton had a child together on June 12, 1916, Melvin Lee Newton, born in Birmingham, Alabama. The couple later had another son they named for his father, Benjamin Newton. Both were dark-skinned like their parents and half-brother E.S.

* * *

We now know more about the identity of Walter's biological father, thanks to modern science. The largest single source of DNA for Walter Newton's son Melvin was identified as 31 percent Ashkenazi Jew. The same would presumably be true of Huey and other siblings no longer alive. That does point to Walter as half Jewish as the family understood. The family was also correct in their understanding that his last name was Simon, although they had no idea where he lived or anything else about him.

Recent DNA analysis indicates that Walter's father was a member of the German Jewish family of Joseph Simon, who lived in the neighboring community of Demopolis, Alabama, at the turn of the 20th century. One of Joseph Simon's descendants found a surprising DNA match with Melvin's youngest son, David Lautaro Newton, and then shared with David the history of the Simon family.

The Simons can be counted among a growing number of families that have begun discovering unknown branches of their family tree through DNA analysis. A similar recent search for ancestors by cousins of Black Panther Party Communications Director Kathleen Neal Cleaver determined that she was related to Judge Lewis Shepherd, a well-known White civil rights advocate at the turn of the 20th century in Chattanooga, Tennessee.

The Simons' ancestors were all German Jews. Joseph Simon's father, Elias Simon, emigrated to Baltimore in the slave state of Maryland with his wife and their children in 1845 from Hess-Darmstadt, Germany. Joseph would be the youngest, born in Baltimore in 1853. Though the background of Walter's father was not known to the Newton family, they had reason to believe Jews in America came from a history of persecution. Historically, Jews in Hess-Darmstadt were "Kammerknechte", which meant serfs of the emperor. The emperor or his designees oversaw "Judenordnung", the regulation of Jews who, under various rulers, were subject to legal restrictions until the mid-nineteenth century. The Simons became part of a wave of German Jews emigrating to the United States at that time.

Jews who came to the rural South in the first half of the nineteenth century often started out making a living as traveling peddlers, a valued service in high demand. They peddled their wares from town to town and used their savings to start their own stores. They were so few in number wherever they settled that they usually were viewed as non-threatening additions to rural communities eager for better access to merchandise.

The largest Jewish settlement in Alabama had been established in the port of Mobile in the 1820s. Other

Jewish transplants found homes in scattered areas throughout the state. For the most part, Jews in Alabama readily adapted to Southern culture. When Alabama seceded in 1860, about 150 of its Jewish citizens joined the Confederate Army. In the years that followed the Civil War, most Alabama towns with significant populations had one or more Jewish businesses in them.

As Joseph Simon grew up in Baltimore, he must have learned of Jewish entrepreneurs in Alabama. The most prominent of these businessmen were the Lehman Brothers, who co-founded the New York Cotton Exchange in 1870. The acclaimed recent play, "The Lehman Trilogy", traces that Jewish banking dynasty's spectacular rise back to the opening of a general store selling dry goods in Montgomery, Alabama in 1844. The store's founder was fresh off the boat, 22-year-old Hayum Lehmann, the son of a Bavarian cattle merchant. Starting out in America, he Anglicized his first name to Henry and shortened his last name to Lehman.

Soon, Henry invited two younger brothers to join his business in Montgomery, which evolved into lucrative financing and trade in highly valued cotton stocks. Over more than a century and a half the Lehman Brothers firm rose to become the fourth largest investment bank in America -- before imploding in the biggest bankruptcy in history during the financial crisis of 2008.

Back in the 1870s, the Lehman family's phenomenal success would have been widely known. Yet times had changed dramatically since the 1840s when Henry Lehman launched his original store in Alabama, including a bloody War Between the States that involved hundreds of thousands of casualties and devastated the Southern economy. During the war the border state of Maryland remained in the Union, but many of its citizens maintained close ties to the Confederacy. Some key battles took place in Maryland. Most of its soldiers fought for the North, but a substantial number joined the Rebel army.

After the Civil War ended in 1865, Federal troops kept the peace in former Confederate states to protect newly enfranchised Black citizens. During that tumultuous Reconstruction Era, Southerners became wary of Northern "carpetbaggers" seeking to exploit business opportunities or help empower recently freed slaves. "Carpetbaggers" got tagged with that label because they often carried cheap cloth suitcases fashioned from carpet remnants. That turbulent time ended in 1877 with the withdrawal of federal troops following the disputed 1876 election of President Rutherford Hayes. Black citizens lost many of their newly gained rights as Southern Whites sought to roll back society to its antebellum heyday.

Soon after Joseph Simon married in Baltimore in 1878, he and his wife moved to Prairieville, Alabama, where he became a mule trader. The mule trade had been active in the rural South since the 1820s. Farmers purchased mules for pulling plows, operating cotton gins and bringing produce to market. Prairieville was about ten miles from Uniontown where Alice's family lived. Joseph later moved his family to nearby Demopolis. The well-traveled plank road from Demopolis to Uniontown was a route that a mule trader from Demopolis in the early 20th century could be expected to pass along frequently.

Joseph Simon was 49 in the summer of 1902 when Alice got pregnant, but he has proved not to be Walter's father. Instead, further research into the Newtons' paternal ancestry showed the closest DNA match came from Joseph Simon's son, Solomon Kaufman Simon, born in 1883. Solomon was nineteen in the summer of 1902. He may have sometimes driven the mule wagon for his father or accompanied him on his routes. He likely met Alice at her family farm. Indeed, the two teenagers might have crossed paths there on multiple occasions over several years.

We do not know whether Solomon's sexual relationship with Alice was consensual. Southern White males in that era did encounter few if any constraints against doing whatever they wanted with Black females. But we now know more about Solomon Simon which raises questions about the rape story Huey was told.

Solomon went away to college and became a chemist. In 1906, he married a 22-year-old Jewish woman from Ohio. He proceeded to pursue his career and raise his family in Georgia. Solomon became a successful entrepreneur and at one point headed a pecan processing company. Unusual in the South in those days, his closest friend and business partner was Black.

In his later years, Solomon made a point of passing on words of wisdom to his oldest grandson. Solomon advised the young teen that there was nothing wrong with having close relationships with Black women. That could indicate fond memories of time spent as a teenager with Alice. In 1901, when Solomon was 18, Alabama outlawed interracial marriage. If a consensual relationship existed between Solomon and Alice in 1902, it would have violated a serious social taboo -- conduct teenagers could find tempting. Solomon's grandchildren consider the alternate rape story inconsistent with his character.

This recent revelation from Melvin Newton's newfound White cousin, Jon Simon Sager, gave Melvin reason to seriously question the rape account Huey and others in the family had long accepted, but Walter Newton had himself been skeptical about. All that the DNA evidence points to is that 19-year-old Solomon Simon was the biological father of 17-year-old Alice's son born on March 28, 1903. Solomon, whose marriage produced two daughters, may never have learned that he had a son. There would be no known contact between the families for well over 100 years.

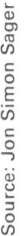

This photo from the 1970s is of Walter's nephew Jon Simon Sager and his wife Avis and her niece Lela whom they helped raise. Jon's mother was Walter's half sister Edith Simon whom he never met, the daughter of Walter's father Solomon Simon, whom he also never met. The families only connected during research for this book.

The Move to Southern Arkansas

WALTER later said that the Black community in Uniontown had made life difficult for his mother raising a light-skinned son. That may have been what ultimately prompted Alice and her husband to move to Arkansas when Walter was a young teen. Life there for Walter would not improve. At the time, the nation as a whole sought to treat anyone not 100 percent White as if they belonged to a distinct, inferior species.

Whatever the catalyst for the Newtons to leave Alabama, they counted among more than 170,000 African-Americans known to have left the state in the start of what later became known as the Great Migration. 22,000 left in the first decade of the twentieth century, nearly 71,000 would leave in the second decade and over 80,000 from 1920 to 1930. Many were greatly encouraged by glowing descriptions of Northern job opportunities like those published in Robert Abbott's widely distributed African-American newspaper, *The Chicago Defender*.

Yet, for the Newtons, the destination was not an exodus from the Deep South. Walter Newton's stepfather was a farmer. Dominated by plantation owners, Southern Arkansas was an equally hostile environment to that of Alabama. Several lynchings were documented in the early 1900s in Ashland County, Arkansas where the Newtons moved. In 1908, an outraged White mob had lynched a Black man named Ernest Williams in Parkdale, Arkansas (where Ben and Alice Newton would settle with Walter, E.S. and Melvin, and where Walter and E.S. would both later choose to get married). The reason offered for Williams' murder was simply to make an example of him for his use of language the mob deemed "offensive."

MSNBC newscaster Chris Hayes in his book, *A Colony in a Nation*, captures the brutal message succinctly: "To desecrate the dead is to humiliate the living, and humiliation may be the most powerful and underappreciated force in human affairs." The joyous celebration of mob law and White supremacy had begun gaining popularity in the South in the mid-19th century as a way to intimidate the growing anti-slavery movement. For many decades thereafter, rowdy crowds gleefully participated in ghastly revenge for the real or imagined crimes of their hapless captives. Each macabre gathering constituted the fit "barbarous" end to a "barbarous criminal."

The continuing animosity between Whites and Blacks in Ashland County made life quite difficult for Walter with his light skin in an otherwise dark-skinned family. Walter later told his daughter Doris that he also suffered beatings from his stepfather.

As a young teen Walter became a field hand. Black kids who he picked cotton with called him "the White boy." When he asked his mother to make them stop, she was helpless to do so. The teens he worked with told him: "White boy, why don't you leave here?" Alienated by his stepfather and persecuted by other fieldhands, Walter left home in 1915 at age 12. Hopping on a train, he became a hobo. That was an exceedingly dangerous undertaking in 1915 as it would be for decades to come — most infamously in the case of the Scottsboro Boys, as Huey and his brother Melvin later became quite aware.

Lessons in Courage

WALTER spent most of his teen years hoboing, which taught him to learn how to survive hostile encounters with courage and self-possession. Most likely on those journeys he took comfort in the Bible. He found great solace in the Scriptures, especially in the life and teachings of Jesus, the stories of the prophet Moses from the Book of Exodus, from David and Goliath in the Book of Samuel, and of Samson in the Book of Judges. He read and reread the heroic exploits of Moses, David and Samson for inspiration.

As a child, Walter would have been exposed to Sunday sermons that compared the lives of poor Blacks in America to the life of Jesus. Preachers noted that Jesus, too, was a minority by birth, a poor Jewish boy raised as a disfavored subject of the pagan Roman Empire. Yet Jesus forged a life of rectitude, stood up for himself, and gained a following for his extraordinary piety and good deeds. The comparison gave Walter strength. When Walter ran into situations where he considered himself wronged, he had no qualms about holding his own one-on-one with a White or Black teenager or grown man, for that matter. If Jesus could risk death for preaching the word of God, if Moses could kill an abusive Egyptian slave master, and David could face down the giant Goliath, then Walter, though slight of build, could stand up for himself, too.

Perhaps Walter realized that David had a tactical advantage over the giant. As an experienced slinger, David outsmarted Goliath by avoiding the expected hand-to-hand combat. Instead, he aimed a stone at the slow-moving giant's exposed forehead and felled him from a distance. Historian Robert Dohrenwend later opined that "Goliath had as much chance against David as any Bronze Age warrior with a sword would have had against an [opponent] armed with a .45 automatic pistol."

Walter especially admired the strength God gave Samson against his enemies. Samson was a biblical superhero — a man so strong and unafraid he could strangle a lion barehanded and take on an entire army of Philistines. Even Samson's betrayal and loss of power was instructive. Like Walter's ancestors, Samson had become a slave to his enemies, but that did not stop him from praying to God, regaining his strength and wreaking vengeance on his captors. Yes, it did cost Samson his own life. To Walter, that was a noble ambition — to live with courage and purpose, unafraid of dying. That was what Walter believed that Jesus himself stood for.

Walter was an avid follower of politics. He had to be well aware that President Woodrow Wilson had instituted a draft in May of 1917 when the United States joined "the War to End All Wars" in Europe that we know today as World War I. War preparations were everywhere and Black soldiers were accepted as both volunteers and draftees, though they mostly served in supply lines to support White troops. (In June of 2023, the Pentagon renamed Fort Polk in Louisiana Fort Johnson to acknowledge the extraordinary heroism of a Black soldier who did serve valiantly on the frontlines in World War I, Medal of Honor winner Sgt. William Henry Johnson. In contrast to Johnson, Confederate Lieutenant General Leonidas Polk, for whom the fort was earlier named, was a wealthy, ill-trained son of a plantation owner, notorious for his lack of success on the battlefield.)

Fortunately for Walter, he was too young to serve. In 1917, the government only required men between 21 and 30 to register with local draft boards. Walter was just 14. Even when the age limit was extended in September of 1918 to draft eligible 18-year-olds, he was just 15. The war ended in November of that year and so did the draft. The risk of having to serve in the military was no longer a concern for Walter when the eighteen-year-old got off yet one more freight train in the summer of 1921 at its last stop in Monroe, Louisiana where he looked for work as a dishwasher. Obtaining directions to a popular café in the Black section of town, he both found a job and met the love of his life, Armelia Johnson.

II.

Armelia Johnson's Background

Armelia's Ancestry

WALTER NEWTON was three-and-a-half years old when his future wife was born on September 17, 1906, in Monroe, Louisiana. Monroe was the seat of Ouachita Parish in a largely rural area of the state near the Arkansas border. Indigenous people had occupied land along the Ouachita River for thousands of years before they were chased out by the Indian Removal Act of 1830.

Black slaves had started arriving for sale to White owners in 1719. Major shipments of slaves — sold to Europeans by the Kingdoms of Whydah and Dahomey in modern-day Benin — arrived in New Orleans. The slaves mostly came from the Congo, Benin and Senegal. Perhaps, among them was a Senegalese ancestor of Armelia Johnson on her father's side brought to work as a field hand on a Louisiana plantation.

Armelia was the first child of John Johnson and Estella McElroy Johnson who had married in 1905, when Estella was 21 and John about 25, both in the first generation of their families born after the 13th Amendment freed all slaves. Estella's birthplace, the small town of Oakwood, Texas, was founded in 1872 as a stop on the railroad about 80 miles directly east of Waco. She met John Johnson after she moved to Monroe with one of her eight siblings, her older brother Isaac Burnett.

Unlike her brother, Estella went by the last name of their stepfather Sam McElroy, a farmer born in 1855 in Alabama, likely as a slave. Unlike most African-Americans raised in the South at the time, Sam learned to read, though he could not write. His wife Martha could do neither. Estella's birth father, Jordan Burnett, was also born in the 1850s. Martha was born in the midst of the Civil War, both presumably into slavery. Martha's parents had arrived in Texas from Virginia, likely transported as the property of White owners.

On Martha's and Jordan's marriage certificate he was listed as mulatto, making him the ancestor most likely to have provided the genes Melvin Newton inherited that indicated he was 3 percent English/Northern European and Irish. This small percentage of White ancestry in Armelia's family history came as a surprise to the Newton family who always attributed their bi-racial heritage solely to Alice Newton's rape story.

Armelia's father, John Johnson, was a native of the then tiny town of Carencro, now a suburb of the city of Lafayette, Louisiana. He was born around 1880 when Carencro already had long-established sugar cane plantations and two sugar mills. Carencro also boasted a number of nearby cotton plantations. The town had cotton gins powered by horses as well as a steam-powered gin. Cotton bales were transported for sale from the Carencro railroad station. The sugar mills both closed in 1900 which might explain why he moved to Monroe.

Ouachita Parish was originally much larger than it is now. It has been divided into eight smaller parishes, including Morehouse Parish and West Carroll Parish where the Newtons would later live. In the nineteenth century, as Monroe grew in size from the extraordinary success of cotton plantations, White settlers either brought slaves along with them or bought slaves after they arrived. Monroe got its permanent name from the first steamboat to dock there on the Ouachita River in 1819, the "James Monroe."

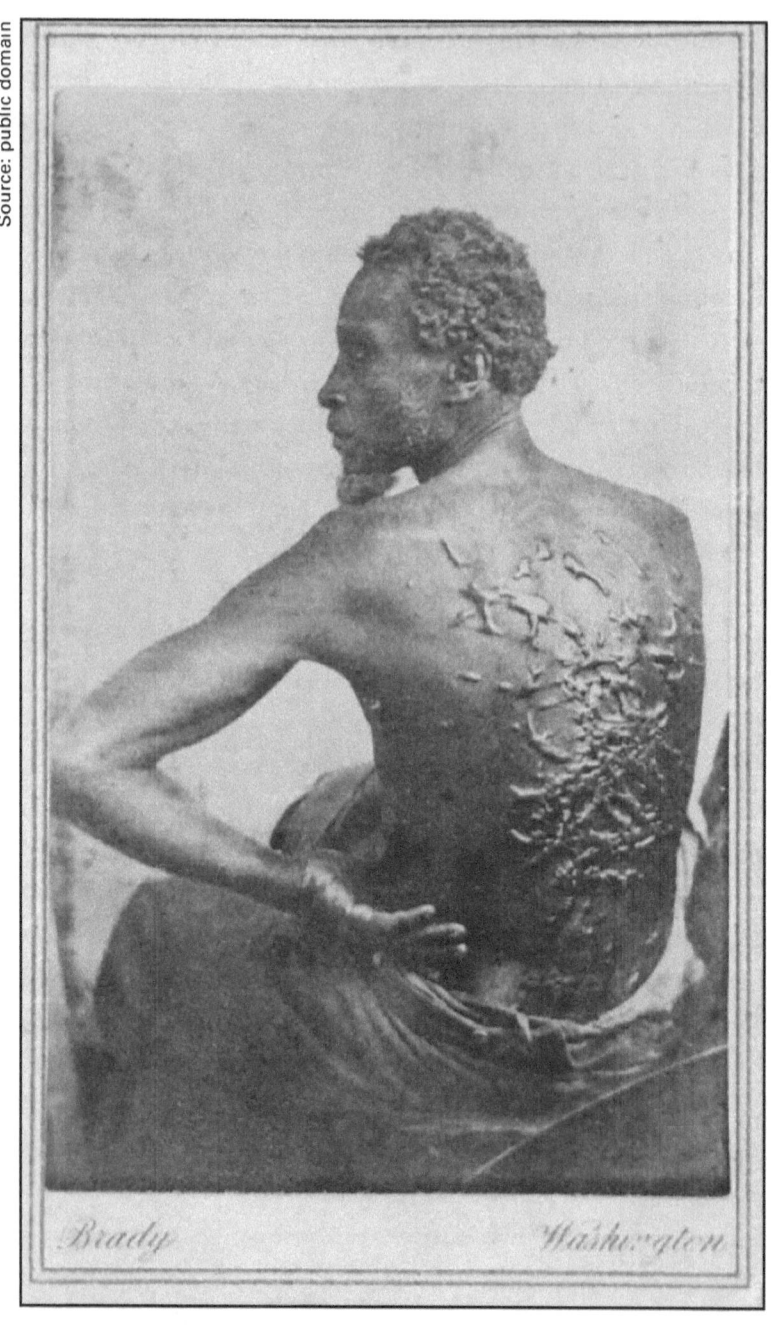

Photo of slave with extensive whip marks on his back, widely circulated by abolitionists in the 1860s.

If there were any free Blacks on board, they likely were limited to riding on the outside deck so as not to offend White passengers, a practice that was true for decades in both the North and South.

Estella and John Johnson may have heard from older Black residents of Monroe that the city had not always been as racist as they were experiencing. Under new laws following the Civil War, freedmen and women in Louisiana had the right to integrated public accommodations and transportation, intermarriage with Whites, and integrated schools. In 1872, the state legislature even elected a Black Union officer, P.B.S. Pinchback, as the state's first Black Senator, the son of a former slave and her prior White master. Mississippi's legislature had already elected two Black Senators.

But in a sign of the incoming Jim Crow era, Pinchback was successfully challenged by White Democrats and never served as Senator. Instead, he became Lieutenant Governor and acting Governor during Reconstruction. Black Codes were soon enacted to reverse all of these civil rights gains. Over the objections of Pinchback and other civil rights champions, segregation was mandated in hospitals, restaurants, fountains, public schools, libraries, parks, public toilets and cemeteries. Poll taxes and biased literacy tests decimated the ranks of Black voters while candidates were selected in Whites only primaries. That was the Monroe that Estella and John Johnson moved to in the first decade of the 20th century and what Armelia experienced growing up.

Today, about 46,000 people reside in Monroe, the vast majority of whom are Black. At the time that Armelia was born, Monroe had just a few thousand residents, a small fraction of the size of the metropolis of New Orleans more than 280 miles to the southeast. By the time Armelia was four years old, Monroe had about 12,000 residents, about a third of whom were Black. Monroe then remained under the strict control of the far wealthier majority White population, as was the rule in other Southern towns dominated by wealthy White cotton plantation owners.

In 1910, Armelia and her parents lived at 195 Jackson Avenue (sometimes listed as Jackson Street) in Ward 3 of Ouachita Parish. It was located just a few blocks below Monroe's main thoroughfare, Desiard Street, on the south side of the railroad tracks. Desiard was an early 19th century French trapper who lived on Bayou Desiard, which he had already named for himself. The bayou later became the principal source of water for the city of Monroe. The Johnsons likely knew that Jackson Street was named for President Andrew Jackson.

The section of Ouachita Parish the Johnsons and Burnetts lived in was known as Monroe's New Town or, frequently, Colored Town. In 1910, Stella's oldest brother Isaac Burnett and his wife Annie Fennell Burnett lived in New Town with Raford McAroy, one of Isaac and Stella's stepbrothers, and Raford's wife Jess. Their home was less than half a mile from Stella and her husband John at 608 Hall Street. Everyone in the family called Annie by her nickname "Sissy."

By 1910, John Johnson was in his early thirties working as a farm laborer. Estella, at age 25, worked as a laundress at a city laundry. Doris recalled being told that her grandfather was a small, good-looking man and a gambler whom Stella dominated. Doris had no memory of meeting him.

Six years later, when Armelia was 10, Monroe became the natural gas capital of the world. With the influx of industry and job opportunities, the population of Monroe and Ouachita Parish would increase dramatically in the coming decade.

For entertainment, since 1890, Monroe residents could attend the Lyric Theater for stage plays, orators and vaudeville. Neither performers like the popular "coon shouters", nor crowd-pleasing traveling lecturers like Thomas Dixon were meant to appeal to Black patrons. The Lyric was renamed the Lyceum in 1909 and showed silent movies as well, frequently those produced by D.W. Griffith for national distribution. The seats were segregated by law with colored patrons relegated to the balcony. John may have gone there on occasion, but he more likely spent his leisure time in the area known as "Five Points" where many Black men hung out, especially on weekend nights.

Five Points was located around 18th Street and Desiard Street. It originated after a huge fire in Monroe back in 1871 consumed over sixty buildings and reportedly caused about $650,000 in property damage. That destruction prompted the city government to create a Fire District. New wooden buildings were quickly constructed near the railroad depot at Desiard and Jefferson Streets for the large number of Black residents of Colored Town displaced by the fire.

Five Points became notorious for its gambling houses, houses of prostitution and saloons. No doubt, John was among the many boxing enthusiasts of his era — big fans of Jack Johnson, the reigning Black heavyweight champion from Galveston, Texas. In the 2005 PBS video, "Unforgivable Blackness: The Rise and Fall of Jack Johnson," filmmaker Ken Burns describes how, in the early years of the 20th century, the bald, six-foot-five-inch Texan became "the most famous and notorious African-

American on Earth."

The legendary boxer had a penchant for breaking social taboo, including flaunting his frequent sexual exploits with White women. Jack Johnson was constantly in the sports news. In 1908 he had shocked White boxing fans around the globe by beating the current World Heavy Weight Champion, Canadian-born Tommy Burns, in a historic inter-racial match in Sydney, Australia. On Independence Day 1910, the world-renowned son of slaves — whom Muhammad Ali would later cite as his own role model — challenged retired American heavyweight champion James Jeffries in "The Fight of the Century." The Johnson–Jeffries match-up marked the first interracial heavyweight title fight in the United States. Prominent sports writers like novelist Jack London assumed that Jeffries, though long past his prime, would wipe the "smile from Johnson's face."

The controversial contest was filmed in Reno, Nevada, before an all-White audience that security guards first checked for weapons. Energized by spectators' shouts urging Jeffries to "kill the nigger," Johnson won handily. Jubilant Blacks took to the streets. Race riots followed in more than half the states across the country. Twenty-three people died, most of whom were Black. Hundreds were injured. A feature-length movie of the historic fight was soon distributed across the country and internationally, though many cities prohibited its showing. Monroe was likely one of them. (Church groups outraged at the moral depravity of the sport soon prompted Congress to ban interstate distribution of any boxing movies, a law that remained on the books for nearly three decades.)

In January 1911, the hard-drinking Galveston Giant

made more negative news by marrying Etta Duryea, a White socialite divorcée from Long Island. It was when Johnson openly cheated on his wife with a White prostitute that the boxer was targeted for the first prosecution under the Mann Act, the recent federal law banning interstate transportation of women for immoral purposes. Alienated from her family and depressed by Johnson's highly publicized sexual infidelities, his wife put a gun to her head and killed herself. Johnson then married the prostitute, and the Mann Act charge had to be dropped. (Another one would later stick.)

Public outrage prompted Georgia Representative Seaborn Roddenberry to introduce a federal constitutional amendment in January of 1913 to ban interracial marriage in all states as it was already prohibited in Georgia and Alabama, among others. Though the amendment failed to gain traction, Jack Johnson's escapades fed into the ongoing narrative of amoral Black men dishonoring White women.

In that tense, racially charged atmosphere, Black communities remained insular, relying on one another for mutual support. Stella's brother Isaac opened a grocery store in 1915 with $75. Fancy Groceries and Market was located next door to Isaac and his wife Annie's new home at 2800 Jackson St. As he rose in prominence, Isaac became a Deacon of the Mt. Nebo Missionary Baptist Church, conveniently located close by at 2930 Jackson St. Meanwhile, Estella and John Johnson had three more daughters: identical twins Orell and Ozell, born in mid-August 1912, and Jessie Mae, born in 1916. Stella helped out in the popular café Isaac operated. It was also easy to attract Black patrons to the grocery store when the alternative was to go to White neighborhoods and wait in long lines where Black customers would be the last ones served. Isaac's business flourished as Monroe doubled in size. But as Monroe grew, its racial divide was only reinforced.

Armelia's uncle Isaac Burnett ran a very successful grocery market and café in Monroe. His sister Stella Johnson, Armelia's mother, worked there in the 1930s.

The Infamous Lynching History of Monroe

IN THE SPRING of 1919, George Bolden, an illiterate Black man in Monroe, was accused of pinning a vulgar message to the door of a White woman whose husband had been the victim of a shooting by a Black man the year before. The message was signed with Bolden's name. Bolden was a carpenter, painter and paperhanger probably well known in the neighborhood as a handyman. The note should have been seen for what it was — a cruel hoax. Like more than a quarter of Monroe's Black population, Bolden could neither read nor write. He signed his name with an X. The note had an obvious intent — to give an excuse for yet another lynching to punish Black men for real or imagined sexual advances on White women.

A large mob of the woman's armed friends surrounded Bolden's home on April 29, 1919, and shattered his leg with a bullet. He escaped to St. Francis Sanitarium in Monroe where his leg was amputated in the Colored ward — a separate building from the White ward. The mob tracked him to the sanitarium, intent on finishing him off, but scattered after the police arrived. An officer gave the nuns and nurses a gun for protection if the mob came back, which it did. When one of the women fired the gun as a warning shot the crowd again dispersed except for one member. The women held him in their custody until the police showed up. Not much later the police somehow let him go.

For Bolden's own safety, the badly injured carpenter spent the remainder of that night in the city jail. The following day Bolden's wife took him to a train which the two boarded for Shreveport, Louisiana, about a hundred miles away. The mob learned of Bolden's planned departure. A cohort on the train caused it to make an emergency stop on the outskirts of Monroe. Bolden was pulled off the train and shot to death, leaving his bereft widow to continue the now pointless journey West alone. No perpetrators of the crime were ever prosecuted.

Black subscribers to the *Chicago Defender* in Monroe like Uncle Isaac could read the details of the murder of Bolden and coverage of other horrific news during the "Red Summer of 1919". That year, bloody race riots erupted in 26 cities across the country, mostly in the South, from May through October. Apart from riot victims, 83 lynchings were recorded in 1919 — the highest number in any year. The biggest deadly riots occurred in Washington, D.C. and Chicago.

In the spring of 1919, the *New Orleans Times-Picayune* dubbed Monroe "the lynch law capital of Louisiana." The horrific lynching of Bolden had a chilling effect on many Black families, prompting them to leave the city, like John and Stella did within the year. Stella's brother Isaac stayed and kept his grocery and café in Colored Town, but he remained quite fearful of White men. He had no way of knowing Bolden's murder would be the last recorded lynching in Monroe, one of 21 documented lynchings in the city and 38 in Ouachita Parish.

The Parish posted the third-highest lynching record in Louisiana and the fifth-highest total of *any* parish or county in the South. Other Northern Louisiana parishes were not much better. Together, they totaled three of the five worst lynching records of all parishes and counties later investigated by the staff of the Equal Justice Initiative in Montgomery, Alabama. The New Orleans *Times-Picayune* described the murder of George Bolden as "the Monroe Horror." It would figure prominently in the NAACP's efforts to pass a national anti-lynching law.

In Chicago, the riots started in August after a Black 17-year-old named Eugene Williams floated on a raft in Lake Michigan on a hot summer day near an unofficially Whites-only beach. He was stoned off of his raft and drowned. For almost two weeks afterward street violence ensued. Gangs of White teen-age rioters focused their attacks on homes and businesses in Black neighborhoods, leaving about 1000 African-American families without homes, several hundred injured and 50 killed.

Bobby Seale, Huey Newton's co-founder of the Black Panther Party for Self-Defense, heard his mother describe her personal experience observing similar violence that summer of 1919 in her own hometown. She vividly recalled living through riots in Jasper, Texas, the heart of the state's historic Ku Klux Klan territory. Of more concern to the Black residents of Monroe would have been the devastating race riots that began on the first of October 1919 in Elaine, Arkansas, 200 miles to the northeast. Historians have since recognized the Elaine massacre of Black sharecroppers as the worst in Arkansas history and among the deadliest in the entire country. The slaughter occurred in Phillips County about 125 miles north of Portland, Arkansas where the Johnsons had moved. At the time, only about a tenth of the local population around Elaine was White.

The night before the massacre began about 100 Black sharecroppers and farmers held a union meeting at a church near Elaine with a White lawyer who was helping them seek higher prices for the cotton they picked. Armed lookouts wound up in a confrontation with a White deputy sheriff and railroad guard who showed up uninvited. Shots were fired resulting in the death of the guard and injury of the deputy sheriff.

That year of 1919 was also the year of the First Red Scare — widespread fear among the White Protestant majority of Americans of radicals and anarchists thought to be inspired by the recent Bolshevik revolution in Russia. Rumors were quickly spread in Phillips County that the unionizing efforts were Communist-inspired and portended an imminent bloody Black worker revolt.

By morning, Arkansas's governor sent a posse to arrest the Blacks involved in the shooting. Hundreds of incensed White volunteers from surrounding counties swelled their ranks. Over 500 federal troops were also dispatched to round up hundreds of Blacks, most of whom had not even attended the union meeting. Between the aggressive actions of the troops and the vigilantes one hundred or more Blacks wound up killed. A total of five Whites died. Yet only Black men were prosecuted.

Ida Wells-Barnett investigated the carnage and determined that the state was engaged in a cover up. Her report detailed torture and indiscriminate murders almost entirely by White men. When the first twelve Black prisoners were sentenced to die, their fate became a cause célèbre for the NAACP. Ultimately, following successful appeals, their executions were avoided. Whether the federal troops committed any murders remains a divisive issue to this day, but in the fall of 2019 the victims of the massacre were honored with a memorial and recognition on the Arkansas

Civil Rights Heritage Trail in the state capital.

While the slaughter of sharecroppers in Arkansas gained national attention, public outcry fell on deaf ears among the majority of Southern Whites. Cruelty was the point. Often crowds of revelers, including children, watched a victim be tortured and mutilated. Sometimes, their human prey was left to burn to death in agony after which mob members would cut off souvenir fingers or other body parts and pose for pictures. Lynchings were also often advertised in newspapers, celebrated in gruesome postcards and by word of mouth throughout the South. Many White residents remained eager for advance notice of the next lynching so they might also enjoy a picnic. Black families told and retold such searing incidents.

Over the rest of that century, Monroe's race relations did change, but not enough according to one of its Black senior citizens. In 2011, 99-year-old Joseph Sharp gave an interview about Monroe. Born and raised in Ouachita Parish, Sharp compared Monroe when he was growing up in the early 20th century to Monroe nearly a century later when it had a Black mayor:

> "Monroe is still a racist White controlled town existing with this "colored people are niggers" bag. They don't call you nigger to your face anymore, but they still treat you like that. . .. The Black mayor seems to be doing a pretty good job. I won't say the Blacks and Whites love one another, but they get along and they don't have physical altercations. There was a time when a Black person walking downtown had to get off the sidewalk when he met a White person. If two Blacks were

walking together, one had to get behind the other when approaching a White. Oh, Lord have mercy, I've seen a lot of changes."

In 2018, the Equal Justice Initiative established a national memorial in Montgomery with 805 steel bars suspended from an open-air structure, representing all the parishes and counties in various states where lynchings were documented — with the names of victims and the dates of their murders etched into them. The park also includes 805 matching steel blocks laid out for visitors to walk around. A mile from there, across the street from its headquarters, EJI established a museum dedicated to documenting the history of lynchings and published the details in *Lynching in America: Confronting the Legacy of Racial Terror*.

In addition, EJI has collaborated with communities across the country to place markers memorializing victims at the sites of known lynchings. This allowed the identifiable targets of terrorism to be more easily remembered — a long-overdue response to more than a century of glorification of Confederate leaders and streets and sites named for them. This effort to publicize the victims prompts many more people to ask why honors have for so long been bestowed on defeated secessionists who were bent on perpetuating slavery. One of the EJI markers commemorates the barbaric, unprosecuted mob murder of George Bolden. Armelia was a young teen when that happened. It had to be chilling. Soon after, her parents moved Armelia and her three younger sisters to a small town in Arkansas.

III.
Arkansas

The Move to Southern Arkansas

BY 1920, the Johnsons had moved to the river town of Portland in South Central, Arkansas. Although the murder of George Bolden had terrorized the Black residents of Monroe, the most likely final straw triggering the Johnsons' move to a more rural area was the pandemic of 1918-19.

What became known as the Spanish flu caused approximately 55 million deaths worldwide from 1918 to 1919. By 1917, Monroe had grown to 35,000 people. During the height of the pandemic from August of 1918 until April of 1919 about 1,100 Monroeians caught that flu; 36 were recorded as having died from it. To keep the flu from spreading, the government ordered closure of schools. Businesses and churches also closed. The Johnson family had strong reasons to relocate to reduce the chances of exposing their four daughters to deadly disease.

John Johnson, at age 40, hired out as a field hand, likely on a cotton plantation, in 1920. Stella, then 32, worked on their own home farm. Armelia was 13. It must have been miserable for her to leave friends in Monroe for the relative isolation of a small farm in Portland Township in Ashley County, Arkansas watching after her three younger siblings and tasked with helping with the gardening, sewing and cooking.

The fear instilled by the fate of George Bolden would not have been eased much in their new location. Portland Township was also terrorized by White mobs. Fear of lynchings would not have been much different in

Southern Arkansas than in Monroe.

Even the name Ashley County reflected the area's racist and violent past. The area took its name from a White plantation owner. Massachusetts-born Chester Ashley had arrived in Little Rock in 1820 when Arkansas was still a territory. Ashley was 30 and quite ambitious. He quickly rose to be the most prominent lawyer in the state. With his earnings, he invested in plantations in southeast Arkansas, the delta where the Johnsons would later live.

Chester Ashley needed many slaves to operate his plantations. His Massachusetts roots did not get in the way as he adapted himself to life among Arkansas's elite, growing wealthy from slave labor. He then turned his attention to politics and got himself elected U.S. Senator in 1844. Ashley suddenly died four years later while still in office. The state then commemorated him in 1849 by naming the area surrounding his plantations in his honor.

The 25,000 Black residents of Ashley County had good reasons to be quite frightened of their White neighbors. On May 30, 1909, a man was lynched at Portland, where the Johnsons would settle a decade later. On August 26, 1927, a man named Winston Pounds was seized by a mob near the small town of Wilmot in Ashley County and hanged from a tree. Sheriffs' deputies had charged him with having "attacked a young married woman." It went without saying that she was White — no such concern would have attended an alleged attack on a Black woman.

When the excuse was an accusation of rape, the grotesque lynching ceremony was particularly emboldened. It publicly avenged the indignity presumed to have been endured by a defiled White virgin or faithful wife who likely would otherwise be forced to testify in open court and undergo the humiliation of having to relive the brutal crime. Most of all, devoted sons of the Confederacy wanted to send a strong message to the federal government. Regardless of what the detested Reconstruction Amendments purportedly dictated, the progeny of former slaves were not citizens entitled to trial by a jury of their peers, equal protection or due process rights afforded to the master race — period.

John Steelman, the man who later became President Harry Truman's chief of staff, grew up in the county just north of Ashley. As a graduate student in 1928, Steelman wrote his dissertation about the history of lynching in Ashley County. The first occurred in a sawmill town named Crossett where a Black man was lynched for allegedly committing murder. Without a trial, the crime was never proved in court. That same fall, another lynching occurred allegedly for "assaulting Whites."

Walter and Armelia Meet and Marry

HUEY wrote in *Revolutionary Suicide* that his parents met after their families moved to Arkansas. Arkansas records confirm that the pair were married on August 8, 1921, in Parkdale, Arkansas, which is now part of the town of DeBastrop. DeBastrop, in turn, is where Ben and Alice Newton probably lived ever since they came to Arkansas sometime before 1915.

Parkdale and Portland, Arkansas, where the Johnsons lived in 1920, were 26 miles apart but at different elevations. Ashley County is roughly divided by a bayou with timberland, including Parkdale and DeBastrop, on one side, and farmland on the other, including the Mississippi River delta where Portland was located.

When Walter Newton and Armelia Johnson married, both lied about their ages. He listed his age as 21, and Armelia listed hers as 18. Walter was close to 18 and a half in August of 1921 and Armelia was actually a month shy of 15. The two of them later reported their real ages at marriage when they were interviewed by a 1930 census taker. By then, Armelia had been married more than eight years and was the mother of four children.

Huey's older sister Doris disagreed with his account that their parents met in Arkansas. She said she heard from her mother that she first saw Walter in Monroe, Louisiana. Doris always believed that was true. Her mother said she was living with Aunt Sissy Burnett in Monroe in 1921. If so, Armelia may have moved there to work part-time in the Burnetts' café while going to high school. Maybe she and her mother were just visiting for the summer. In any event, as Doris heard it, Walter Newton showed up at the café in the summer of 1921 looking for a job washing dishes. He spied Armelia there and asked Sissy who the girl was. Sissy said she was her sister-in-law Stella's daughter. Walter said: "I'm going to marry her." Aunt Sissy told him to keep away from Armelia or "Stella's gonna kill you".

Doris understood that Stella was then also staying with her brother Isaac's family. Armelia told Doris that her mother warned her: "Better not go down there messing with Walter." After Walter had only been working at the café for a week, he asked Armelia to marry him. Armelia was gentle and kind by nature but attending church together on Sunday might have sealed the deal. Walter could tell that Armelia was as religious as he was and must have been quite pleased that she, too, was literate. He must have seen from talking with her that she was very bright, polite to her elders, and had a good sense of humor. Fortunately for him, Armelia was likely desperate for change and accepted the offer of this handsome stranger for an unknown future together, starting out broke.

Stella, though much displeased, apparently gave her reluctant consent to the marriage. Jessie later recalled playing outside with her dolls while her older sister got married in a church. Jessie would have been five at the time. Since the pair listed Parkdale on their marriage certificate as their place of residence, the church was also likely in Parkdale, probably the church Walter's mother Alice and his stepfather attended. Walter went back to work as a field hand like his stepfather did.

Walter and Armelia lived in Arkansas for seven years before moving back to Monroe. That may also have been where Walter worked for a brief time as a brakeman for the Union Saw-Mill Company railroad in addition to his farm work. Founded in 1904, the railroad was a huge enterprise initially holding 90,000 acres of timberland and growing to 340,000 acres. Its main office was 140 miles almost due north of Ashley County, but its railroad ran south to Parkdale, and the company had a bi-racial workforce.

Neither Melvin nor Doris was aware of the seven years their parents lived in Arkansas. Doris said her dad worked at some point as a brakeman for the Union Saw-Mill Company but never realized that was a company located in Arkansas. Her mother never mentioned living anywhere but Louisiana before moving to California. It's not surprising they had no idea their parents spent time in Arkansas. The experience was apparently miserable for both of them, especially Armelia, who spent much of her teens and all of her early twenties in the state. Melvin said that when he was in high school and received an assignment to research family history, his mother refused to tell him any stories.

The racial tension that underlay Ashley County's history of lynch mobs undoubtedly played a role in Armelia's extreme distaste for life in rural Arkansas. Since 1900, five lynchings were recorded through 1927 while the Johnsons lived in Portland and the Newtons lived in Parkdale. But Armelia's parents had a pressing reason to move back to Louisiana.

The Great Mississippi Flood of 1927, a horrendous natural disaster that inundated the delta areas of Southern states, would hit the record books as the nation's most devastating river flood. Over the course of several months, it wound up covering 27,000 square miles with up to 30 feet of water. Ashley County delta towns like Portland were right in the flood's path. The cost of the damage amounted to a range of $4.2 to $17.3 billion in today's dollars. Historians documented the deaths of 127 people in Arkansas out of 500 lost lives from that flood. Far more suffered damage — about 630,000 people in Arkansas, Mississippi, and Louisiana. Hardest hit were African Americans, of whom 200,000 or so lost their homes and had to find temporary quarters in relief camps.

Walter had other reasons for disliking Arkansas. It was hard for him to get by, even when he worked long days. Unless the farmer provided housing, the pair would have started out married life staying with Ben and Alice Newton. The two teenagers could not have afforded their own place when they arrived in Parkdale in 1921. Yet that must have been awkward; Walter had left home at twelve to make his own way in the world partly because of the abusive way his stepfather treated him.

Armelia's parents lived about 25 miles away in Portland so Armelia could see them and her younger sisters only on occasion. There was also an opportunity to meet people at church on Sundays in Parkdale's Baptist Church. But the rest of the week would have been quite lonely for Armelia since Walter would not let her take a job outside their home.

Armelia never became close to her mother-in-law. Both would have kept busy tending to a vegetable patch, feeding chickens, gathering eggs, and milking the cows. Indoors, there were chores, too: sewing, cooking, and canning vegetables and fruit to consume out of season. Armelia likely also spent some of the time watching after her young brother-in-law Melvin. Whatever spare time Armelia had, she liked to sit down with the Bible or a novel.

Within a little over two years, Armelia had her own child to look after. The Newtons' first son, Lee Edward, was born on November 28, 1923 when Armelia was 17. His father's half-brother Melvin Lee Newton was then seven. Walter honored him by naming his first-born Lee. Lee Edward was just a toddler of two when his sister Myrtle was born on December 17, 1925. She was dark like her petite grandmother Alice, though she seemed to favor her mother's and grandmother Estella's build and facial features.

Armelia kept busy. Being the oldest daughter in her family, she already had years of experience helping care for her younger sisters, but she still felt like a kid herself. She very much enjoyed playing with her babies. Armelia also had learned to be a good cook, a skill she may have honed with her Aunt Sissy at the café where her mother Estella later worked as well. Armelia liked to make smothered chicken and dumplings, sweet potatoes, cornbread and black-eyed peas. With leftover cornbread, she made cush the next day, adding onions and gravy, all fried together and doctored up with spices. Cush became a staple. She also made sweet potato pies on occasion.

For holidays and other special meals, Walter liked to bake cakes. Walter and Armelia took what comfort they could with homemade treats and their growing family, but they were only too happy to leave Arkansas behind when the opportunity arose.

IV.

Back to Louisiana

The Johnsons Return to Monroe

FOLLOWING the Great Flood, it was no wonder that the Johnsons moved back from the tiny town of Portland to Monroe, where they still had family they could rely on. Isaac Burnett offered Stella a small shotgun house he built behind his own much larger house at 2900 Jackson St. adjacent to his market and café. Stella went to work for Isaac. His business continued to thrive as Monroe's population more than doubled from 1920 to 1930.

Back near the gambling dens of Five Points, John Johnson likely reverted to his old habits. Doris believes Stella confronted John often about his gambling losses. On one memorable occasion, John had promised to buy shoes for the children with his winnings but came home having lost all his money. He then hid under the house. He claimed a barking dog kept him from coming out of his hiding place. Estella was through trying to make him "do right." Doris recalls that her own family was back in Monroe by then. Her father told his father-in-law: "John, why don't you leave." And John did leave.

At some point, Stella was confronted by a claim that her husband had secretly placed a mortgage on their small house. Mortgages were exceedingly rare in those days, especially for the simple wooden shotgun homes on concrete blocks that poor folks built for themselves or rented from the builder. Stella found out that John was dying in New Orleans and went to see him. Doris says her grandmother told her that she asked John point blank on his deathbed if he put a mortgage on their house. He swore he never did.

Doris developed a far dimmer view of her prosperous Uncle Isaac than did the community at large. As she remembered him, he was so big and fat, he took up most of the couch when he sat on it. She also remembers that he had a knot on the back of his head. She found him intimidating. Doris also understood from her grandmother Mama Stella that he treated her poorly. Mama Stella told Doris that her Great Aunt Hattie in Brownsville, Texas was wealthy. When Hattie died, the family was supposed to share the inheritance. Doris remembers a White man from Texas coming to the house to offer to buy Hattie's land from Isaac. The presence of the White man scared her, as did all Whites back then. But Isaac, despite his fears, refused to sell the land.

Mama Stella thought she was entitled to a monthly check but told Doris she got nothing. Instead, Isaac kept the inheritance. His sister gathered paperwork in preparation for a lawsuit against him but never filed it. Instead, she gave the documentation in a cloth valise to Armelia who asked Jessie Mae to hold onto it. After Mama Stella remarried and was widowed, she went to live with Isaac and his wife Sissy but let her children and granddaughter Doris know she still bore a grudge. Jessie Mae's son Eddie wound up saving the paperwork for Mama Stella's claim to the inheritance for years before it got lost in a move.

The Newtons Move to West Monroe

HUEY'S second oldest sister, Leola Newton, was born on June 22, 1927, in Ala Ray, Arkansas, just two months after the catastrophic Mississippi River flood. She turned out to be the only one of the children who was light-skinned like her father. The family was not likely to have been affected directly by the flood, which mostly submerged property in the delta region of Ashley County. The Newtons still lived in the higher wooded area that the flood zone did not reach. Yet sometime within a year or so after Leola's birth, the Newtons picked up and moved to West Monroe, Louisiana to live near Mama Stella again.

When Walter and Armelia left Ouachita Parish for Arkansas in 1921, the population of the parish was a little over 30,000. By 1930, it was more than 54,000. Nearly 19,000 were Black. Walter was better off in searching for work than many others. Aside from his manual labor skills, he was literate, unlike close to 20 percent of the Black population in Ouachita Parish. The literacy rate was somewhat better in Monroe itself — five out of six Black residents could read and write.

In addition to day labor, Walter became a part-time preacher at the Bethel Baptist Church located at 230 Washington St. in West Monroe, walkable from their new home. He considered it a calling. Walter felt that he was receiving messages from God that compelled him to the ministry just as the prophet Moses had been chosen by God to accept the Ten Commandments and, at God's bidding, to free his people from bondage. Lee, Myrtle and

Leola attended the church with their mother. Armelia would have dressed them up and herself worn a dress and hat as did all the other women going to church.

Walter enjoyed planning ahead and letting the parishioners know what he planned to focus on in his sermons. Yet he often got inspired at the last moment to address a different subject entirely. He attributed the last-minute changes to guidance from God through an inner voice that dictated the subject of his talks. Lee must have been extremely proud to watch his father's passionate sermons inspire the flock. Myrtle was not quite old enough to pay attention. Leola was still a toddler, too young yet to join in the singing of hymns and spirituals. Armelia also now had her own mother nearby. It was a bit of a hike across the bridge to visit Mama Stella (whom the family had started calling "Muzz") and Armelia's younger sisters on Jackson Street but still walking distance.

In the summer of 1928, Armelia became pregnant again. Walter, Jr. was born at home on March 17, 1929, in West Monroe and nicknamed "Sonny Man". This was just a year after "Sonny Boy" aired for the first time, the 1928 megahit that Al Jolson performed as a Blackface minstrel in "The Singing Fool." Too many Black men in the south suffered from being called "boy" no matter their age. The son named for Walter Newton would be called "Sonny Man" from infancy – a little man, never a boy.

The 1930 census shows Walter, age 27, and Armelia, age 23, living with Lee, aged 6, Myrtle aged 4 and 3 months, Leola age two and Walter, Jr., a baby in Ward 5 in Ouachita Parish. Their crowded household also included 24-year-old E. S. Newton, Walter's younger sibling. Walter believed E.S. to be a half-brother but later learned that he was a stepbrother from Ben Newton's earlier marriage. The two men, though not blood relatives, shared deep knowledge of the Scriptures, a love of Gospel music and a strong work ethic.

Sonny Man now had a cousin in Monroe almost his age. Armelia's youngest sister Jessie Mae had a baby daughter in 1929 she named Ruby Jewel. The father was a married man named Amos Lawson. Jessie Mae was just 13 herself. Muzz would raise Ruby Jewel Lawson to adulthood.

Although the Newtons' home was urban now, there were no streetlights or signals at street corners. The dirt roads in West Monroe were narrow with ditches for drainage on either side unlike the paved streets and sidewalks that were characteristic of the more affluent White neighborhoods of the city. That made it hard for the family members to steer clear of the mud while walking to church. The lack of lighting also meant people in West Monroe mostly made sure they were home by dark. Walter Newton was quite protective of his wife. No matter how tight their finances became, he would not allow Armelia to work outside the house for fear of her safety.

Not surprisingly, with high unemployment, Monroe had a very high crime rate in the 1930s. Yet it would not provide a public defenders' office for decades and Black defendants were seldom able to afford private counsel. Louisiana still incarcerates a higher percentage of its residents than any other state. Today more than 9 out of 10 Louisiana criminal defendants are represented by overworked public defenders. In the 1930s, the quality of representation was far worse, and the jury would be composed of all White men who could be expected invariably to side with the prosecutor. Unsurprisingly, arrest and jailing of Black men far exceeded the percentage of White arrestees. The White newspapers fed on the disproportionate Black arrests to brand Black men as far more dangerous. A Black accused of a capital crime stood almost no chance even when he got to face trial rather than a lynch mob.

In 2011, 99-year-old Monroeian, Joseph Sharp, recounted the fate of a neighbor who wound up being the last man legally hanged in Monroe. Antoine Antoine was convicted of killing a White man whom Antoine alleged had attacked him first. His plea of self-defense was not accepted. (Indeed, historically self-defense had never been a viable plea North or South for a Black man who killed a White attacker.) Antoine was hanged on the fourth-floor gallows at the courthouse on St. George Street in Monroe, the same floor where the jail was located.

The use of the Monroe courthouse for hanging stopped after arrests mushroomed to the point that the parish needed to build more courtrooms. Then the city transferred all court-ordered hangings to the capital. Hangings in Baton Rouge ended in 1941 due to adoption of electrocution as a more modern means of execution. Meanwhile, extrajudicial lynchings continued throughout the South without legal redress.

***

Walter and Armelia arrived back in Louisiana prior to the Wall Street crash in October 1929 that launched the Depression. While living in West Monroe in 1930, Walter supported his family by working with his stepbrother E.S. in a gravel pit. Both men had been quite fortunate to find work. By 1930 almost half of the Blacks in the parish were unemployed. In Monroe, work was slightly easier to come by — 43 per cent had no jobs. Both income and sales in the parish sank by two-thirds in just five years. Walter would find employment at different times in a carbon plant and a sugarcane mill, as well as sharecropping on cotton plantations. During that time property values in Ouachita Parish fell by a third. Income from retail sales and farming dropped closer to two-thirds. Sharecroppers and tenant farmers proliferated as farms were foreclosed upon or bought out.

The country as a whole was reeling. During the first three years of the Depression, national income fell by more than half. The cotton market tanked. As devastating as that was for the White population, it was far more so for Blacks. Black professionals in the South were far fewer in number than in the North and mostly consisted of poorly compensated clergymen or teachers. Half of all Blacks in cities across the country would be unemployed by 1932. A year later, so would 25 percent of Whites. Government relief became a necessity for the hardest hit. That included roughly half of Black families in the North and a higher percentage in the South. Yet persisting through adversity was something Blacks had long been accustomed to. One survivor described the Depression as nothing new: "The Negro was born in depression. It only became official when it hit the white man."

Life Under the Kingfish

WHEN the Newtons moved to West Monroe the new governor of Louisiana was Democrat Huey Pierce Long, nicknamed the Kingfish. Walter paid close attention to politics even though he could not vote. By the mid-1930s, nationwide, fewer than one out of 25 African Americans counted among registered voters. In 1932, these traditional Lincoln Republicans felt abandoned by their party and endorsed Democrat Franklin D. Roosevelt for President. Yet Southern Democrats were ardent segregationists and would be for decades to come.

Long himself openly embraced racism but held himself out as a champion of the poor, fighting corporate greed. During his term as governor from 1928 to 1932, Prohibition under the 18th Amendment to the Constitution was still the law of the land. Yet it had little if any impact in Louisiana. Like his predecessors, Governor Long had no intention of enforcing it. Moonshine and bootlegged beer remained readily available for the entire time the sale of alcohol was officially banned. That was not an issue Walter Newton cared much about. He seldom drank and never to excess.

What impressed Walter during the Depression was that Governor Long launched huge public works projects, including modern highways, and broadened the scope of social programs. Yet the Kingfish's tenure was mired in scandal with accusations of corruption and acting like a would-be dictator. Impeachment proceedings for abuse of power did not result in conviction.

Four years as governor established Long as the

unrivaled political boss of Louisiana. By 1932, he had fired hundreds of state employees loyal to his rivals and replaced them with his own supporters. Long was then elected United States Senator and used that office as a platform for his presidential ambitions.

After helping FDR win the election in 1932, Long became a vocal critic of the new President for not doing enough for the poor. Long was expected to challenge FDR in the Democratic primary in 1936. But in September of 1935 Long was assassinated by the son-in-law of a political rival whose career Long had torpedoed by arranging for the gerrymandering of the man's home district.

Despite the racism that pervaded state and local politics, Governor Long was revered as a populist who got things done. He impressed Walter and other Black Louisianans as well as poor Whites because of the major public improvements he caused to be implemented. Walter could see that Long talked the talk of racism but actually helped lift Black people up. Improvements like free books for schools benefited the children of both Black and White Louisianans.

Yet another example that Walter particularly admired was the creation of jobs for Black nurses to treat Black patients at White hospitals. Long's rationale to White constituents was to make sure White nurses did not have to touch naked Black men's bodies. Long also gave impetus to the creation of Black hospitals, professional training for Black doctors and nurses and hiring of Black doctors. All of this was justified to his White constituents as protecting the sacred tradition of segregation.

The first federally-funded medical facility for Blacks in Washington, D.C., was the Freedman's Hospital established during the Civil War. As of the turn of the twentieth century, only about forty such hospitals had been established in various states with predictably inferior equipment. By 1922, there was only one Black hospital all the way from the nation's Capital to New Orleans that experts in the field considered "well-equipped." Today, the Freedman's Hospital is known as Howard University Hospital, just one of three traditional Black hospitals still in use.

Even though the facilities and pay at Black hospitals created by Governor Long were never designed to be truly equal to those at White hospitals, Long achieved both better health care for Black patients and far more medical careers for Black aspirants. He may have also saved a number of Black women from being sterilized without their knowledge in White hospitals. They might go to the hospital to give birth and wake up having had a hysterectomy or tubal ligation. It was a medical practice in the late 1920s and 1930s sanctioned by legislation in many states to curb reproduction by minorities and the poor, a policy long advocated by leading eugenicists.

Birth control advocate Margaret Sanger was famous for promoting birth control as a way to produce "less children for the unfit." The Newtons were a large, working-class Black family — a category that appalled Sanger. She was convinced: "All of our problems are the result of overbreeding among the working class." Eugenics was endorsed by White politicians, doctors, lawyers and judges across the country. After the Supreme Court in 1927 endorsed forced sterilization in *Buck v. Bell*, 274 U.S. 200 the adoption of state laws allowing that procedure resulted in surgical sterilization of over 62,000 people nationwide, mostly women of color.

Black women in particular were a target, making Margaret Sanger a popular speaker at KKK gatherings. Her agenda was made explicit in a private letter to a prominent doctor who also advocated birth control as a way to improve the gene pool: "We don't want the word to go out that we want to exterminate the Negro population..."

Giving birth at home with help from a midwife, as Armelia did, had some advantages. For one, home births were a way to avoid being subject to an involuntary hysterectomy, a common procedure in hospitals. Fortunately, for others, in 1942, a more enlightened panel of the Supreme Court unanimously held that the imposition of compulsory sterilization on a man convicted of being a habitual offender (in this case a chicken thief) violated the due process and equal protection clauses of the Fourteenth Amendment. The high court noted that white collar felons such as embezzlers and those guilty of political crimes were exempted from that law. Only by analogy did women targeted by compulsory sterilization laws later obtain that same constitutional protection as men.

By 1944 there would be 124 Black hospitals across the country that served only "colored" patients – still less than a fifth of which garnered full approval for their surgeries. (Most hospitals in the South would stay racially segregated until 1966, when President Lyndon Johnson forced compliance with the Civil Rights Act of 1964 by making integration a condition of future Medicare funding.) Yet thanks to the leadership of Governor Huey Long, by the early 1930s there had been a general increase in accessible medical care for Black people. Pioneering television journalist Belva Davis, who was born in Monroe, got the same positive impression of Huey Long from her parents' generation that Walter Newton had.

The two families knew each other and followed parallel paths out of the South. Born Belvagene Melton on October 13, 1932, Belva was the eldest of four children. Her mother was only 14 at the time, just five years older than Lee Edward Newton. Her father and Walter Newton may have worked at the same sawmill or possibly met when Walter Newton served as a part-time Baptist minister. Perhaps the Newtons attended one or more performances of Belva's father's popular gospel quartet. When Belva was a young teen, her family would move to Oakland, California in the same community to which Walter later moved his family. In 1967-1968, as a cub TV reporter, she would cover Huey Newton's arrest and trial from a different perspective than most other mainstream journalists.

The Move to Bastrop

IN 1930, the Depression had no end in sight, which was likely a major factor in Walter Newton's decision to move from Monroe. Like so many others, he wound up as a sharecropper, in his case picking cotton in nearby Bastrop.

Back in Monroe, Walter had quickly developed a reputation for standing up for himself in ways that struck some people as brash and reckless, earning him the moniker "Crazy Man". He later told his children that he acquired the nickname after he got into a dispute with a younger White boss over the way he was performing a task. The boss threatened to resort to whipping to bend him to his will. Walter challenged his boss as not being man enough. Walter's surprising display of backbone ended in a way that made bystanders perceive him as foolhardy. Standing up for himself against oppressive bigots was a way to get killed. Walter was happy to embrace that "Crazy Man" reputation since it tended to protect him from further aggression. He found that White bullies preferred easier targets.

Melvin thinks that his dad may only have survived so many confrontations with White men in the South because he was himself half-White. Another story Walter told his children demonstrated even greater courage. He had been in a car with other Black workers acting a bit rowdy on their way home. They happened to stop along the way across from a house where a White woman spied them from her porch. Soon a White man emerged from the front door wielding an ax. He accused them of making fun of her. The driver of the car immediately took off down the block. But Walter wanted to go back and face the man. The driver let him out and Walter returned to meet the fellow heading their way. Walter asked him what he planned to use the ax for. The man said he was just displaying it for his sister's benefit. Walter considered that answer good enough. He had stood his ground and made a point.

Sharecropping in Bastrop would have meant a bit more space for a garden to feed their family with homegrown produce. A move out of Monroe also meant that Walter and his family joined a different local Baptist church. There were several in Bastrop, but it was more likely they joined St. Matthews Baptist Church in the adjacent village of Mer Rouge where Walter Jr. was baptized. Mer Rouge, French for Red Sea, was located in Morehouse Parish on the outskirts of Bastrop on the same railroad line. The boundary between the village of Mer Rouge and Bastrop is the large and imposing Red Hill. The Newtons' home in Bastrop, situated at the bottom of that hill, was walking distance from the parish school in Mer Rouge that Lee Edward and Myrtle could now attend.

The school was a two-story brick building built in 1925, serving not just as a school but as a community center for that rural area. Residents were invited to numerous events there over the years the Newtons lived in Bastrop. (The school is now listed in the National register of Historic Places). Leola went there, too, when she was old enough. (In her forties, Leola returned to show her children where she had lived and walked to school and made sure to take them by the ice cream shop in Mer Rouge by the railroad tracks that they used to frequent. It was still operating).

The Newton family arrived in Bastrop in time for Doris to be born at home on October 21, 1930. The family would remain in Bastrop for nearly ten years. Leola, Sonny Man and Doris would attend the same parish school in Mer Rouge. One of their schoolmates was Katherine Jackson, a year younger than Myrtle. Katherine walked to school with both Myrtle and Leola. Lee Edward quit elementary school to help Walter pick cotton so she might not have met him yet. But, as an adult, Katherine would move to Oakland, California and marry him.

Myrtle quit school early to help her mother out in the garden and in the house with meals, chores and watching the younger children. The Newtons' third son Melvin David Newton was born on December 17, 1937, Myrtle's 12th birthday. His first name was for Walter's half-brother. His middle name may have been bestowed in honor of the Biblical David.

All of the children appreciated Armelia's calming influence when things bothered them. They knew she loved them all dearly. Hugs and kisses were plentiful. She was fun to spend time with; yet she was a strict disciplinarian. They all learned to do the chores she assigned them, not wishing to face the consequences if they didn't.

When Sonny Man was old enough, he picked cotton with his father and older brother. Leola and Doris assisted in the garden and indoor chores. But Myrtle, as the oldest daughter, was expected to help out the most. By now, it may have been apparent that Myrtle suffered from asthma. Leola did, too, making it hard for both of them to work for much time in the garden. It is not likely the family had access to any medical care for their condition.

In their spare time, the children loved playing games with Armelia — indoors and out, checkers or jacks; outdoors, swinging on an old tire hung from a tree. One of the treasures the family acquired was a hand-turned gramophone to play 78 records. Lee Edward started making a record collection of his own. Armelia greatly enjoyed being a stay-at-home Mom, interacting with her children and watching them dance. Yet Myrtle lost out on some of her childhood. It rankled when she was stuck inside cooking and cleaning while her mother played with her younger siblings outdoors.

Compared to Monroe, Bastrop was still a relatively small town. It had a population of about 5100 when the Newtons moved there in 1930. Even that was a large increase from its earlier population of just 1200 residents in 1920 before the paper mills came. Under 10,000 live there today, the vast majority of whom are Black.

Bastrop had been named for a land speculator named Felipe Enrique Neri, who called himself the Baron de Bastrop, though his claim to nobility was suspect at best. De Bastrop apparently fled Holland for fear of being prosecuted for embezzlement. He arrived at Fort Miró in the late 18th century and received a land grant there which gave rise to a colony near the Ouachita River.

The roughly nine square mile town of Bastrop was incorporated in 1857 and became the seat of Morehouse Parish. Although Bastrop bordered on swampland, it had enough suitable ground to lay tracks to connect to Monroe by rail when Bastrop was established as the parish seat. Likely due to the rail line, Bastrop became a base for soldiers recruited for the Confederacy during the Civil War — until January of 1865.

Fittingly, when Bastrop fell to the Union Army, it was conquered by an expedition of 3,000 former slaves from Vicksburg. The ex-slaves formed the 3rd United States Colored Cavalry, which was led by Union Colonel

Bastrop, Louisiana was captured in January of 1865 by 3,000 former slaves from Vicksburg who had joined the Union Army in January of 1865. The ex-sloves formed the 3rd United States Colored Cavalry, which was led by Union Colonel Embury Osband, a White officer, as was the rule for other Black units in the Union Army. Vicksburg itself had fallen on July 4, 1863, allowing the Union to control the Mississippi River.

MEN OF COLOR
TO ARMS! TO ARMS!
NOW OR NEVER

Three Years' Service!

FAIL NOW, & OUR RACE IS DOOMED

ARE FREEMEN LESS BRAVE THAN SLAVES

Embury Osband, a White officer, as was the rule for other Black units in the Union army. Vicksburg itself had fallen on July 4, 1863, allowing the Union to control the Mississippi River. That triggered implementation of the Emancipation Proclamation issued by President Lincoln the preceding January: "all persons held as slaves within any State or designated part of a State, the people whereof shall then be in rebellion against the United States, shall be then, thenceforward, and forever free . . . ."

Slaves who remained in the South during the Civil War could only become free if and when their location fell into Union hands. Less than two months after Vicksburg fell, President Lincoln realized that "the emancipation policy, and the use of colored troops, constitute the heaviest blow yet dealt to the rebellion." So the fall of Vicksburg precipitated the fall of Bastrop at the hands of the 3d United States Colored Cavalry in January of 1865.

The courthouse in the town center of Bastrop was built in 1914. It is still there today. At the back of the courthouse, Bastrop also opened the Rose Theater, which remains an entertainment venue. The Newtons loved Gospel music. One popular performer was Zeke Lee, a native of Bastrop known for his gospel quartet. His stepdaughter, Jacquelyn Cliffortene Hilton later went to the same elementary school that Doris attended in Monroe. Another well-known family in Bastrop was the Smiths, who had five sons. One of them, Arthur Smith, was a blacksmith much in demand for shoeing horses and forging tools. Years later, Arthur Smith and his wife Bertha formed close connections with the Newtons after the Smiths moved to Monroe.

When entering Bastrop from any direction you could

smell the strong sulfuric odor. Sulfur was in constant use as part of the local paper mills' manufacturing process. The huge increase in population from 1920 to 1930 was due in large part to the arrival of this new industry. Back in 1921, the Bastrop Pulp & Paper Company built the second paper mill in the area. It added another mill shortly afterward with the goal of establishing Bastrop as the "paper mill center of the South." In 1927, the International Paper Company bought the mills and became the largest employer in Bastrop for decades to come. At their peak production, the mills employed 1100 people. The unfortunate byproduct was the sulfuric acid that seeped into the water supply, making the taps run yellow. The mills have since closed.

Bastrop's population grew quickly in the 1920s due in part to the new paper mills and, in 1927, to the influx of refugees from the Great Mississippi Flood to the relief camp established in Bastrop. The Newtons' home in Bastrop was a small shotgun house with two bedrooms. The family had two cows, some chickens and pigs. They also maintained their own vegetable garden. Some families had fruit trees as well from which they could lay up a supply of preserves.

Throughout his years in town, Walter had more interactions with White men that kept his reputation as a "crazy man" intact. Once, when he believed a White shopkeeper had defrauded him, he spread the word in town about what had happened. The irate man drove to the Newton's home to confront him. Walter knew that the fellow kept a gun in his glove compartment. He situated himself on the passenger side running board where he could make sure the fellow could not reach for his gun as they talked. He then told the man: "If you hit me a lick, the other folks will have to hunt me down because you'll be lying here in the road dead." That put an end to it.

Sometimes when both parents went somewhere together, Lee Edward was left to supervise his younger siblings. Doris had three scary adventures when she was small that might have caused her death or severe injury. The first was when Doris was 4 or 5 and almost drowned. Her parents left her and Myrtle under Lee Edward's supervision. All of the older children had responsibility for younger siblings. Lee Edward was 11 or 12; Myrtle was about 9. Leola was about 7 and may have accompanied her mother and father.

Their parents owned a little boat and warned Lee Edward not to go messing with it in the river. Lee promised them he would obey their instructions. But as soon as their parents left, Lee Edward broke the lock where the boat was stored. He took the boat to the river by a bridge. Doris and Myrtle went with him. Doris flipped into the water. Myrtle caught her by the hair and rolled her on the riverbank to get the water out. Doris remembered that her parents were so mad she thought they wanted to kill Lee Edward.

A year or so later, Doris was about 5 or 6 when she was playing near the fireplace at home. Her mother was working with other women gathered for a quilting bee. Suddenly Doris's sleeve caught fire. Her mother was concentrating on sewing a quilt and did not notice Doris catch fire until another woman screamed, "Armelia!" The other woman grabbed Doris's dress and pulled it off over Doris's head. Armelia passed out from the close call.

Monroe in the 1930s

THE NEWTON FAMILY still maintained frequent contact with their relatives in Monroe. Walter may even have commuted there for work at some point after the family moved out of West Monroe. Muzz was happy to board whichever of the children Armelia wanted to go to school at Mt. Nebo's or Colored High or to work in Monroe. Sometimes a child might stay with Uncle Isaac and Aunty Sissy. Lee Edward moved into his own quarters after his own stay with Muzz.

In her autobiography, *Never In My Wildest Dreams*, newscaster Belva Davis describes life in Monroe in the 1930s: mired in "the depths of the Great Depression, the reign of Jim Crow, and [experiencing] the "Flood of the Century" on the Ouachita River. Surprisingly, despite the continuing racial tension, Black and White Monroeians actually found themselves working together by necessity to combat the devastation caused by that flood.

The Ouachita River flood in February 1932 was worse for locals than the 1927 Mississippi River flood. It overflowed sandbags and submerged more than a fourth of Monroe in polluted water. The water stayed above flood level until the middle of April, prompting government health warnings to people in the flood districts. If they were not vaccinated, they were likely to catch typhoid. The flood forced both Black and White families into tents on higher ground. Several formerly segregated neighborhoods wound up having men stand side by side piling sandbags on the levy to contain the flood and living in integrated campsites – only to revert to segregation when the flood waters subsided.

Once life got back to the usual pattern, the KKK still had the capacity to enforce strict unstated rules of behavior. Belva recalled that Blacks who worked in White homes in the 1930s when she was a child headed straight for the back door. They never knocked on the front door for fear that it would bring retribution for acting dangerously "uppity."

When the flood receded, Klansmen were still often on the prowl. Belva noted in her autobiography: "It was said in Monroe that Negroes woke up every morning fearing that they might be lynched, while Whites woke up every morning fearing a Negro uprising."

Belva's parents lived in a single story, shotgun house probably much like the Newtons. In her case, it was located on a dirt road called Solomon's Alley, a dozen blocks on the north side of the river. Even by the late 1940s, similar homes had no indoor plumbing. They used a wash pan to do dishes, visited an outhouse during the day, keeping on the lookout for rats and snakes, and kept a chamber pot or "slop jar" in the house to use at night. Families took their baths in a galvanized tub.

Belvagene lived with a childless aunt as a toddler, which had the benefit of her own bedroom, a luxury the Newton children seldom, if ever, enjoyed. When Belvagene's aunt died of tuberculosis, she wound up sleeping on a blanket on the floor.

Like other women in her family, Belvagene's mother earned just $4 weekly working long days as a laundress at G. B. Colley's Monroe Steam Laundry alongside dozens of other women. The conditions likely did not differ much from those Stella Johnson had endured as a laundress in 1910. The women still suffered through unbearable heat and steam every workday in order to provide freshly starched bed linens, shirts and other clothing for the mostly White patrons of the laundries.

Belvagene's father worked at a sawmill. The nearby lumberyard was rat-infested, a health hazard common in Colored Town. Belva recalls that sawmill work was dangerous. Mill workers often lost their fingers or hands working there, but her father was more adept and fortunate. He had started as a young teen. By the 1930s her father had developed the expertise to work with the most complex machinery at the mill and was earning $30 per week – several times what laundresses made. Yet, like Stella's husband John, Belva's father brought little of it home.

At the time, Five Points was owned by the very same White family that owned the lumber mill. The saloons and gambling houses lured the mill workers to gamble or drink away their earnings. Belva's father was among those who spent weekends at Five Points. He had a temper and wound up in jail on many weekends, though he was bailed out by Monday, likely by his boss, so he could head back to work on time. Belva's father also became a Gospel singer in quartets, spending some of his earnings on suits for his gigs and using hair pomade to slick down his hair to attract the ladies in attendance.

* * *

At some point, Walter Newton took a job in Monroe working for a carbon company, presumably United Carbide and Carbon Corporation. It was established in 1917 shortly after a major new natural gas source was found that greatly expanded local industries. Among other things, starting in 1920 the company made antifreeze for automobiles. Monroe then became prosperous enough to introduce streetcars. In that Jim Crow Era, most streetcars accepted only White riders. Blacks could only board those with a Black star insignia. Given the paucity of "Black star" cars, when one came along passengers were often squeezed in like sardines. Yet it was well worth waiting for. Among other things, this new mode of public transportation made it far easier for Monroeians to catch the latest picture shows.

Walter's brother E. S. was a ladies' man for whom movies on weekends were a great destination. First-run films lured teenagers, too. Lee Edward, Sonny Man and their sisters could take in movies either in the theater in the Bastrop town center or in Monroe when staying there. Immersed in Hollywood extravaganzas, they could forget for a few hours the second-class treatment that characterized their lives.

In Monroe by 1930 the Paramount Theater on Desiard Street was the place to go with or without a date. The movies, of course, would always star White actors and actresses. The Lyceum Theater that folks frequented in the teens and twenties had itself been bought out by Paramount and remodeled in 1929 for the advent of talkies. The Lyceum could seat 1100 patrons, but the Paramount was far larger. It attracted sell-out crowds to Hollywood blockbusters that included the box office hit "Dr. Jekyll and Mr. Hyde" in 1931 that wound up nominated for three Academy awards; "King Kong" in 1933, dubbed "the greatest horror film of all time"; and Cecil B. De Mille's epic "Cleopatra", which was the highest grossing film in America in 1934.

At first, the Paramount had two ticket windows manned in the same location by one cashier, who served White patrons before switching to sell tickets to those in the colored line. That evolved into two booths with separate cashiers accessed by separate entrances. The Whites came in through the majestic front double front doors. The Whites also sat in upholstered seats on the ground floor, some up front in orchestra seats.

The colored entrance was through a side door. The Black customers climbed five flights of stairs that, by the early 1930s, reeked of urine. The staircase led up to the wooden seats in the balcony. Many teenagers from Colored Town would head there on the weekend if they had any money to spend. An attendant stationed in the hall made sure everyone had bought a ticket.

Black patrons who needed to relieve themselves during the show were directed to a bathroom upstairs, but the toilet was usually clogged. Using the stairwell to pee in may have been out of desperation or perhaps a form of protest, but it made the walk up most unpleasant for others consigned to the balcony. Once seated in the dark, however, some of the patrons, mostly teenagers, got a more targeted revenge. They occasionally tossed popcorn and soda over the rail onto White patrons below, knowing they could never be caught.

Zion Travel Baptist Church Survives its Own Civil War

AS Uncle Isaac established himself solidly in the Black middle class and helped his sister's family, they all watched from the sidelines an eye-popping rift among African-American Baptist churchgoers. The circles Uncle Isaac traveled in included one of the most highly respected members of Monroe's Black community, William Frederick Sherman. Sherman was a member of the NAACP, a deacon in the Zion Travel Baptist Church and a member of the PTA, who also taught Sunday school and acted as the church historian. His day job was running elevators at the Bernhardt Office Building as well as janitorial work.

Sherman's granddaughter Margaret Ann Jackson was a contemporary of Walter Newton's older children who went to the Mt. Nebo Church School. When the Mt. Nebo Church school closed, many members of its student body wound up at the new school on Jones Lane, so the Newtons had reason to know Sherman as well. He became deeply involved in both city politics and church activities and wound up representing many Blacks denied voter registration who required three registered voters to vouch for reinstatement of persons removed from the voter rolls.

Zion Travel Baptist Church in the early 1930s was one of the oldest and largest Black Baptist churches in Monroe. It dated back to 1871 — just six years after the end of the Civil War. Its second long-term pastor, Warner Washington Hill, took the pulpit in 1904. He was a revivalist who brought in many new congregants with boisterous efforts to engage the flock. Yet he turned out to be quite divisive. In 1932 a violent feud erupted in the flock that had been simmering for some time.

In February 1932 the church leaders were among the many community organizers focused on the emergency caused by the Ouachita flood. A group of unhappy members decided to seize the opportunity of Warner Hill supporters' absence to oust him as pastor. The dissidents ironically designated their group "the Harmony Club". Hill wrote a letter seeking the support of a local judge to prevent the takeover. The Harmony Club responded by filing an action for injunctive relief to block Hill from the pulpit. Hill counterclaimed and lost. His supporters met in the meantime and reinstated Hill. But the feud did not end there.

The Harmony Club had abstained from the church election to prevent a quorum of attendees. The Club members won their injunction and got the judge to hold Hill in contempt for relying on an invalid vote to stay as pastor. Hill would not accept that result. In June of 1932 he tried to conduct a sermon from the pulpit and wound up arrested for "disturbing public worship." The situation appeared so contentious that the White superintendent of police then intervened and closed the church down. He reopened it in August after a new vote of the congregation rejected Hill's leadership and instead installed as the new pastor Madison James Foster, the long-time principal of Monroe Colored High School where over 1100 sons and daughters of Colored Town went to school from kindergarten through eleventh grade, including Sonny Man and Leola.

Every Black family in town knew Madison Foster. The dispute became the talk of the town even among those who did not read the newspapers but simply gathered at places like Isaac's café and grocery store or attended Mt.

Nebo Church where Isaac was a deacon. As the year progressed, the split allegiances among members of Zion Church had both sides refusing to speak to one another.

Professor Foster, as he came to be called, had risen to statewide prominence as President of the Louisiana Colored Teachers Association. Around town, he dressed to impress with gold cufflinks accessorizing his suits and starched, collared shirts. Both he and his wife were widely admired among the middle class in the Black community. Those reading the widely distributed *Chicago Defender* could often find Prof. Foster quoted in the columns covering Louisiana news. To the Harmony Club, Foster represented an obvious, highly respected choice to take over the leadership of the Church. He was definitely not a Holy-Roller like Pastor Hill.

Foster had come to Monroe with his wife Ottie back in 1905 and became long-time members of the Zion congregation. Ottie was herself the daughter of a preacher. Madison grew up reciting from the Scriptures as entertainment for the guests of his foster parents. Foster may not have talked much about his youth. He had been raised by a White family in New Iberia who helped him get a college degree at Leland College in New Orleans. That was where he met and married Ottie, who was also then earning her teaching degree. In the 1930s, she served as President of the Golden Seal Embroidery Club and was often featured in the society pages of Monroe's Black newspapers for her role in various community events.

When Foster took the pulpit of Zion Travel Baptist Church on Sunday, September 4, 1932, and started reading from the Scriptures, four women approached him to insist that he stop. They were among the diehard congregants who still supported Hill. Foster had no intention of yielding to their demands. The attempt to halt the service outraged Harmony Club members, who had suspected something of the sort might happen. Angry parishioners on both sides of the dispute left their seats and broke out in fights.

The situation quickly got worse when a Hill supporter named James Dugans brought out his handgun. George Daniels, the President of the Harmony Club, then ran for his own weapon. Daniels had stashed a gun in a nearby house in the expectation that Hill supporters would "shoot up the church if Foster preached." Daniels was not wrong. When he returned, Daniels found his daughter lying wounded on the church floor. Dugans then shot Daniels, who returned fire. Dugans wounded three other parishioners before he fell dead from a bullet wound. Daniels' daughter died the next day.

Much to the horror of peaceful Black Baptists in the city, the Monroe Superintendent of Police again shut down the church amid outrage in the White community about the unfathomable turmoil that had just erupted in a place of worship. Walter Newton could only watch from the sidelines and hope the controversy would die down quickly. The Superintendent soon determined that Dugans was the instigator of the deadly violence and only charged Daniels with bringing a concealed weapon to the church. By November 1932 the superintendent of police would reopen the church after new elections in which Hill could not participate. Prof. Foster and his family had escaped the August confrontation unharmed and stayed active in the church. Frozen out of any leadership role at Zion, Hill and his followers launched their own rival church, Triumph Baptist. Black Baptists throughout the area could breathe easier as the White community calmed down.

The Monroe Monarchs — A Glimmer of Integration

IN the 1930s professional and college sports absorbed the South. E.S. Newton was a particular fan of baseball. Leland Foster, the oldest son of Prof. Foster, was a star pitcher in college who many locals thought might make it to the Negro Leagues. Leland spent a lot of his free time in pool halls. Armelia's father, John Johnson, could easily have run into him there.

An inveterate gambler, John Johnson was drawn to the racetrack at Forsythe Park just two miles northwest of the Johnsons' home near the river. The track also served as a baseball field. The home team was the White Monroe Twins, who belonged to the Cotton States League. The stands had separate seating for White and Black attendees. Since 1930 it also had artificial lights — the first ever in Monroe. Fans could now watch games in the cooler evenings instead of the blazing sun. But the lackluster Monroe Twins were not as huge a draw in 1932 as the amazing Monroe Monarchs, an African-American team that occasionally played night games there, too.

African-Americans had participated in baseball games since the sport originated shortly before the Civil War. Most teams played in the Northeast, but New Orleans had early teams, too. In the Reconstruction Era they competed against White teams, but that was no longer true in the era of Jim Crow. In the late 1920s, a semi-pro Black team from Monroe played in the segregated Dixie League. After they became affiliated with the Kansas City Monarchs, they became known as the Monroe Monarchs, playing in the Negro Southern League. In 1931 the Monroe Monarchs won the Texas-Louisiana minor league championship. Then came their spectacular 1932 season.

In 1932 thousands of Black and White sports fans thronged to see the Monroe Monarchs. They had just been included for the first time as a major league Negro team. Given its small population of just 26,000 and its location in the segregated Deep South, it took all the owner's persuasive abilities to get Monroe included in the big leagues. Other teams were located in urban hubs with far greater fan bases.

During the Roaring Twenties, Black service industries had mushroomed in cities like New York, Chicago and Philadelphia. Black professionals and successful entrepreneurs helped grow the Black middle class, which supported the growth of Black entertainment. Once the Monarchs won their place in the most competitive league, the prowess of the Monarchs gave locals a jumbo shot of civic pride in the heart of the Depression.

In 1932 the Monarchs' winning record gained a following in the White sports pages as well as Black newspapers. Their home field was Casino Park located on the corner of 29th and Hope Streets in the Booker T. Washington District just outside the eastern city limits of Monroe. It had once been a cotton plantation. The stands seated 3,500 fans in a field on the south side of the Kansas City Southern and Union Pacific railroad tracks that ran along Desiard Street just a couple of miles from Jackson Street where the Burnetts and Johnsons lived. Awkwardly, for the few women fans who showed up, there was no women's bathroom.

In 1931, the Monroe Monarchs began playing at Casino Park, constructed on a field recently acquired by Texas millionaire Fred Stovall, whose oil and gas drilling company had a bi-racial workforce. Casino Park boasted a lot of action. In addition to the baseball field, it had a community center, dance hall and swimming pool.

Much to his parents' chagrin, Leland Foster liked to hang out at juke joints. E.S. Newton did, too. Like the Blues, jukes dated back to the latter half of the nineteenth century. Plantation owners sometimes provided space where Black slaves could relax in their free time. Juke joints later began appearing as pop-ups in old buildings at crossroads in the rural south near sharecroppers and small farms. They also appeared in cities like Monroe where segregated dance halls like the one at Casino Park allowed patrons to let loose drinking and dancing, enjoying soul food and sometimes gambling.

Fred Stovall was a newcomer who had moved to Monroe to oversee his gas drilling company. His corporate office was on Desiard Street near North 10th Street in the middle of the city where the streets were paved and level, unlike the dirt roads that dominated Colored Town. Stovall also financed the Negro Southern League and a feeder team for the Monarchs called the Drillers, who worked for Stovall's gas drilling company. The Drillers played at Casino Park when the Monarchs were on the road.

The 1932 season proved to be a major landmark in local race relations, if only for a short reprieve from enforced segregation. At the time, the impact of the Monarchs' season was similar to what later occurred in South Africa a year after apartheid ended. New President Nelson Mandela realized that hosting the Rugby World

Cup would bring Blacks and Whites together. Rooting the team to victory became a huge bridge builder across the racial divide as the Springboks went on to win their first Rugby World Cup in June 1995.

Monroe in the 1930s remained just as segregated as the rest of the state. Blacks still had separate entrances at entertainment venues, had to climb to the balcony of movie theaters and were kept separate from Whites everywhere that could be accomplished. Yet White newspapers began regularly reporting on the Monarchs' games and began identifying with the team. White reporters were far less likely to talk about the Monarchs as a "Negro" team. Instead, they began to call the players "Monroe" or say "we" when describing the team's exciting 1932 season.

At Casino Park, normally a rope divided White and Black spectators, but at a home game halfway through the 1932 season Stovall noticed the White half of the bleachers was far less than full. Meanwhile, Black patrons crowded into every seat on their side, and more were seeking a place to sit. Stovall ordered the rope removed to allow the Black spectators to fill in the gaps. The stands would remain undivided for the rest of the season.

Monroe-born Prof. Thomas Aiello, author of *The Kings of Casino Park*," highlighted the extraordinary symbolism of dropping the rope: "Not only does it say something about the population of Monroe and its ability to come together in a very difficult time, it also says something about the Black population of Monroe and its resilience in the face of some really overwhelming odds. . ... The team's winning ways created an eagerness for whites to interact with Negro League baseball, which was previously unheard of." The team traveled in style in new Ford automobiles purchased by Stovall. He also housed them at Casino Park. The season ended in September with the unofficial Negro World Series of 1932 against the Pittsburgh Crawfords whose roster included megastars Josh Gibson, Satchel Page and Cool Papa Bell — all later inducted into the Negro Leagues Hall of Fame. Sportscaster Paul Letlow described one memorable moment in that series:

> "Out in what would have been left field there is a railroad track that runs east to west . . . In that world series, Josh Gibson, the great slugger, hit a home run. And there was a train passing by at the time. And a player, Augustus Saunders, who I interviewed years ago, told me that a home run ball landed on the train and traveled all the way to Jackson, Mississippi." [A different source claimed the ball only made it to the next town].

Lee Edward was nine that year. Perhaps Uncle E.S. took him to see one or more of those riveting games as he later brought his own children along with him to his beloved Detroit Tigers stadium. The Monarchs only lasted through 1932 as a major league team before reverting to minor league status, then disbanded around 1935. What stuck with Black attendees was that for one extraordinary season a common love of baseball integrated the stadium.

Bastrop in the Late 1930s

WHEN Melvin Newton was born on December 17,1937 at home in Bastrop, his older sister Doris recalled that the midwife who came to deliver him was Miss Phoebe. The family soon performed a ritual that likely derived from African ancestors. Melvin was "given" to his older sister Leola, who was ten-and-a-half.

Though Myrtle spent the most time raising Melvin, Leola would be tasked with helping feed the baby and watching out for his safety in the house and in the yard. That designation had not been an option for Lee Edward when Myrtle, Leola and Sonny Man were born, because Lee Edward was too young at the time. Now, Lee Edward was needed to work in the field with his father. Doris could not remember a time that either Lee Edward or Myrtle went to school. They both quit in elementary school to help out their parents when Leola, Sonny Man and Doris were quite young. In addition to babysitting, Myrtle did most of the washing, cooking and ironing for the family.

Melvin remembers very little of life before moving to Oakland, California when he was 7. His recollections of Bastrop seem dreamlike. He vaguely recalls a neighbor woman who lived on the hill above their house. He would have been no older than three when they left Bastrop. Their cousin Earl, who lived nearby with his mother, sometimes came over to play with his young cousin. Melvin remembers Earl taking him for a ride on his bicycle when Melvin was about three.

Going forward, as Melvin and Leola got older, she became his trusted advisor. They would share a close lifelong bond. He sometimes called Leola Sister-Mom in recognition of her role as a third parent. Leola absorbed her father's teachings and set the same example: give family members unconditional love, always believe in yourself and your dreams, work hard, stand straight and proud, smile and dig deep for courage. Leola would practice on Melvin and later convey those same messages to her own children.

Doris recalled that there was a Black club in Bastrop called The Dragon on the nearby hill that blared out music at night, as other juke joints did on the Chitlin Circuit throughout the South. Walter and Armelia were not fans. They strongly preferred church music and encouraged their children to sing hymns. Doris recalled that the Dragon had sawdust on the floor, a common, cheap way to cover floors using the piles of leftover sawdust from the mills. Yet how Doris knew what the floor looked like inside the Dragon is unclear since she said her mother would have whipped her if she ever went in. Melvin is not sure the place is still there — he and his second wife, Barbarette, went back to find his home in Bastrop decades later, but did not look for the Dragon.

The rare surviving Black juke joint can still be found in Bay St. Louis, Mississippi — the 100 Men Hall Blues Club. It proves just how much these humble gathering spots can serve as hotbeds for local culture and burgeoning musical trends. The club originated as a community group for mutual assistance among local Black citizens in 1894. The building itself dates back to 1922 and became a stop on the Chitlin Circuit, now a landmark on the Mississippi Blues Trail. Many famous Black musicians traveled that circuit throughout the Southeast and Midwest. In the 1930s, the Chitlin Circuit included, among other performers, Count Basie, Moms Mabley, and Billie Holiday.

* * *

When Doris was eight, about a year after Melvin was born, she found herself in grave danger once again, this time because of a nasty-tempered bull. The family was staying with her Uncle Jack in Monroe. Doris attended the Mt. Nebo Church School where her Great Uncle Isaac was a Deacon. It was the same school then attended by gospel singer Zeke Lee's eight-year-old stepdaughter Jacquelyn Cliffortene Hilton, whose family had also moved back from Bastrop to Monroe.

Doris had joined some other children in a pasture near her Uncle Jack's house, gathering close to a jicama tree to get buckets of water. But the kids made the mistake of running straight past a turf-defending bull, which charged them, forcing them to drop their buckets and flee. Left behind, little Doris was scared to death. Luckily, the bull chased the kids who were running instead of Doris. She crawled under the fence and took a longer route home even though she risked the wrath of her parents by arriving home after 6 p.m. If they had no good excuse for being late, the penalty was going to bed without dinner. That was likely for the children's own protection — not being out after dark. Doris thought she would arrive home before her mother but was mistaken. Her siblings and her parents all got home before she did. Her brother and sister told her:" The bull didn't want you, he wanted us."

* * *

Living in Bastrop with its sulfuric air pollution, Armelia may have noticed that both Doris and Melvin suffered from bouts of asthma like Myrtle did. As her mother's full-time helper, Myrtle became skilled in cooking country meals for both small and large gatherings. Leola also helped share cooking duty at home. When Doris got old enough, she started contributing her own specialty of fried chicken and rice.

Walter pleased his children by baking pineapple cakes for special occasions and other cakes for the holidays. He was happy to oblige Melvin's taste for chocolate and other family members' favorites, including coconut cake. When the family bought flour from the mill, it came in print bags. That popular marketing strategy allowed women to wash the sacks out when they were empty and make dresses from them.

Huey told an anecdote in *Revolutionary Suicide* about Lee Edward as a teenager that his father had relayed to Huey. It happened around 1938 when Lee Edward was 15 and the family was still living in Bastrop. Father and son went to work at a local sugarcane mill owned by an imposing White man. The mill may have been affiliated with the Godchaux company founded in the nineteenth century by Leon Godchaux, "The Sugar King of the South."

The process of refining cane sugar started with grinding the harvested stalks in a continually running machine. On his very first day, Lee Edward was assigned the exhausting task of keeping the grinder constantly fed. Otherwise, friction in the engine's gears would cause it to burn itself out. Although the speed of the grinder had been reduced to make it easier for Lee Edward, after a few hours he could not keep up. By late morning, disaster happened. The engine began to burn out. The owner was furious and immediately started berating the teenager. Walter ran over, shut the machine down and came to his son's defense.

When Walter repeated the story to his younger children, they were impressed with their father's boldness. Walter told them: "The white man was over six feet tall and weighed 200 pounds." Even so, Walter was undaunted. He insisted that the job should have been given to an adult, not a boy. Walter then decided Lee Edward needed to work somewhere else.

Walter Newton and his eldest son Lee Edward at about the age of 15 around 1938 when the family was living in Bastrop.

Sharecropping in Oak Grove

AT ninety-two, Doris retained strong memories of life in the family's next home in Oak Grove, the parish seat. She was ten in 1940 when they moved there from Bastrop. The two oldest boys helped Walter with sharecropping. Myrtle helped raise the younger children.

The Newton household moved into a two-bedroom house at 413 Ward 3, in West Carroll County, Louisiana. Melvin recalls they had no running water and relied on an outhouse — just as the family had in Bastrop. Some local families relied on sulfur sprinkled on the ground to deter snakes. Melvin has a clear picture in his mind of his father driving a mule wagon back and forth from the fields with the harvested cotton. Walter never knew that his own father likely descended from a White mule trader.

One way to envision what it was like living as a sharecropping family in North Central Louisiana in the early 20th century, and in Southern Arkansas for that matter, is to find a book of folk-art paintings by celebrated artist Clementine Hunter. She was born in the late 1880s, the eldest of seven children of Creole French-speaking sharecroppers, and the granddaughter of slaves. Her beloved maternal grandmother was half African-American and half Native American, born in Virginia and brought to a plantation in Louisiana.

Hunter spent most of her own life on Melrose Plantation, on the Cane River in Natchitoches Parish about 109 miles southwest of Monroe. Fortunately for Clementine, Melrose had far more benevolent ownership than the plantation where she was born, Hidden Hill Plantation, later renamed Little Eva Plantation.

Investigative journalist and civil rights activist Lamar White, Jr., described Hidden Hill Plantation as a "cruel and dehumanizing place for Blacks and Creoles like young Clementine." It became known as Little Eva Plantation because it was renamed for a character in Harriett Beecher Stowe's novel *Uncle Tom's Cabin*. The plantation was reported to be one of the inspirations for that best-selling novel.

Hunter was a talented quiltmaker and prolific, bilingual artist who never learned to read or write. She lived to be 101. Her artwork hangs in numerous prestigious museums throughout the United States and in the Louvre. But she got a late start to her career. As a child she only had one year of segregated schooling, where the strict discipline deterred her from any further attendance. At the age of eight, she began working in the fields alongside her father. Over time, Hunter graduated from fieldhand to gardening and housework as a maid, accomplished seamstress and talented cook. Hunter married twice and had seven children.

In 1939 Hunter was still employed at Melrose plantation, which was then operated as an artist colony. One day, while cleaning, Hunter discovered a set of paints and brushes left behind by a guest. By then in her fifties, Hunter began creating from memory more than 5,000 folk art paintings of plantation life. Hunter sketched Black sharecroppers picking cotton, harvesting pecans, washing clothes, attending church and engaging in other routine activities she witnessed and participated in as a child and adult. Rarely did Hunter include a White person in her paintings. It is unlikely the grueling manual labor changed much from plantation to plantation or over the decades even under kindlier owners.

Clementine lived mostly in poverty and never ventured more than 100 miles from her rural home. Yet she depicted joyous occasions, including baptisms and weddings and a spirit of camaraderie among those she painted, like the strong family bonds that the Newtons developed in similar circumstances.

***

The town of Oak Grove had no paved streets, just dirt roads with rocky surfaces. It had a movie theater and a grocery store. Blacks were not allowed in either one at the same time as Whites. The Rex Theater only sat Black patrons upstairs.

The family raised their own chickens and pigs and still owned their two cows. They also grew their own vegetables. The White farmer for whom Walter picked cotton accommodated the family by adding onto the house he provided for them to create more space for the family of eight. Lee Edward stayed with the family for the first couple of years before he left to take a job in Monroe and live with Mama Stella.

Life was tough. The family drew great comfort from each other's company and did not miss having others to turn to for entertainment. They regularly attended church and at home had each other for entertainment. Doris played checkers and dominoes with Armelia, but Walter would no longer play checkers with her because she beat him.

Leola's godfather was a man named Augustus Moore. He told Armelia that their rural home on the outskirts

A print of an oil painting by internationally renowned Louisiana folk artist Clementine Hunter painted in the 1950s, Remembering "Wash Day" at the plantation in Louisiana.

of Oak Grove was not safe from wildlife. That must have scared Doris since she had to walk through the woods regularly to get to school. Leola was afraid of animals and particularly disliked snakes. Melvin only saw a snake once in a field. But once was enough. He found encountering a snake as terrifying as his sister Leola did. Augustus Moore suggested they needed to move to avoid the children being eaten by a bear.

Walter had no fear of wildlife, just as he had no fear of White men. If need be, like Ida Wells, he had a shotgun and knew how to use it. He taught his sons as well when they got old enough to handle one. All of his children were prepared to defend their home if need be.

Walter instilled in all of his offspring the fierce pride of being a Newton. He taught his sons to line up with their shotguns if a White man came to bother them. Those without guns picked up rocks to throw. Lee Edward reinforced the principle that Newtons always stood up for themselves in teaching self-defense to his younger siblings. He gave his brothers tips on boxing and wrestling skills and showed his sisters how to put tacks in the soles of their shoes so they could add a sharp sting to their kicks if anyone gave them trouble. Fortunately, no one ever threatened the family home, possibly because of the reputation Walter had developed for taking no guff.

Walter grew secure enough in his new surroundings that he accepted a hunting trip with several White locals. The men apparently thought they would have some fun at Walter's expense, quizzing a Black preacher about his views on the origin of man.

If any of the men had attended public high school, the standard biology textbook then in use taught that there were five races of men "each very different from the other in instincts, social customs, and, to an extent, in structure ... the Ethiopian or negro type, originating in Africa; the Malay or brown race, from the islands of the Pacific; the American Indian; the Mongolian or yellow race, including the natives of China, Japan, and the Eskimos and finally, the highest type of all, the Caucasians, represented by the civilized White inhabitants of Europe and America."

The concept of White superiority was not a problem for Fundamentalists, but the reference to evolution in that textbook conflicted with what they learned in Sunday school. The men who took Walter Newton hunting all had to have been well aware of the 1925 Scopes "Monkey" trial in Dayton, Tennessee. The sensationalized case in the heart of Bible country had gotten extensive national coverage in newspapers and on radio and the lecture circuit. In that trial, the teaching of evolution from that same high school biology book was famously challenged as a summertime attraction to bring tourists to Dayton.

"The timeless debate over science and religion" pitted three-time Presidential candidate William Jennings Bryan, a devout Christian, against famed Progressive infidel Clarence Darrow. Before a national audience who tuned to radio coverage of the trial, the two giants on the American lecture circuit debated biblical Creationism — historically taught in public schools as well as Sunday school — versus evolution, Charles Darwin's scientific explanation of *The Origin of the Species*.

Walter's White interrogators now wanted to challenge a Black preacher for laying claim to the same Creator that they did. How could Blacks have descended from Adam and Eve, whom they assumed were White? Did

Adam also mate with a gorilla? Despite the fact the men were all armed and capable of doing him harm on any pretext, Walter managed to get away with a quick retort: "Adam must have been a low-life White man to have had sex with a gorilla."

It would have been interesting to have gotten Walter's comment on the June 13, 1925, cartoon about the Scopes trial published in *The Chicago Defender*. He could well have seen it since *The Chicago Defender* had been for many years one of the leading Black newspapers in the country avidly devoured by a national readership. The cartoon was captioned "Disbelievers in the Evolution Theory." It showed two monkeys huddled together on a tree limb overlooking a White lynch mob celebrating a hanging. One monkey asks the other, "Joe, do you believe fiends like these are descendants of ours? Joe emphatically responds: "No!"

Huey's "Outdooring Ceremony"

IN Oak Grove, Melvin slept on a cot in the kitchen. There was also a crib in the house for Huey when he was born on February 17, 1942. Like his older siblings, Huey was born at home. It had been a long and difficult pregnancy. When the midwife showed up to help Armelia that day, Melvin took an immediate dislike to her and crawled away to hide.

Shortly after Huey's birth the family performed a more elaborate "giving" ritual for their new baby son than when they designated Leola as Melvin's guardian. Melvin only retains quite hazy memories of that ceremony. This time, Sonny Man, who was just shy of 13, was given the honor of being the first in the family to bring the new baby outdoors.

That ritual, which customarily takes place eight days after birth, has a long history among the Gadangme People of Southeast Ghana, which was the area where nine per cent of Walter Newton's ancestors from Africa originated. Walter could have heard about that tradition from his mother or from friends with Ghanaian ancestry. Either way, he felt it was well-worth emulating.

The Gadangmes called the ritual "kpojiem ɔ", which is derived from three words: "Kpo" meaning "yard", "dzie" from 'dze' meaning "come out" or "appear", and "mɔ" which refers to a person. So, kpojiemɔ means "take or bring the child out into a yard." It is referred to in English as "the outdooring ceremony". Scholar Ernest Tetteh describes it in *The Outdooring Dedication and*

Naming of an African Child: A Ceremony of the Gadangme People of Southeastern Ghana. "[The]beautiful ceremony [is] to symbolically introduce a new-born baby to God . . . as well as to the mysteries of the seen and the unseen world . . . ." It is "at this outdooring ceremony that the baby is dedicated and given a name (family identity). Hence, a child is not recognized as part of the family without the ceremony."

During the outdooring, male infants would be circumcised, and female infants would have their ears pierced. The ceremony is traditionally followed by a feast, welcoming the child as a member of the tribe. The Ghanaian ritual bears a strong similarity to a traditional Jewish baby-naming ceremony after birth where a male baby is also ritually circumcised and received into the religious community.

Huey later understood the special honor his parents intended to bestow when they named their youngest son after "the Kingfish" Huey Pierce Long. He may well have wondered as an adult if they bestowed him with the middle name Percy instead of Pierce in order to avoid cursing him with the Kingfish's fate. Walter apparently did harbor some concern about naming his son for a victim of assassination, but the esteem he and Armelia held for their former governor won out.

Huey was told by his parents what took place during his simplified "outdooring" ritual with Sonny Man: "He took me outside, hauled me up onto the back of a horse, and circled the house while the rest of the family followed." More likely, Sonny Man mounted the horse first, steadied himself and then one of his parents carefully handed him the swathed, tiny baby to hold as his father led the horse slowly around the house. One can imagine that Walter also made one of his special occasion cakes for Huey's outdooring.

The joy of that celebration gave way to grave concern a few months later when Huey got so sick that Armelia was afraid he would die. It was hard to find a doctor, but one did come to the house to see Huey. The doctor quickly figured out that Armelia's baby had a bowel obstruction. Doris said the doctor "put soap up his butt" and it did the job. There was "shit everywhere." When Armelia saw the results, she broke out in a wide grin: "He's gonna live!"

Not only did Huey thrive after that scary bout of ill health, but he delighted the whole family with his quick mind. He started talking at a very early age. Armelia doted on her "little prince". His sisters did, too, but teased him for his beautiful baby face. They told him he should have been born a girl.

Lee Edward and the Simmons Family

SHORTLY after the Newtons moved to Oak Grove, Lee started seeing a neighbor's girl named Cleaster Simmons, whose father was also a sharecropper. Joe Simmons had the unenviable task of raising twelve children by himself. As a teenager, Lee liked to take as many of the kids as could pile on for a high-speed horse and wagon ride. The older children in the two families played with each other and sometimes got into fights. Lee and Myrtle were particularly prone to instigating mischief. On at least one occasion, they placed a cat on a hot stove to watch it jump off and run away. Myrtle later regaled her children with stories of their exploits, which included snatching things that did not belong to them and having to give them back. As the preacher's kids, such behavior could not be tolerated by Walter. They earned frequent whippings for their misdeeds.

The boys wrestled and boxed. Doris grew up petite like her grandmother Alice, but full of spit and vinegar. On her way to and from school as a young teen, Doris got her aggression out with some well-placed kicks aimed at the Simmons' boys' shins, while wearing her prized white, majorette boots. Myrtle liked to egg Doris on: "Kick 'em Doris, kick 'em!" It was not a fair match up. The Simmons boys were strictly admonished by their father that they would get whipped if they ever fought with a girl, so the boys just took Doris's kicks without retaliating.

Lee Edward had grown in his teens to be thin and good-looking. He resembled his grandfather John, Stella's

Lee Edward as a young adult

slightly built husband. As the eldest son, Lee now preferred the family to call him "Brotha." When it came to schooling, the children went off in all directions. Oak Grove did not have a high school. Black and White children were segregated for elementary school and then the White children were bussed to Monroe for high school. When they first arrived, Doris walked to a one-room schoolhouse, which also had an outhouse. Melvin later went to the same school for a year or two before they moved away. Their older sister Leola and Sonny Man had already gone to stay in Monroe with their grandmother. That move allowed Sonny Man to attend the Colored High School.

Alice Newton came to visit the family in Oak Grove sometimes. Doris remembered Alice's raggedy suitcase, likely an old carpet bag. The kids loved her visits because she always brought cookies and candy, but Armelia found the visits to be an ordeal. Alice complained so much that Armelia asked Walter to ask his mother to leave. At some point after being widowed, Alice entered into a second marriage to a man named David Carter and moved to Chicago. She would remain in Chicago for the rest of her life.

In the fall of 1942, Cleaster became pregnant with Lee's child and, on May 21, 1943, gave birth to a daughter named Ester Lee, honoring both of her parents. (Later, their daughter added an "h" to her first name). Huey was then not yet a year-and-a-half old. Lee Edward was 20 and had moved to Monroe to get work in a lumber mill where he cut the wood into slats and loaded the slats on trucks. He soon left the South for a better-paying, wartime defense job in Portland, Oregon.

Cleaster separately moved with Esther to Monroe to live near her aunt and uncle, Bertha and Arthur Smith, the blacksmith who had relocated from Bastrop. Mother and daughter spent a lot of time with the Smiths, who grew quite fond of Esther. As Esther later learned, her mother liked living in the fast lane. Cleaster and her friends drank heavily. Esther still recalls her mother having her pour beer for Cleaster's friends when Esther was 3 or 4. She also recalls walking down the street with her mother and pretending to be a paperboy. As a preschooler she thought that was a wonderful job to have.

One night in 1947, Cleaster became so ill that an ambulance was called. It took both Cleaster and Esther to the hospital with Cleaster vomiting frequently on the way. The staff sat the little girl by herself on a bench while the emergency room focused on Cleaster's worsening condition. The next thing Esther remembers is her great aunt and uncle arriving to take her to their home. They told her Cleaster had died. Now 80, Esther assumes the cause was alcohol poisoning. She remembers the funeral and seeing her mother's casket lowered by straps into her grave.

Esther never saw a photo of Cleaster, but at no time felt deprived as a motherless child. The Smiths smothered her with love and gladly raised Esther to adulthood. Walter and Armelia Newton would not meet their first grandchild until she was nine. Lee Newton would not meet his first daughter until she was an adult.

Estella Johnson, Armelia's mother whom family called "Muzz".

Life in Monroe with Muzz

ARMELIA'S sister Jessie moved to Chicago and left her daughter Ruby Jewel behind. In the windy city, she found work by day in a warehouse and at night as a dancer in a strip club. Jessie returned to visit every so often and brought school clothes and other gifts for Ruby Jewel. Doris left to go to live with Muzz and Ruby Jewel in Monroe for a year when she was in her early teens. Melvin was then about five or six. His mother assigned him the task of looking after his little brother. Melvin took that job very seriously. When they were outside in the yard, he had to make sure the toddler did not wander off or get hurt. It was a responsibility for the baby in the family that Melvin carried with him into adulthood.

Doris remembered Muzz as a stern disciplinarian, much harsher than Armelia and Walter. In her early nineties, Doris still had a vivid memory of getting whipped by her grandmother for some long-forgotten transgression. She was just wearing a thin nightgown at the time, and it hurt a lot. It was helpful to have Ruby Jewel for company, but Doris also witnessed Muzz go after Ruby Jewel with a stick after the two girls went for a bike ride against Muzz's instructions. Ruby Jewel had fallen off the bike and hurt herself, but Muzz was more concerned about being disobeyed than she was about her granddaughter's injury.

Sticks, belts and paddles were commonly put to use on children in those days. In Muzz's case, her own parents had both been born into slavery. They may well have considered beatings the normal way to ensure obedience of children. White parents considered paddling an appropriate discipline tool for their own children. Throughout the nineteenth and first two-third of the 20th century paddling at school was also common punishment for misbehavior. Today, corporal punishment has largely fallen into disfavor, but the holdouts in the United States are largely in Southern states.

Doris was sure that her own mother had never experienced Stella's harsh beatings. Armelia was, by nature, gentle and highly respected. It was quite possible Armelia never did anything to raise Stella's ire — except to marry Walter when she was not quite 15.

To escape from Muzz, Doris turned to "Brotha" Lee Edward for help. He was then still working in Monroe in the lumber mill. She complained to Brotha about her grandmother's harsh treatment, and he promised to get Doris sent back home. At some point, Doris moved in with Aunt Sissy and Uncle Isaac. By the end of the year, Doris did get to go home.

Armelia by now had grown quite unhappy at the family's situation. Often when her husband was out in the field, she shared with Doris her worries about their future. She told Doris she hated living as a sharecropper. Armelia often cried and considered packing up and leaving Walter. Doris recalled her mother exclaiming "Lord Jesus, help me, Father." Somehow, Armelia soldiered on.

V.
Westward Bound

Walter Decides to Join the Exodus

WHEN Walter decided he would uproot his family from Louisiana for California during World War II, he had reason to assume the move would improve their situation. But he could not have predicted how profoundly this relocation would impact the lives of both of his youngest sons. The hardships they would endure in the ghettos of Oakland, like those experienced by Bobby Seale when his family moved to the East Bay from Texas in the early 1940s, would bear painful similarities to the blatant discrimination their families fled from in the South. But packing up and leaving the South behind would also provide far more opportunities. Most significantly, the move would acquaint Huey with similarly disaffected inner city youths frustrated by the pacifism of the civil rights movement as he came of age in Oakland's racial tinderbox in the turbulent sixties.

It is hard to imagine the formation of an armed Black Panther Party for Self-Defense in 1966 had Huey Newton and Bobby Seale not met each other in Oakland, the city that federal officials in Washington, D.C. greatly feared would become the next Watts after the Watts District in Los Angeles exploded in devastating riots in 1965.

What finally prompted Walter to leave the South behind? Over the years, he had to have paid close attention to the growing exodus from the South to pursue a better life. Best-selling author Isabel Wilkerson noted in *The Warmth of Other Suns: The Epic Story of America's Great Migration* the stunning impact such mass departure had on the remaining labor force in the South:

"When the people kept leaving the South resorted to coercion and interception worthy of the Soviet Union . . . .. Those trying to leave were rendered fugitives by definition . . . .. In Albany, Georgia the police tore up the tickets of colored passengers waiting to board. In Summit, Mississippi, authorities simply closed the ticket office and did not let northbound trains stop for the colored people waiting to get on. . . ..

Instead of stemming the tide, the blockades and arrests 'served to intensify the desire to leave and to provide further reasons for going,'[quoting sociologists Will Weatherford and Charles Johnson]."

The church where Walter was an assistant pastor was full of gossip about community members who uprooted themselves and moved north. One family in particular that Walter knew from Monroe would have generated a lot of talk — that of John Melton and his brother-in-law, Ezra.

Ezra had been a meat packer for a local division of Armour & Co., one of the largest meat packing companies in the country. In 1937, Ezra and his wife Pearline opened a small grocery store, another welcome addition to Colored Town, enabling their friends and neighbors to avoid lengthy trips to White-run groceries. But Ezra could only afford to run the new store part-time while he continued working at the meat packing plant.

Ezra soon became disabled from a severe back injury caused by a swinging side of beef. One can imagine how bad a blow he might have received from such a carcass, weighing around 300 pounds. The injury sidelined him from working at the plant, depriving Ezra of cash needed to maintain the new grocery. It also forced him to move with his wife and niece Belvagene, whom they were then raising, into the small house the Melton family already shared with other relatives.

What followed was another example of the "crazy nigger" stories that the Black community often gossiped about. Ezra brought suit against Armour for damages. As far as anybody knew he was the first Black to sue a White employer in the history of Monroe. In fact, for decades in the nineteenth century Blacks were banned from testifying against Whites. Though that law was no longer on the books when Ezra went up against Armour, public pressure against bringing any such suit remained intense. Ezra somehow found a White lawyer and a judge receptive to his claim. He won an award of $2,000 in compensation for his injuries.

Ezra's victory was Pyrrhic. His lawyer quickly learned that not a nickel of the judgment would be paid. Instead, he found out that a mob was gathering to tar and feather Ezra for his impudence. The Meltons feared a far worse consequence. They all knew about the last lynching in 1919. That very night, Belva's father persuaded all the men in the family to flee and plan to rendezvous in Oakland, California. Some of them had access to cars. They may have grabbed a copy of the most recent *Negro Motorist Green Book* to take with them to know where it was safe to stop on the way to California.

Ezra hopped onto a freight train to escape a White mob Hell bent on teaching him a lesson for daring to sue over a work injury at a branch of one of the largest meat plants in the country. Within the next six months the women and children followed by train.

The same year of 1940 when the Melton clan left for California was when the Newtons had relocated to Oak Grove. Walter was back picking cotton with his sons Brother and Sonny Man. The girls sometimes picked cotton, too, though they mostly worked in the garden and helped with the cooking. Walter had to realize that he was frequently in situations where he, too, could be targeted as a "crazy nigger" for repeatedly standing up for himself. He saw no prospects for a better future in Northern Louisiana and knew Armelia was extremely unhappy with his return to farming. He also had to know that in many Southern communities Whites had prevented Blacks from leaving town and depleting the local manual labor force. It might take careful planning should he try to leave.

Walter also must have been aware of the migration during the Depression of a million or more poor White tenant farmers evicted or fleeing from the Dust Bowl in the 1930s. They toiled in fields of the Great Plains as he did in Louisiana until a spate of severe droughts and wind erosion turned previously fertile soil to a barren wasteland. Then, the Okies, as some took to calling them, took to the road to seek similar jobs in California's farmland.

Walter would have been quite interested in the fictionalized version of the Okie migration to California that won John Steinbeck the 1939 Pulitzer Prize and a National Book Award. Steinbeck's novel, The Grapes of Wrath, told a tragic tale Walter could imagine poor working folks like himself enduring — a family that left Oklahoma to pick crops in California only to face poverty and exploitation in California's fertile agricultural valleys. And they were White!

What Walter may have since learned from folks who had already migrated to the West is that the California legislature responded to the glut of impoverished newcomers

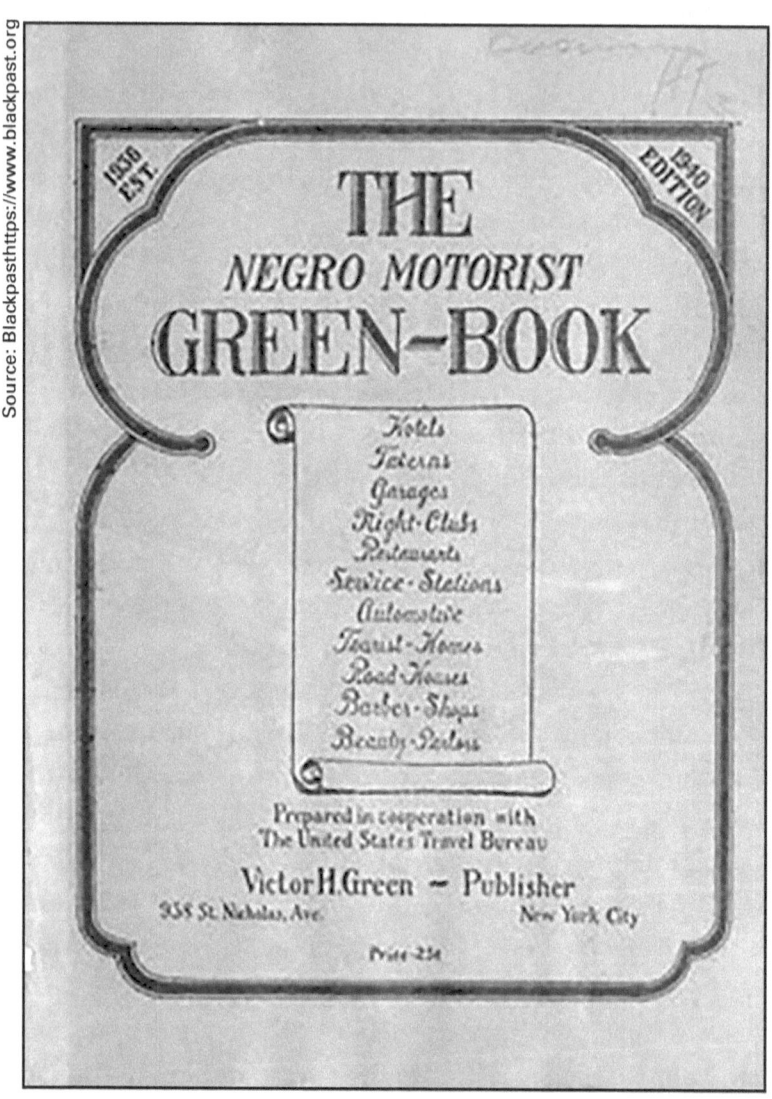

The Green Book was a guide for Black motorists to safe places to stop while traveling through the South in the mid-20th century during the Great Migration. It was created and published from 1936 to 1966 by an African-American mailman, Victor Hugh Green, who lived in New York City.

by passing a law making it a misdemeanor to bring an indigent person into the state. That law hit the news in January of 1940 when a California resident drove to Texas to bring his unemployed brother-in-law to stay with his family in California. All the brother-in-law had was $20 to his name, which he spent on the way West. Ten days after he arrived, the brother-in-law applied for government aid. That was how Edwards got caught, tried and convicted of importing his indigent brother-in-law to California. The case had major implications across the country.

As the United States edged closer to joining the Second World War in Europe, Walter heard through members of his church about the executive order signed by President Roosevelt in June of 1941 to prohibit discrimination in war industries. It was signed under pressure from labor unions and civil rights activists who were planning a march on Washington for July 1, 1941. The march was intended both to challenge unfair wage disparities and to protest ongoing discrimination in the military. One of the leaders was A. Philip Randolph, President of the Brotherhood of Sleeping Car Porters headquartered in Oakland, California. Randolph had co-founded that union in 1925 as the first Black labor union in the country.

Anyone who took a ride on a Pullman train knew that railroad baron George Pullman employed only Black men as porters for his trains and required them all to answer to the name "George." Frustrated by their low pay and onerous working conditions, the Sleeping Car Porters union had grown to 18,000 members in the United States and Canada.

A keen observer looking to leave the South, Walter was a grateful beneficiary of the union's lobbying efforts to pressure Roosevelt into issuing his historic executive order. When the United States officially joined World War II in December of 1941, the number of job opportunities tripled in the next three years as factories were required to speed up defense production, giving high priority to tanks, planes, weapons, and ships.

Other welcome news came from the United States Supreme Court in November of 1941. The high court ruled that the California law making it a crime to bring an indigent into the state violated the interstate commerce clause. Concurring justices in *Edwards v. California*, 314 U.S. 160 (1941) would have gone further and declared that individual citizens had a personal right to interstate travel.

Walter closely followed the war's progress on his radio. He also learned more about job opportunities. Besides the government, another major employer was Kaiser Industries in Oakland. The situation looked promising. In early 1944, Armelia's younger sister Jessie moved to Oakland to live with her second husband Eddie James Ento. They had met and married in Monroe before he went into the military. Eddie was now stationed at the Oakland Army base as a forklift driver. Walter could stay with Jessie and Eddie until he got settled in one or another wartime job. So, Walter planned to join around 50,000 other Black workers from Louisiana, Texas and Arkansas who headed to the Bay Area. Once he got situated, he could save enough to bring out his wife and family. Apparently, during World War II, Northern Louisiana was relatively easy to leave.

Doris had heard about earthquakes in California and did not want to move there because she was scared of being caught in one. Armelia told Doris her father was trying to make it better for her — and for all of them. At 14, Doris preferred the known to the unknown. As it turned out, the risks were often less extreme than those they were leaving behind. And yet Doris was right to fear for the safety and well-being of her family in California.

The Closet Slave State of California

WALTER had reason to believe he was headed to a far more racially tolerant society when he left Louisiana for Northern California. If so, he was in for a rude surprise when he arrived. Like many other Blacks who crossed the Mason-Dixon line before him, Walter's eyes would open to the truth observed by Fire-Eater William Yancey, "the "Orator of Secession," in the lead up to the Civil War. The distinctions between slavery in the South and grueling employment practices in the North (and West) were more in name than in substance.

A crucial difference by the time Walter arrived in California was that the North and West were evolved enough to have abandoned extreme racist practices. The people of those regions had condemned lynching and extended the right to vote to minorities. But California still prohibited interracial marriage and continued to reinforce de facto segregated housing and schools. Walter would also soon find out that working conditions weren't that much better "out West" than what he'd faced back home.

Walter arrived in a part of the United States with its own entrenched form of institutional racism, which echoed the state's long and bloody history of conscripted labor, dating to the age of colonialism and European conquest. But the racism originally targeted Mexican and Native Americans.

European explorers in the 16th and 17th centuries believed that the peninsula of Baja California and what later became the state of California was an elongated island. The Spanish named the New World discovery after the heroine of an early sixteenth century Castilian novel, Las Sergas de Esplandián (*The Adventures of Esplandian),* which told of an idyllic island nation of Black Amazons headed by a virgin warrior queen named Calafia (sometimes spelled Califia).

Las Californias were populated by nearly 300,000 indigenous people. The bounty of the territory of California could only be harvested with intense human labor. Historian Jean Pfaelzer notes that "under four empires — Spain, Russia, Mexico, and finally the United States — 770 miles of land grew as a slave state. . . . Each empire imported its own system to possess diverse human beings — California Native Americans, Alaska Natives, African Americans, Chinese girls, and convicts. . . . Legal and extralegal slavery thrived side by side in California where brutal forces of involuntary servitude and human trafficking have endured for centuries . . . ."

Frederick Douglass called slavery "a hydra-headed monster." Prof. Pfaelzer used that same analogy: "Throughout the history of California, the hydra has gorged on numerous systems of legal and illegal slavery . . . . Slavery secured the conquest of California; it settled the land and fostered its wealth. . . . The story of California is a history of 250 years of human bondage. California thrived because it welcomed, honed, and legalized numerous ways for humans to own humans."

By 1850, California already had a small number of Black slaves brought in by their masters, as well as free Blacks who sought a better life. The census taken that year counted 92,597 residents — 99 percent White and 1 percent Black. The census did not include any of the approximately 150,000 Native Americans who remained from the nearly 300,000 who occupied California when the first White explorers arrived. Up to half of the indigenous population had perished from illness and malnutrition. Historian Tony Platt attributes that high rate of death to "despair" as well as "contagious disease facilitated by a mission system that was authoritarian and brutal, marked by 'the sight of men and women in irons, the sound of the whip, the misery of the Indians.'"Following the discovery of gold in California in January 1848, "White gold miners saw enslaved Blacks hauling rocks, building sluices, and panning for gold. . .. Many free Blacks had traveled west, already schooled in abolitionist struggles; they had not expected to meet enslaved Blacks forced to assist the gold miners."

Though California's political leaders included a mix of slave owners and abolitionists, California came into the union as a "free state" under the Compromise of 1850. Its Constitution expressly guaranteed that slavery would not be tolerated. Based on that assumption, Frederick Douglass joined with other abolitionists urging runaway slaves and free Blacks to head west to gain civil rights. Thousands more came, only to endure a rude welcome that, in some ways, foreshadowed Walter's experience when he and his family tried their luck in the Golden State.

In 1850, control of the California Legislature was in the hands of pro-slavery Democrats. Following the contested adoption of a Constitution decreeing intolerance for slavery, the Legislature eviscerated its promise by enacting the Testimony Exclusion Laws of 1850. These laws strictly prohibited "Blacks, mulattoes and Indians" from testifying against Whites in either civil or criminal cases. As noted by historian Tony Platt:" Because Native people could not testify in court against Anglos, the law in effect encouraged entrepreneurs to kidnap and sell them as unpaid apprentices to farmers, ranchers and miners." That same latitude was afforded Whites seeking to enslave Blacks. Essentially, the Legislature imposed a civil rights ban on any Black or Native American who could not get a White witness to vouch for their claim.

The Exclusion Laws were soon invoked in court by a White man named George Hall, sentenced to die based on eyewitness testimony of three Chinese immigrants who swore they saw him murder Chinese miner Ling Sing. Hall's lawyer appealed the death sentence to the California Supreme Court. The all-White-male panel, by a two-to-one decision, reversed Hall's conviction. The majority interpreted the prohibition against testimony by "Blacks, mulattoes and Indians" also to prohibit Chinese-American witnesses despite no such language appearing in the statute.

Writing for the court, Chief Justice Hugh Murray's rationale was that, if the judiciary did not determine that the Legislature meant to consign Chinese-Americans to the same legal oblivion as Blacks and Indians, Chinese-born U.S. citizens might soon show up "at the polls, in the jury box, upon the bench, and in our legislative halls." In retrospect, his xenophobic opinion has been condemned for "containing some of the most offensive racial rhetoric" to be found in California appellate case law and "the worst statutory interpretation case in history."

By the time of the Supreme Court decision in *People v. Hall* in 1854, the California Legislature had passed a

Fugitive Slave Law declaring that any Black person who had arrived in the state as a slave before California entered the union remained the legal property of whoever owned them when they came. Even provably free Blacks feared being bought, sold and shipped South since they lacked the ability to access the courts to challenge their captor. That was exactly what had happened to kidnapped New Yorker Solomon Northup, who, in 1853, published his harrowing memoir in *Twelve Years a Slave* (the basis of an Oscar-winning 2012 film of the same name).

Northup was kidnapped in Washington, D.C. in 1841 and spent a dozen years enslaved in Louisiana until he surreptitiously alerted friends in New York who helped him get free. The problem was far from unique to Northup. New York had already adopted a law providing assistance to kidnapped New York citizens sold into slavery. After New York's governor helped Northup obtain his freedom, Northup sought legal redress against his kidnappers. But he was stymied by a similar testimonial bar in Washington, D.C. to the one adopted in California. Northup had since become a popular abolitionist speaker. Free Blacks in California would likely have been aware of his cautionary tale. Many contemplated fleeing to Mexico or Canada where free Blacks had already established communities, thanks to the Underground Railroad.

The situation in the "free" state of California during its first decade did not preclude owners of more than a thousand slaves from bringing them into the state. Most were forced to assist fortune-hunters flocking to the Gold Country of the Sierra Nevada foothills. When gold mining started to become mechanized in the 1850s, slave labor in the mines was no longer in demand. As more settlers arrived a new market opened up: "slave owners rented their enslaved men out to work as servants in new households or as cooks in hotels and restaurants . . .. Profits from slavery in California now came from the wages the enslaved turned over to their owners – a version of the southern "Sunday system" that allowed enslaved men and women to earn money on the weekends." Slaves were still their masters' property in California but could earn their freedom by paying off their owners.

After the Thirteenth Amendment to the Constitution freed all slaves in 1865, California imposed laws similar to the Black Codes and Jim Crow laws adopted in the South." Popular culture reinforced racism in California as it did elsewhere in the nation. Through the first few decades of the 20th century, Black face entertainment thrived in the theaters. In 1912, the marching band of Berkeley's University of California paraded in Black face. The epic racist 1915 film "Birth of a Nation" was filmed mostly around Los Angeles.

Not much had improved by 1944 when Walter arrived to work in Oakland and stayed with his sister-in-law and her husband in nearby South Berkeley. Black families were still excluded from almost all other parts of Berkeley and consigned in Oakland to live in a similar ghetto in West Oakland.

Starting Out Again in Northern California

WALTER did not own a car at the time of his move to Oakland. Long distance travel by himself was, in any event, much safer by train. There were few public places while traveling through Texas where Black drivers could safely stop for a bathroom break, get a bite to eat or spend the night on the road. But train travel was demeaning. Until the West-bound train left the South, Walter, like all other Black passengers, had to put up with woefully inferior accommodations. In *The American Dilemma* published the same year that Walter left the South for good, Swedish author Gunnar Myrdal summarized what he learned from all the Black rail travelers he interviewed in the United States: "It is a common observation that the Jim Crow car is resented more bitterly among Negroes than most other forms of segregation."

Walter must have had to keep reminding himself he was leaving the most humiliating experiences of segregation behind. Black passengers paid the same price as White travelers but got no luggage rack, no lounge area and only access on some trains to a partitioned small section of the dining car. Many packed their own food rather than take chances at stops on being able to get served — often around the back by the kitchen door. Yet riding in a crowded car seated with his luggage under his feet was better than when Walter once rode hobo in freight trains. At least there was a small bathroom. By design on long-distance Pullman trains, the White passengers had two larger ones.

The train would have been quite crowded and included many men like himself, seeking a new job and a new life. It likely took the better part of three days before they arrived at the Oakland main terminal. When they arrived, they disembarked from a track outside the 16th Street station in West Oakland, a majestic stone building of classical design that had served passengers on the Southern Pacific Railroad since 1912. Jessie Mae and her husband Eddie were no doubt there to greet him. Eddie had been injured in an accident and remained in Oakland for the duration of the war. The scene must have been quite chaotic. One Oakland resident recalled:

> "We'd go down to the 16th street station after school to watch the people get off the trains, and it was like a parade. You just couldn't believe that that many people would come in, and some didn't even have luggage; they would come with boxes, with 3 or 4 children with no place to stay . . . and they would ask everyone if they had any place to stay or could they make some space into rooms."

For the most part, other newcomers did not have a local relative as Walter did. To assist them with lodging opportunities, the city of Berkeley, just north of Oakland where the University of California had its main campus, had already created an Emergency Housing Committee. Local civil rights advocates like African-American pharmacist William Byron Rumford went further. They formed an inter-racial welcoming committee to help families from the South adjust to their new environment. (Before he ran his own pharmacy, Rumford had been the

Oakland's 16th Street Station built in 1912 became the main train station in the city long before the Newtons arrived.

first Black hired at Oakland's Highland Hospital, working as an assistant pharmacist).

Neither Rumford nor other volunteers could remedy the fact that accommodations for the onslaught of newcomers were simply in too short supply. Hardly any local Whites would accept Blacks into their homes as boarders or let apartments to Black tenants. White families also resisted having Black workers from the South live in their neighborhoods. They mounted fierce political opposition to temporary, low-rent housing complexes the federal government had begun opening in 1941 as a wartime redevelopment project. Those going on record objecting to local housing projects included the city of Berkeley, its neighbor Albany to the north, and the University of California.

Reporter Gary Kamiya recently noted that many White residents openly voiced fears the projects would lead to integrated city schools. ["When World War II brought Blacks to the East Bay, Whites fought for segregation".] As a result, most new Black arrivals found housing only in the most undesirable locations. In Berkeley, that meant the flatlands below Shattuck Avenue, in the vicinity of Jessie Mae's home on Mabel Street near Ashby and San Pablo Avenues.

Melvin recalls visiting his Aunt Jessie in her house on Mabel Street after the war. In West Oakland, the new arrivals poured into similarly neglected neighborhoods. West Oakland became crowded. The vacancy rate in Oakland had dropped to almost zero in the fall of 1942. "Workers slept outdoors, in 24-hour movie theaters, in shifts in the same bed, in trailer parks, even in chicken coops."

Walter would make sure his family had a place to live before he brought them out. His first order of business was to get a job. The Oakland Naval base was still hiring in the late spring of 1944. Walter at 41 had an advantage over many competitors. He could read and write and was in good physical shape with years of experience in a variety of both skilled and unskilled jobs.

Racism in the local workforce was still a major issue. When war production first increased the need for more labor, White unions had collaborated with management to freeze Black workers out of steady jobs. President Roosevelt's unprecedented wartime Executive Order 8802 in the summer of 1941 had banned discrimination by the government or defense industries based on race, creed, color, or national origin. Yet unequal pay and other discriminatory employment practices continued. It soon turned out that institutional discrimination against Black Navy enlistees led to horrific consequences.

Two months after Walter arrived in Oakland, a major explosion shook the East Bay. Five thousand tons of ammunition exploded in Port Chicago, less than 25 miles from where he worked at the Naval shipyards, rattling windows fifty miles in every direction. It was the worst disaster of World War II to occur on continental United States soil. Munitions improperly loaded by overhead nets onto cargo ships suddenly ignited on July 17, 1944, destroying two ships and adjacent docks. The devastating accident wiped out 320 men, almost two-thirds of whom were African-American. The explosion wounded over 400 others. It accounted for fifteen percent of all African-American casualties suffered in naval duty during the war.

Outraged members of the African-American community saw this atrocity as proof the Navy and the U. S. government considered the Black workers expendable.

There was no disputing that the highly undesirable and manifestly dangerous task of handling explosives was assigned largely to untrained, predominantly Black sailors in segregated units. They worked in conditions that many likened to a slave labor camp. Hundreds of sailors, both White and Black, refused to return to active duty in Port Chicago after the devastating explosion. Many of the resisting White sailors were transferred.

Fifty Blacks who refused to go back to work in conditions that violated federal regulations were charged with mutiny, a federal crime that could be punished by death. Shortly afterward, they were tried and convicted but sentenced to hard labor and 15-year prison terms rather than death. Most likely, those lesser sentences were prompted by the scathing national publicity stirred up by NAACP lawyer and future Supreme Court Justice Thurgood Marshall.

Marshall observed that controversial court martial trial, which took place just west of Oakland on Treasure Island in the San Francisco Bay. Outraged by what he saw, Marshall arranged to represent the convicted seamen on appeal. After the war, he succeeded in getting most of their sentences reduced significantly. The bad publicity surrounding this disaster also caused the Navy to begin desegregating its units in 1946. It would take fifty years before the last surviving mutineer received a presidential pardon from President Clinton for his felony conviction. The rest of the Port Chicago 50 were posthumously exonerated in July of 2024.

***

It is easy to envision Walter having another goal beyond a steady job when he arrived in California in May of 1944 — to register to vote for the first time ever. Encouraging the congregation to vote would have been a high priority of the Baptist church he joined, as it was for other Black churches. For that opportunity, Walter had another reason to appreciate FDR's executive order that brought him to a new job in California. Recently, the war appeared to be going quite well for the United States and its Allies. FDR's popularity running for an unprecedented fourth term in November 1944 propelled voters across the country to once again vote for him by a convincing margin, this time to "finish the job." (In 1948, the Great Migration would swell the ranks of Black voters enough to enable Democrat Harry Truman to squeak to an unpredicted victory as FDR's successor).

Supporting FDR would have been easy for Walter. Local races in 1944 presented less palatable choices. Governor Earl Warren's immediate predecessor, Culbert Olson, had been the only Democrat to win that office in 40 years. As the State's Republican Attorney General, Warren had taken the reins back from Olson with a decisive victory in 1942 after Warren spearheaded the forced removal of Japanese-Americans. A far smaller number of Germans and Italians were also sent to internment camps. Locally, the mayor of Berkeley had been a Republican since 1919. The same was true of Oakland for the past three decades. The state also had yet to elect its first Black representative in Sacramento. (That would be pharmacist William Rumford from Berkeley in 1948).

Although the political scene was an improvement on the entrenched White power in the South, Walter could see that the East Bay of California harbored a similar racial divide. In West Oakland, the Black community had created its own culture and business district like many of the newer residents had previously grown accustomed to in the South: restaurants, cafes, stores, barber shops, churches, schools and entertainment. Basically, West Oakland was its own city within a city, not unlike Colored Town in Monroe or other Black ghettos in Southern cities.

Walter surely heard about a race riot that broke out on a Key System streetcar in downtown Oakland in 1943, just a year before he arrived. The Key System (the predecessor of today's AC Transit) was a privately run elaborate streetcar and bus line system that served several cities in the East Bay and connected to San Francisco via the Bay Bridge as well as by ferry. During the war, when gas rationing severely limited car travel, Key trains carried more than 25 million passengers across the Bay.

The 1943 riot was inspired by a "Zoot Suit" riot in Los Angeles, where servicemen had attacked Mexican-American immigrants wearing the showy, wide-lapelled Zoot suits with padded shoulders that first became popular with African-American and Italian men. Walter had likely encountered some high-fashion men in Five Points wearing Zoot Suits. The amount of cloth that went into Zoot suits was considered extravagant during wartime and criticized as unpatriotic. Similar "Zoot Suit" riots occurred in other cities, involving White soldiers attacking Blacks. The Oakland riot grew to a mixed-race mob of 2,000. A local newspaper, *The Observer*, commented:

> That riot on Twelfth Street the other day may be the forerunner of more and larger riots because

we now have (a) a semi-mining camp civilization and (b) a new race problem, brought about by the influx of what might be called socially-liberated or uninhibited Negroes who are not bound by the old and peaceful understanding between the Negro and the white in Oakland, which has lasted for so many decades, but who insist upon barging into the white man and becoming an integral part of the white man's society."

Walter was one newly arrived, bi-racial man who felt entitled to "barge in." He would never accept that American society should just be the province of White men.

Walter Newton would never accept that American society should just be the province of White men.

Oakland's History

THE South had become unlivable for Walter and his kin due to persistent unemployment, racism, and xenophobia worsened by economic conditions. Yet, in myriad ways, Oakland's history from the mid-19th century and into the Civil Rights era, often evoked bitter memories of the South. Hunger for cheap labor led to poor working conditions for Blacks, and, in the wake of the Great Migration, bitter resentment from Whites who felt they were competing for the same positions. Oakland even had an entrenched chapter of the KKK.

In 1852, when Oakland was incorporated with fewer than 1,500 people, most settled by the waterfront. Only a few were of African descent. But when Oakland became the terminus for the transcontinental railroad in 1869, the population began to expand exponentially. Large numbers of immigrants from Europe, most of them from Portugal and Ireland, flooded the city. The new arrivals also included a small percentage of Italians and Germans, African-American and Chinese railroad workers, Mexicans and Japanese immigrants.

For the first few decades of the twentieth century, Oakland's White population kept growing. At first, Catholics dominated the city, but in the 1920s political corruption led to Protestant control, led by members of the Ku Klux Klan. By then the KKK was gaining enormous ground politically across the country, winning Senate seats and governorships in a number of states. The group's membership nationwide swelled to over four million members, dwarfing prior right-wing movements in the country's history. Thousands lived openly in Oakland. However, their primary local target at the time was Catholics, perhaps in part because of the marginal presence of African Americans in their communities.

The KKK burned crosses in public parks and other gathering places to attract attention to their political agenda — unlike the Deep South where the KKK preferred to terrorize Black churches and homes. In 1924, over 8000 Ku Klux Klan members held a cross-burning ceremony in the Oakland Auditorium. That boldness echoed a Fourth of July multi-state gathering that same year of 20,000 Klansmen at a convention in Long Branch, New Jersey, who burned crosses and hanged in effigy New York's Governor Al Smith. Smith drew their wrath for daring to propose — without success — that the Democratic Party 1924 presidential platform condemn the KKK's violence against Blacks and Catholics. The Oakland KKK leaders were as corrupt in governing as the prior administration had been. In just a few short years, the KKK lost control of the city. (Its most egregious lawbreakers were prosecuted by Alameda County District Attorney Earl Warren, who went on to become California Governor in 1942 and ultimately Chief Justice of the Supreme Court.)

During the Depression, unemployment had hit about as hard in the Oakland flatlands as it did in Monroe. The Pullman porters continued to expand the nascent Black middle class. Yet, by 1940, the census listed just over 302,000 residents in the city, almost all of them still Whites of European ancestry. Oakland listed a total of 8,462 Blacks, up less than a thousand from 1930.

Belvagene Melton's family was among the relatively tiny Black populations in Berkeley and Oakland. Even fewer lived in San Francisco. Black families made up only 2.9 percent of the general population. All other minorities combined added up to only another 5,765 people. In 1940, most minorities in Oakland still lived in essentially the same areas they had occupied since the turn of the century, alongside poor White families in the flatlands of industrialized Berkeley and West Oakland.

Among those "flatlanders" was the cartoonist Morrie Turner, born in Oakland in 1923, the son of a Pullman porter. Turner would later base his internationally syndicated comic strip "Wee Pals" on his integrated working-class neighborhood as a child. The only non-Caucasian, racially homogenous neighborhood in Oakland was Chinatown, one of the oldest in the country, which occupied sixteen blocks between the Oakland waterfront and Lake Merritt near the city's downtown hub. In East Oakland, minorities tended to be servants of White families until the wartime influx of newcomers overwhelmed the available housing in the Brooklyn Basin. Then Blacks began occupying the southern part of the city near the Oakland airport and San Leandro.

Walter must have quickly learned that the police enforced strict segregation in Oakland just like they did in Louisiana. As long-time Oakland resident William Patterson later commented: "If you traveled outside of your sector, you got stopped." The well-to-do lived in upscale neighborhoods in the city's center by manmade Lake Merritt, on the Berkeley border to the north and in the Oakland hills to the east. In the business boom of the 1920s, citizens had raised funds to erect a "Necklace of Lights" of lamp posts illuminating Lake Merritt at night, but it went dark during World War II and would not be refurbished for decades.

Many of the most influential White businessmen actually lived in Piedmont, an affluent virtually all-White oasis of a bedroom community completely surrounded by the Oakland hills. In the late 19th century, Piedmont's residents had simply refused to have their community absorbed by the larger city as towns like Brooklyn, Montclair Village, Fruitvale and Melrose had done.

The Oakland establishment not only feared the mass of new Black residents but had been waging a running battle with White labor unions. There had been major bloody strikes during the Depression, but a moratorium on strikes during World War II. Within Oakland, a Republican machine held enormous sway in politics. The engine for that machine was the city's newspaper of record, the *Oakland Tribune*, which occupied its own twenty-two story tower, the Tribune building, then the tallest structure in the city.

When Walter Newton arrived, California's governor was Earl Warren, the former District Attorney of Alameda County and a good friend of fellow Republican political heavyweight William Knowland, the owner of the *Tribune*. Locals called Knowland "The Power in the Oakland Tribune Tower." Walter must have picked up on the "shadow power base" of the city — the numerous White men's service clubs that provided golden opportunities for political and business networking and admitted no minorities or women as members. The Ku Klux Klan, though less prominent, still had members in Oakland in the 1940s, some of whom maintained political clout.

It would have been obvious to long-time residents and new arrivals alike that West Oaklanders such as Walter had no seats at the table. City Council members were elected citywide by the White supermajority. Most, if not all, of the winning candidates were hand-picked by Joseph Knowland and endorsed by the *Tribune*. The city council members, in turn, chose the mayor from among their number. Oakland politics was a closed system — and Blacks had no way into that inner circle.

Much as in the South, Blacks could not eat in most restaurants in downtown Oakland or shop at a dime store or sit at a lunch counter, much less buy or rent a home in a White neighborhood In fact, many homes throughout the Bay Area and the state as a whole had deeds with restrictive covenants prohibiting sales to non-Caucasians, most often invoked to bar prospective Black buyers. A fairly typical restrictive covenant for an Oakland neighborhood association read: "No persons of African, Japanese, Chinese, or of any Mongolian descent, shall be allowed to purchase, own, or lease said property or any part thereof or to live upon said property or any part thereof, except in capacity of domestic servants of the occupant thereof."

In looking back seventy years later, Melvin Newton compared Oakland to a traditional Jewish ghetto, one for Black people to protect Whites from being contaminated by the rabble that had migrated from the South. The hub of West Oakland was Seventh Street along which the electric Key Train System carried commuters to a ferry to San Francisco. Black professionals opened offices along Seventh Street, but at night, vice predominated. Near the railroad yards bordering Seventh Street were pawn shops and houses of prostitution, tucked into rows of blues clubs, bars, barbeque joints and gambling establishments. Many Pullman porters lived nearby the railroad's Oakland terminus. They had their own gambling parlor, "The Shasta."

The first Black-owned music venue, the Creole Café, launched in 1918 to promote New Orleans-style jazz and big band music. Three years later the Lincoln Theatre opened, advertising both vaudeville shows and movies. During Prohibition, West Oakland's version of speakeasies thrived on Seventh Street as "after-hours clubs", many owned by Charles E. "Raincoat" Jones.

Walter would undoubtedly soon hear of Raincoat Jones, a veteran of both the Spanish-American War (as an infantryman) and World War I (as a cook), who participated in the Alaska Gold Rush before he came to Oakland. Jones made most of his fortune money-lending, bootlegging during Prohibition, and running gambling rooms. He then invested in several blocks of commercial property on Seventh and Eighth Streets in West Oakland between Wood and Willow Streets.

In his many conversations with Black co-workers at the Naval base, Walter surely heard stories of Raincoat Jones's soft heart for needy folks. Jones and a small group of successful business friends made it a point to support enterprises that the Black community needed, collecting start-up money for a pharmacy. He was also rumored to have helped hard-up workers with their union dues and to have offered down payments on occasion to assist Black families in buying a home.

One of the establishments Jones reportedly backed would become internationally known — the **Slim Jenkins Supper Club** owned by Harold "Slim" Jenkins. Among the talented performers he featured in his club was **Saunders S. King**, whom Walter likely had heard of before. In the late 1930s King could be heard on NBC radio singing with the Southern Harmony Four Gospel Quartet. In 1942, King's "S.K. Blues" on his innovative electric guitar became a national sensation.

By the 1940s, Slim Jenkins was recognized as the unofficial "Mayor of West Oakland." Walter would have been interested to learn that Jenkins, thirteen years his senior, was from Monroe, Louisiana. Jenkins had come to Oakland just after World War I, where he started out waiting tables. In 1933, Jenkins had been savvy enough to open a liquor store at 1748 Seventh Street on the very day Prohibition was repealed. (One assumes bootlegger Raincoat Jones' assistance might have been the boost Jenkins needed).

As his business expanded, Jenkins later added a market and the Slim Jenkins Café. His nightclub boasted a swanky restaurant, as well as a banquet room. Coat and tie were required as a multi-racial mix of well-to-do patrons came to hear some of the nation's top singing talent, Billie Holiday and Nat King Cole among them. High-profile nightclub guests included President Franklin D. Roosevelt and William Knowland, as well as Republican mayors. Like Jones, Jenkins cultivated cozy relations with the local White political machine. He was known for his largesse in supporting Republican office seekers. It was definitely good for business.

When Walter arrived in town, Seventh Street had long since become one of two centers of West Coast Blues. By the 1940s alcohol sales were legal once again, but gambling in California was not. Jenkins' likely patron, Raincoat Jones, still operated gambling halls during those years with a wink and a nod from the White police whom he paid off with discreet delivery of regular packets of bribes.

Walter lacked the temperament for rowdy Seventh Street nightlife. As in Monroe, he found more rewarding ways of socializing and building a community. In his spare time from work, Walter needed the familiar comfort of organized religion. It was also one of the best ways for him to make new friends. He joined the Antioch Missionary Baptist Church in West Oakland on 7th Street. (It later moved to 14th and Filbert). The congregation included about 200 members.

The pastor, J. L. Thomas, kept a sign in the pulpit: "PRAYER CHANGES THINGS." With Walter's extensive knowledge of scripture and eagerness to serve, he soon became an assistant minister, as he had been in Louisiana. Aside from helping with passing the plate and other tasks assigned by Pastor Thomas, Walter would substitute for the pastor when he was ill and regularly handle services on Sunday night.

Walter fervently believed prayer was the path to salvation. At church, whether you were plagued by sickness, or work injury or financial difficulties, everyone prayed with you for healing. For Walter and other congregants in West Oakland, the church remained the principal steadying force in their lives just as it did for their relatives and friends at the churches in the South they left behind.

The church offered camaraderie, stability, solace and hope. It reinforced family and extended family and friends as what made life worth living in good times and bad. During that year, Walter saved enough money from his job at the Oakland Naval Yard to send for Armelia and four of their children in the late spring of 1945. His grounding with a new church family provided the prospect of reinvention and renewal in the Golden State.

Walter's Family Takes the Train West

AFTER Walter left for California, Armelia stayed on in Oak Grove with the small boys, Myrtle and Doris. They scraped by with the vegetables and fruit they grew and their farm animals. War rationing limited the amount of butter, sugar, canned milk and other supplies that could be bought. During those precarious times, Armelia heard from Walter that he had saved up the money to bring the family out West. She may well have wondered how long the job at the Naval base would last if and when the war ended. She faced many unknowns. Armelia was especially concerned about leaving her mother and other family members behind.

Nineteen-year-old Myrtle was happy to accompany her mother and help out with the younger children. At the time, she was in a troubled relationship with a man named Scott Ward, which the move West gave her an excuse to end. The next oldest sibling to join Armelia was Doris, who was fourteen-and-a-half. Then came the two little boys – Melvin, who was nearly seven and a half, and Huey, who was three. They waited until school got out in May, packed up and went to stay for a few days with Muzz until it was time to leave. Seventeen-year-old Leola would stay behind for now with Muzz and Ruby Jewel. Sonny Man stayed with Uncle Isaac, who had grown quite prosperous. Isaac had no children of his own and wanted Sonny Man to succeed him running his businesses when he retired.

The family, like Walter, had no choice but to board a segregated train in the South. At least at first, everyone in the family had a seat. Jim Crow cars were notoriously ill-kept. Sometimes, White conductors spat tobacco juice on the seats. The ride was long, and as usual the Newtons would have had to be resourceful just to have sufficient food for the journey, especially at a time when dining cars were Whites only. Trying to get served food at stops could be downright hazardous.

Armelia had reassured Doris that their new home would be a better place for them. Yet Armelia continued to agonize about leaving her mother and many of her relatives. But at least some indignities — including segregated cars — would cease as the journey progressed. After one stop, Melvin took immediate notice when White people got on to share the same car with them. The precocious seven-year-old told his family: "Oh, we must have crossed the Mason-Dixon line." That dividing line between segregation and integration was something Melvin had already learned about. Now there was no room for the family to sit. All the seats were taken, Whites having priority.

Huey was also precocious and liked to talk. He saw two seated White sailors and said, "Hi." He was wearing his own sailor suit, which likely emboldened him. A White sailor saluted the cute little boy. "You're one of us!" Huey said, "I'll give you a quarter if you give my mother a seat." The sailor took the quarter and put it in his ear. Armelia got the seat, picked up Huey and put him on her lap. Myrtle and Melvin were standing where their mother could see them. The other sailor chivalrously got up and offered Doris his seat. Myrtle would have benefited from one, too. Unbeknownst to her family, she was pregnant when she left Monroe.

That overcrowding only lasted a couple of hours before they arrived at a station where they switched trains. When they disembarked, the sailor told his captain he wanted to introduce his little friend. The captain assumed the new friend was a girl the sailor met on the train. He was surprised to see a small African-American boy. The sailor took the quarter from his ear and explained how Huey had paid him for his mother's seat. That was the last time they saw the sailor, but the friendly interchange left a good impression on the family.

Many hours later they reached their destination. When the family finally got off the train in Oakland at the 16th St. station, Walter and a friend arrived together to meet them in an old car, presumably owned by the friend. Piling in was a tight squeeze with three adults, two teenagers, two small boys and the family's luggage. Armelia, Myrtle and Doris had to be anxious about what was in store for the family in this new setting. Melvin was just excited to take it all in. Huey was all eyes, too, and totally ingenuous.

Huey at the age of 3 in the sailor suit he wore in the spring of 1945 on the train from Louisiana to Oakland, California.

Melvin at the age of 7 shortly after the family arrived in California in the spring of 1945.

VI.

THE PUSH AND PULL OF FAMILY

The Family Settles in Oakland

WALTER'S friend drove them to their first apartment, on Third Street in West Oakland. It was close to an intersection with the major artery of Grove Street that led several miles North to Berkeley. The site was also not far from the city waterfront facing the island of Alameda in the San Francisco Bay. On the way, Armelia must have wondered how different Oakland was going to be from Monroe. She would soon discover that the differences were slight. The moment they arrived they were relegated to a Black ghetto. Grove Street in Oakland then served as a de facto color line with Blacks on one side and Whites on the other. (In a nod to progress in 1983-84, Grove Street was renamed Martin Luther King, Jr. Way in both Berkeley and Oakland).

There was an obvious reason the apartment Walter had found for his family was still available — it faced the adjacent train track with its round-the-clock traffic. The ground floor, three-bedroom flat housed all six family members who were now in Oakland: Walter and Armelia, Myrtle and Doris and Huey and Melvin. The two girls and the two boys each shared a bedroom. But the apartment had no place for them to cook meals. Instead, the family shared a kitchen with other tenants and had to put their family name on meat stored in the communal fridge.

Myrtle worked as a maid to help support the family, herself and the baby in her womb. Armelia had always been able to rely on her oldest daughter to help her out with the younger children. Left at home overseeing Doris and the boys, Armelia quickly grew quite unhappy and resented the noisy trains that rattled past their home all day and disrupted their sleep each night.

Myrtle may have tried to cook traditional recipes she had learned in Louisiana, but she and Armelia were forced to take turns with strangers in the use of the kitchen. The situation became so intolerable that the family soon moved to a small, two-bedroom basement apartment on the corner of 5th and Brush Street in West Oakland where the Nimitz Freeway is now.

Compared to their previous flat by the railroad tracks, this one was more peaceful, though it was not much of a step up in terms of privacy. Their new place had a cement floor, a kitchen and, on the opposite side of the apartment, a washroom with a tub, but no washing machine. The only bathroom belonged to the landlord, Mr. Johnson, who lived above them in the one-story house. The family shared that with him, creating an awkward and inconvenient situation for them both.

The two boys sometimes amused themselves by catching stray cats. They took them upstairs on the back porch of Mr. Johnson's quarters and tossed them down to the ground to see if it was true cats landed on their feet, and they did — at least most of the time.

Walter and Armelia slept in one bedroom; the children all slept on wall-to-wall cots in the other. Money was stretched thin. Sometimes they would eat cornmeal cush twice a day. It was Doris's responsibility as the only older sibling at home in the summer of 1945 to look after both younger brothers. Doris and the little boys spent most of the day outdoors. They seldom had any store-bought toys, but at least they had a backyard where they could play in the dirt.

Already at seven, Melvin felt a special responsibility for his little brother's safety, knowing that Huey was their mother's precious baby and "kind of the darling of the family." The Newton family remained closely knit, with few outside friends except at church. Relying on Doris to join in their fun did not always go smoothly. She could play catch with the boys but when she got annoyed, she would lose patience and hurl the ball straight at them.

Armelia took a while to catch on to Doris's lack of affinity as a teenager for babysitting. When her mother was out, Doris decided she would become Queen Doris. She took a sheet, wore it like a cape and ordered the boys to fetch her water or fix her a sandwich. She threatened to beat them up if they did not do her bidding. One day, the boys had more than enough and mutinied. Instead of taking orders from her, they jumped her and tore up the sheet. When Armelia got home and heard what happened, Doris got in trouble for threatening the boys. They were not faulted for tearing up the sheet. From then on, Armelia took the boys with her rather than let Doris babysit.

The Central Role of Religion in the Newtons' Family Life

AS SOON as the family settled in, they started attending church on both Sundays and several weekday evenings. Melvin joined the Young People's Union. He and Huey also went to Sunday School. The whole family worshipped together on Sunday. Myrtle and Doris showed up in dresses and hats. The family also sang in the choir. Doris only mouthed the words because she knew full well that she could not carry a tune.

Melvin joined the junior choir as did Huey when he was old enough, though Huey, like Doris, only mouthed the words. He, too, could not carry a tune. But, to his parents' delight, Huey very much enjoyed participating in church plays. He was phenomenal at memorization, though he later confessed to having great difficulty reading.

As they got older, the boys also served as ushers at church on Sunday in their official roles of Junior Deacons. The pastor counted on young male members to assist him while they were learning the elements of the service. Their job was to announce the sick roll, help elder members get seated, and pass the plate for donations at each service. Melvin was baptized by Pastor Thomas and Huey would be baptized when he turned twelve, a rite the older siblings had all undergone in Louisiana.

During services, the boys sat in chairs near the pulpit. They listened quite attentively to Walter's sermons on Sunday evenings and when he handled the regular Sunday service. Walter's talks were always quite animated, full of references to fire and brimstone for unrepentant sinners. He liked to wave his arms and move around as he spoke. Huey was quite frightened as a young child listening to his father condemning impious people to Hell. But he and Melvin also listened attentively when Walter admonished the congregation that: "He who can make the rhyme repeat itself can also rewrite it." No one needs to remain in a rut. They can redirect their lives in a better direction.

Walter's favorite sermon told the story of the prodigal son from the Gospel of Luke, a story of sin and redemption. Walter could relate to the father with two sons: one who stayed with his family, always worked hard in the field and remained God-fearing; the other, who took off on adventure and indulged for years in sin. The story focused on the prodigal son's return after he had become a penniless wastrel. Perhaps this parable brought to mind men and boys from Walter's hoboing days.

In the Biblical story, the father joyously embraces the prodigal son and celebrates the occasion with a special feast. The jealous older brother, who had never strayed from fealty to both God and family, is taught a lesson about God's mercy and love for sinners who seek forgiveness. Huey and Melvin greatly preferred Walter's frequent retelling of the stories of David and Goliath, and of Samson. These tales gave them heroes to identify with.

Walter and Armelia Newton pictured around 1954. Walter is holding his Bible.

In Oakland to Stay

IN EARLY August 1945, President Truman took the extraordinary step of authorizing war planes to drop atomic bombs on the Japanese cities of Hiroshima and Nagasaki. He was persuaded it was necessary to avoid a costly land invasion where heavy troop losses were expected. Coupled with Russian gains against the Japanese, the devastating bombings triggered Japan's surrender on August 15. World War II was over. But Walter still held on to his job at the Naval Base, even as peacetime cutbacks began.

Stability was especially important considering that Walter and Armelia were searching for ways to improve their family's circumstances, including their living quarters. During this time, Walter had an unexpected, and bizarre, run in with an FBI agent while working at the Naval Supply Station. Doris recalled the strange experience many years later.

It all started when a White co-worker became friendly with her father. Over the course of about six months, the fellow bought Walter lunch, took him to the movies and inquired with interest about Walter's family. One day, shortly after the family arrived in Oakland, the man put his hand on Walter's head so he could examine Walter's skull behind one of his ears. He was looking for a scar but found none. The man then revealed that he was an FBI agent trying to track down a man who resembled Walter.

Walter heatedly replied: "You son of a bitch!" Walter seldom swore and punished his children when they did in his presence, but this was too much. "What the Hell?" he said. The experience made Walter leery of the FBI, long before he learned of their efforts to track Huey's activities two decades later.

Meanwhile, the family kept growing. In November 1945, Myrtle, who still lived with them, had a baby boy, Jimmy. Her parents wanted to have Sonny Man and Leola join them, too. Family was everything to the pair, a feeling strongly shared by their children. The two older teens arrived after school got out in 1946. Fortunately for the family, the Newtons managed to find a spacious flat in West Oakland. It was located on property owned by Beth Eden Church on Magnolia Street at its intersection with 10th Street. At last, the family members had privacy and space. This house was the first nice place they had ever lived in, with three bedrooms, its own kitchen and even a small yard outside.

In this new and comfortable home, while Sonny Man enrolled in Oakland Tech for his senior high school year, Melvin and Huey built on their close friendship. The two fantasized about going into construction together. Later, they envisioned themselves hanging out shingles as a pair of professionals. Melvin dreamed of being a doctor and Huey aspired to become a dentist, like the Wilson brothers who set up their practices in West Oakland.

Unlike his sister Doris, who said she "didn't learn shit" in high school, Melvin absorbed his parents' high value on education, loved school, and had as his goal graduating from college. In class, he found some material off-putting. He found that he could not relate to *Little Black Sambo,* which was, at that time, a staple in elementary schools across the country.

The story — one of the few texts at that time to center

on a non-white character — told of a dark-skinned South Indian boy who was accosted by tigers. To avoid being eaten, he gave his new clothing away piece by piece to these predators. Then the tigers chased each other around a tree and turned themselves into ghee — clarified butter. Little Black Sambo's father scooped up some of the ghee and the family ate it with pancakes.

The edition widely distributed in America drew Little Black Sambo as an African boy with a "pickaninny" hair style. It was extremely popular through the mid-twentieth century and inspired a board game, a dart game with Little Black Sambo as the target, and a cartoon version. Later, severe criticism from poet Langston Hughes and others convinced the publishers to redraw the illustrations, change its title to *Little Brave Sambo* and rename other characters in the story.

Melvin also recalls the school including in its curriculum the story of the tar baby in Uncle Remus's tales of Br'er Rabbit. Though the tales of Uncle Remus were based on West African folklore, the best-selling nineteenth century versions by Georgian Joel Chandler Harris presented African-Americans as unsophisticated children. Harris used pidgin English for the dialog of Br'er Rabbit, Br'er Fox and Br'er Bear and downplayed the harshness of slave life on plantations.

Disney turned the tales of Uncle Remus into its 1946 release, "Song of the South" which soon had kids across the country whistling "Zip-a-Dee-Doo-Dah. (In recent years the dated film has been condemned by critics for its racist caricatures. Disney never released it for streaming and closed its animated Splash Mountain ride based on Br'er Rabbit and other Uncle Remus characters in favor of a more modern-themed replacement).

Melvin never had a Black teacher until he went to college. He became a model student, wanting to learn from his teachers and assignments as much as he could. His favorite after school activity was visiting the library. When Huey started school, his experience would be markedly different. Melvin later took martial arts classes as an adult and realized that his approach to racism in school mirrored successful moves against adversaries in Taekwondo and White Crane – deflect the impact and send it in another direction. Huey did not follow that path. He was quick to anger, while Melvin was slower to ignite. When Huey felt affronted, he clashed head on at school with whomever he found abusive.

Though Huey had early dreams of a conventional career path with his brother, his temperament, combined with the hostile environment he encountered in his new hometown, changed his outlook. Huey came of age at a time when relations between West Oakland's Black youths and the local police were getting ever worse. A combination of changing demographics and entrenched racism was to blame.

One part of the problem was a dire need for suitable housing. The Newton family was lucky to find a spacious home after the war ended. West Oakland was becoming increasingly crowded. During World War II, the government had constructed temporary housing for Black shipyard workers and their families near the Navy Yard in the island city of Alameda, a nearly all-White town separated from Oakland by an estuary. The officials segregated these housing projects from the White population of the city. Yet city leaders still worried about "the problem of the increased negro population" which Alameda's mayor attributed to "the influx of war workers and the housing shortage." When these jobs ended after the war, the projects closed down and many of the residents poured into West Oakland.

With increased unemployment, the crime rate in West Oakland started to rise. The city police department responded with national recruitment efforts. Many successful applicants were White Southerners. Not surprisingly, these new recruits would handle crime in the Oakland flatlands much in the same way law enforcement was carried out in Black communities of the South.

Black men in West Oakland began to view the White policemen who patrolled their area as a hostile, occupying army. They knew it was common for Black arrestees to receive a beating before making it into jail. It often made no difference if they cooperated with the arrest or how minor the charge might be. In fact, as later revealed in an investigation of Oakland police abuse, on paydays, police often would park outside the West Oakland bars that cashed checks for workers. Police would arrest some patrons on charges of drunkenness. In the privacy of the prowl cars, officers would beat and rob them of their week's earnings before turning them in at the West Oakland police station.

Labor strife was also on the rise. Aside from increased unemployment and higher crime rates, the end of the war also meant the end of the moratorium on strikes. In early December 1946 several hundred women retail clerks picketed two downtown Oakland department stores for equal pay and a union contract. The Alameda County Central Labor Council followed up with a call for a walkout by all of its members until union demands were met. Over the next two days, supporters went on a self-declared "work holiday" that started small but soon mushroomed to over 100,000 employees enjoying a respite from work — more than a quarter of the city's population.

Within 24 hours, the walkouts shut down most businesses in downtown Oakland, leading the City Council to declare a state of emergency. The council members put tough-minded Mayor Herbert Beach in direct charge of the police and fire departments. Mayor Beach saw this general strike as an attempted revolution. He quickly hired beefy strikebreakers to supplement the police. One observer detailed what followed:

> [S]ome 200 Oakland and Berkeley police, many in riot gear, swept down the street. They roughly pushed aside pickets and pedestrians alike as they cleared that block and the surrounding eight square blocks. They set up machine guns across from the stores, while tow trucks moved in to snatch away any cars parked in the area.

Standing protected on the sidelines, nodding their approval, were key local men in power, bent on crushing this populist uprising: the police chief, city council members, representatives of picketed department stores and, of course, the anti-union group's acknowledged leader, Joseph Knowland of the *Oakland Tribune*. In Louisiana, Walter had often seen Whites abusing Black workers. It must have been shocking for him to see White strikers and their supporters facing a similar threat of community-sanctioned violence.

In the 1940s, members of Oakland's growing Black middle class opened their own branch of the NAACP to address community concerns. The Oakland branch of the NAACP did not just challenge discrimination in the courts. It also organized picketing of City Hall to call attention to blatant exclusionary practices by White businesses and homeowners.

By the 1950s, the NAACP was inviting Black youths to the West Oakland community center to plan their own activities. The adult council focused on gradual empowerment. They taught the teenagers Robert's Rules of Order to conduct their own meetings and reminded them that Oakland's Juvenile Hall was just across the street. Kids could either learn how to work within the system to make change or wind up in Juvenile Hall. But many Black youths growing up in West Oakland at the time — including Huey Newton — would chafe at the idea of working within a racist system that made self-advancement, decent housing, and fair wages an unattainable dream for many residents.

Maintaining Close Ties Through Daddy and Mother

THOUGH tensions were simmering in Oakland, the family mostly focused on their personal lives. Myrtle became involved with a man in Oakland in 1946 and had her second child, Patrick, in April of 1947. Armelia looked after both grandsons while Myrtle continued to work. Doris stayed at McClymonds for two years. Like Myrtle, she was much more interested in boys than school. One day when the family had been in Oakland for perhaps a year, she met a young man named Glen Godfrey, three years older than Doris. Glen worked in Alameda for the Navy and came by their house with a friend who knew Myrtle.

When Glen first spied Doris, she was playing hopscotch. She was barely 16. He drove back to see her again when her mother was sick in the hospital with the flu. Glen, a good-looking young man with an infectious smile, whistled at Doris from the car and pulled up. He urged her to get in, but Doris told him her father would whip her if he caught her in the car when Glen dropped her off. Undeterred, Glen suggested she get in anyway and he would let her out a few blocks away so she could walk home. Doris relented, but when Glen asked for her phone number, she could not provide one. The Newton family did not then have a phone. Doris was quite afraid of her father's reaction if he found out.

On a later occasion, Doris borrowed Glen's leather coat and wore it to a church event which she thought her father would not be attending. When she saw that he was in the church, she ran home to take it off. Her friends laughed at her embarrassment. Meanwhile, Glen told a friend, "They'd have to kill me to keep me from seeing her."

Myrtle soon married a new boyfriend, James Seymour. The Seymours joined her parents at their new flat and stayed in the third bedroom with Myrtle's two little boys. The Newton family stayed comfortably housed there until 1948 when Beth Eden Church needed the land for expansion. Then Walter and Armelia were forced to move on short notice to a cramped, one-bedroom apartment on 17th and Castro. The only bedroom served as a sitting room during the day. That was the room where Walter and Armelia slept. Melvin and Huey slept in the kitchen.

By the time the family moved to 17th and Castro, Leola had also married and both older daughters were living elsewhere with their husbands. Armelia's mother, Muzz, came out to visit during that time and likely stayed with Jessie and Eddie Ento in Berkeley. Melvin recalled her regaling them at length with stories of their Monroe relatives. They found the tales fascinating.

In October of 1948, Myrtle would have her third and last child, her daughter Patricia Seymour. Until then, Doris had been staying with her parents and younger brothers at their apartment, sleeping on a cot in the sitting room that also served as her parents' bedroom. Doris got married to Glen in July of 1949 and moved to segregated housing in Alameda. After all three girls left home, Huey and Melvin regularly did the dishes. The daughters would come back frequently to visit their mother and help out with chores.

Family ties remained strong. Walter and Armelia remained the unquestioned patriarch and matriarch of the Newton family. Everyone in the immediate family called them Daddy and Mother except Leola's husband,

James Carr, who addressed Walter as "preacher."

Armelia would greet all of them with a kiss and a hug, saying "Give me some sugar." Gregory recalled Daddy making the same request of his grandchildren, followed by a long hug that scratched each grandchild's face as they came into contact with his bristly chin.

When gathered at their parents' home, the siblings and their spouses would crowd into Armelia's kitchen, eating and telling stories. There was always plenty to talk about. Leola shared revealing stories from working alongside White co-workers. Because of her light skin Leola was often mistaken for White. Some of her co-workers spoke openly in front of her about their negative attitudes toward Black people, having no idea of the personal affront she experienced.

Many family stories were from earlier days in Louisiana. The joy the Newton family took in recounting past colorful events reflected the long history of storytelling among African tribes that permeated their genes. Embellishments were expected, making it hard sometimes to tell fact from fiction. Doris particularly acquired a reputation for embroidering her tales, but the ones she told the same way over and over had the ring of truth.

This storytelling prowess never diminished during Doris's long life which ended in the fall of 2023. Her funeral was a chance for her many admirers to tell stories of their own. Her celebration of life occurred at a Black-owned mortuary in Oakland, the city where she had spent most of her life since she arrived in California as a teen. Funerals for members of the African-American community in Oakland still appear to differ little from those in the Deep South. A *New York Times* reporter noted in 2012:

"If Sunday [when the faithful attend church] remains the most segregated day in the South, funerals remain the most segregated business . ... [T]he races tend to bury their own."

There is a widely repeated African saying, "When an elder dies, a library burns to the ground." Since time immemorial, the African continent was a land of oral tradition with cultural heritage passed by word of mouth between generations. In West African culture, which was a major source of the Newtons' genetic heritage, a venerated storyteller was called a Griot. He memorized the details of significant events and performed songs and dances at ceremonial gatherings. Women who sang at such ceremonies were called Griottes.

At Doris's memorial the tradition of storytelling was on display once again. Her niece Terrez told those gathered at the service how critically important Doris was to her life. Doris had been a devoted godmother to both Terrez and Tracy. She had taken Terrez to care for as a newborn when Leola became ill after giving birth. From then on, Doris played the role of a second Mom to Terrez, offering strong opinions as a lifelong advisor with uncompromising views on proper grooming and behavior, including dressing up and wearing lipstick whenever she went out in public.

Most telling was an incident told by Doris's nephew Lautaro that occurred a few years before Doris's death at age 93. She and Glen had been married for more than sixty years when he began suffering from dementia. Melvin's youngest son cracked up the attendees at her celebration of life by recounting an exception to the strong bond that connected his aunt and uncle until the day Glen died in

January 2021. One day when Glen was in his early nineties, he insisted on taking the car keys to go on an errand although he was no longer capable of driving. He and Doris got into a heated argument, and she pushed him down. Glen grabbed the keys and pushed her back. Not sure what else to do, Doris called the Oakland police.

Other family members in the house prevented Glen from leaving. When two officers arrived, they asked who had started the physical altercation. Doris said she did and was promptly arrested — standard department policy in cases of domestic violence. When they put handcuffs on Doris, her hands were so small that the cuffs easily slid off. For the first and only time in her life, Doris wound up spending the night in jail. Soon after Doris's release, she faced a court appearance. One of her three granddaughters accompanied her to the hearing. There was no way Glen intended to press charges, so the case was dismissed — with the judge assuming the defendant was Doris's granddaughter, not the tiny, elderly woman who sat next to her.

In this author's view the police response demonstrated deficiencies that continue to this day in department recruitment and training, which the inclusion of far more personnel with social working skills could have resolved. Undoubtedly the incident will be a story told and retold by family members, a tale that Doris herself recalled with amusement when asked if she had ever visited her brother Huey in the Santa Rita jail. She said she had not, but she and Melvin exchanged knowing eyerolls about her overnight stay at the same jail when she was almost ninety. Doris would have provided great fodder for Griottes, though she would have declined to sing for an audience.

Huey probably had the most inherited talent that could have qualified him as a Griot in times past. Early on, he began to exhibit phenomenal memorization skills, though he, too, would have had to leave the singing to others.

Keeping Up
with Extended Family

SETTLING into their life in West Oakland, the Newtons still tried their best to maintain ties with the loved ones they left behind. Armelia occasionally took trips back to Louisiana to visit her family. In 1952, she booked a train to Monroe with Myrtle and her daughter Patricia, who was then four. They were accompanied by Armelia's sister Jessie and her almost-three-year-old son Eddie. Eddie still remembers how enamored he was with the big train they boarded at the Western Pacific and Santa Fe Railway station in West Oakland. It was a long ride to Louisiana.

Partway on their journey they switched trains to an all-Black car as they entered the segregated South. There were lots of family members to connect with, and not all of the reunions were pleasant experiences. Myrtle's husband James Seymour was also from Monroe and his family still lived there. Aunt Jessie's daughter, Ruby Jewel, was still living with her grandmother and likely still working as a clothes presser in a laundry, as she had been in 1950.

Ruby Jewel, then in her early twenties, took her toddler brother Eddie to visit a friend. He became fascinated with an open-flame heater and badly burned his arm before the adults realized the danger he had placed himself in. Muzz was furious at Ruby Jewel. Jessie was more understanding of her daughter's benign neglect. Muzz also directed her temper at Patricia. When the four-year-old accidentally broke a cherished ornament, Muzz whipped Patricia's behind so hard that Myrtle moved Patricia to her paternal grandmother's home for the rest of their stay.

During that same trip to Monroe, Armelia was introduced to Arthur and Bertha Smith, who were raising Armelia's oldest grandchild. They had made the effort to connect with Esther's great grandmother Muzz and great uncle Isaac Burnett and wanted Armelia to get to know her granddaughter. Armelia and Bertha hit it off and remained in telephone contact when Armelia returned to California.

That summer Armelia invited the Smiths to drive out to California and visit with them in Oakland so they could meet the rest of the family. The two women became lasting friends. The Newtons were still living then on Castro Street. Esther had no television at home so that was an exciting new experience. She retained fond memories of her newfound relatives. From then on, just before school started in September, Esther received a care package at home in Monroe of school clothing that Armelia sent her daughters to pick out for Esther. Armelia made sure to get contributions from Lee toward those clothing packages.

By the time Esther connected with the Newton family, her father was married to Katherine Jackson, the neighbor from Bastrop who had as an adult first moved to Detroit and then Oakland. Katherine had a son Lawrence born in 1950 when she and Lee Edward got together in Oakland. In October of 1951, they had a daughter whom Lee named Armelia after his mother. He had already adopted her brother Lawrence.

Walter kept up with his own family in Arkansas. When Walter headed West in 1944, his half-brother E.S. was still living in Parkdale, Arkansas. He remarried in February

1946 to a woman named Bernice Rogers who already had seven children from her own first marriage. Throughout his life, E.S. was just as religious as Walter. He taught his children Sunday School and brought them all with him to the church he regularly attended after he moved to Detroit. Walter must have gotten a kick out of E.S. telling him that the pastor at New Bethel Baptist Church was Clarence Franklin, a nationally known preacher and civil rights advocate known as the man with the Million-Dollar Voice.

In 1956, Clarence Franklin's fourteen-year-old daughter Aretha would complete her first album, "Songs of Faith" that she recorded in Detroit at her father's church. Most likely E.S. was there that day, among others, to hear Aretha Franklin's extraordinary rendition of gospel music. E.S. shared Walter's lifelong love of Gospel, a spiritual mainstay for them both through good times and bad.

The Move to a Mixed Neighborhood

THE NEWTONS continued to put down roots in a city that was riven by political strife, economic hardship and racial stratification. Mayor Beach's brutal response to the 1946 Oakland strike caused a major political backlash. Opponents ushered in a change to the city charter to have the mayor elected directly by Oakland's citizens, independent of the city council. West Oakland still lacked any influence.

Businessman Clifford Rishell won the 1949 election and two reelections, serving until 1961. He became known as "Ambassador of Goodwill for Oakland" and "Oakland's Super Salesman" —- the man who brought in the Oakland Raiders football team. All the while, Rishell and the city council ignored the growing slums of West Oakland and the brutal treatment the police inflicted on anyone they arrested there.

The police understood that their primary role was to protect property owners. They had the authority to shoot to kill anyone suspected of being a fleeing felon, including those suspected of car thefts and burglaries where no victim was put in physical danger. Traveling their beats in patrol cars rather than on foot as they had done in the past, the almost entirely White male police force instilled fear and hatred among the residents. When Walter went to work for the City of Oakland Street Department in the late 1940s, he got to know who was in the police force. He was dismayed by what he learned. He told Melvin in 1952 or 1953 that there was then only one Black patrolman on the entire city payroll. Walter befriended him until he found out that the officer's job was limited to arresting Black suspects.

With Sonny Man's help, in 1952 Walter bought a house on 47th Street in North Oakland. Located in an integrated neighborhood, it was actually a duplex. Walter could only afford the mortgage by renting out the apartment on the first floor. The family moved into the two-bedroom unit on the second floor. Huey and Melvin shared a bedroom, and the other was occupied by their parents. This was a major achievement. The Newtons were among the minority of Black families that could afford their own home.

By 1960, almost two-thirds of White families would own their own homes — thanks in large part to post War, mass-produced suburban developments restricted to White occupants. Meanwhile, Black homeownership was only 38 percent. (During the recent pandemic, Black homeownership sunk back again to barely two out of five families).

Increasingly, during the 1950s and '60s, the cities became disproportionately Black and the suburbs White. In the early 1960s, Oaklander Morrie Turner had not yet debuted his syndicated cartoon "Wee Pals", the first integrated comic strip. The fledgling cartoonist's day job was working as a rare Black clerk in the Oakland Police Department. One day, Morrie answered the phone and took a message meant for a White co-worker. The caller obviously assumed Morrie was also White. The message? "The niggers are taking over Oakland."

* * *

None of the Newtons' adult offspring moved in with them in their North Oakland home. By then, Sonny Man

Walter "Sonny Man" Newton, Walter and Armelia's second son

had relocated to Southern California. Leola, Myrtle and Doris all lived with their husbands and children in Berkeley and Oakland. Brother Lee had moved from Aunt Leola's home in Berkeley to West Oakland where he then lived with Katherine and their two children.

Despite Walter's best efforts to keep the family afloat, Melvin and Huey both realized how his debts weighed him down. "The bills" were why they could not buy coveted toys. Yet Walter had a telephone installed. He managed to afford a television with rabbit ear antennas. Huey watched cartoons, the Howdy Doody Show, Hopalong Cassidy and the Mickey Mouse Club. Melvin favored Gunsmoke and Dragnet. Their father also liked Western tv series but was most interested in the news. Armelia loved daytime soap operas and watching Perry Mason.

Walter and Armelia bought most of their appliances in installments, with interest sometimes doubling their cost. After a vendor disputed one of the mailed payments, Huey and Melvin were tasked with hand-delivering payments to the stores so Walter would have receipts as proof. Walter sent the boys once or twice a month to hand over the money in envelopes.

At home, Walter spent much of his spare time working in his vegetable garden and keeping the hedges trimmed with help from the boys. The backyard was his domain; the house was Armelia's. The daughters still came weekly to do dishes, clean windows or other needed chores for Armelia. On occasion, Myrtle's daughter Patricia as a small child would stay overnight with her grandparents. She has a memory of one such time when she was about three and Mother took her to Huey's elementary school where they were having a maypole celebration. Huey would have been about nine.

As Huey got old enough to help with kitchen duties, Armelia asked him to clean the oven for her. It pleased her immensely that he did so whenever she asked. She apparently overlooked the fact that Huey often tried to shirk his other chores by riding off on his bicycle to leave Melvin taking out the garbage or washing the dishes.

* * *

Back when she worked in a nightclub, Aunt Jessie was quite petite. She still weighed under 100 pounds when she arrived in California in 1944, but she had since gained a lot of weight, particularly after she had her second child, Eddie Ray Ento, in October of 1949. Eddie was born twenty years after Jessie gave birth to Ruby Jewel. As Eddie grew older, behind his mother's back, Eddie started calling her "Big Jess."

By 1953, Aunt Jessie had gotten divorced from Eddie Ento but still lived in Berkeley with her preschooler. She would often come to visit Armelia with little Eddie in tow. Doris would bring her son Glen. Glen went by the nickname Ricky that Doris had wanted to name him at birth. Ricky was just a few months younger than Myrtle's daughter Patricia, and four years older than Eddie. The boys enjoyed wrestling and sometimes heading across the street to play by the creek. Though Huey was several years older, he joined them on occasion. Ricky often stayed overnight with his grandparents and became one of his grandfather's favorites.

Lee sometimes dropped off Armelia and Lawrence for an hour or two visit with their grandparents when they were preschoolers. Unlike her cousins, his daughter Armelia recalls her grandmother never warming to her. She never offered the two any treats. Armelia instead ushered them out to play in the backyard even as she was offering her husband something to eat. Little Armelia never could fathom why. She always understood that Lee Edward was her biological father, but there was gossip among the women in the family that Lee Edward was only her stepfather. Somehow her grandmother took offense, apparently believing that someone not born with any Newton blood was named after her. Huey did not share that attitude. Armelia remembers her older cousin as a teenager giving her small change on occasion to go buy a candy bar.

***

Ricky and his sisters found time spent with both Huey and Melvin delightful, especially when the two uncles babysat them at home. The pair of teenagers would play games in the yard with their two nieces and nephew, take them to movies and other outings. Melvin very much enjoyed spending time with his young relatives. Huey did, too. Eddie most enjoyed the visits to his Aunt Armelia's when Melvin was home. Eddie somehow found it fun that Melvin would often put his cousin Eddie and nephew Ricky each in a headlock and give them noogies.

On weekends, Melvin and Huey would pick up Myrtle's three small children to take them to Antioch Baptist Church where Walter was still an assistant pastor. On Saturdays, the kids had rehearsals for Easter and Christmas performances of songs, poetry and plays. Huey had been a star performer when he was their age, but Patricia hated having to learn her lines.

On Sundays in the early '50s, the three little ones went

to Sunday school. The best part for Jimmy, Patrick and Patricia was the attention they got from their youngest uncles. Melvin and Huey would grab them on the sidewalk and turn them each upside down before loading them into the car. Myrtle, standing in the doorway, would scold her brothers for the rough-housing, especially when she saw Patricia with her good dress hanging upside down as she was dangled by her feet. That never stopped Melvin and Huey.

Practically every weekend the family would get together. At the beginning of every year the family would decide who was going to host Thanksgiving, Christmas and other special gatherings. It soon became the custom for many of the clan to head to Myrtle's for an after party following a gathering at their parents' home. They felt far more uninhibited at Myrtle's than when their father was looking on. Myrtle always had plenty of alcohol and food on hand for anyone who was still hungry. She herself was much more gregarious when she was drinking.

At home or elsewhere the family gathered, Myrtle delighted in serving fried chicken, macaroni and cheese, greens, potato salad, and sweet potato pie. The kids happily drank strawberry Kool-Aid made with 7-up and lemons. Oftentimes on Sundays, a plate would have to be made up for Daddy because he spent the better part of the day at church. While the adults traded stories, the grandchildren might play in the backyard or sometimes have a dance contest in the living room. Mother took particular delight in watching her grandchildren dance. Aunt Jessie may have judged the contest, relying on her experience as a professional dancer, though the moves being evaluated would have been quite different from the routines she had performed in Chicago.

Debra recalls her grandfather preferring to sit in the living room watching his favorite Westerns. When she came with her parents, Walter would order her to take a seat with him, so she would not overhear the adult banter in the kitchen. Though he had raised his children not to use profanity, Doris was not alone in acquiring the habit of swearing like a sailor.

Debra was afraid of being yelled at by her grandfather, so she did as she was told and never budged. If Sonny Man was there, he would take charge of the music. Brother Lee preferred Western country music to rock and roll or the Blues. Once, their partying attracted a neighbor knocking on the door to join in the fun. Lee answered with a curt dismissal: "You are not invited. We party by ourselves."

Huey and Melvin Follow Different Paths

IN THE FALL of 1948, Huey had gone to first grade at Lafayette Elementary School where Melvin was in fifth grade. It was the only year that the two would attend the same school. As the baby in the family, Huey was spoiled by his mother and did not take well to having to conform his behavior when the teacher instructed him to do so. The school had a sandbox in its playground. One day Huey came in from recess and took off his shoe to empty out sand before regaining his seat. The children were allowed to do that, but they still had to be seated on time. In front of the class, the teacher punished Huey for his tardiness by hitting him on the head. He threw his shoe at her.

That incident resulted in a parent-teacher conference, the first of many. Walter and Armelia took every school summons seriously. But Walter always wanted to hear both sides of any dispute, whether it was between his children or between one of his offspring and a teacher. Only then would Walter pass judgment. If he thought Huey was in the wrong, he would be punished by his parents as well as by the teacher.

Armelia grew to hate the way teachers treated Huey as a troublemaker, with little academic potential. She knew he was smart. Later, it turned out that there was only one elementary school teacher who brought out Huey's best efforts. Mrs. McClaren had previously taught Melvin at Lafayette and remembered him fondly. She never shouted at students but remained soft-spoken and encouraging. For Mrs. McClaren, Huey wanted to live up to her expectations of Melvin's younger brother.

Growing up, Huey felt severely handicapped by his light complexion and medium build, with a nose inherited from his White grandfather. His handsome bi-racial features, coupled with a high-pitched voice and a funny name, were serious liabilities on the streets of Oakland. Kids on the block may not have heard of Louisiana's demagogue Governor Huey P. Long, for whom he was named, but they teased Huey "Pee" Newton unmercifully.

The torment continued throughout elementary school. He quickly developed thin skin. Even with his older brothers, Huey's first reaction to a fearful situation was to go on the attack. Melvin recalled Sonny Man one Halloween tried to scare Huey as a child by menacing him while wearing a grotesque mask. Huey surprised him by pouncing and flailing at the frightening sight.

Starting in 1950 when Huey was eight, a new cartoon character hit movie screens and then comic books, growing in popularity over the next several years. The character was Baby Huey, a huge, guileless duckling wearing a diaper and frilly baby bonnet. That may have contributed to Huey being called a baby in school. Yet there was a different reason classmates mocked him for his baby hair. His mother had taken to plastering his remaining baby hair to his forehead with pomade to give him bangs when she groomed him for school. That continued for years. No wonder Huey got into a lot of tussles with the other children at school. His reputation as a brawler with a hot temper started in early childhood and would follow him around for the rest of his life.

Though Huey had admired professional boxers since the age of five, he never got involved in organized sports.

Nor did he learn to dance or carry a tune, but he did display talent for playing the piano. When he was twelve, his parents arranged for three years of classical training. They hoped he would play the piano at church. Among the pieces he practiced were Rimsky-Korsakov's "Flight of the Bumblebee" and selections from Tchaikovsky's *Nutcracker Suite*. Though adept at his piano lessons, he became increasingly restless at school.

Melvin had a different reaction. Like Huey, as he grew up Melvin became ever more aware of racism in the public schools. When Melvin attended Oakland Tech High School in the 1950s, it had an established dual track system. Still focused on the best education he could get, Melvin knew he wanted to take the college preparatory courses. But the counselors told him to take wood shop and other less intellectually challenging courses where all the Black students were being steered. Melvin agreed to take wood shop, but he also insisted on college prep. He soon discovered there was only one other Black student on that same competitive and academically rigorous track. He credited his parents' support and encouragement for motivating him to accomplish his goal.

Huey, at the age of fourteen, practicing at the piano in 1956

The Impact of Emmett Till's Murder

AS HUEY continued to get into mischief, Walter and Armelia must have been reminded how fortunate they were to no longer live in the Deep South. The gruesome lynching of fourteen-year-old Emmett Till in Money, Mississippi made national news during the last week of August 1955.

Emmett Till was just seven months older than Huey. He was visiting relatives in LeFlore County, Mississippi on a summer trip from his home in Chicago. His mother had warned her only son when she put him on the train South that he needed to exercise extreme care around the Whites he encountered there. Like Huey, Emmett did not always listen to his mother's advice.

The Newtons could imagine Huey doing what Till was accused of — whistling at a pretty White woman he encountered in a grocery store. He may have been just trying to show off his bravado to his young cousins. Raised in a major city where such a boorish compliment was not uncommon, Emmett had no idea that a wolf whistle in rural Mississippi would cost him his life. When the woman's husband and his half-brother learned about the incident from onlookers, they tracked Emmett down at his great uncle's home, kidnapped him, tortured and shot him, tied a piece of metal to his head, and shoved his body into the Tallahatchie River. With Till's mother's permission, *Jet* magazine and *The Chicago Defender* widely disseminated photos of her son's mutilated corpse.

Black teens in Oakland, like others across the country,

saw the grossly disfigured remains displayed in *Jet* magazine and had nightmares. Melvin was in his senior year of high school at the time. The horrific image made an indelible impression. Huey's new best friend David Hilliard, who later became the Panther Party chief of staff, was just twelve at the time. Looking back at eighty, Hilliard realized that Emmett Till's murder jump-started his political awakening. He assumed it had a similar effect on Black teens across the country. Emmett's mother, Chicagoan Mamie Bradley [later known as Mamie Till-Mobley], would subsequently co-author *The Death of Innocence: The Story of the Hate Crime That Changed America*.

The extensive publicity ensured thousands of mourners attended Till's open casket funeral in Chicago. But it did far more. Emmett Till's death prompted belated national attention to the desperate need for federal civil rights legislation. Civil rights activists began mobilizing across the country. Emmett's mother sent a telegram to President Eisenhower urging that the Commander in Chief ensure that "justice is meted out to all persons involved in the beastly lynching of my son." She received no response. Yet LeFlore County officials reluctantly yielded to outside pressure for a murder trial once attention focused on the prime suspects: the husband of the pretty White storekeeper Emmett had dared to whistle at, and the husband's brother, motivated to take vengeance for the teenager's perceived impudence.

While a murder trial was promised, its outcome was preordained. The pair of defendants were acquitted after a short, kangaroo-style proceeding before an all-White-male panel of equally racist neighbors and friends. The prosecutor even tried to raise doubt that the disfigured corpse was really Emmett Till, despite his mother having recognized the ring the corpse wore that had belonged to her deceased ex-husband. The unmoved jury panel deliberated only an hour, including a soda break, before they acquitted the two men. Not long afterward, the exonerated men brazenly sold their story to *Life* magazine. They freely admitted killing Emmett after they no longer risked prosecution due to the doctrine of double jeopardy.

Even after the adoption of Civil Rights laws in the United States, efforts to make lynching a federal hate crime kept failing until passage of the Emmett Till Anti-lynching Act in the spring of 2022. In the meantime, starting in 2008, successive memorial plaques were placed at the site on the shore of the Tallahatchie River near Glendora, Mississippi where Emmett's corpse was found. The plaques had to be replaced because they were repeatedly vandalized. The last replacement in 2021 was a 500-pound bulletproof sign.

On July 25, 2023, the date that would have been Emmett Till's 82d birthday, President Biden belatedly answered Mamie Till-Mobley's plea for justice. He dedicated three monuments to Emmett Till and his mother at sites henceforth guaranteed federal protection: the riverbank where Till's mutilated body was dredged up; the county courthouse where the shocking exoneration of his murderers took place; and the church in Chicago where Till's mutilated remains were displayed to the world. Any attempts to damage the new memorials now constitute federal offenses.

Walter and Armelia would not live to see the national memorials dedicated to Emmett Till and his courageous mother. Nor would they witness the posthumous public tributes to their troubled young son Huey, whose rise to power and fame was still more than a decade away. At the time he entered high school, they had no indication that Huey was headed towards anything but trouble.

Huey Reaches a Turning Point in Junior High

BLACK STUDENTS were in the minority at Santa Fe Elementary School and Woodrow Wilson Junior High School in North Oakland. In sixth grade, Huey soon bonded with David Hilliard, who lived around the corner from the Newtons. David was the youngest in a family of twelve children. He had just arrived from Alabama with his parents to accompany two of his brothers who had obtained jobs at the Oakland Navy base during the Korean War. It soon became a regular habit for David to drop by the Newtons' house every afternoon after school. He looked forward to a warm welcome. Armelia would offer him a bowl of collard greens, a piece of cake, or both. David began to view her as his second mama.

Armelia and Walter figured that David might be a good influence on Huey. David recalls that Huey memorized and recited famous lines from literary works to impress the girls in high school. Melvin helped Huey by reading them aloud or playing recorded versions for him on their record player. Two of Huey's favorite sources were Shakespeare's *Macbeth* and an English translation of verses attributed to Persian astronomer-poet Omar Khayyam.

David observed how annoyed the boys on the dance floor became when Huey attracted girls to his corner poetry readings from the *Rubaiyat*. But girls were often drawn like moths to the flame by Huey's recitation of the suggestive, centuries-old verses: "Your hand can seize today, but not tomorrow; and thoughts of your tomorrow are nothing but desire. Don't waste this breath, if your heart isn't crazy, since 'the rest of your life' won't last forever." What girl could not fall for: "When Time lets slip a little perfect hour, O take it for it will not come again."

Walter and Armelia still hoped Huey would go to college like Melvin, the only one of Huey's older siblings ever to get a college degree. From Huey's perspective, shortcuts to an easy life were more appealing. For a little while, Huey had a paper route. That ended when his customers' subscriptions suddenly came to a halt because Huey was pocketing their payments.

His father expected Huey to emulate his own work ethic as Melvin did. But Huey took the opposite lesson from his father's example. He believed that racism ensured that Black men had a steep, uphill climb to make a living in mainstream society. They wound up with little to show for it, no matter how hard they worked. The rougher elements of Oakland acted as a magnet to Huey, as they had with his oldest brother, Lee. Huey had numerous fights with neighborhood toughs, establishing a formidable reputation on the street.

Walter got suspicious of Huey's behavior and decided that his youngest son was up to something. Walter stayed up one night and heard Huey tapping at the boys' bedroom window on the second floor, trying to wake Melvin to let him in. Huey must have been standing on a ladder when Walter caught him and gave him a beating, one of many he meted out to his son. Armelia also whipped Huey for transgressions, though hers were not as painful to endure. Huey realized they both acted out of love. He did not resent their efforts to keep him on the straight and narrow. But neither did he heed their commands.

The Hammer Incident

DESPITE his parents' urging and Melvin's example, Huey became an indifferent high school student, often skipping school to spend hour upon hour in the pool halls. Doris recalled that Huey often talked Melvin into doing his homework for him. Melvin doesn't remember doing that, but while attending Oakland City College, Melvin still lived at home and willingly did Huey's bidding. Melvin only realized later, when he read *Revolutionary Suicide,* that Huey wanted to get thrown out of class so he could avoid being exposed for "not learning what was supposed to be learned."

Misbehavior in class and truancy got Huey suspended from Oakland Tech in his sophomore year. In his junior year, his parents enrolled him in Berkeley High, using Myrtle's address as his home address, though he actually still lived with them. But trouble followed him. Not long after he started at Berkeley High in 1958, Huey was accosted by a group of Black students who accused him of trying to lure away their girlfriends. As a new, good-looking classmate, Huey had aroused their jealousy when he chatted with several girls one day after school.

When the teens appeared prepared to jump him, Huey struck first and hit one of them in the jaw. Lee Edward might have taught him it was an advantage in a street fight to catch an adversary by surprise. That would be Huey's go-to move in adulthood as well. Against a group of teens bent on teaching him a lesson, it was a bad move.

Having instigated fisticuffs, he suffered an onslaught of blows in retaliation, leaving him bleeding and with several loose teeth. The other boys then fled before the police arrived. Huey refused to name his attackers to the responding officer. It was against his principles. Instead, he began plotting his revenge.

When Huey's parents brought a doctor to the house to see to Huey's injuries, Huey told him: "You ought to see the other guys." The next day Huey brought a hammer to school and an inoperative handgun belonging to his father. He had sneaked out of the house with both weapons to scare his attackers with. At lunch break, Huey hit one of his attackers with the hammer and then brandished the gun to intimidate the others. Questioned again by a policeman about this second incident, Huey told the officer he did not intend to kill anyone. He was "just going to break their backs." Not surprisingly, Huey's actions got him suspended from Berkeley High and referred to juvenile court.

True to his Solomon-like disposition, Walter waited to pass judgment until he spoke with the principal, the police and with Huey. Walter and Armelia agreed that Huey had a right to defend himself, but he was wrong to bring weapons to school. Huey spent a month in the Juvenile Hall. When the detention was up, Walter took Melvin along to pick Huey up. Berkeley High had meanwhile discovered that Huey lived in Oakland and refused to readmit him. Huey went back to Oakland Tech.

Armelia grew increasingly worried. Huey's reckless streak was patent. He kept playing hooky with his parents having no idea what he was up to. Huey later admitted that he was driving and drinking long before he was old enough. At night, after his parents went to bed, he swiped his father's car keys and sneaked out of the house. Sometimes, it was to do a favor for Myrtle who found herself needing a ride home late at night and counted on her little brother to come to her rescue. Walter and Armelia still hoped Melvin's example would put Huey on the path to finish high school and chart a righteous path forward.

Huey Takes Lessons from Melvin

MELVIN was still living at home and had some influence over Huey. After graduating from high school, Melvin had enrolled in the National Guard. It involved summer training sometimes in the desert and weekend training during the rest of the year. During the week Melvin attended Oakland City College, which was walking distance from his parents' home. There, he focused on vocational training to pursue his interest in becoming a social worker. As a side interest, Melvin picked up the art of hypnosis from a classmate. Melvin then taught it to his younger brother. Huey was no longer his little brother since Melvin's adult height was just five-and-a-half feet, and Huey had grown to five-feet-ten.

An apt pupil when the subject interested him, Huey practiced at parties putting friends under a spell. He realized how easily people would execute orders to get down on all fours, or bark like a dog. They also could be stuck with a needle or pin and evince no reaction. Huey later studied the skill more intensively on his own. He once hypnotized himself and asked Melvin to place a lit cigarette on his arm. It resulted in a serious burn that Melvin immediately regretted inflicting.

By his senior year in high school, Huey had an eccentric Afro-Filipino girlfriend named Dolores with whom he would have a stormy, on-and-off relationship for the next four years. Huey loved to debate. So did Dolores and Melvin. Dolores often visited the Newtons' home and accompanied Huey and Melvin to other family gatherings.

To his parents' relief, despite distractions, Huey managed to obtain his high school degree, though Armelia was upset that counselors told him "he was not college material." Though he graduated in the bottom half of his class, Huey was still better off than most of his contemporaries. One third of young Black males in Oakland were unemployed high school drop-outs, six times the national average.

After graduation, Huey held a number of short-term jobs. He worked one summer at the Del Monte cannery in nearby Emeryville, where Leola and Doris were then employed. From time to time, Huey hired on as a construction worker or longshoreman, though he did not last long at any of these jobs. That included the work his father obtained for him as a street cleaner for the City of Oakland.

Melvin encouraged Huey to take college courses. He shared with Huey what he was taught in an introductory philosophy course that included Plato's *Republic*. After Melvin explained Socratic dialogue to him, Huey was intrigued enough to plow his own way through it. For the first time in his life, he felt engaged by the written word. Huey would later claim that he was completely illiterate until then and had faked the ability to read and write in high school. Melvin knew that was an exaggeration but did not discount Huey's insistence that he suffered as a child from undiagnosed dyslexia.

Plato's philosophy presented an alternate and appealing construct to the religious parables Huey was raised on. He had grown disaffected with church teachings. Plato and Socrates grappled with many weighty subjects from a secular perspective: love, justice, reality and illusion. Huey was particularly drawn to the parable of prisoners in a cave who mistook silhouettes on the wall for real objects that firelight had projected as shadows. Plato concluded that philosophers knew the difference between illusion and reality and had a duty to educate others imprisoned by self-delusion.

Huey's high school graduation photo. At the time, one third of young Black males in Oakland were unemployed high school drop-outs, six times the national average.

Huey's Beatnik Phase

SINCE Myrtle's and Melvin's birthdays both fell on December 17th, when Melvin turned 21 the Newtons rented a private basement venue to celebrate the two with a potluck, music and drinks. Their parents were proud to see Melvin follow up on his two-year degree in sociology by attending San Jose State where he pursued a bachelor's degree. There he concentrated on studying sociology, those who committed violent crimes, probation, parole, and prisons. His parents hoped Huey would follow Melvin's lead toward a respectable career path.

Melvin no longer lived at home. Rather than tackle a lengthy commute from Oakland, Melvin joined thirteen other students who stayed in a large Victorian house off campus in downtown San Jose that one of them had leased. Melvin shared a bedroom with one of his housemates. Doris did what little she could to help Melvin with expenses. Mostly, Melvin found ways to finance himself.

At Oakland City College Melvin had joined Phi Beta Sigma, an historic Black fraternity founded at Howard University in the early twentieth century with chapters that spread to colleges across America. Melvin had already joined the Oakland chapter of Phi Beta Sigma at Merritt College. San Jose State had one, too. Armelia saw it as a good sign when Huey enrolled in Oakland City College as his brother had, walking distance from home. Like Melvin, Huey joined the Phi Beta Sigma fraternity.

Much to his parents' dismay, Huey soon grew a scruffy beard like Beatniks were doing in the late 1950s to rebel against conformity to societal norms. Walter insisted that

Huey shave it off, but Huey refused. Outraged, Walter knocked Huey down.

Huey then left home in his first semester. He began sharing a flat near the campus with William Brumfield, also known as Richard Thorne, a co-founder of the Sexual Freedom League and later an abusive cult known as Om Lovers.

Thorne was charismatic and anti-establishment. He believed that divesting oneself of property was a cleansing experience. At this time, Huey's efforts to support himself took a dark turn — he began taking other people's property. He turned from paying jobs to petty burglaries from unlocked cars, parking lot robberies, selling stolen property and, for several months, pimping. Thorne attracted many young women who shared his views on promoting sexual freedom. Huey enjoyed their favors, too, and offered them for a price to acquaintances.

Yet this period of criminality coincided with intensive immersion in philosophy and militant politics in classes Huey took part-time. He was especially interested in the recent Cuban revolution and guerrilla leader Ernesto "Che" Guevara. Huey now made "Cuba Libre" his drink of choice and thirsted to gain more knowledge.

Life-Changing Tests of Fraternal Loyalty

BY 1961, Lee had moved to Redwood City in San Mateo County on the San Francisco peninsula, where he sought work as a janitor for Chope Hospital. Having quit elementary school to work with his father in the cotton fields, Lee feared he could not pass the written test portion of the exam. Melvin agreed to take it for him and aced it. Lee did a fine job in the interview. The hospital never discovered Melvin's role and offered Lee the position. Lee would keep it until he retired in 1995. In gratitude for helping him secure that job, Lee told Melvin there was an opening for a social worker in San Mateo County that also required passing an exam. Melvin took it and was awaiting his results when he faced another loyalty test, this time to Huey.

At the time, Melvin was living at home after graduating college. He decided to go to a dance one Friday night and unexpectedly found Huey there, still sporting the Beatnik goatee his father had objected to and still living with Richard Thorne. The atmosphere in the club was tense. Melvin could see that Huey was getting into an escalating confrontation with a known gang leader. Looking around the room, Melvin also noticed a number of thuggish men he assumed were gang members. They appeared ready to attack Huey at any moment. Melvin headed home and got his father's handgun, likely the same inoperative weapon Huey had brought to school to confront bullies at Berkeley High. Melvin didn't bother to check if it worked. He only wanted to scare the gang off by brandishing it.

When Melvin got back to the dance, Huey and the gang leader were facing off outside. Melvin got between them, but he was four inches shorter than Huey, who was himself about four inches shorter than the gang leader. The two barely noticed Melvin as they glared at each other over his head. One of the gang members hefted a long piece of wood and swung it at Melvin and Huey — just missing both of their heads. Melvin pulled out the gun and waved it around, causing the gang to back off. In those days carrying a gun was uncommon. None of the gang members had one.

When Huey pulled a machete out, Melvin had an alarming realization. He was still awaiting the results of his exam and police might arrive at any minute. If he were arrested, the job opportunity in social work he had worked so hard for would disappear. Instead of staying to ensure Huey's continued safety, Melvin raced to his borrowed car and headed home just before the police arrived at the dance, called by someone who saw the drawn gun. Huey had put his machete away by the time the police showed up. When they asked for the man who wielded a gun, Huey sent them in the wrong direction. Disaster averted. At the age of eighty-six, Melvin reflected that his whole career could have gone down the drain if he had stayed even another minute.

The Afro-American Association

IN 1962, Huey joined a study group started by Berkeley Law graduate Donald Warden, who would later change his name to Khalid Abdullah Tariq al Mansour. The Afro-American Association was an informal gathering of Black men who met regularly at Warden's home. At the time, Warden also hosted a radio program with the same name. Among the study group's members were future Congressman and Oakland mayor Ron Dellums, and Thelton Henderson, a young civil rights lawyer, who decades later became the first African-American judge to head the District Court for the Northern District of California. Huey, at 20, was the youngest member of the association. In this setting, he was there to learn and listen — and on his best behavior.

In their high school days, the participants had learned American history from a White perspective. When interviewed in 2013 for the film project "American Justice on Trial", Judge Henderson described how those meetings of the Afro-American Association enabled the group to gain insight into their own history at a time when no such offerings existed in college curricula:

> We'd learn about our heritage. The premise of the Afro-American Association was that Blacks should not accept the white historical version of a Negro... [The name] Afro-American was very consciously decided to reflect our African heritage, rather than whatever a Negro had come to

mean. So, we started studying our heritage and read a bunch of very, very interesting [books] that I had never read . . . Marcus Garvey, W. E. B. Dubois, E. Franklin Frazier – author of *The Negro Family in the United States*. It was a very exciting and eye-opening period for me.

Judge Henderson remembered Huey quite well from those meetings:

A very bright young man. A very respectful young man . . . He came to learn, and he was a quick learner. He contributed a lot, and I've always imagined that many of the ideas he got for the Panthers' philosophy and some of the interest areas that they had, came from those meetings at the Afro-American Association.

Huey relished the group's focus on the works of Leftist political writers like Dubois, James Baldwin and Jean-Paul Sartre. The group likely read James Baldwin's "A Letter to My Nephew" in which he advised his younger brother's teen-aged son: "Please try to remember that what they believe, as well as what they do and cause you to endure, does not testify to your inferiority, but to their inhumanity and fear."

Huey embraced the association's pride in its members' African heritage, including the teaching of Swahili. He brought the books home and turned the tables on Melvin. By then, Melvin was again living in Oakland after graduating from San Jose State in 1961. Huey reveled in introducing his older brother to works Melvin had never read before.

In the fall of 1962, Huey started holding forth frequently at a lunchtime speaking platform adjacent to the community college. The speakers at this corner forum had become known as the Grove Street orators. Huey liked to expound on the Cuban revolution, hand out "Fair Play for Cuba" flyers and criticize President Kennedy's Cuban blockade and the history of American colonial power.

National events were also catching the Newton clan's attention. At the time, mixed race sit-ins and Freedom Riders in the South were on the national news. In late December 1962, Dr. Martin Luther King Jr. drew a crowd of thousands to the Oakland Auditorium. Doris and Melvin were enthralled to hear King in person. Huey may have been there, too.

King had previously visited Oakland and Berkeley for speaking engagements that raised money for his civil rights efforts. On one of those trips, King was invited to dine with the local President of the NAACP who lived with his family in the almost entirely White city of Alameda. The Oakland police had to be notified in advance because they otherwise had a practice of stopping Blacks driving across the bridge from Oakland to question them on their purpose in going to Alameda.

This time more than 7,000 people came to hear King make an historic address to commemorate the upcoming 100th anniversary of the Emancipation Proclamation. Sixty years afterward, Doris still recalled what she wore on that historic occasion, her favorite black dress. Dr. King took the opportunity to focus on themes he revisited eight months later in his world-renowned "I Have a Dream" speech at the Lincoln Memorial before a quarter of a million participants in the March on Washington for Jobs and Freedom.

Huey must have been aware of that momentous speech. But when he co-founded the Black Panther Party for Self-Defense in 1966 it would be with open disdain for the pacifism King espoused. The Panthers would deride King as a bootlicker until King came out in 1967 against the Vietnam War and launched a poor people's campaign. By 1962 when King enthralled Oakland crowds with his vision of a future integrated society, Huey had long since rejected the Biblical instruction in Jesus's Sermon on the Mount to turn the other cheek. Having goaded his own religious father to punch him when words failed to win an argument, Huey itched for confrontation both personally and politically.

The Violent Clash with Odell Lee

BETWEEN 1961 and 1964, Huey had been arrested on misdemeanor charges more than once. He managed to talk his way out of all but one theft conviction. In the spring of that year, he faced his first serious charge, resulting in his conviction for assault with a deadly weapon. Melvin believed Huey might have avoided the charge if other witnesses had come to testify on Huey's behalf.

Despite his physical fitness, Huey escaped the 1963 Vietnam War draft with a 1-Y psychiatric exemption. He attributed that designation to his outspoken criticism of racism in the military. His parents must have been quite relieved. Anyone with a 1-Y classification could only be called up in the event of a declared war or national emergency. Congress never elevated the Vietnam conflict to an official declaration of war.

At age 22, Huey, who was just above average height at five-foot-ten, did not intimidate anyone by sheer size. But his adversaries learned to fear his temper and the violent way he settled real and perceived slights. By 1964, he had already cultivated a fierce reputation on the street. Huey was aggressive in expressing his political views and took offense easily at personal digs. He shared with Melvin a conversation he had with their father about fighting to defend one's honor.

Huey wanted to know Walter's view, as a preacher who embraced the Golden Rule, what the proper response was to being dissed. "What do you do if your brother offends you?"

Walter said, "You don't strike your brother. You try to reason."

Huey pursued the question further: "What if he continues to offend you?"

Walter replied: "Well, he's not going to continue to offend you."

Huey persisted: "Yeah, but what if he does?"

Walter gave Huey the answer he was looking for: "Then he's not your brother. You strike him down."

The incident that got Huey arrested on felony assault charges happened at a birthday party Melvin and Huey had attended at the home of a relative of their fraternity brother, Tom Broome. Most of the people there were relatives of the Broomes or were Phi Beta Sigma fraternity brothers. Huey had gone to school with one of the guests, Margo Lee, who came to the party with her husband Odell, a man neither of them knew. Odell Lee looked intimidating. He had a long scar down one side of his face from his ear to his chin and he exuded attitude.

When others began dancing, Huey, as usual, did not participate. Instead, he initiated an animated rap session. Melvin stood nearby and heard the contentious interchange between Huey and Odell. For whatever reason, Odell took great offense when Huey recited a phrase in Swahili he had learned from Don Warden. Odell responded with one in Chinese. Huey insisted that he and Odell were both Afro-Americans.

At that moment, Huey happened to be standing at the buffet table. He ignored Odell and headed to the kitchen to grab a steak knife to cut his meat since the only utensils set out for guests were plastic. Odell grew more incensed when Huey began to walk away. He angrily grabbed

Huey's left arm to turn Huey around to face him, saying: "Don't turn your back when I'm talking to you."

Huey retorted: "Don't you ever put your hands on me again" and turned away once more and picked up a knife. Knowing his brother's temper, Melvin feared what might happen next. Odell again forced Huey to face him and reached for his own hip pocket. Expecting Odell to draw a switchblade, Huey took his steak knife and stabbed Odell several times in the neck while Odell held onto Huey with his right hand. Melvin jumped in and pushed Odell into the corner of the room. By then, Odell was bleeding heavily. Odell got up and charged Huey again. Melvin got between them and took the knife from Huey.

As the two brothers headed for the door, somebody asked Huey, "Why did you cut him?"

Melvin responded: "He cut him because he should have cut him" and backed Huey outside.

Melvin's instinct was family loyalty as his father and mother had taught him. He believed Huey had overreacted but also considered Odell a dangerous man who had instigated the confrontation. Melvin wanted Huey to press charges, but Huey refused to go to the police, just as he'd declined to name his attackers at Berkeley High. Alerting authorities to handle attackers violated his code of ethics.

Odell spent several days in the hospital. Huey heard that upon his release Odell wanted to come after him for revenge, so Huey began carrying a gun. No such attack occurred. Instead, to Huey's surprise, Odell filed charges against him for assault with a deadly weapon. At the trial, Huey asked for a lawyer to advise him, but insisted on representing himself before the jury. He had taken courses in law at night and mostly had success representing himself on misdemeanor charges. The judge told Huey his choice was all or nothing: either to let a lawyer represent him or to conduct his own defense without legal help.

Turning down a lawyer was a bad idea. When Odell took the stand, he denied reaching for a weapon in his pocket and explained that his scar did not come from a prior knife fight but from an automobile accident. All Huey was able to present to the jury was his testimony that he acted in self-defense in the belief he was about to be attacked and Melvin's support as an eyewitness.

Tom Broome later recalled seeing what went down between Odell and Huey. In his view, Huey would have gotten off if he had a decent lawyer. Broome thought "there was so much provocation that a third-grade attorney could have beaten the case or at least had it reduced. Huey didn't know how to go about it, made a fool of himself and wound up with a felony conviction to boot." (That 1964 felony conviction would emerge as a basis for attacking Huey's credibility at his 1968 trial.) Melvin blamed Tom Broome and other fraternity brothers for not coming forward. Yet Melvin realized Odell was related to the party's hosts, which made them reluctant to take sides.

Following the guilty verdict, the Newton family scraped up $1,500 for Huey. Melvin told Huey that this money was available either for bail or to hire a lawyer to represent him at sentencing but not both. It was his choice. Huey chose to have his family pay for a lawyer at sentencing. Huey thought he might get Sonny Man to post bail because of their strong sense of kinship dating back to the outdooring ceremony, but Sonny Man was unreachable. As a result, Huey was taken to the Alameda

County Jail pending his sentencing hearing.

As it turned out, Huey made a good choice by having his parents pay for an attorney. The judge could have sent him to prison for a year or more, but the lawyer helped Huey get a reduced sentence of six months at the Santa Rita jail. Even so, Armelia was beside herself that her baby son had gotten himself into such trouble that he was now going to spend six months in jail. That may have been when she started a closet habit of drinking sherry, keeping her consumption a secret from most of her family. Doris knew something was wrong when she came by the house to do chores for her mother and Armelia would take to her bed.

Reconnecting with Esther Lee

IN 1961, Bertha asked Walter and Armelia if they and Lee would agree to allow the Smiths to adopt Esther, who had just turned 18. The Smiths wanted to make sure that Esther would inherit their property when both of them died. The Newtons had no problem with the adoption since the Smiths had raised their granddaughter. Lee had no objection.

Esther Lee Smith graduated from Colored High School in Monroe where two of the older Newton siblings had gone. (It had undergone a name change to Carroll High at a new location in the 1950s when Esther attended it). After graduating, she enrolled in Southern University, where she met Lennon White, became pregnant and married him. Their son Tony was born in 1963 and their daughter Tonja in July of 1964.

Immediately after her daughter's birth, Esther reached out to her grandparents in Oakland to let them know she was desperate to get out of her marriage. They responded without hesitation, inviting Esther and her babies to come live with them. Esther took her toddler son and not quite two-month-old daughter on the train to California in September 1964 to join the Newton household. At the time, only Huey lived at home, shortly before he went to jail.

In June of that year, Melvin had married his girlfriend Joyce Thomas, whom he had met at a fraternity party. Most of his fraternity brothers were already married by then. In 1959, Huey's good friend David Hilliard had married Patricia ("Pat") Banks whom he met at a fraternity party through Melvin. David was not a fraternity brother. He had quit school before obtaining his high school degree and went to work to support his wife Pat and new baby. When Melvin married Joyce, she was 21 — five years younger than he was — and still lived at home. Her widowed mother thought Joyce was too young to marry but they ignored her.

The Thomas family belonged to the Church of Christ, which did not permit musical instruments at services, while Melvin, as a Baptist, had grown up with piano music at church. This posed a challenge for Melvin, who had to find a wedding venue that both families would find acceptable. In the end, he settled for Chapel of the Chimes on Adeline Street, which led to some family gossip about this odd choice of venue. Unbeknownst to Melvin at the time it was mostly used for funerals.

As the first daughter-in-law, Joyce quickly bonded with Armelia. Melvin, meanwhile, joined Joyce and her mother at their church services in an effort to strengthen his relationship with her family. But he quickly found the fundamentalism of the Church of Christ too far from his own religious views. The newlyweds started quarreling almost immediately. Soon, a major rift developed between them. Melvin later reflected that getting married at a funeral parlor might have been an omen.

While Melvin was finding married life a difficult adjustment, Esther enjoyed an exceptionally warm welcome from his parents. Armelia loved babies and now had her first grandchild and two great grandbabies. With only two bedrooms, the Newtons offered Esther and her children Huey's room, while Huey graciously agreed to sleep on the living room couch. Armelia had covered the couch in protective plastic, which must have made it quite uncomfortable. Yet Huey undoubtedly got a kick out of having a beautiful niece to introduce to his friends. Esther bore a close family resemblance to Huey and was barely a year younger than he was.

Armelia looked after the babies to allow Huey to bring Esther to check out the Oakland City College campus on Grove Street where Huey was a student. Huey impressed Esther with his knowledge almost as much as Melvin did. She interacted less with Melvin and his wife Joyce but often saw their infant son Gregory when Armelia babysat. Esther considered Melvin to be brilliant. He was also the quietest and most subdued of her uncles and aunts.

To increase her job opportunities, Esther enrolled at the community college to continue toward a degree. Meanwhile, back in Monroe, her husband Lennon White was bent on reuniting with Esther and their two young children. Soon afterward, he came out to Oakland and convinced Esther to get back together with him. He moved the family to Berkeley to live with his aunt and uncle.

Once Lennon arrived, he started hanging out with Huey. Lennon began absorbing Huey's radical political views just as Huey was developing ideas for activism. Two years later, Lennon White would be one of the first contemporaries Huey turned to when he and Bobby Seale decided to form their own Black militant group.

After Esther obtained her college degree, she started working for the Social Security Administration. The elder Newtons and the Lennon White family kept in close touch. Armelia insisted on continuing to cover expenses for Esther and her daughter Tonja for diapers and formula and other essentials. Lennon's aunt and uncle took care of Lennon's and Tony's needs.

Living in Berkeley, Esther also developed a bond with her now divorced Great Aunt Jessie — another tribal connection. Getting by wasn't easy, but they helped each other out as much as they could. The family got together weekly, cementing their ties. They bolstered each other's resilience to life's vicissitudes and established deeper roots in their adoptive hometowns of Oakland and Berkeley.

Family Ties Bolster Endurance

AS the extended Newton family worked hard to get by in California, living mostly in segregated neighborhoods, they found great comfort in mutual support. By 1964, Myrtle, whom most family members now called "Sista" or "Aunt Sista", started trading off with Leola and Doris hosting get-togethers. Esther and Lennon, when he joined her, enjoyed the frequent family parties.

Doris and Glen had just bought a new home in the Oakland hills for themselves and their three children near the zoo. It was by far the most spacious place for extended family to gather. The drawback was that Doris insisted on keeping it looking pristine — as if no one lived there. The family had a better time crowding into Myrtle's apartment in Berkeley where the liquor flowed freely, and the atmosphere was far more relaxed.

Myrtle always volunteered to cook. In addition to a big pot of greens and ham hocks, she liked to include chitlins and pigs' feet, among other dishes from the Louisiana backcountry. Sonny Man was the only sibling who refused to eat pork products. Leola thought that was because he had been traumatized as a toddler watching a pig being slaughtered for family meals. But Sonny Man was also the most health conscious of his siblings. He prided himself on keeping fit and eating mostly vegetables.

By 1964, Huey and his girlfriend Dolores spent hours at a time with new sparring partners – his mother's nephew Jake and his girlfriend Betty. Jake Ward was Aunt Orell's son, who moved to the Bay Area from Monroe in 1964 shortly after his mother died. Her twin sister Ozell had died in 1955. Both twins' deaths hit Armelia and Jessie hard.

Huey also now had his first car, which Melvin nicknamed the Gray Roach. Riding with Huey was an adventure. He liked to scare friends by racing the Gray Roach across railroad tracks to beat an oncoming train. That game resulted in a few near misses. His reckless streak became ever more noticeable as he grew older.

At family gatherings Armelia and Walter continued to preside as "Mother" and "Daddy" to all of their offspring. Walter told his nephew Eddie Ento to call him "Buddy." One could always tell when Sonny Man was around because he took control of the music, playing Blues or his favorite new songs — "Little Red Rooster" and "Mustang Sally." To the rest of the family, Esther's father, Lee Edward, responded to "Brotha" or "Uncle Brotha." He would bring his record player and stack of records and sit in the corner to listen to his own discs. The family learned to tolerate hearing his favorite songs over and over whether they wanted to or not.

These weekly gatherings comforted the family members during their difficult adjustment to a new life out West. They were starting to realize that California wasn't all that different from Louisiana in its commitment to White supremacy.

Later that fall of 1964, Esther experienced racism California style. On the ballot was Proposition 14, an initiative sponsored by the California Realtors' Association to amend the state Constitution to undo the impact of California's pioneering Fair Housing Act of 1963. The highly controversial act was the crowning achievement of the state's first African-American Assemblyman,

Berkeleyite William Byron Rumford. Rumford had engineered the passage of the first state law in the nation to prohibit discrimination by home sellers and landlords on the basis of race, religion, sex, national origin, ancestry or marital status.

The backlash came swiftly. The main aim of putting Proposition 14 on the ballot in 1964 was to protect landlords and sellers from getting sued if they refused to allow a Black family to purchase or rent a home in an all-White neighborhood. Proposition 14 was endorsed by the American Nazi Party, White Citizens' Councils, and the National States' Rights Party, whose motto was "White Men Unite." This punitive effort had much in common with contemporary efforts to protect those who oppose gay marriage.

A majority of residents of Alameda County voted against Proposition 14, but it passed statewide with over 65% of the vote. At least, the Newtons were living in one of the most welcoming counties in the state, despite how far short it fell in promoting racial equality. Walter and Armelia's duplex in a mixed neighborhood was one of the signs of progress.

VII.
A NEW ERA

Survival Lessons from Solitary Confinement

BY THE FALL of 1964, Huey Newton's path was starting to diverge from that of his large and close-knit family. His violent altercation with Odell Lee led to a brutal and isolating experience in prison that he would later describe as a proving ground and a source of his political awakening.

Before Huey was sentenced to the Santa Rita Rehabilitation Center for stabbing Lee, he spent one month in the Alameda County jail. Looking back, Huey recognized that the torment he endured while incarcerated there forced him to learn the secrets of surviving in prison unbroken. He viewed it as essential training for enduring maximum-security lockup when he later co-led the Black Panther Party.

In the Alameda County Jail in late 1964, Huey started out as a jail trusty, an inmate allowed special privileges outside his cell in exchange for good behavior. But Huey's contempt for authority soon became evident. Trusties assisted guards with their duties, such as delivering inmate meals. But shortly after Huey arrived, the prisoners organized a food strike against the bland meals they were served. In a coordinated effort, they threw bowls of gloppy pea soup against the barred doors of their cells leaving large pale green splashes on the corridor floors and walls. The administration targeted Huey as a likely instigator. He was the only trusty who participated in the protest. As they correctly surmised, Huey had the ability to pass the word along as he performed his meal delivery duties from cell block to cell block.

Huey had started out incarcerated on the main line. As punishment for being an apparent ringleader of the protest, Huey wound up on the harshest level of confinement, "the soul breaker." There were two such cells at the jail, each just 4 ½ by 6 feet with walls painted black, and blood-red rubber tiles on the floor. The cells were smaller in size than a circus lion cage. Huey later described being stripped naked and left there in the dark without a blanket and only a sliver of light visible under the solid steel door. There was no bunk, not even a wash basin, just a four-inch hole about the size and depth of the cup on a golf green for inmates to relieve themselves.

Guards delivered a half gallon of water meant to last for a week, cold pea soup twice a day and an unappetizing vegetable patty once daily. Periodically, an officer would stop by to offer a reprieve if the prisoner promised he would now follow prison rules. The expectation was that, after a few days, anyone consigned to the soul breaker would volunteer to obey prison authorities — either that or start screaming for release. Prisoners were offered no showers, no family visits or interaction with anyone but prison officials on their brief daily stops at his cell. Such inhumane isolation rooms were later outlawed at the instigation of Huey's future criminal defense lawyer, Charles Garry.

In 1964, Huey did not yet consider himself a revolutionary. But he was stubborn. Despite the desperation he felt after a couple of days in solitary, he determined not to give in. To avoid sleeping in his own overflow waste surrounding the cell's slimy hole, he minimized his water and food intake. To avoid sinking into a deep depression, he forced himself to recall his most pleasurable memories. That was also how Huey had dealt with overwhelming situations as a child. But those remembered incidents began to fill him with anxiety. He then tried exercising in his cramped quarters. There was enough room for push-ups. By the end of the second week Huey felt in total control of his thought processes.

In keeping with prison practice, following fifteen days in isolation, the guards transferred Huey back for one night to his prior cell, permitted him to shower and had him examined by both a doctor and psychiatrist. When he still remained defiant, they returned him for the rest of the month to the soul breaker, which he endured unabashedly. It was an experience from Hell that Huey liked to retell, especially to new girlfriends. They always reacted with empathy and awe.

After the sentencing hearing, Huey was transferred to the Santa Rita jail to serve the rest of his six-month sentence. The Santa Rita correctional facility was a converted Army base just over twenty-five miles southeast of Oakland. Huey started out there in the honor camp where prisoners were trusted to bunk together in minimum security, not separated into cells. They also had opportunities for exercise in the yard and visits from family and friends. Melvin and Leola came as often as they could. Other family members also visited Huey in the first few weeks. Despite Huey's cultivation of a tough street image, he relished their show of unconditional love.

One day, Huey saw a familiar face, a neighbor who went to the same middle school in the 1950s as Huey and David Hilliard. Anwar Hasan arrived at the jail after facing a choice: $400 in fines for unpaid parking tickets or a month in Santa Rita. Too poor to pay the fine himself, he opted to save his parents their hard-earned money by taking jail time instead. Huey approached Anwar and passed on words of advice for stomaching life inside Santa Rita: "Don't eat the pork."

Walter and Armelia had to hope that serving this sentence would convince Huey to take a less combative path forward. But the event at Santa Rita that made the biggest impression on Huey had the opposite impact. In early December 1964 Huey was enjoying some fresh air in the Santa Rita prison yard. Through the barbed wire fence, he saw incoming busloads of arrested Free Speech Movement demonstrators from U. C. Berkeley. Hundreds of White students and activists had flouted authorities by taking over a campus building in protest of restrictions on political activity. Huey admired the statement they made.

Huey was unable to resist his own mini-rebellion against prison rules. Not long after seeing the busloads of jailed protesters, Huey got into a dispute with a Black trusty who was serving food and thwarted Huey's attempt to take seconds. Huey then bashed the man on the head with a tray. Not surprisingly, Huey wound up with similar punishment as he had received in the Alameda jail — serving out the rest of his sentence in maximum security with no family visits.

At Santa Rita, that meant being sequestered in the Graystone building in its "cooler." There, Huey used the same coping techniques he had developed previously in solitary confinement in the Alameda soul breaker. But this time he refused to keep silent about the wretched conditions. The guards grew tired of Huey complaining daily about the poor quality of the food and how cold the cell was. The prison administration's solution was to transfer him back to Alameda County Jail in late January 1965 to finish his last month once again in the soul breaker.

The Birth of the Black Panther Party for Self-Defense

HUEY NEWTON stayed close with his family. Yet with every passing year, he was becoming more determined to forge his own rebellious way in life. Upon his release from jail, Huey was determined to empower himself by learning as much as he could about California's criminal laws. Immersing himself in the legal system had been on his mind since his disastrous attempt to represent himself at trial the prior fall. To this end, he returned to Oakland City College and took a course taught by Assistant District Attorney (and President Ronald Reagan's future Attorney General) Edwin Meese III. Huey quickly proved an extraordinarily apt student, particularly when the subjects were the constitutional rights of suspects and the dos and don'ts of California's open-carry gun laws.

Back before he went to jail, when Huey gave talks about the Cuban revolution as one of the Grove Street orators, one of the listeners was part-time student Bobby Seale. Seale was more than five years older than Huey. Like Walter Newton, Seale's family had arrived in the East Bay in 1944, and for similar reasons — to seek a better life. In 1955, Seale dropped out of Berkeley High School to join the Air Force. He served three years and left with a dishonorable discharge for getting into an altercation with a White officer. Seale had since become a highly trained sheet metal mechanic in the aerospace industry, but when he connected with Huey in 1965, he was actually hoping to make a career out of stand-up comedy.

Like Huey, Seale had a recent but intense interest in history and radical politics. To that end, Seale became a charter member of a new West Coast chapter of the Revolutionary Action Movement ("RAM"), a secretive organization based in the East that advocated guerrilla warfare. RAM took as its inspiration a new book, *Negroes with Guns*. Its author, former NAACP leader Robert Williams, was a strong proponent of armed self-defense. The book was based on his community in North Carolina's recent efforts to protect itself from attack by White racists. In 1961, Williams fled his home state of North Carolina to live in Castro's Cuba. He had since begun regularly broadcasting his militant views to Blacks in the South via "Radio Free Dixie."

As Huey became more politically active, he started seeking out close friendships — and finding political comrades — that felt like the kind of dependable brotherhood he enjoyed with Melvin. But unlike Melvin, who forged a career path within the existing system, Huey was bent on radical change.

At Oakland City College, Huey became one of the Grove Street orators singing the praises of the recent Cuban revolution. He drew Seale's rapt attention. The two quickly bonded. Huey admired Seale's skill with rifles, his dishonorable discharge from the military for insubordination, and his shared interest in revolutionary politics. Huey still had his family of origin, but Bobby Seale became his comrade in arms. The pair sought out like-minded radicals. But Seale's cohorts in RAM did not share his view of Huey, whom they regarded with suspicion because of his parents' home in the more integrated neighborhood of North Oakland.

Newton and Seale soon joined disaffected Blacks on campus who founded the Soul Students Advisory Council (a forerunner of the Black Student Union). They published a new radical political and literary magazine called *Soulbook*. Among the Advisory Council's founders was Leftist scholar Louis Armmond, who had become one of the handful of Black activists in the early Free Speech Movement. At Armmond's instigation, the Council opposed the drafting of Black soldiers for the Vietnam War and organized hundreds of people to attend an anti-war rally. The Council also lobbied for courses in Black history and pushed for the hiring of African-American faculty.

Armmond introduced Bobby Seale to the writings of the late Afro-Caribbean revolutionary Dr. Frantz Fanon. Fanon had participated in the successful Algerian overthrow of French colonial rule. The insurrection began in 1954 and took until 1962 to achieve its goal of independence from France. The members of the Soul Students Advisory Council studied Fanon's *The Wretched of the Earth* like the Bible. Here was a blueprint, taken from recent successful experience, for how a liberation movement could be started from a condition of perceived total subservience.

Fanon called violence "a cleansing force." He wrote in *The Wretched of the Earth* that violent action "frees the native from his inferiority complex and from his despair and inaction. It makes him fearless and restores his self-respect." If violent revolt could work against the French in Algeria, why not for American Blacks? Seale read and reread Fanon's *The Wretched of the Earth* and recommended it enthusiastically to Newton. Newton was the first among the Grove Street orators to make a public connection between the Algerians' overthrow of an oppressive regime and what might be possible for Blacks struggling in Oakland.

Huey and Bobby Seale soon befriended another radical from Oakland City College. Richard Aoki, a Japanese American Army vet from West Oakland, was two years younger than Seale. Aoki had hung out in the late 1950s with Sonny Man and Lee Edward, though he was closer in age to Melvin. Known then as a streetfighter, Aoki had become radicalized after his family was forcibly removed from their Oakland home during World War II and interned for three years at Topaz (Central Utah) War Relocation Authority Camp. He and his family were among the 127,000 Japanese Americans who were forced into such camps for the duration of the war.

Huey was particularly impressed by Seale's and Aoki's facility with firearms because of their military training. Aoki also let Huey and Bobby know that he had ready access to a supply of guns. Seale was especially motivated to take action after the assassination in February 1965 of his hero, Black nationalist minister Malcolm X, a leading African-American critic of Reverend Martin Luther King, Jr.

In the early 1960s, Malcolm X had inspired large numbers of disaffected young Blacks across the country with his call for aggressive pursuit of racial justice. Malcolm X rejected the pacifist approach of Mahatma Gandhi that Dr. King advocated. Malcolm X had been the leader from 1952 until 1964 of the radical religious and political Nation of Islam. Launched in Detroit in 1930, it had gained far more traction under Malcolm X with his melding of street smarts and scholarship, urging change "by any means necessary — the ballot or the bullet."

Huey and Bobby had been enthralled by speeches in Oakland by both Malcolm X and World Heavyweight

Champion Cassius Clay. Both strongly advocated Black empowerment. Huey and Bobby heard Malcolm X when he was a featured speaker at McClymond's High School in West Oakland. Two of Huey's sisters had attended the school in the 1940s when no such invitation would have been extended to a Black radical.

The Nation of Islam drew much more public attention when Cassius Clay became affiliated with it. In 1964, Clay converted to Islam and changed his name to Muhammad Ali, as the extraordinary boxer would thereafter be known. Malcolm X had a bitter falling out with the Nation of Islam that same year. In 1966, three members of the Nation of Islam would be convicted of gunning him down, but two would be exonerated in 2021. Doubts linger to this day as to who was actually behind the assassination of Malcolm X.

* * *

It was after Aoki transferred to U.C. Berkeley that Huey and Bobby joined the Soul Students Advisory Council where they were first introduced to the writings of Dr. Frantz Fanon. Seale later pointed to the moment in 1965 when he and Huey focused on the impact of Dr. Fanon's writings as the true genesis of the Black Panther Party. Using Fanon's book, *The Wretched of the Earth*, as their guide, they would later recruit to their cause the "lumpenproletariat." The term was coined in the mid-19th century by Karl Marx and Friedrich Engels, authors of *The Communist Manifesto*. It described unorganized members of the underclass, often with criminal records – among them, thieves, prostitutes and violent felons.

In March of 1966, Huey and Bobby got into minor trouble with the Berkeley police for their activism. Seale was standing on a chair on a Berkeley street corner haranguing passersby with revolutionary poetry. As an officer started to arrest Seale for disturbing the peace, Huey reached for the officer's gun and was arrested for interfering with Seale's arrest. The incident was covered by the local underground newspaper, *The Berkeley Barb*. That article gave Huey and Bobby their first publicity for railing against the establishment. The next month Muhammad Ali made national news when he was arrested for resisting the draft for the Viet Nam War.

That same summer of 1966, a new federal jobs program was launched in Oakland to employ inner city youth. Oakland had been awarded funding as a measure aimed at preventing a repeat of the devastating riot in the Watts neighborhood of Los Angeles in 1965 and race riots in other cities in 1966. Superior Court Judge Lionel Wilson headed the Oakland jobs project as Chairman of the city's Economic Development Council. (At the time, Wilson was also the first and only Black judge in the county). Wilson hired Seale to supervise eighty at-risk high school students at the North Oakland Anti-Poverty Center. Seale brought Huey in to assist him.

Starting in June, a major rift among civil rights leaders in the South caught both Huey's and Seale's attention. The Southern Christian Leadership Conference (SCLC) spearheaded by Martin Luther King, Jr. had affiliated a new student organization promoting civil rights through peaceful means. In June of 1966, the Student Nonviolent Coordinating Committee (SNCC) was headed by Stokely Carmichael, a Trinidadian by birth, whose family moved to the Bronx when he was a young teen. Carmichael was a freshman at Howard University when he joined the campus affiliate of SNCC and became one of the first Freedom Riders. The first week of June 1966, King and Carmichael joined civil rights activist James Meredith in co-leading a March Against Fear starting in Memphis, Tennessee. Their intended destination was Jackson, Mississippi but Carmichael quit after a sniper severely wounded Meredith on the second day of the march.

Carmichael then drew national outrage when he called for an aggressive new strategy to seek Black Power. He disavowed prior White allies and encouraged inner city youths to form Black Panther organizations, named for the panther symbol used by his own voting rights organization in Alabama. The panther was said to defend itself vigorously, but not to engage in an unprovoked attack. That was actually a myth. Panthers are adept as a species at stalking and launching unprovoked attacks on their prey. Carmichael promoted the black panther across the country as a powerful symbol of defiance. By August of 1966, the panther logo was beginning to be used by organizers of Black militants in a number of cities.

In September, Bobby Seale joined the new Black Panther Party of Northern California based in San Francisco. He quit soon afterward after finding it too tame for his liking. Instead, he and Huey got together to create their own political platform with Richard Aoki. Aoki was then attending the University of California at Berkeley. Together, the three hammered out a 10-point platform using the Nation of Islam's "What We Believe" as a model. Huey and Bobby refined their version of the program at Seale's home near campus and at work in the

Anti-Poverty Center. Then the two showed up at Melvin's door in married student housing at U.C. Berkeley where he was studying for his master's degree in social work.

As Melvin's wife Joyce cared for their one-year-old son, Gregory, Melvin listened to Huey and Bobby explain their plan to form an organization using the Black Panther logo recommended by Stokely Carmichael. In this consequential meeting, Huey's two 'families' came together. Huey once again counted on Melvin's support — and was not disappointed.

Dismayed by what they considered the toothlessness of the fledgling San Francisco Black Panther Party, Huey and Bobby Seale wanted to add to their own new party's title the words "For Self-Defense." That phrase would emphasize a far more aggressive message. This new party would carry loaded weapons. (The terms of Huey's probation restricted him from carrying a handgun, but he could still wield a rifle or shotgun.)

Melvin thought the ten-point program was spot on for focusing on jobs, housing, education in Black history, an end to police brutality, resistance to the draft and a demand for trials of Blacks before a jury of their peers. He was quite leery of what would happen if they carried guns but helped them polish the language of their program. The finished platform included a lengthy quote from the Declaration of Independence justifying the right to overthrow "absolute Despotism" after "a long train of abuses and usurpations." Seale's wife Artie and Huey's new girlfriend LaVerne Williams both worked on typing up the platform.

Soon Huey recruited a handful of others, including 17-year-old Bobby Hutton. Huey also asked his long-time close friend David Hilliard, who was married and working since he dropped out of high school as a longshoreman. David turned him down flat: "I ain't got no time for that goddamn shit." David was practically part of the Newton family. Huey never pushed other family members to join him. Yet two in-laws were eager to participate: Myrtle's new son-in-law Steve Johnson (who had just married her daughter Patricia); and Esther's husband Lennon White, who agreed to be the Party treasurer. Steve had a station wagon and agreed to drive the group around West Oakland as they followed the police on their rounds.

At great potential risk, the small group of men drove around West Oakland following patrol cars on their beat. The Panthers stopped their car when they saw someone being arrested so that Huey could get out and read the arrestee his new Miranda rights. The high court had been headed since 1953 by former Alameda County District Attorney and Governor of California Earl Warren. Under his leadership, the Supreme Court had recently established the right of arrestees to remain silent and their right to counsel. Huey made it his mission to make sure Black men being arrested in West Oakland knew about these rights. Each time Lennon stopped the car where an arrest was underway, Huey's armed associates stood watch, carrying loaded long arms the legal way Huey had taught them. The guns were pointed straight up or straight down. The police grew livid at these tactics.

As a new bride, Patricia did not appreciate Steve's preference for riding around with her uncle and his friends over spending time with her. Esther was not keen on Lennon's participation, either. It made her very nervous. One day Esther discovered their preschoolers playing in the closet tossing paper money around. It came from a brown paper bag Lennon had deposited there to serve as the Party's makeshift piggy bank.

In the spring of 1967 the Black Panther Psrty had not yet set up this headquarters. The Party would grow dramatically in 1968 with all the publicity surrounding Huey's trial.

The Sacramento World Stage Debut

IN FEBRUARY 1967, newspapers ran fearful headlines after the Black Panthers provided an armed escort of Malcolm X's widow from the airport to the offices of the Leftist magazine, *Ramparts*, in San Francisco. The Panthers also won a new radical supporter, Ramparts staffer Eldridge Cleaver, a recently released California inmate who had just published to great acclaim his collection of essays written in prison, *Soul on Ice,* after the best-selling book appeared serialized in *Ramparts*.

That April the local press covered a Panther rally in a Black neighborhood in Richmond protesting the death of Denzil Dowell. Dowell was unarmed and suspected of fleeing from burglary when he was shot by a Contra Costa County sheriff's deputy. The Panthers featured Dowell's death in the first issue of their underground newspaper, which would quickly become the Panther Party's principal source of revenue. This followed on the heels of headline-grabbing riots in San Francisco's tenderloin district in September 1966 following the police shooting death of a joyriding teenager.

Meanwhile, Huey allowed himself to be used for mythology and image-making to increase his range and influence. An iconic photo of Huey would appear in every later issue of the Panther paper, showing him seated on a wicker throne atop a zebra rug in the living room of Cleaver's then fiancée, civil rights lawyer Beverly Axelrod. She had engineered Cleaver's release from prison that past December and arranged for the publication of his book *Soul on Ice*. Both she and Cleaver were now eager to help the Black Panther Party gain far more attention and adherents. At their instigation, Huey posed with a spear in one hand and a rifle in the other — an image he later found cringe-worthy.

On April 30, 1967, the Panthers garnered another blaring headline: "Oakland's Black Panthers Wear Guns; Talk Revolution." It was accompanied by photos taken of Seale and Huey on the San Francisco State campus, both legally armed. In response to police urging, a California Assembly member from the affluent, small East Bay city of Piedmont proposed a new law that would prohibit most open carry of firearms in cities throughout the state. That gave Huey an idea for a bold response. Seale could lead an armed group of Panthers and members of Denzil Dowell's family on an eighty-mile drive to the State Capitol in early May to oppose the bill and introduce to the world the Panther Party and its 10-point program.

The entourage packed loaded guns in the trunks of their cars, planning to display them on arrival. Eldridge Cleaver, on assignment to cover the event for *Ramparts* magazine, went along with no gun. Huey wisely accepted the recommendation of his associates to stay behind at his parents' home in Oakland. He remained on probation from his 1964 conviction. They did not want to risk their leader being charged with violating its terms and sent back to jail. He hoped there would be television coverage so he could watch the bold confrontation he had set in motion.

On May 2, 1967, Bobby Seale led 23 other men and 6 women in a caravan of six cars to Sacramento. Many of them brought rifles, 12-gauge pump action shotguns and Magnum .357s. Seale wore a .45 caliber pistol on his hip. Some had slung on bandoliers of ammunition. Following Huey's strict instructions, when they emerged from their cars and collected their long arms, they kept them pointed straight up or down at the ground as they marched toward the Capitol building. Huey had counseled Seale that if someone fired upon him, he should shoot back. Luckily, the startled police did not respond to this provocation with force. If the cops had opened fire, the result would have been the early extinction of the Black Panther Party for Self-Defense. It was just one instance of Huey showing reckless disregard for the consequences of his ideas.

Stunned cameramen and reporters followed the relatively unknown group of Black militants as they made their way into the Capitol building. All the while, TV cameras were rolling, and photos were snapped. The guards stopped a few of the Panthers upon entering the building and took away their guns but returned the weapons later on. White NRA members had often been allowed to wear holstered guns into the Capitol. A few did so that day as well.

To the immense relief of the Assembly members, Capitol police quickly ushered out their unexpected Black visitors without any violence. On both the way in and out of the Capitol building, Seale stood on the Capitol steps to read to the media Huey's "Executive Mandate Number One." It accused the California legislature of seeking to keep the Black community "disarmed and powerless" while police repression increased throughout the country.

That afternoon, Huey came inside from doing yard work at his parents' home to observe the breaking news out of Sacramento. He reacted with glee at the success of what he called 'shock-a-buku' — sudden moves that kept the enemy off balance.

As the Panthers drove out of Sacramento, the police arrested them on a variety of minor charges and took them to the city jail. Bobby Seale would soon receive a several-month jail sentence on charges stemming from that trip. The day after the Panthers' armed appearance at the Assembly, major California newspapers ran the front-page story with headlines such as "Armed Men Invade Assembly," "Guns in Capitol" and "Armed Foray in Assembly Stirs Wrath." Other media both nationally and abroad picked up the startling story. By the time of the Panthers' astonishing May debut, Louis Armmond had left for the East Coast fully committed to armed revolt. He had seen hundreds of thousands of protesters marching in the streets in the past couple of years which made him think the United States was headed toward a general insurrection.

Armmond's belief intensified when he read New York newspaper headlines about the armed militant Blacks who showed up at the California Capitol talking of revolution and carrying guns. Neither Armmond nor the revolutionaries he worked with expected the Oakland Panthers to be the vanguard of their revolution. Melvin actually had a similar view to Armmond's. He believed that Huey envisioned the Panthers' leadership role as largely symbolic. Melvin reflected that: "[Huey] saw the guns as something that was spectacular and something to draw attention and to draw people in. He didn't see it as something that would be used to take on the United States."

All of the publicity his brother generated made Melvin nervous:

> "It got a lot of press, which was Huey's object. He wanted . . . a colossal event, and the colossal event really was a recruitment effort. . . . [But] to

go to Sacramento with the guns [was] a two-edged thing. . ... [I]t got the publicity and the attention of the youth that wanted to be Panthers . . .. The other side of it was that it . . . drove some people in the opposite direction. . ... I would not have done it, but it was done. . . . . I'd never thought the guns served a good purpose."

It may have been that very same night; Melvin was in the kitchen where Huey sat at one end of the dining table and their father at the other. Walter was trying his best to dissuade Huey from continuing to engage in dangerous confrontations with the police. He warned Huey he could be killed. Huey responded that he felt the Party platform was well worth defending. Using his father's teachings against him, Huey made it clear that the threat of death did not faze him: "Jesus did it." Melvin saw how Huey had left his father feeling checkmated. He himself felt that the police were now primed to dig Huey's grave.

National Race Riots and Local Anti-War Protests

LATER in May, Huey talked David Hilliard into helping him raise bail for the Sacramento arrestees. Huey used a speaking fee he received from San Francisco State to buy a block of marijuana to divide into matchboxes for the two of them to sell. They both knew that Huey was still on parole from his 1964 conviction and could have been sent back to prison if caught with marijuana. David asked him what they would do if the police stopped them. Newton laughed and responded, "We shoot them. You know, we fight." David was not eager for any such deadly confrontation. Fortunately, they did not get stopped.

The Panther Bill, as the new restrictive California gun law was nicknamed, passed quickly as emergency legislation. It was signed in June 1967 by Governor Reagan. From then on, the Panthers and most others could be arrested for carrying loaded guns within city limits. The new restrictions took effect just as the nation began to endure the "long, hot summer" of 1967 when more than 150 race riots erupted in cities across the country. The widespread uprisings prompted President Johnson to establish a blue-ribbon panel to study the root causes of inner-city violence.

Remarkably, no uprisings happened in Oakland like the riots that summer in so many other cities. Instead, Black community leaders in West Oakland made plans for a belated Juneteenth Day festival in August 1967 in DeFremery Park, the largest park around. It was a favorite gathering place for West Oakland residents. (The 19th of June 1865, when Texas slaves first learned of their freedom, had long been celebrated among Blacks in the South. Those who resettled elsewhere in the country introduced it to other states. It became a national holiday in 2021 at the direction of President Biden).

The organizers invited only African-American entertainers and speakers. Among the political officeholders were San Francisco Assemblyman Willie Brown (later Speaker of the State Assembly and then Mayor of San Francisco); State Senator Mervin Dymally (later Lieutenant Governor of California) and Berkeley's new anti-war Council Member Ron Dellums. Dellums would go on to a long career in Congress capped by service as Mayor of Oakland.

The Oakland police assumed they would provide security but were officially asked not to monitor the festival. Instead, the organizers turned to the Black Panthers. The Panthers had recently begun building community support by lobbying for traffic signals at dangerous intersections, acting as crossing guards and by disseminating their platform.

The Panthers' 10-point program largely echoed long-desired goals of the entire Black community. As reporter Belva Davis observed: "Better education, food for the kids that go to school and . . . not to have to go to school hungry. I mean, they were just fundamental rights and to deny that the things that they were asking for were needed would have been hypocritical." The police were affronted by the deployment of Black Panthers as security for the event but reluctantly acquiesced. This incident turned a new page in local police-community relations. Established Black families were now openly shunning official security offered by the city and showing greater comfort in protection by a militant Black group that considered the police the Gestapo.

* * *

All of the racial riots across the country that summer were taking place amidst increased anti-war activity. Beginning in 1964, Muhammad Ali had begun drawing increased public attention to the Nation of Islam. In 1966, Ali began making headlines as part of the anti-war movement when he refused to submit to the draft. Living in Oakland and Berkeley, Huey and Bobby Seale were situated in the forefront of the Vietnam War protests.

The third week of October 1967 marked a major two-pronged initiative. In coordination with a planned march on the Pentagon, a coalition of Bay Area activists launched "Stop the Draft Week." They planned several days of massive demonstrations designed to shut down the Oakland Army Induction Center, one of the largest such facilities on the Pacific Coast.

On the first day, some three thousand protesters blocked the center's entrance, leading to more than a hundred arrests. The following day, twice as many demonstrators blocked the doorway and the surrounding streets. An estimated 250 Oakland policemen, sheriff's deputies and highway patrolmen broke through and dispersed the crowd, spraying mace and swinging batons. The bloody confrontation injured many protestors.

The stand-off between police and overwhelmingly White students amazed younger West Oakland Blacks. They thought head-bashing was not something police did to Whites. Belva Davis covered the mêlée as a young reporter for a San Francisco TV station. She knew she was witnessing history: "The Bay Area felt like ground zero in a generational battle for the soul of the country." Walter and Armelia may have been reminded of the huge labor strike just after World War II that they had observed being brutally suppressed.

Armelia must have grown more fearful about what might happen to Huey, who was back living at home. He still cleaned out her oven when asked. He even helped Walter out again working in the yard and regularly delivered envelopes of bill payments. Yet Huey had no paying job. He kept late hours at bars and social events fund-raising for the jailed Panthers. In those excursions he was often accompanied by either Emory Douglas, the editor and graphic artist for the fledgling Panther newspaper, or David Hilliard, or both. David had still not decided to join the Panthers.

Doris heard from her mother that a family on their parents' street let the police take over their house to keep a lookout for Huey. Walter was incensed. He had misgivings of his own about the Panthers, but he did not like anybody messing with him and his children. Then, in late October, Armelia's worst fears were realized.

The Predawn Shootout and Huey's Arrest for Murder

ON the night of October 27, 1967, Huey asked Emory and David to join him again and head out for a night of drinking at local bars. Both begged off. Emory had already agreed to monitor a dance. David had set up a late-night poker game fund-raiser at his home. He was hoping to obtain the rest of the money needed for Bobby Seale's bail. Huey talked another longtime friend, Gene McKinney, into accompanying him instead.

In the early morning of October 28, 1967, Melvin was at home in his apartment in North Oakland with Joyce and his two-and-a-half-year-old son Gregory. It was a Saturday, so Melvin expected to sleep in, freed from his weekday schedule. At the time, he was employed as an Alameda County social worker helping people with mental and physical disabilities. An insistent knock on his door surprised him. He rose to open it and found his father there, looking extraordinarily distressed.

Walter told Melvin that the Oakland police had just stormed his home looking for Huey. He and Armelia were the only ones there. They had no idea where Huey was. The officers told them that one policeman had been wounded, and another died following a shootout with their son on Seventh and Willow in West Oakland. Soon Walter and Armelia learned that Huey was at Kaiser Hospital — near death with a bullet wound in his stomach.

Melvin quickly got dressed and went down to the scene of the shooting. He didn't know what he expected to find. There was still blood on the street, but Melvin didn't see anything else. The police had already removed the blood-stained law book with Huey's name inscribed in it that the first responders found near Officer John Frey as he lay dying. Melvin walked up and down near where a mammoth new post office was being built. He gained no insight into what had happened until he spoke with David Hilliard.

Huey and Gene McKinney had been at Hilliard's poker party at his house in West Oakland around 2 a.m. before heading out in Huey's fiancée's Volkswagen to get something to eat on Seventh Street. Hilliard recalled: "The next thing I know I hear somebody banging on my door saying, 'Open the door. Huey has been shot. We've got to take him to the hospital.'"

Once he was helped inside, Huey was conscious enough to argue with his friends not to bring him to the hospital. He feared that he would end up in the gas chamber. But they were not about to let him die:

> So, when he comes into my house all bloody . . . my brother and my wife are putting towels around him trying to stop the bleeding until we could get him in the car to take him to Kaiser Hospital, which happened to be only 10 minutes away. We were rushed to do that because he was bleeding and blanking out — just becoming unconscious.
>
> So, we put him in the car, took him to Kaiser, drive to emergency. I go up and I bang on the door . . . and I'm screaming, 'There is a man dying out here. He's been shot. You have got to bring a gurney.' They bring a gurney, put Huey on it.

David and his brother June fled from Kaiser Hospital before anyone identified them or their car.

Doris was also still in bed when she first heard about the shooting. Her mother called, obviously quite upset. Doris had a premonition that something terrible would happen because a bird had flown against her windowpane. Her grandmother Muzz had once told her that it was a bad omen. When Armelia told Doris that Huey had been shot in a confrontation with police, Doris jumped up and got dressed to drive to her parents' home. When Doris arrived, her father had already returned home from alerting Melvin.

After Myrtle heard the grim news, her daughter Patricia came over to her apartment to console her. Myrtle was in shock. Sixteen years his senior, Myrtle viewed herself as Huey's second mother. Myrtle later left for her parents' home to comfort Armelia. The Newtons knew by then that Huey was undergoing surgery at the hospital and had already been charged with murder.

While others in the family sought updates on Huey's condition, Doris fielded calls to her parents' house. Armelia became furious at anyone telling her something negative: "You ain't nothin' but a damn liar." But Armelia told Doris she would die because of Huey getting into stuff and going to jail. The shooting immediately dominated the front pages of the afternoon newspaper. The telephone kept ringing. David Hilliard came over as soon as he could. Armelia was distraught. She told David he had to help Huey. David promised he would get Huey freed. He decided then and there to become a Black Panther.

After surgery at Kaiser Hospital, Huey was transferred to Highland Hospital where he was kept under close police watch. As he began his recovery, he was able to have family visits. Huey was quite agitated by taunts from the officers guarding his hospital room. He complained to visitors that they shook his bed and threatened his life.

Armelia's first thought was that they should get Perry Mason to represent her son. She had watched the TV program often enough to know that Mason never lost a case. It had to be explained to Armelia that the defense lawyer she admired was a fictional character. Melvin and his sister Leola immediately went to work looking for a highly skilled local criminal attorney for their younger brother. At the recommendation of Huey's trusted friend Beverly Axelrod, they met with Leftist lawyer William Patterson, who happened to be in San Francisco when the shooting occurred.

Patterson was the President of the American Communist Party and the head of its legal defense group. He had come to San Francisco to visit his long-time friend Dr. Carlton Goodlett. Like Patterson, Goodlett was a fellow Leftist. Dr. Goodlett published the *San Francisco Sun Reporter*, a newspaper founded in 1944 that aimed to serve the influx of Blacks arriving in the Bay Area. Dr. Goodlett was also a friend of veteran San Francisco criminal defense lawyer Charles Garry. Patterson immediately offered the Newton family help from the American Communist Party to fundraise for Huey's defense. He strongly recommended that they hire Charles Garry to defend Huey — which they promptly did.

Patterson viewed Huey's defense as one that could be promoted to educate the public about continuing entrenched racism. Patterson's own mother had been born into slavery. As a young lawyer, he had helped make history advancing the cause of the nine Black teenagers who became known as the Scottsboro Boys. Their defense precipitated a major milestone in criminal justice after they were sentenced to death on false accusations of gang rape in 1931 on a train traveling through Alabama. Huey and his lawyers agreed that they would handle his defense as an opportunity to challenge the justice system — comparing Huey's prosecution to the historic Scottsboro cases.

Drawing Parallels to The Landmark Scottsboro Boys' Cases

THE MISCARRIAGE of justice in the Scottsboro Boys' prosecution had two enormous consequences on appeal. More than half a century after the Fourteenth Amendment declared that all citizens were equal under the law, the Supreme Court finally established the right of Black citizens to be included in the jury pool. It also established the right of all indigent death penalty defendants to have competent counsel to represent them. William Patterson saw Huey's prosecution as another historic opportunity to expose systemic racism in the justice system. Patterson's involvement greatly enhanced Huey's plan to frame his court case as a stage to promote the Panther Party's platform.

The case of the Scottsboro Boys was of particular relevance to Huey. Like those nine unlucky teenagers, Walter Newton had spent much of his teen years hopping on and off freight trains in the Deep South. His quest was the same as theirs — seeking temporary menial jobs to eke out a living. Walter had been quite lucky not to face potential death at the hands of racists making up lies about him in those hobo days — like those that condemned the Scottsboro Boys.

In March 1931, the nine Black youths were arrested by Jackson County Sheriff Matt Wann and his deputies after boarding a freight train headed to Memphis from Chattanooga, Tennessee. There had been a number of other Black and White teen-aged boys on that train, desperate to find work during the Depression. The train took them over the Alabama border through Paint Rock where it stopped following a race fight among some of the youths. Most of them jumped off the train before it got to the station.

Several White boys summoned the sheriff to the Paint Rock station. The sheriff's men found a total of nine remaining Black youths in several different cars. The boys did not even know each other. The sheriff's men also found two White prostitutes in a different car. One, Ruby Bates, was 17; the other was 21-year-old Victoria Price, who feared being arrested for violating the Mann Act [transporting a minor girl across state lines for immoral purposes]. To protect herself, Price falsely accused all nine of the youths of raping her and Bates.

None of the sheriff's men compared where Price and Bates were found when the freight train was stopped versus where Price and Bates said they were raped. Nor did the investigators consider where the accused Black teenagers were located when the train stopped (in several other cars). The Black teenagers were brought to the county seat of Scottsboro and barely escaped lynching even after a doctor examined Price and Bates and verified that neither of the young women showed evidence of sexual assault during the time they were on the train.

Locals instantly spread false rumors that one girl had her breast bitten off. A lynch mob gathered at the jail and demanded the boys be turned over for hanging. Officials led by Sheriff Wann only dispersed the angry crowd by threatening to kill anyone who tried to grab one of his prisoners. But Wann tried to appease the mob by promising a quick trial "to send them to the chair." No matter how predetermined the outcome, the crowd considered trials in court too good for their targets. However, they yielded to Wann's show of force backed up by National Guardsmen.

Five days after their arrest, the Scottsboro Boys were indicted by an all-White male jury. Barely a week later, the group of teenagers faced trial — the same day as a county fair. The governor again sent armed guards to protect the prisoners with machine guns and bayonets. Permits to enter the gallery to watch the trials of the Scottsboro Boys became the hottest ticket in town. A standing-room-only crowd of White men filled the garrisoned courthouse.

Some 10,000 proclaimed defenders of Southern womanhood gathered outside awaiting the quick end of the trials. In this case, the women they claimed to put on a pedestal were prostitutes who accepted customers of both races. Their real goal was a celebration involving multiple lynchings. The court conscripted an unprepared out-of-state real estate lawyer to appear in court for all nine boys. The judge paid no mind to the conflicts that made joint representation unethical.

One of the Scottsboro Boys had succumbed to pressure to implicate the others in the false rape claims in a futile effort to avoid the death penalty. A single lawyer could not possibly represent competently both that boy's interests and those of the remaining eight defendants. After back-to-back, hurried group trials riddled with prejudicial errors, all nine were convicted in a total of five days. Eight of the Scottsboro Boys were sentenced to death; Eugene Williams was spared because, at 13, he was too young to qualify for the death penalty.

With William Patterson's participation, the Scottsboro Boys case soon became a major cause among civil rights activists, primarily in the North. Execution was stayed pending appeal, first to the Alabama Supreme Court, and then to the U.S. Supreme Court. At the time, William Patterson, a young civil rights champion from Northern California, already worked for the International Labor Defense (I.L.D.) affiliated with the Communist Party U.S.A. The ILD brought the Scottsboro Boys cases to the United States Supreme Court. A new trial was ordered in which a veteran volunteer defense attorney set up a 32-foot model train on a table for the jury to see exactly where the accusers and the defendants were located when the train stopped, convincing a second judge that Price and Bates were lying.

Patterson saw the Newton case as another vehicle for attacking systemic racism in America's criminal courts. His involvement in Huey's defense proved an enormous boost to the elevation of the Panther leader onto a national and international platform. Patterson's experience as a civil rights advocate predated the Scottsboro Boys case. In the 1920s, he had joined efforts to prevent the infamous 1927 execution of anarchists Sacco and Vanzetti in Massachusetts for their alleged roles in a payroll robbery and murder. That was an even more comparable historic case which Huey's lawyers would invoke. With supporters worldwide, Sacco and Vanzetti became international symbols of American injustice. Their executions in 1927 had set off major protests around the world, highlighting the prejudicial misconduct of the trial judge and prompting major judicial reforms.

With the repercussions from the executions of Sacco and Vanzetti still a searing memory, the briefs on appeal to the Supreme Court in the Scottsboro Boys cases detailed the blatant errors committed in the trials of the nine boys — all defended by the same woefully inadequate counsel before the same White-male jury. The first death penalty trial had lasted just two days; the other three trials had lasted only a day apiece. This time, the shocking lower court record produced landmark results. The Supreme Court finally declared that the right to counsel guaranteed by the Sixth Amendment in 1791 meant that defendants in capital cases deserved *competent* counsel at the state's expense if they could not afford their own lawyers. The U.S. Supreme Court also decided that the all-White jury was unfair because the local jury pool unconstitutionally excluded all Black citizens.

William Patterson was eager to come to Huey Newton's defense because he saw it as a key opportunity to highlight the lack of progress in more than thirty years since the Scottsboro Boys case. In those three decades, entrenched racism made it all but impossible for Black people to get a fair criminal trial. Jurors who wound up seated in death penalty cases remained almost exclusively White males. Patterson understood that those skewed juries should have been abolished long ago. Black defendants deserved the chance to face a jury of their peers.

William Patterson and Beverly Axelrod agreed that veteran criminal defense lawyer Charles Garry had the best chance of making the Newton trial as historic as that of Sacco and Vanzetti and the Scottsboro Boys. Garry was a close friend of Patterson's friend Carlton Goodlett, and a mentor of Axelrod's. Both were members of the San Francisco Lawyers Guild.

Like Goodlett and Patterson, Garry was a long-time Lefty. He had gained fame defending accused Communists during the McCarthy era and later successfully defended a string of murder trials. His firm, like that of Bob Treuhaft in Oakland, was a rare partnership of White lawyers that routinely accepted Black clientele. When Melvin and Leola met Garry, he impressed them with his record. He had never lost a client to the death penalty.

The family resisted the suggestion by several Black Panthers to opt only for a Black lawyer. The Panthers favored Clinton White, one of the top defense lawyers in the Bay Area, or maybe John George, who was then representing Huey's fiancée LaVerne Williams in her efforts to get her impounded car back. George had previously represented Huey on misdemeanor charges. But Garry's experience keeping clients from being executed won out. Seale confirmed that Garry had won some two dozen murder cases. What was a huge plus as well was that Garry, unlike Clinton White, was willing to work without a hefty down payment — actually, no down payment at all.

After meeting Huey in Highland Hospital, Garry became convinced that Huey needed immediate protection from his police guards. He then met with Melvin, who asked Garry: "Did he do it?" Garry told Melvin he never asked Huey that question. Melvin then realized that he shouldn't ask either. There was nothing Melvin could do with more knowledge about the shooting one way or another and he did not want to interfere with Garry's handling of the defense.

Meanwhile, Melvin had other important tasks to undertake for his younger brother. Patterson had just helped Melvin and Leola create a fund-raising defense committee for Melvin to head. Melvin and Leola then quickly arranged for private nurses 24/7 to watch over

Huey, including Joyce's sister Delores Casey. Melvin wrote checks from the defense committee to pay for this care.

David Hilliard immediately quit his job to devote all his time and energy to honoring his promise to Armelia. For Hilliard, the Newton family was his family. He first focused on how to mobilize community support for Huey. Soon he and Eldridge Cleaver's new fiancée Kathleen Neal began driving a borrowed van around West Oakland. They used a bullhorn to spread the news that yet another Black man was facing murder charges in a racist legal system.

Shortly after the shooting, the Panthers obtained from a newspaper photographer the extraordinary photo he took on the morning of October 28 in Kaiser Hospital. It showed Huey writhing in pain after being handcuffed to a gurney on his way into surgery. Unlike the cropped version that had gone out on the *San Francisco Examiner*'s front page, the original photo showed a startled police officer in the foreground. The Panthers featured that photo in a widely distributed pamphlet. The caption was what William Patterson had hoped for: "Can a Black man get a fair trial?"

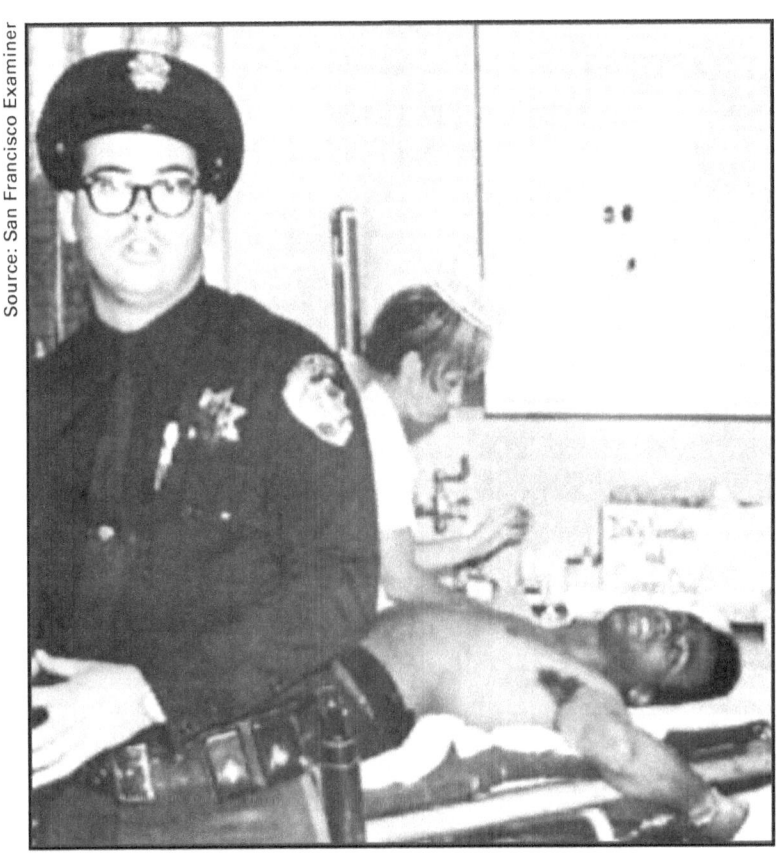

This photo was taken by a newspaper photographer for the San Francisco Examiner in Kaiser Hospital as Huey was being wheeled into surgery on Saturday, October 28, 1967. The Panthers quickly reproduced it on a flyer with the caption "Can a black man get a fair trial in America . . . defending his life against a white policeman?"

Dead Man Walking

GARRY'S associate Fay Stender quickly filed a motion to keep Huey in the hospital until he recovered. Yet the hearing could not be scheduled before the police moved Huey from Highland Hospital to death row in the maximum-security prison at San Quentin in Marin County. It was a safety precaution the county had employed before with perceived dangerous defendants awaiting a murder trial. Meanwhile, the shocking transfer to death row made Huey's family all the more anxious to visit Huey. Melvin and his father made immediate plans to drive to San Quentin, but Armelia could not bring herself to go there.

Despite the grim surroundings, Huey surprised his father and brother by letting them know he was fine with his situation. At least on death row he was left alone to have a peaceful recovery. Huey told Walter and Melvin that whenever he was removed from his cell for any reason, a guard walked in front of him and another followed close behind. Each time, one of them would announce: "Dead man walking." Huey soon learned that was the same protocol for anyone on death row. But for Melvin it was shocking. His mother's baby had not yet been to a trial in which the defendants were officially presumed innocent. Yet Huey was already experiencing life on death row — as if the gas chamber were his destiny.

That Huey faced certain execution was, in fact, the assumption of almost everyone following the case. Just a little over six months earlier the media had covered the first execution under the watch of Governor Ronald

Reagan. (It would turn out to be Reagan's only execution as governor.) Reagan had campaigned as a strong supporter of the death penalty. An African-American named Aaron Mitchell was on death row when Reagan was sworn in. Mitchell was convicted of killing a White policeman in a January 1963 shootout after trying to rob a Sacramento bar. Interviewed the day of his execution on April 12, 1967, Mitchell told reporters: "Every Negro ever convicted of killing a police officer has died in that gas chamber. So, what chance did I have?"

When Huey's defense team appeared before an Alameda County judge, they vigorously objected to Huey being held at San Quentin until trial. As a result, the sheriff transferred Huey to a jail cell in the courthouse on the shores of Lake Merritt where he would spend the rest of his pretrial incarceration. That was a major victory because it placed the Panther leader close to both his family and his growing number of Panther supporters.

Huey would get frequent visits now that he was being held less than four miles from his parents' home in North Oakland. The jail was also just over a mile and a half from DeFremery Park in West Oakland where his supporters would gather. Huey's presence in a nearby jail reinforced the intensity of Kathleen Neal and David Hilliard's efforts to galvanize community support for his cause.

The Family Rallies to Huey's Side

ALMOST the entire Newton family would soon mobilize on Huey's behalf. Melvin chaired the fund-raising effort from the outset, working with the Panther Party to organize community support. Yet he resisted joining the Party. Melvin admired their police patrols, but harbored serious concerns about where it would all end. At one point he told Panther Party newspaper publisher and sketch artist Emory Douglas, "I see a lot of blood with the guns." Emory Douglas was as aware of the life-threatening stakes as Huey was. He replied, "To the horse's brow." Melvin responded, "Wow." He understood that meant a commitment to let flow whatever amount of blood it took.

The first pretrial hearing Huey attended was in mid-November. At his lawyers' insistence, the judge allowed Huey to change out of his regulation jail jump suit to attend the court session. Sonny Man had been pressed into service to pick out suitable clothing since he was the most fashion-conscious member of the family. Huey wore slacks with a blue shirt and green jacket. Sonny Man would add to Huey's wardrobe for later appearances, knowing that the way defendants dressed could create a strong impression on a jury.

As Huey's prosecution moved forward that fall, Melvin called a press conference to appeal for support. He did not anticipate being asked if he was also a Black Panther. But when that question was posed to him, he quickly realized he had no choice about what he must say. If he said "No", he would be asked for an explanation that might hurt his brother's case. Faced with no other good option, Melvin said, "Yes." He would remain Panther Party Minister of Finance for about a year before quietly withdrawing from that role.

Meanwhile, Doris, Leola and other siblings were among Huey's many visitors seeking to keep his spirits up in the Alameda County Jail. Their mother Armelia was too sickened by the situation to visit her son there. Huey tried to cheer up the family members and friends who came to see him in the visiting room on the tenth floor of the courthouse. He never appeared to be engulfed in self-pity or fear.

Melvin had already told family members that Garry did not want them to ask Huey anything about the case. Garry was concerned that Huey might say something that would work against him at trial. Alex Hoffmann on the legal defense team often joined Huey to keep him from answering the probing questions of visitors, knowing that the defendant's answers could cause trouble for him later on.

When a British reporter interviewed Leola, she impressed him with her dignity as she described the unfairness of the proceedings to date. She praised her brother's commitment to improving race relations, and rejected the assumption that Huey was anti-White, explaining that their own father was half-White.

It remained to be seen if Huey could get a fair trial. Huey's fiancée La Verne Williams was also interviewed. She thought Huey was being railroaded. She described to the reporter how she had been hounded by phone calls, followed on the streets and otherwise targeted with attempts at intimidation because of her support for Huey. Melvin had little time to spare beyond his job as an Alameda County social worker and efforts at fund-raising. He had a wife and young child to support. Yet his primary focus was on his little brother's dire situation and its effect on their parents. In spite of his time pressures and many commitments, Melvin managed to orchestrate a major event held at Oakland Auditorium celebrating Huey's 26th birthday in February 1968. The family received plenty of help from the Panthers, who invited the SNCC leadership from Atlanta, Georgia.

Black Panthers showed up en masse to the celebration, thereby guaranteeing both close police and FBI surveillance. The Panthers also drew strong press interest. Doris and other family members helped with ticket sales. Sonny Man came back from L.A. for this rally, so all six of Huey's siblings were among the 10,000 people who filled the auditorium that night.

By then, Huey represented the Party's soul. The audience was used to seeing him featured in each issue of the Panther newspaper seated in a wicker throne. That throne now sat empty on the stage. Most of the speakers expected Huey to be sentenced to death for murdering a cop. Those who addressed the crowd from the stage that night often referred to Huey in the past tense, as if he were already dead.

Among those taking the podium, only Charles Garry gave a measure of hope. The key, he said, would be to get an impartial jury as guaranteed by the Constitution. But few in the crowd thought that was possible given the history of seating White male juries of "one's peers." Racially skewered juries constituted one of the ten points of grievance highlighted in the Panthers' program. James Forman of SNCC warned that if Huey was executed, the ensuing unrest and violence would be enormous: "The sky is the limit."

Panther recruit Janice Garrett-Forte, who served as Bobby Seale's secretary, understood the significance of "The Sky's the Limit" and the empty chair. "We would do anything necessary to avenge [his death] . . . warfare on the streets, against the establishment . . . {I]t would push us to the brink of fighting in our communities . . . against the establishment . . .. We all had weapons."

Armelia was bashful by nature, and uncomfortable with any public speaking, even at her local church. She reluctantly agreed to take the podium after Doris reassured her she could do it. She told the packed auditorium: "I am Armelia Newton. That's my baby you have gathered here for. I wish I could hug and kiss everybody in here one by one for helping my baby." Garry stood behind her, ready to assist if she ran out of words. Armelia talked briefly. But her personal appeal was extraordinarily effective.

Stokely Carmichael, wearing an African robe, urged other Blacks in that racially mixed audience to adopt an ideology solely for Black people. (He would later move to Guinea and change his name to Kwame Ture). Many other Blacks in attendance wore dashikis. Carmichael ended by proclaiming, "Brother Huey belongs to us . . .. Carmichael continued, "He is flesh of our flesh, he is blood of our blood . . .. Brother Huey will be set free — or else.

Bobby Seale sits next to an empty wicker throne on the stage at the Oakland Auditorium on February 17, 1968 at the fundraiser for Huey Newton's defense. The event took place just a few blocks from where Huey Newton was jailed awaiting his murder trial for the death of Officer John Frey. Seated to the right of the throne are SNCC leaders Stokely Carmichael and H. Rap Brown who flew in from Atlanta. Partially visible on the right is future Congressman Ron Dellums.

Armelia was bashful by nature, and uncomfortable with any public speaking, even at her local church. She reluctantly agreed to take the podium after Doris reassured her she could do it. She told the packed auditorium: "I am Armelia Newton. That's my baby you have gathered here for. I wish I could hug and kiss everybody in here one by one for helping my baby."

Assassinations Inflame the Community

IN FEBRUARY 1968, as Huey Newton faced a trial for his life, a blue-ribbon Presidential Commission was making national headlines. It provoked debate across the country with its report on the sorry state of race relations. Released in February of that year, the Kerner Report, named for commission chair Otto Kerner, governor of Illinois, was considered so topical and controversial that it was turned into a bestselling book.

One of the report's most provocative sections zeroed in on the lack of diversity in police forces across the country. It cited those lopsided demographics as a major societal problem. The panel placed most of the blame for urban unrest on "White racism . . . for the explosive mixture which has been accumulating in our cities since the end of World War II."

The panel also criticized the press for reporting the news through "White men's eyes." It warned that the nation was "moving toward two societies, one Black, one White — separate and unequal." The panel proposed controversial major investments in the nation's inner cities like the pilot jobs program that had employed Huey and Bobby Seale in Oakland.

The racial tensions outlined in the report became even more ominous just two months later. On April 4, a gunman assassinated the Reverend Martin Luther King, Jr. Doris was among the myriad followers of Dr. King who wept at the news. Coverage of the assassination preempted regularly scheduled television programs. Meanwhile, widespread looting and firebombing broke out in major cities, prompting more than 60,000 National guardsmen to be deployed to enforce curfews and restore peace.

President Johnson declared a National Day of Mourning for Reverend King and ordered flags flown at half-mast. It marked the first time that honor was bestowed for the death of a Black man in America. It was only the third half-mast salute ever noted for *any* private citizen. Just days earlier Johnson had startled the nation by announcing his decision not to seek reelection. That left the Democratic field wide open. The murder of the country's most famous pacifist halted presidential candidates in their tracks as they absorbed the enormous impact of this tragedy. Gathering African-American leaders to the White House, the President vowed that King's dream had not died with him. President Johnson declared that the dream would become a blueprint for united action to assure young Blacks that the "fullness of life" would not be denied them "because of the color of their skin."

The Kerner Report's recommendations soon gained adherents as more White leaders blamed pervasive White racism for Dr. King's death. They vowed to work together with Black communities to address "the white problem." From the Panthers' perspective, the assassination proved they were right. King's martyrdom could only swell their ranks with newly outraged Blacks. Some White men in Oakland anticipated violence and ran to buy guns.

King's death was also a game changer for national anti-war activists. More war protesters now embraced the Black Panthers as the quintessential African-American voice against the war. Large numbers of White anti-war demonstrators became full-throated supporters of the "Free Huey" movement.

After King's murder, President Johnson convened a special joint session of Congress to address new proposed legislation. Meanwhile, Katherine Hepburn won an unexpected Oscar for best actress in *Guess Who's Coming to Dinner?* This comedy drama involved liberal White parents surprised by their daughter's announced engagement to a Black doctor portrayed by Sidney Poitier. Just four years earlier, Poitier had won the first Oscar ever awarded to a Black leading man. The groundbreaking 1967 film about interracial marriage proved exceedingly popular at the box office. Its timing paired well with the Supreme Court's 1967 decision that finally ruled anti-miscegenation laws unconstitutional.

At first, Oakland remained relatively calm with Bobby Seale urging people not to invite any police action. Then Eldridge Cleaver did the opposite. Eager for a clash, Cleaver brought with him a number of Panthers including their youngest recruit, 17-year-old Bobby Hutton. David Hilliard, whom Huey had named the Panther Party's Chief of Staff, reluctantly went along.

Cleaver led three carloads of armed Panthers seeking to confront any local officers they could find. That quest ended badly with the police intercepting their mission. The police arrested all of the Panthers except Cleaver and Bobby Hutton. The two of them holed up in a house in West Oakland and began an armed standoff. After about ninety minutes, the police tear-gassed the house. Cleaver and Hutton both decided to surrender. Clever emerged naked to prove he held no weapon. Hutton was too shy to leave the house naked. He came out wearing a coat and met with a barrage of gunfire, killing the unarmed youth in the street. His death caused shock and uproar in the Black community.

On Sunday afternoon there was a pre-planned "Free Huey" rally at DeFremery Park on Adeline Street. A shell-shocked Kathleen Cleaver spoke in her husband's stead since he remained jailed. The biggest Panther gathering so far became an impromptu memorial celebration for Bobby Hutton. A formal funeral on April 12, 1968, drew over 2500 community members joined by Hollywood star Marlon Brando. Melvin wrote a tribute to Bobby Hutton that he offered to give at the gathering on behalf of Huey. Huey later included the tribute in the preface to *Revolutionary Suicide*:

> Li'l Bobby was the beginning — the very first member of the Black Panther Party. He gave not only his finances; he gave himself. He placed himself in the service of his people and asked nothing in return, not even a needle or a piece of thread. He asked neither security nor high office, but he demanded those things that are the birthright of all men: dignity and freedom. He demanded this for himself and for his people.

> Like a bright ray of light moving across the sky, Li'l Bobby came into our lives and showed us the beauty of our people. He was a living example of an infinite love for his people and for freedom. Now he has moved on, and the example he gave will serve us as a beacon that lights our way and leads us on in the struggle for life, dignity, and freedom.

We salute Li'l Bobby and his family for what they have given us. He was the beginning of the Party. Let us make sure that his thinking, his desires for his people become a way of life.

Yours forever,
HUEY P. NEWTON
Minister of Defense
Black Panther Party
April 1968

Brando later accompanied some Panthers on a neighborhood patrol and offered $10,000 in bail for David Hilliard's release. It was then that Hilliard first realized the Panthers had gained Leftist celebrity status. The death of Bobby Hutton also galvanized mainstream Blacks in the community to support the Panthers in their opposition to the police. The Panthers honored Hutton as their first martyr. His death marked the real beginning of their movement. Suddenly far more youths arrived at their headquarters interested in joining the Panther Party. Church congregations began to pass the hat and women in the Black community started to collect money for their support.

Huey's trial had been set for May but was postponed because of the turmoil in the community created by the shocking deaths of Reverend King and Bobby Hutton. The trial was reset to begin in June, but yet another assassination helped force a new delay. This time the victim was Presidential candidate Senator Robert Kennedy, gunned down at the Embassy Ballroom in Los Angeles after a rousing campaign speech. Gun violence was going to be on everyone's mind in California. Huey faced execution for the shooting death of a policeman. The Oakland community had recently honored Officer Frey with an elaborate funeral that reinforced the significance to the city of a peace officer killed in the line of duty.

VIII.

The Trial

The Internationally Watched Trial Begins

HUEY relished the upcoming confrontation. He could count on both his nuclear family and his adopted family of Panther supporters to be out in full force to support him. By the start of the trial in mid-July, Huey had full confidence in his legal team. Garry had a well-deserved reputation as a street-fighter in the courtroom.

At Huey's insistence, in addition to their ordinary trial preparation, both Garry and his co-counsel Fay Stender had read Panther literature and the works of revolutionary writers who had inspired them. These included, first and foremost, Frantz Fanon. Garry, in turn, identified with Huey as the son he never had. In Fay, Huey stirred both a maternal instinct and sexual attraction, emotions he had cultivated from their first encounter. She was as devoted to Huey's freedom as if he were family and worked day and night for his acquittal.

Huey recalled his disastrous attempt to represent himself in court in 1964. This time, he trusted his counsel to put on the aggressive defense he desired. He would sit tight and follow their instructions. Huey also put his faith in the protestors outside the court. He hoped they would escalate the stakes with their revolutionary chants, making any jury think twice about condemning him to death.

The "Free Huey" committee had already kicked into high gear. On Sunday, July 14, a huge mixed-race crowd of Panther supporters and curious locals of all ages gathered at DeFremery Park for a four-hour picnic and rally. Many attendees now called it Bobby Hutton Park in honor of the fallen Panther. Helmeted Oakland police circled the block in patrol cars, on foot and in hovering helicopters. *Life* magazine reporter Gilbert Moore was its first and only Black newsman at the time. Moore realized that was why he had been sent out from New York to cover the high-profile trial. Observing the extraordinary turnout of law enforcement, he thought the police were "awaiting a signal to declare open war upon the savage citizens below."

Melvin addressed the crowd along with SNCC's James Forman, Bobby Seale and the Cleavers. Surprisingly, Eldridge Cleaver had been released from jail in early June — the first time anyone had heard of the Adult Authority losing a parole revocation case. The moment he was out of custody, Cleaver immediately bolstered community support for Huey. At the July 14 gathering at DeFremery Park, he urged the attendees to show up in force again at the trial starting the next day.

Not surprisingly, the mainstream press responded with alarmed headlines. On Monday morning, July 15, 1968, the *Oakland Tribune* proclaimed that the city's main courthouse looked like a "besieged fortress." Sheriff Frank Madigan supervised historic security efforts, including armed deputies standing outside every entrance with walkie talkies, mace and batons. Large security nets were draped across steps leading up to the building. All but one entrance was locked. The Oakland police and National Guardsmen stood by, backing up the deputies.

The trial was set to take place on the seventh floor — the only courtroom that would be in use there for the duration of the highly secure proceedings. As a precaution the stairwells from the sixth and eighth floors were sealed. Only one elevator served the seventh floor, with an armed guard standing sentry. Meanwhile, thousands of chanting Panther supporters had gathered outside before dawn, some carrying signs with warning messages: "Free Huey or Else"; "If Anything Happens to Huey, the Sky's the Limit." For the opening day of *The People of the State of California versus Huey P. Newton, LIFE* magazine paired reporter Gilbert Moore with photographer Howard Bingham. They both later wrote books about the trial. The duo were but two of many media representatives drawn to cover the guaranteed headliner. Reporters came from London, the *New York Times*, the *Boston Globe*, network and local television and radio crews, wire services, *TIME* and *Newsweek*, as well as underground newspapers.

As one of the principal organizers of the huge crowd surrounding the courthouse, Kathleen Cleaver was astounded that the state got to call itself "The People." She thought the protesters she was rallying outside the courthouse were "the people." Her role was to attract so much press coverage and political heat that it would be extremely difficult for Huey to get the death penalty.

John Burris was then a local college student. He later pursued a successful legal career standing on the shoulders of the Panthers as a civil rights attorney focused on police abuse cases. Reading about the case, Burris wondered if Huey Newton acted in self-defense. He said, "I didn't have a view that [any] Black person could get a fair trial in Oakland." Burris figured that a Black revolutionary like Huey Newton did not have a chance in Hell. When the trial proceedings started, Judge Monroe Friedman ordered all the media representatives and spectators to undergo security screening. This was the first time the court had ever taken such measures. All the benches in the courtroom were filled, and not just with supporters. The Panthers in attendance could tell the audience included a number of plain clothes policemen and FBI agents.

Huey's fiancée LaVerne Williams, his siblings and his Episcopal priest, Father Earl Neil of St. Augustine's Church, all sat up front. Neil had a special connection to the Panthers, whom he allowed to meet regularly at his church after members discovered their headquarters were bugged.

A bailiff brought Huey in handcuffs down the stairwell from the tenth floor and escorted him into the courtroom, where the cuffs were taken off. Prosecutor Lowell Jensen made the customary request to the judge to order that all witnesses be excluded from the courtroom until they were called to the stand. He also asked the court to prohibit any display of support for Huey in the courtroom. Leaflets, buttons and signs were already seen everywhere outside the courthouse. Garry, in turn, objected to the unaccustomed security measures. He argued that they created an atmosphere of fear and intimidation. He argued that the extraordinary precautions would give members of the jury panel the impression that Huey Newton was a dangerous killer before the trial even began.

Yet when the first batch of potential jurors filed into the courtroom later that morning, they did not get a negative impression of Huey. At his lawyers' request, the judge had allowed him to replace his jailhouse garb with civilian clothes. Huey had entered the courtroom dressed in a black turtleneck with a sharp, gray suit chosen by

Sonny Man. Though it was sweltering outside that afternoon for Panthers wearing their signature leather jackets, Huey welcomed the outfit his brother had selected for him. The air-conditioned courtroom was kept at a chilly 60 degrees. Huey shivered, but not with fear. His people had his back.

Newton family's collection of pins worn when Huey was incarcerated.

The Battle to Select a Jury of Peers

NEWTON'S defense team understood they faced an uphill battle when it came to picking a jury that might choose to spare the Black Panther leader's life. They had ample reason to worry about the ethnic, political and sociological make-up of the "jury of one's peers." The team knew they were in for a bureaucratic slog. Three weeks of potential jury questioning followed, based on a long list of questions that Newton's lawyer Fay Stender and sociology professors from Cal had collaborated on.

Huey's family members were impressed by this pioneering effort to expose racial bias. One idea Stender and her consultants came up with was to inquire how potential jurors voted on Proposition 14 in 1964. They considered it a proxy for the prospective jurors' views on race. Though a majority of residents of Alameda County voted against allowing housing discrimination by sellers and landlords, Proposition 14 had passed statewide by a nearly two-thirds vote.

In 1966, the California Supreme Court had struck down Proposition 14 for violating the 14th Amendment of the United States Constitution. A bare majority of the U.S. Supreme Court affirmed that ruling in May of 1967. Judge Friedman disallowed questions that sought to pry into how individuals had voted on Proposition 14 or how they felt generally about race relations. Yet he agreed that potential jurors could be asked about their awareness of the recent Kerner Report on racism, their exposure to the term Black Power and familiarity with the Black Panther Party.

Garry also used the time to remind the jury panel that reality was not like the popular *Perry Mason* television show. (Armelia was not there to get that message.) It was not Huey Newton's burden to prove who killed Officer Frey and have the true killer confess on the stand. Throughout that selection process, Huey sat next to his lawyers and Ed Keating, publisher of *Ramparts* magazine. Keating had a law license and planned to write a book about the trial from the defense perspective. Huey could be seen sometimes whispering to Charles Garry or taking notes. Often, he turned to smile at his family and friends in the audience.

As the days progressed, Huey dressed to impress. He alternated between wearing his gray suit with a brown suit and mustard-colored turtleneck and slacks and a turtleneck with a sport jacket also hand-picked by Sonny Man. But Sonny Man himself seemed oblivious to any need to make a good impression. Much to the amusement of his relatives, Sonny Man showed up one day in the middle of the morning session. He unsteadily sauntered up the aisle, obviously drunk. His teen-aged niece Debra started to giggle nervously, as did some of the other family members in attendance. Fortunately, Judge Friedman was indulgent, waiting for Huey's older brother to take his seat before resuming the proceedings.

For the spectators and reporters, the days of repetitive questioning of potential jurors often seemed tedious and yawn-inducing. Not so for the lawyers, who considered jury selection the key to the entire racially charged case. Clarence Darrow, the nation's most famous defense lawyer of the early 20th century, put that observation starkly in one of his own most racially charged cases back in Detroit in 1925.

Darrow was also defending a Black man accused of murdering a White man. Upon finishing jury selection, Darrow said: "The case is won or lost now. The rest is window dressing." *LIFE* reporter Gilbert Moore observed that Charles Garry approached the task of selecting his client's death penalty jury from the mostly White residents who turned out for jury duty like a man "stuck in the apple orchard with a taste for oranges."

The trial judge would excuse for cause any juror who exhibited bias or other disqualifying information. In addition, each side had been granted twenty peremptory challenges which they could use to excuse potential jurors for any reason without having to explain why. In deciding when to use his peremptory challenges, Garry drew from a list of close to 300 questions Stender and the sociology professors from Cal had prepared. This curated list of questions helped eliminate those with ties to law enforcement, racially exclusive clubs or conservative political causes.

During the entire jury selection process, Garry asked minorities only a few softball questions. He excused no minorities but relentlessly grilled White men he assumed were racist. Jensen, for his part, challenged every working-class Black. The result of the slog through nearly 160 prospective jurors was far from the traditional jury of twelve White men who until then generally comprised a "jury of one's peers" in criminal cases. Seven of the ultimate panel of twelve jurors were women, most of them middle-aged. Two were widowed mothers; three were married; one was a Latina, and one was Portuguese-American, married to a Latino. Of the five men, three were minorities, including one Black banker, a Cuban-American machinist and a Japanese-American lab technician.

Looking back, jury expert Karen Jo Koonan realized the diversity of that jury was "absolutely pioneering.... It just was unheard of." Yet Garry remained dissatisfied. He said that he "finally accepted a jury with a few people on it I would not want to have lunch with let alone let them decide Huey's fate." Jensen was relieved when Garry used up his last challenge. The prosecutor had feared they would not be able to seat a jury after so much polarizing pretrial publicity.

Melvin spoke often with Fay Stender and understood that the revolutionary composition of the Newton jury had benefited from three major legal cases decided just in the prior three months. In April, a local judge had made a surprising decision, declaring a juror IQ test an unconstitutional example of socioeconomic bias, targeting and disqualifying minorities living in the flatlands.

In early June the United States Supreme Court issued a landmark decision from the Midwest that Newton's defense team had been following on appeal. A majority of the Warren court ruled in *Witherspoon v. Illinois* that jurors who questioned the wisdom of the death penalty as public policy could still be seated. Their inclusion would be premised on their pledge that they could vote for execution if the facts warranted it. Stender explained that this new ruling would give Huey's legal defense team a much better chance of seating a high percentage of women and minorities in Huey's case. Both groups were known to harbor far more doubts about the wisdom of the death penalty than White males.

Lastly, just a week before Huey's trial began, another local judge made headlines declaring a mistrial in a criminal case. The judge found that the prosecutor had improperly dismissed all Black potential jurors. With that recent case in mind, Garry made a point of standing up and stating the juror's race for the record every time Jensen dismissed a Black candidate for the jury. This dramatic stance impressed both family members and Panthers in the audience, though most Panthers remained outside demonstrating as Kathleen Cleaver did.

Jensen kept middle-class banker David Harper as the only Black on the jury. He trusted Harper and thought he could be fair. But Jensen also was mindful he needed to protect himself from Garry's repeated charges of racism. As Jensen anticipated, Garry immediately sought dismissal of the entire panel because it did not consist of Huey's peers from the flatlands. Judge Friedman denied that motion. He ruled that a jury of one's peers meant a group of people who came from a cross-section of the entire community, not just one segment of the population. He also denied Garry's motion for a mistrial based on the selection of four White jury alternates.

Melvin Newton kept in close communication with Fay Stender. At the time, it was rare for a woman lawyer to be involved in any felony trial, let alone a death penalty case. But Stender was well-prepared for the constitutional issues the case would raise. She had clerked for the California Supreme Court. Later she worked in private practice on death penalty appeals under the tutelage of Garry's law partner, Barney Dreyfus. Dreyfus was a renowned constitutional scholar. Melvin appreciated her skills and dedication to freeing his brother. He could tell that she provided the backbone for the defense, working long hours to draft and type up all the motions throughout trial.

The biggest question among spectators when the jury was seated was what to think about the lone Black juror. David Harper looked like he could have been Huey's more mainstream older brother. The Panthers assumed the thirty-five-year-old banker was an Uncle Tom. Yet they understood why Garry had chosen not to challenge him. Garry was making a statement about trusting any and all minorities over Whites. Garry and Stender were less concerned about Harper. They actually thought Jensen might have made a mistake leaving David Harper on the panel.

Huey decided he would closely observe Harper's reactions as the evidence unfolded. Throughout the trial, Huey would gaze at Harper for signs of his inclinations but could not take his measure. Huey wondered if the banker was actually an Uncle Tom like other Panthers then thought. Was he "blinded by the crumbs the system offered him" or was he a brother who, like the Panthers, seethed at the unfairness of a racist society?

Jury foreman David Harper

Opening Statements

THE first week of August, the death penalty trial began in earnest. Huey was buoyed to see his father show up for the first day. Walter Newton sat behind Huey with his six other children, La Verne Williams and Father Neil. It was not surprising that Armelia could not stomach joining them there. The proceeding was just too painful.

Several members of Huey's family continued to show up to support him in court. But not all of his loved ones could handle the crowds, the crush of the press and the strain of the trial. Some could not break free from the pressures of their daily lives to watch proceedings that could drag on for another month or more. Myrtle's daughter Patricia was home tending to her first-born toddler, Kim. Her husband Steve, who had driven for Huey and his friends when the Panther Party was first launched, was now working full-time at the Travis Air Force Base. Both of them would have to get by on secondhand reports. So did other family members who cared about Huey's fate but could not attend.

The Newton family who made it to the courtroom that first day had the bracing experience of watching prosecutor Lowell Jensen present his case first. Armelia was right not to attend as Jensen provided evidence to convince the jury that Huey should die. Jensen had the burden of proof. He outlined the basic facts as the prosecution saw them. A police officer had been killed during a car stop in the line of duty. He was shot by an ex-felon with a history of violence and known animosity toward the police.

Jensen noted that Huey Newton had reason to fear imminent arrest for violating the terms of his parole. Jensne told the jury that Huey Newton was carrying a prohibited handgun when the police stopped him for traffic violations. The police found marijuana in the car. When he got out of his car, Newton pulled his gun on Frey. The two men then grappled over Frey's gun. Newton used Frey's gun to shoot both Frey and his back-up officer Herbert Heanes. Heanes shot back and wounded Newton before collapsing from his own wounds. Frey's murder justified the death penalty. In addition, Newton was guilty of assaulting Heanes.

Jensen informed the jury that Newton had a passenger in his car when it was stopped. The two of them fled on foot and commandeered a car at gunpoint after finding it parked around the corner. Jensen promised to produce an eyewitness to the shooting who would identify Newton. Jensen would also put the kidnap victim on the stand.

Huey and Charles Garry immediately huddled together in whispered conversation as if this was news to them. They had actually known about Dell Ross, the alleged kidnap victim, since they got access to Ross's grand jury testimony in November 1967. On the eve of trial, they also learned the identity of the alleged eyewitness to the shooting. He was an AC transit bus driver named Henry Grier. The fact that both prosecution witnesses were African-American was problematic for the defense.

Most observers in the courtroom could not imagine how Garry would respond to the damning picture Jensen had just painted. The presentation had to have made Huey's family sick. Given his turn, Garry was true to his streetfighter reputation. He stood up and jabbed back.

Jensen had zeroed in on the morning of the shootout. Garry gave it the back of his hand. Spectators noted Garry's supreme confidence as he claimed Newton was not guilty of any of the charged crimes. At times, Garry would take his glasses off and wave them for emphasis.

Garry dwelt upon Huey's life history, his decision to join the Black Liberation Movement and then to form the Black Panther Party with Bobby Seale. Seale showed up for the first time that day and sat down with several other Panthers. Garry read the jury the Black Panther Party's 10-point platform. He asserted that their stand against police brutality got the Panthers singled out for persecution. Jensen repeatedly objected to Garry's charges of police harassment, but Garry was allowed to continue.

Garry told the jury that the deceased officer, John Frey, was a well-known racist who had no justification for stopping Newton that October morning. Frey had done so only to abuse the Panther leader yet again. Frey then precipitated the shootout in which he died. Garry recited the death threats Newton received from police officers while in the hospital, replete with vulgar terms, including "nigger" and "Black bastard." The veteran trial lawyer then summed up what he intended to show in defense of the murder and assault charges. Newton did not fire a gun at any time on that date. He did not kill Officer Frey. He did not shoot Officer Heanes, and he had no knowledge of any marijuana found in the car.

Like the spectators, the jurors listened intently to both opening statements. Two veteran trial lawyers had just laid out for their consideration starkly contrasting versions of what went down in the predawn of October 28, 1967 — and Huey Newton's life hung in the balance.

When court adjourned that day, Rush Greenlee, the only Black reporter from the *San Francisco Examiner*, singled out Walter Newton and pressed him to answer questions about his son's trial. Walter was a reluctant interview subject. He expressed his contempt for newspapers, saying they always printed lies. When asked for his view of the charges his son faced, Walter exclaimed: "Now that's a damn fool question. Of course, I don't think he's guilty."

As one of the few other Blacks among the reporters present, Gilbert Moore from *Life* magazine was torn by conflicting reactions: Huey Newton was too smart to have shot Officer Frey in cold blood when he knew the police watched his every move. But then Moore pictured the early morning scene with Newton facing an oppressive enemy spewing hatred. Where did all the bullets come from that resulted in one dead and two wounded participants? Moore could not believe the Panther leader had not fired a shot. He thought to himself, "You can bullshit the judge and the jury and the press all you want to, but I'll bet a million dollars you shot John Frey." Raw emotion then bubbled to the surface as Moore pondered the huge flag behind the judge: "Do I really give a damn? I hope to God he did shoot him. Shoot him, Huey! Shoot him dead! Kill him for me, Huey, kill him for us. Revenge is ours, saith the Blacks."

The Prosecution Puts on Its Case

LOWELL JENSEN confidently started testimony on Monday August 5 with a police dispatcher. The dispatcher played an official tape-recording made less than half an hour before the predawn shooting on October 28, 1967. Officer Frey requested a "rolling 36" auto license check on the Volkswagen bug just spotted on 7th Street in West Oakland and learned it was "a known Panther Vehicle." Frey told the dispatcher he was going to stop it at Seventh and Willow, while awaiting backup from another police patrolman. The dispatcher's office identified the car as owned by LaVerne Williams, whom the police assumed was a man.

Jensen then had the dispatcher skip minutes later to the second officer, Herbert Heanes, shouting for immediate assistance. That was followed by audio of the officers who arrived shortly afterward to find Officer Frey dying in the street and Officer Heanes slumped wounded in his car. On cross-examination Garry pointed to time lags in the tape that gave Frey ample opportunity to use the stop as an excuse to harass the car's occupants.

Next came a pathologist who pointed out on a model torso the path of four or five bullets that he concluded had struck Frey, one of which was found still in his body at the autopsy.

Jensen then called Gilbert De Joyos, the first officer to arrive at the scene after the shooting. De Hoyos had been cruising on the next block, so it took him only 30 seconds to get to Seventh and Willow. There, he spied two parked police cars and a Volkswagen. Frey was lying on the street bleeding by his own patrol car and pleading for help. Then De Hoyos and another arriving officer heard Heanes moaning in the other police car.

The stage was set for Jensen to call Heanes himself to the stand. He was dressed in his uniform, which juries always found impressive. The jury paid close attention as Heanes testified that Frey had asked the driver of the car he stopped to identify himself. The driver told him he was La Verne Williams. Heanes then walked over to the driver's window and immediately recognized Huey Newton. Many other patrolmen already knew Huey Newton by sight, though Frey did not.

The two officers asked Newton to get out of the car. Frey intended to arrest Newton for falsely identifying himself and for failure to produce his license. Heanes said Newton was compliant but when he got out he walked "rather briskly" back to the second of the two parked police cars about thirty feet away. Heanes then said Newton "turned around and started shooting." Asked to identify Newton in court, Heanes pointed to "the gentleman in the gray coat" at the defense table.

Garry insisted that Heanes get down from the stand and touch the man he saw that morning. Jensen was caught off guard. He had never seen a lawyer make such a request before. Any witness would be uncomfortable having to identify an accused murderer by physical contact. Heanes walked over and touched Huey's shoulder as Huey remained motionless. That afternoon, Garry aggressively challenged Heanes' account with his very first question on cross-examination. "Did you shoot and kill Officer Frey?" Heanes recalled only firing one shot and saw nobody fall. Garry reminded him that his gun had fired two shots. Heanes said he had no idea what happened to the second shot. He also admitted he never saw a gun in Newton's hand. He had only heard gunfire from Newton's direction. At the time, he was more focused on Newton's passenger, standing with his arms raised on the curb by the Volkswagen.

Garry had Heanes and Huey Newton get up to reenact where they stood that morning. Garry portrayed Officer Frey. He then asked Heanes if the gun might have been fired by a different civilian on the scene, much shorter than Newton. Heanes had not noticed any such person. The cross-examination succeeded in introducing doubt that Huey Newton had shot Officer Frey.

The next day Jensen produced his eyewitness, 40-year-old bus driver Henry Grier. Grier was six-foot-one and a 200-pound Navy veteran. Grier testified that when his bus stopped at Seventh and Willow at about 5 a.m. on October 28, he had a clear view of two policemen and a male civilian illuminated by his bus lights. At Garry's insistence, Grier walked to the defense table to place his hand on Huey's shoulder to identify the civilian he saw that morning. Huey again remained still.

Returning to the stand, Grier testified that he saw Newton whirl and pull a gun from inside his shirt. He identified the same bloody white shirt Heanes had earlier identified in court as the one Newton wore that morning under a dark jacket. The civilian fired the gun and the other policeman fell. Grier then swore he saw the civilian fire "at least three or four shots" into the back of the first policeman and then flee the scene. The next day, Garry focused on gutting Grier's testimony. He used for his guide a chart Stender had prepared showing key inconsistencies between Grier's courtroom testimony and what Grier told the police in a sworn statement shortly after the shooting. Back then, Grier said he got his first look at the scene from a distance of thirty to forty yards. In court, he said fifteen to twenty feet. Grier had originally described the civilian as light-skinned, no more than five feet tall and weighing about 125 pounds. The man wore a light tan jacket, dark shirt and a dark hat. In his first statement, Grier had told police the civilian pulled a gun from his jacket pocket. In court, Grier described the civilian pulling the gun from his shirt. Grier also contradicted his first statement that he saw the gunman run off through the construction site for the nearby post office.

Garry again reenacted the shooting, this time with Alex Hoffmann on the defense team playing Officer Frey. Grier demonstrated that he saw Frey fall on his stomach when he had originally told the police he saw Frey fall on his back. Garry belligerently asked if Grier knew what an Uncle Tom was. That prompted Jensen to rise with yet another objection to Garry's badgering of a prosecution witness. By the time Grier left the stand, many observers were left wondering how the bus driver could be sure that Huey Newton, who was five-foot-ten and weighed 155 pounds, was the same civilian Grier saw wrestling with the officer that morning. To the amazement of onlookers, the testimony of the eyewitness to murder now appeared shaky.

That afternoon a police technician testified about evidence found at the site of the shooting: two fired 9-mm shells, two buttons, a police citation book with a partly written ticket, and a blood-stained California criminal law book inscribed with Huey Newton's name. Garry stipulated that the book belonged to his client.

On Monday August 12, Jensen called his second star eye-witness, the alleged kidnap victim, Dell Ross. Here was the man Jensen told the jury had been sitting in his parked convertible near the corner of Seventh and Willow when Newton and his companion leaped into the convertible. Jensen had told the jury in his opening statement that the two men then ordered Ross at gunpoint to drive them away.

Reporters' antennae perked up again. They were well aware of Ross's devastating grand jury testimony identifying Newton as the shooter. They assumed Ross would clinch the prosecutor's case. Ross, a Black man in his mid-thirties, came to court dressed flamboyantly with his eyes hidden behind dark sunglasses. When Jensen asked: "Where were you on the morning of October 28, 1967?" Ross shocked the whole courtroom, Jensen and the judge by refusing to testify on Fifth Amendment grounds.

From there, things only got worse for Jensen. Ross surprised the judge and prosecutor again by showing up with his own counsel. Ross's Berkeley lawyer was in partnership with a close friend of Fay Stender's from the Lawyers Guild. The judge temporarily sequestered the jury and heard arguments from counsel. Jensen was uncharacteristically irate. He could not fathom how a kidnap victim could claim he would expose himself to prosecution if he testified. The next morning, Judge Friedman granted Ross immunity. Ross retook the stand before the jury. He again refused to give any details of the morning of his kidnapping.

With growing exasperation, Judge Friedman explained to Ross that he now risked a citation for contempt of court. Ross said, "Send me to jail then." Jensen tried a different tactic. He sought to refresh Ross's recollection by having him read the grand jury transcript. Ross replied, "I can't read." Jensen then started reading Ross's previous grand jury testimony about two men who jumped into his parked car. The one in the back carried a gun and threatened to kill Ross if he did not do as he was told. The backseat passenger then said, "I just shot two dudes. I'm shot." Jensen, referring once again to the grand jury testimony, also described Ross taking a look at a police photograph of Newton and then identifying him as one of the two people who entered his car.

Garry repeatedly objected that this reading was improper because Huey Newton's defense counsel had not been allowed in the grand jury proceeding. But Judge Friedman overruled Garry's objections, allowing the jury to hear Jensen read Ross's entire damning grand jury testimony. Garry moved for a mistrial. Judge Friedman denied the motion. Although Jensen was sandbagged by Ross's sudden lack of cooperation, the press still reported that the prosecutor had won a key battle. It seemed that, by reading Ross's incriminating grand jury testimony to this jury, Jensen had backed Newton into a corner, the *Oakland Post* reported, "like a rat in a trap." But that view would change dramatically after Garry rose for cross-examination.

Garry asked Ross if he recalled being in Garry's law office in San Francisco in late July. Garry played a tape. The jury, press and spectators listened intently as Garry identified the voice on the tape as Ross. The taped voice acknowledged appearing before the grand jury and giving a statement to the police. He claimed both the grand jury testimony and prior statement were coerced and "not true." The man on the tape recanted his statement about seeing Newton holding a gun and denied hearing Newton speak. Ross claimed that he was "kinda out" in the back seat of his car and in no shape to make such detailed observations about Newton.

Jensen was convinced that Garry had tampered with the witness and could barely contain his fury. When Garry concluded his cross-examination, and Jensen tried to get Ross to identify his signature on the police statement, Ross said: "I see some writing here, but I don't know what it is." Stymied, Jensen excused Ross as his witness. That moment turned out to be pivotal in the trial. The fact that the jury heard Ross's grand jury testimony without meaningful cross-examination was a bell that could not be unrung. This would be listed as one of three key errors the defense successfully argued on appeal. Huey suppressed any cocky reaction to Garry's masterful theatrics.

The next day, Jensen turned to the ballistics evidence and put Police Crime Lab Director John Davis on the stand. The jury paid rapt attention as Davis testified that unburned gunpowder deposits on Frey's uniform revealed he had been shot in the back from a distance between six inches and a foot and a half. The only person so positioned was the civilian he had been grappling with. Davis stated that the slug removed from Frey's body appeared to be from the same gun as the bullet that wounded Heanes. Neither could have been fired by Heanes' gun. The powder around Frey's wounds indicated that the shots likely came from Frey's gun, matching live bullets in his holster. Davis identified the two buttons found nearby as like those on Newton's jacket.

Also called to the stand was the emergency room doctor who first saw Newton at the hospital. Garry had Newton stand up for the doctor to identify the entrance wound in his abdomen and the exit wound in his back. His probation officer testified that the probation ended on October 28, 1967, the day of the shooting. That meant Newton was still restricted from carrying a gun or possessing marijuana. A chemist identified two matchboxes found in the Volkswagen as containing marijuana. He also testified he found tiny amounts of marijuana in the right front pocket of Newton's pants. Jensen then rested his case having called 26 witnesses for the State. The defense team thought that the prosecutor appeared deflated. Garry jumped up and called for acquittal on all of the charges.

After the weekend recess, the judge granted the defense motion to dismiss the kidnapping charge since Ross had been dismissed as a witness. But he denied the motions for acquittal of the remaining charges. Having seen Garry's withering attack on key prosecution witnesses, everyone in the courtroom anxiously awaited the presentation of the defense.

The Defense Takes Its Turn

GARRY'S first witness was Tommy Miller, a passenger on Grier's bus who worked at the Alameda Naval Station. He disputed the bus driver's vantage point. Miller had also heard shooting but believed the bus had already passed the police cars by then. He also thought it was too dark to see the faces of the policeman and the man he was grappling with.

Garry also called two friends of Huey's who had seen him on Friday evening October 27, at a bar celebrating the end of his parole. Garry was using this testimony to show the jury that Huey believed his parole had ended the day before the police stopped him. If so, Huey would have had no motive to fear being sent back to prison for parole violation on October 28.

Spectators once again paid close attention when Garry offered witnesses who attested to Officer Frey's past abuse of Black arrestees. In fact, Frey's reputation for racist behavior was so well-established in Oakland that the Panther newspaper once ran a caricature of a pig with Frey's badge number on it. That occurred long before the shooting. Jensen vigorously objected that Frey was no longer available to defend himself against charges that he was racist or had abused Huey Newton. The judge overruled Jensen's objections. Garry was allowed to put on the stand a teenager whom Frey had called a "nigger" and a pimp. The teen said Frey left him to be beaten up by a White man who claimed the youth had just robbed him.

The jury heard another man who had been stopped for speeding. The man testified that Frey had called him a "Black motherfucker." A third man who received a ticket a couple of days before the shootout testified that Frey bragged at the time: "I am the Gestapo." Stender had also tracked down witnesses to a high school career day presentation during which Frey had used the word "nigger." (Jensen would feel compelled in rebuttal to put on the stand one of Oakland's few Black officers to vouch for Frey's behavior on one of these arrests. Yet damage had clearly been inflicted to Jensen's portrayal of Frey as a fallen hero.)

Garry followed these attacks on Frey's character with a surprise witness, Gene McKinney. He was the mysterious passenger who had fled the scene with Huey. Like Dell Ross, McKinney came to court with his own lawyer. After McKinney responded to a few preliminary questions, Garry shocked the spectators again by asking McKinney whether he had shot Officer Frey "by chance or otherwise." McKinney's lawyer advised him not to testify further on the grounds that it might incriminate him. Jensen objected that a witness could not answer several questions and then invoke the Fifth Amendment. Garry suggested that Jensen offer McKinney immunity as he had done for Ross, but Jensen wisely did not take the bait. If Newton's friend McKinney then said he shot Frey, the case against Newton would be severely compromised and McKinney could not be prosecuted.

To Jensen's dismay, Judge Friedman then limited Jensen to cross-examining McKinney on the few answers he had given. McKinney again invoked the Fifth Amendment even to questions asking him to explain how he and Huey Newton had gotten together that morning. Judge Friedman had enough. He held McKinney in contempt and had him hauled off to a tenth-floor jail cell. Following McKinney's dramatic exit, Charles Garry called Huey Newton to the stand.

Huey's Historic Testimony

AFTER the first day the family's presence had been intermittent. But the entire Newton family knew how important Huey's testimony would be. The Panthers were equally anxious to see how forcefully he would promote their political agenda. Garry considered it crucial for Huey to tell his life story and political philosophy to place the shooting incident in context. Even so, Garry knew the high risk involved. When a defendant chooses to take the stand, the burden of proof switches to the defense despite the fact that the judge instructs the jury otherwise. O. J. Simpson "dream team" member Barry Scheck knows that as well. When a defendant chooses to testify, his credibility "becomes *the* issue in the case, not whether the prosecution has proven its case beyond a reasonable doubt."

Huey planned to use his turn on the witness stand to full advantage both for those in the courtroom and the world at large. The high risk in his case was magnified by his criminal record. The judge would instruct the jury that they could disbelieve everything Newton said simply because he had a prior felony conviction. That was why Garry had tried so hard to convince Judge Friedman that Huey's 1964 conviction for the knife attack on Odell Lee did not rise to the level of a felony. Judge Friedman rejected that argument. The jury would be instructed that they could assume someone who committed a prior serious crime would lie about anything. Huey understood the stakes were high, but he showed no sign of cracking under pressure. He was undoubtedly bolstered by seeing so many supporters in the courtroom and being aware of the demonstrators massing outside.

By 6 a.m. on August 22, crowds had again surged outside the courthouse, which had far more security guards stationed outside than any day since the trial began. Gilbert Moore was thrilled to be on hand to witness the scene. Anger erupted as he heard a few Black activists confront White men who arrived first. One of them wanted to know "what the fuck" White boys were doing in the front of the line. The latecomers asserted their own priority. One of them said, "We been standing on line for four hundred years." A panel of glass in the double doors broke as everyone pressed to be among those lucky enough to see Huey Newton take the stand.

Melvin had not attended the trial often because of his work schedule, but he made sure to be there for the day Huey testified. The Panthers and the defense team engineered an enormous turnout that day — a crowd second only to that on the first day of trial.

Gazing upon the full courtroom from the witness chair, Huey shivered from the air-conditioning. Even so, he displayed great pleasure, seeing all the friendly faces in the crowd. He likely also noticed the increased numbers of plainclothes policemen. Dressed like a professor in a turtleneck and sport jacket, Huey was set to use his turn on the stand as if it were a classroom lectern. When prompted by Garry, Huey spoke in a conversational tone with no quaver in his voice. He focused his gaze on juror David Harper. Huey considered his testimony an opportunity to address Harper one-on-one, hoping he could develop a bond.

As Garry began the questioning, Huey flatly denied shooting either officer. He knew the police kept a list of

Black Panther vehicles and that he risked being stopped at any time. Huey had by his count been accosted by police forty to fifty times before. That was one of the reasons he kept his law book handy, as he did that day.

Huey told the jury that he never carried a handgun because that would be an automatic violation of his parole, as would the use of marijuana. The pants Newton wore had been purchased secondhand from Good Will. He claimed he had no idea that there was marijuana residue in the pocket. He never checked the pockets. He also claimed that he was unaware of any marijuana in Laverne's car.

Huey insisted that the only gun he ever carried was a shotgun, which the law allowed. He also said he only carried that weapon when he was on one of his police patrols. He added that he could be expelled from the Panthers if he ever carried a gun when he wasn't on patrol. He could also be expelled if he was ever caught with narcotics. McKinney, who pleaded the Fifth Amendment right not to incriminate himself, knew they had weed in the car. He would only own up to possessing marijuana long after the statute of limitations had passed. The whole court room paid close attention as Huey then told his version of the fatal incident on the morning of October 28:

> "I started to drive down 7th Street and as I made a left turn at 7th and Willow, I noticed a red light in my rear window. I pulled over to the curb and came to a stop. The police officer got out of his car, walked over to mine and said "Well, well, well, what do we have here? The great, great Huey P. Newton.

It must have been two to three minutes later that another officer pulled up behind the first one. The first officer opened up the door and I got out of the car with the law book in my right hand. I leaned on the car with my hands on top of the book and the officer made a frisk in a very degrading fashion.

I said, 'You have no reasonable cause to arrest me.'

He said, 'You can take that book and stick it up your ass, nigger,' and he gives me a straight arm in the face. I went down on one knee and as I was getting up, I saw the first officer draw his service revolver and then I felt a sensation of boiling hot soup being spilled on my stomach."

Huey said he had no memory of anything that happened after being shot until he arrived at the hospital. The whole case now turned on Huey's credibility. The defense team was well aware that if the jury believed Huey knowingly transported marijuana while still on parole, Jensen had his motive for killing Officer Frey. If Huey carried a concealed handgun when stopped by the police as a parolee, he would have been guilty of at least second-degree murder. That was because possession of a handgun brought the felony-murder rule into play. Any death, even an accidental one caused by a felon with an illegal gun constituted second-degree murder. A concealed handgun under Huey's shirt or from his jacket pocket was exactly what bus driver Grier testified that he saw Huey bring out.

Only four minutes of Huey's direct testimony concerned the early morning shooting. Most of his time on the stand, Huey assumed his familiar role as lecturer. He had gotten plenty of experience drawing crowds as one of the Grove Street orators at Oakland City College. Later, he had addressed weekly meetings of new recruits at Panther headquarters. Huey talked at length on direct examination about the poverty of American Blacks after hundreds of years of oppression. Jensen interrupted his presentation several times, objecting that this history lesson was not relevant to the proceedings. But Judge Friedman found Huey's historical overview fascinating and overruled the objections. Newton then told a hushed courtroom:

> "It's the fact that there are twenty-six million people in poverty. It is a fact that a large percentage of Blacks suffer from poor housing. It's a fact that a large percentage are unemployed and unemployable. These are the objective conditions or the facts that exist in the external world. . . . We realize that we are the most brutalized people in this country, and perhaps in the world, but we also realize that we need an alliance with all people who are in oppression."

He went on to explain:

> "The Black Panther Party is not a racist group, . . . we have formed an alliance with many cultural minorities, and even the disillusioned youths in the White majority, and I say disillusioned because the young Whites are now re-analyzing the whole American power structure, and as they analyze hypocrites they see that they have been sold a false bill of goods."

Probably most riveting was his accusation that the founding fathers were hypocrites. He obviously had in mind the statement in the Declaration of Independence that: "We hold these truths to be self-evident, that all men are created equal, that they are endowed by their Creator with certain unalienable Rights, that among these are life, liberty and the pursuit of happiness." All men? Not counting Native Americans and African Americans.

He was also referencing the Preamble to the Constitution: "We the People of the United States, in Order to form a more perfect Union, establish Justice, insure domestic Tranquility, provide for the common defense, promote the general Welfare, and secure the Blessings of Liberty to ourselves and our Posterity, do ordain and establish this Constitution for the United States of America." Huey pointed out that this conception of "We the People" left out minorities as well as all women.

Huey said, "At the very time the British colonists affixed their signatures to their own Constitution, many of them were murdering and enslaving Black people right in this country." He could have added Native Americans to that list of targets for genocide. He could also have noted that at various times in American history, Catholics, Mexicans, Chinese and Japanese immigrants, Jews and other minorities suffered from discriminatory treatment by the White Anglo-Saxon Protestant (WASP) majority. Huey did call attention to the fact that women of all races, religions and ethnicities were unable to vote in national elections until more than half a century after Black men.

Ten of the twelve jurors had reason to identify with the impact of systemic WASP repression of Americans like themselves. But Huey kept his gaze on the lone Black juror, David Harper. Huey wanted to make sure Harper paid close attention as Huey spoke about the Black Power Movement. Most of all Huey wanted Harper to hear what Huey had to say about the role that the Black middle class needed to play to elevate others of their race:

> "The Black Power Movement is a movement to free Blacks from exploitation and oppression. ... Out of the thirty million Blacks in the country about two percent of our people are middle class. . .. Now in order for us to get any changes to the bottom, we are going to have to harness somehow the imaginations, the skills and the abilities of the Black middle class, because they are the only people who really understand our oppression to the fullest extent. And who are willing to do something about it, because they realize that the only reason that they advanced is when the Blacks pushed from the bottom, when the Blacks caused disturbances then poverty jobs are given and the Black bourgeoisie get the administrative position and makes much money, but the Black who actually was the perpetrator of the disturbance gets nothing but maybe a jail sentence."

Huey described how the Party regarded the police:

> "The way the Black Panther views the police is mostly with the matter of — we think that it's a very pathetic situation, that it makes us very sad because we realize that the police are not the real enemy, that the police — they only take orders.

They are the fall guys of the power structure. They go in and do the dirty work for the exploiters and they do it so they can meet the notes on the house and take care of the kiddies and they only take orders.

But the real brutality is not police brutality but social brutality, political brutality and economic brutality. The police are in the community to see that the power structure persists — persists in inflicting these brutalities upon the general community, so we would like to see the police leave our community and we erect our own security forces.

Now, the subjective conditions, how the people view these facts and relate them, if they view the facts and say that — "Well, I think that all peaceful means have been exhausted," then a condition of war will ensue. But if the people view all of these facts and say that — 'But we still have another avenue, we still have a Black Panther Party to form as a national political group and perhaps we can redress our grievance through this political machine that they are going to build,' and that would be the peaceful avenue, that it's possible to take place.

The Black Panther Party abhors violence of any kind, . . . we also abhor the conditions that promote or stimulate this violence. We feel that any time people have to — or people kill each other — that it's a — it's unnecessary and it's sheerly — it's not in the interest of humanity. We think that life is the most precious thing in the universe. It is more precious than property or anything else, because even in the situation of this state where a person — a policeman can execute a citizen under the disguise of a fleeing felon when someone steals a car and the police says halt and he doesn't halt, even if it's a child, that he has a legal right to shoot this individual and kill him. And we stand against this, also."

Few other judges in the country would have allowed this testimony. Garry was extremely grateful for the opportunity Judge Friedman accorded him. Nearly five decades later, Innocence Project co-founder Barry Scheck found it impressive that the judge allowed Garry "to bring out the history of race problems in the United States as a predicate for understanding the defendant . . . in the context of a political trial." Scheck considers the decision a key ruling for the defense that "not all judges would do. . . even to this day." Civil rights lawyer Thelton Henderson was appointed a pioneering Black federal judge by President Carter in 1980. Looking back decades later, Judge Henderson applauded the latitude Judge Friedman granted Garry:

"I think Judge Monroe Friedman, who presided over this trial, did something unusual, and I thought courageous in his . . . evidentiary ruling that Huey Newton could talk about racism as it affected him, as it affected his life, and his view of the world, and his behavior. . . . I don't think there are many judges who would have made that ruling. I think it was the right ruling because I think that one's perception, one's life experiences that affect them deeply and from birth, if you're Black, your racial experiences start as soon as you're interacting with . . . other human beings. I think he made the right ruling, but it was a rare ruling in those days."

The jury appeared to marvel at Huey's dignified and scholarly presentation. His family could not have been prouder. Watching from the spectators' gallery, David Hilliard was greatly impressed:

> "Because then the trial is not a trial. It's actually a classroom for people in court. . .
> He would swivel around from the D.A. and start talking to the jury. He would be educating the jury about our movement, because Charles Garry would say, 'Well, why did you create the Black Panther Party?' So, he turned the chair around. He's not talking to the D.A. He is talking directly to the jury . . . about how we got here . . . a history lesson in the oppression and economic subjugation of Black folks in America, and Huey was very, very adept. . .. So, the jury members would be glued to what he's saying."

Huey also told the jury that the Black Panther Party had adopted rules against drinking or drug use among its members and advocated only peaceful methods of achieving their goals. While Huey gave testimony about the Party's commitment to nonviolence, outside the courthouse beyond the jury's hearing, demonstrators shouted, "Revolution has come — Time to pick up your gun" and "Off the pigs."

Jensen had to realize he was fighting a losing battle

to treat the shootout in a vacuum. SNCC leader Stokely Carmichael conducted a press conference during the noon break. He characterized the proceedings as a political "trial of a Black man . . . trying to liberate his people." Overseas press loved this angle. In London, the *Sunday Telegraph* had just published an in-depth article for its two million readers, analyzing the case in political terms.

But Garry's decision to put Huey on the stand also made his client vulnerable to potentially withering cross-examination. In allowing Huey to speak for himself, Garry gave Jensen the opportunity to focus at length on the events of the fatal morning of October 28. Also, by dwelling on Huey's political philosophy, Garry opened the door wide for Jensen to grill him on the virulent anti-police rhetoric in his writings. That was Garry's greatest fear. Yet it was a risk that he felt he had to take. It was one of the reasons he considered this case so complex to try. Garry knew that Jensen could have introduced those writings whether or not Huey was allowed to take the stand. If Huey's essays were not placed in a political context, Garry considered them inflammatory enough to convict him of murder.

Jensen had all weekend to finish preparing his cross-examination on Monday, August 26. Some of it would be revisiting at greater length the brief testimony about the shooting that Huey gave on direct. But much of it would confront Huey with his history of violence. Jensen would also confront Huey with his own incendiary statements to followers in which Huey targeted the police as enemies to "off."

Jensen started with softball questions designed to put Huey at ease. Jensen was then hoping to make him angry by employing tougher tactics so the jury could see Huey's explosive temper. But Huey had been forewarned by his sister Leola, who had overheard Jensen at a break telling an associate that he intended to provoke Huey. For his part, Huey had to keep calm and focused when forced to retell his version of the fateful interaction with Officer Frey. This time the questioning would come from a hostile opponent intent upon tripping him up.

On his guard, Huey managed to keep his temper in check throughout the grueling cross-examination. His experience finding peace of mind in the soul-breaker came in handy. When asked how he spent the Friday before the shootings, Huey testified that he had a paid speaking engagement at San Francisco State after which he went to his fiancée LaVerne's home. They had a date to celebrate the end of his probation. which he believed was completed that night. But she felt ill and instead loaned him her car.

Huey described going to his then favorite bar, Bos'n's Locker, where he had one rum and Coke. He then left to attend a party at a church social hall where he linked up with his friend Gene McKinney. When they left the party, they went to Seventh Street, intending to stop at an all-night restaurant for some barbecue. They were looking for a parking space when they were pulled over by Officer Frey. Newton described how Frey had frisked him abusively, feeling his genitals. He held out his law book and told Frey there had been no reasonable cause for stopping him. Frey called him a "nigger" and told him "to take the law book and stick it." Frey then "straight-armed" Newton, who stumbled.

The audience perked up when Newton asked Jensen's permission to demonstrate what he meant by being straight-armed. He got off the stand and pretended he was Frey. Newton then pushed Jensen back with his hand extended to Jensen's chin, using obvious restraint to avoid causing the prosecutor to lose his balance. Newton then said, "This is the way it happened. Excuse me," and resumed his seat on the witness stand.

Huey then testified that Frey drew his revolver. He heard explosions. Then, as he had testified earlier, he immediately felt a sensation "like hot soup." The next thing he remembered was crawling onto the concrete platform outside the emergency entrance to Kaiser Hospital. Jensen shifted to the *Black Panther* newspaper and Newton's prior writings. His aim was to repulse the jurors by calling their attention to the most incendiary aspects of the Panthers' philosophy. Jensen pointed out that the Panther paper listed the late Dr. Martin Luther King in a "Bootlickers' Gallery." In response, Newton insisted that this characterization changed when Dr. King came out against the Vietnam War. Jensen then called specific attention to an article Huey had published in the *Panther* newspaper the summer before, called "The Correct Handling of Revolution." Newton had written it as a critique of the 1965 devastating Watts riot in Los Angeles and more recent urban riots. The article Huey wrote included a highly inflammatory passage that started with a description of the Panther Party as the vanguard of the revolution:

> "The Vanguard must provide leadership for the people. It must teach the correct strategic methods of prolonged resistance through literature and activities. If the activities of the party are respected by the people, the people will follow the

example. When the people . . . see the advantage in the activities of the guerrilla warfare method . . . when the Vanguard group destroys the machinery of the oppressor by dealing with him in small groups of threes and fours and then escapes the might of the oppressor, the masses will be overjoyed and will adhere to this correct strategy."

Jensen likely paused for effect before continuing:

"When the masses hear that a Gestapo policeman has been executed while sipping coffee at a counter, and the revolutionary executors fled without being traced, the masses will see the validity of this type of approach to resistance."

Huey's supporters all considered him a hero for such fiery rhetoric It was "off the pigs" taken to its logical conclusion. Huey explained that the article referred to an unspecified revolutionary time in the future. Conditions had not yet risen to the level of impasse where peaceful struggle was fruitless. Jensen also confronted Huey with a poem he had published in the *Black Panther* newspaper the summer before. It was called "Guns Baby Guns!" It displayed the same theme as his essay:

Army .45 will stop all jive
Buck shots will down the cops
will open prison gates
The carbine will stop the war machine
A .357 will win us heaven.
And if you don't believe in playing
You are already dead.

Jensen had Huey read the poem aloud to the jury along with the list of weapons on the same page of the newsletter that the Panthers advocated as necessary for self-defense: an Army .45 pistol, a 12-gauge shotgun, an M-1 carbine, a .357 Magnum pistol and a .38-caliber police revolver. The jury already had heard expert testimony that Frey had been killed with his own .38 caliber revolver.

Huey repeatedly stated the Panther Party was an organization for self-defense working to combat violence. Yes, he gave speeches on Black liberation in which he advocated "taking care of business" on the streets, but he did not intend that to involve execution of policemen. He claimed he had been misquoted in a *Ramparts* magazine article by Eldridge Cleaver entitled "The Courage to Kill" that portrayed him as advocating bloodshed.

Instead of focusing on Jensen, Huey shifted to look at the jury. Huey's gaze fell mostly on David Harper when he launched into long answers. At the end of one such lecture, Huey turned back, and, to his surprise, Jensen was no longer standing there. Huey asked, "Where is he?" before he turned his head and spotted Jensen sitting at the prosecution table. Huey then said, "Oh. There you are. I thought you had left." Jensen said, "No. I'm still here." Judge Friedman rebuked the crowd for bursting into laughter.

Jensen asked about Huey's arrest in Berkeley in March of 1966 along with Bobby Seale. He examined Huey at greater length regarding his prior assault conviction, inquiring whether racism was involved. Jensen knew that Odell Lee, the victim of the assault, had been Black. But Huey surprisingly told the courtroom that his argument with Lee had started as a dispute over ethnic greetings. It escalated when Lee grabbed Huey's arm as

Lee reached into his own pocket. Huey believed he was acting in self-defense when he then stabbed Lee with a steak knife. Without a lawyer when he went to court, the jury had not seen it that way.

One sympathetic lawyer in the gallery told Eldridge Cleaver during a break that he thought Huey was being crucified on the stand like Jesus Christ. Cleaver had responded: "Yes, Huey is our Jesus, but we want him down from the cross."

At the day's end Garry was convinced that Huey had handled himself exceedingly well. Sociologist Bob Blauner, like everyone else on the defense team, was impressed at how brilliant and articulate Huey had shown himself to be. Even Lowell Jensen later conceded that it had been a smart move for Garry to put Huey on the stand in his own defense.

Dr. Herman Blake, sitting in the audience, was almost moved to tears watching Huey testify. There he was with his life on the line, carrying the banner of the Black revolutionary. The professor wrote Huey shortly afterward: "You were absolutely beautiful. Your manner and presentation on the witness stand were the highest manifestation of the integrity of the Black experience. I shall never forget what I saw and heard, regardless of the outcome."

After two days of watching Huey being cross-examined on the stand, Judge Friedman confided to the lawyers in a meeting in chambers: "He could have been a fine young man, It's really too bad." *San Francisco Examiner*'s Rush Greenlee relished covering the remarkable feat that Garry and Newton had achieved:

"[T]he political nature of the Black Panthers seemed to have transcended the stark events of 5 a.m. last Oct. 28. The jury must still decide the fate of Newton — whether he lives or dies, remains imprisoned or is set free — not the question of his politics. And yet in the back of the minds of the jurors, what he stands for may loom large, perhaps larger than the murky evidence pointing to his guilt or innocence. . . . He wishes to stand or fall on the validity of his cause. ...
The testimony inside the courtroom and the evidence outside show all too plainly that the case is at least in part one of people who feel they have been discriminated against and who are not willing to take it any longer."

Greenlee's article proved Garry's strategy had worked. The extraordinary political overtones lent an atmosphere of unreality to the courtroom battle over what exactly happened in the morning shootout.

The Jury Hears From an Expert on Diminished Capacity

ON TUESDAY, August 27, Garry called his last witness, Dr. Bernard Diamond, a veteran forensic psychiatrist on the faculty of U.C. Berkeley. Garry had relied successfully on Dr. Diamond in prior cases to prove diminished capacity to commit murder. His credentials included more than a decade of experience in the Army Medical Corps and two dozen scholarly articles on the subject. He testified for the defense about the reflex shock reaction and state of unconsciousness commonly caused in combat by bullet wounds to the abdomen.

Most significantly, over Jensen's objection, Judge Friedman let Dr. Diamond answer a hypothetical question based on a summary of Huey Newton's testimony. Dr. Diamond was asked to assume Huey had little or no recall of what transpired after he felt a hot flash from the bullet he took in the stomach. Dr. Diamond told the jury that shock of that nature was "fully compatible with a penetrating gunshot wound of the abdomen." But ultimately, it was up to the jury to determine whether the eyewitnesses were credible or not.

Dueling Rebuttal Witnesses

LIKE his sister Leola, Melvin Newton did his utmost to help spare Huey from execution. After Garry rested the defense, Jensen presented four police witnesses in rebuttal to underscore Huey Newton's history of violence and aggression resulting in his prior criminal record. Melvin then came forward as one of Garry's rebuttal witnesses. Melvin's primary purpose was to explain the context of his kid brother's juvenile record.

Soft-spoken, polite and obviously learned, Melvin must have made an excellent impression on the jury. First, he described his own education leading to a master's degree in social work. Then he corroborated Huey's testimony that he had been functionally illiterate in high school, barely able to graduate. Melvin had chuckled to himself when, to the judge's incredulity, Huey insisted that he was unable to read or write even simple words like "cat." Melvin knew that was an exaggeration.

Then, Garry asked Melvin about the hammer incident. Melvin told the jury about the severe beating Huey had endured the day before he retaliated with a hammer against one of his assailants.

Another rebuttal witness, Dr. J. Herman Blake, would later co-author *Revolutionary Suicide*. He provided novel but crucial testimony about ethnic slang. Blake made the case that the provocative language the Panthers used meant something different to the Black community than to Whites. A phrase like "takin' care of business" had multiple meanings depending on the context. It could refer to politics, sex or a variety of other subjects.

Most important to Garry was getting Dr. Blake to explain that "Off the pigs" was not intended literally, but figuratively. It was an exhortation to free the community from police oppression. That was not how Bobby Seale's assistant, Panther Janice Garrett, interpreted "Off the pigs" as she and others kept chanting outside the courthouse. It meant "kill the pigs, kill the policemen. . . . [T]hey were trying to kill us and it was up to us to defend ourselves. So, when we used verbiage like 'off the pigs,' it was if they come at you, then you defend yourself and you shoot back at them."

The Panthers were still waving their revolutionary placards and chanting outside while Prof. Blake testified inside the courtroom. Blake interpreted graphic phrases Huey had used in his writings like "buckshot will down the cops" and "carbine will stop the war machine" as figurative expressions of the desire for an end to police brutality and for peace.

Though many trial observers remained quite skeptical, Garry hoped that the jury would give some deference to an African-American professor's benign interpretation of Newton's writings. Maybe Blake's testimony would undermine Jensen's argument that the writings evidenced motivation to kill Officer Frey.

At the end of the day Judge Friedman invited the lawyers to his chambers to determine the jury instructions he would give. Jury instructions were critical. What would the panel be asked to decide with Huey's life on the line? In chambers, Garry and Stender raised the defenses of unconsciousness and diminished capacity. They argued that the jury should be instructed that Huey had not purposely shot Officer Frey but might have done so unknowingly. Either Huey was not conscious of his acts when he picked up and fired Frey's gun or, after suffering a life-threatening stomach wound, had diminished capacity to understand what he was doing. Officer Heanes had similarly testified about his own lack of memory after he was wounded. The trial judge agreed to give the diminished capacity instruction, but not the instruction on unconsciousness. (The Court of Appeal would later conclude that the defense was entitled to both instructions).

Garry and Stender's battle for these instructions was essential to saving Huey from the death penalty. Frey was killed with bullets fired into his back from his own gun less than two feet away. There was no question Huey was the civilian seen by Grier grappling with Officer Frey before the shooting started. He even left his bloody law book behind. A traditional jury of White men would have assuredly convicted the Black Panther leader of first-degree murder. How a jury of mostly women and minorities would assess the credibility of prosecution and defense witnesses remained to be seen.

Huey's trial would resume with closing arguments the following week. Meanwhile, almost everyone who watched the news was glued to national coverage of the confrontations between police and anti-war demonstrators at the 1968 Democratic Convention in Chicago. Bobby Seale was among the speakers, having filled in at the last moment for Eldridge Cleaver.

Mayor Richard Daley had denied parade permits, rendering all planned protests by anti-war demonstrators illegal. Not dissuaded, ten thousand activists converged on Grant Park in the city's Loop, not far from where the convention was underway. More than a thousand members of the crowd were actually federal and local undercover agents, taking notes on whom to arrest.

Largely at President Johnson's undisclosed direction, Mayor Daley amassed a huge phalanx of troops. To counter the protesters Daley assembled 12,000 uniformed policemen backed up by 6,000 armed National Guardsmen, another 6,000 army troops and teams of firemen. Meanwhile, inside the convention hall, many delegates sympathetic to the demonstrators pushed for a plank in the party platform to end the Vietnam War. Television viewers across the country saw police roughly mishandling some of the delegates and reporters. Shocked at what was happening before his eyes, Connecticut Senator Abraham Ribicoff condemned the "Gestapo tactics."

On August 28, a confrontation erupted in the streets between law enforcement and demonstrators. The police overreacted by tear-gassing and spraying mace on just about anyone in their path. Television news cameras captured more than fifteen minutes of chaos outside the hotel where Vice President Hubert Humphrey was awaiting his nomination for President. Outside the Convention Hall demonstrators shouted, "The Whole World Is Watching." By the time the 1968 Democratic Presidential Convention ended, about a hundred protesters and 119 police officers had been injured. Nearly 600 people were arrested. Much of this had been televised, astounding ninety million Americans with visual images of the chaos.

Everyone involved in Huey Newton's trial had a long weekend to absorb the mind-boggling anarchy in Chicago and ask themselves, "What's next?" Alameda County's sheriff and Chief of Police Charles Gain feared similar violence in Oakland if a murder verdict was announced against Newton. They decided to make a show of overwhelming force. Reinforcements began arriving to multiply the number of police stationed outside the building.

Officers were already jittery after the Panther ambush in April. Month after month of Panther newspaper stories urged followers to "kill the pigs." "Sky's the Limit" placards and speeches surrounded the courthouse each day of the trial. The officers' concern grew even more acute after they heard that the Panthers were stockpiling ammunition. A *Los Angeles Times* reporter observed: "Frustration, fear and anger are straining the nerves of big city policemen close to the breaking point."

Closing Arguments: Villain or Victim?

THE courtroom was again packed for closing arguments on Tuesday morning, the day after Labor Day. Huey's siblings were apprehensive as Jensen once again appeared confident of a murder conviction. He used no notes as he called John Frey "a forgotten man" who had no chance to tell his own story on the witness stand. He had been murdered in the line of duty, only to face character assassination in court.

Jensen sensed the jury's rapt attention and stayed clinical in his approach. He pointed to the torso of the mannequin and the testimony of ballistics expert John Davis as proof. Only Huey Newton was close enough to fire the two bullets into Frey's back that caused his death. If Newton had taken just a brief moment to choose to kill Frey, the killing would meet the definition of premeditated murder.

Jensen referred to the partially written traffic ticket at the scene of the shooting. It showed that Newton had given Frey a false name and had not produced his driver's license. Only when Officer Heanes arrived did Newton identify himself — because Heanes recognized him.

At times, Jensen spoke softly as he paced in front of the jury. At other times, he sounded sarcastic. Jensen vigorously denied any police conspiracy to "get Huey Newton". Jensen told the jury: "Actions speak louder than words." He referred to Huey as a convicted felon who was "no stranger" to violence. Caught with marijuana in his car and in his pants pocket, he had a strong motive to take deadly action against Frey — to prevent his parole revocation. Jensen also pointed out that Newton had been caught once before trying to take a policeman's gun from him.

In his summation, Jensen relied heavily on bus driver Henry Grier's testimony as an eyewitness. He brushed aside all the discrepancies that Garry had shown. Jensen focused the jury's attention to Grier's original statement to the police: "I did get a clear view of his face."

After lunch, the veteran prosecutor explained the law the jurors would have to apply. He described the circumstances that would make one killing murder, another a kind of manslaughter. Jensen compared the situation to a driver deliberately mowing down a pedestrian, recklessly speeding through an intersection or being grossly negligent behind the wheel. Each scenario would involve a different level of culpability in causing a pedestrian's death. Those were all different from a law-abiding driver unable to stop in time when a pedestrian jaywalked.

Jensen then told the jurors the trial had reached a "sad and melancholy". . . "moment of truth." He ended with a request that they find Newton guilty of assault upon Officer Heanes and first-degree murder of Officer Frey. Most of the reporters assumed the prosecutor had the jury convinced. Gilbert Moore wrote that when Jensen finished his remarks, "you could feel the noose tightening around Huey Newton's neck; you could well-nigh sniff the gas chamber fumes seeping up through the floorboards." When Jensen sat down, all eyes turned to Garry. He jumped up and started his final argument with a quote from *Alice in Wonderland*: "The King said, 'The evidence first, and then the sentence.' The Queen said, 'No. The sentence first and then the evidence.'" Garry was animated and emotional. He focused primarily on all the discrepancies in Henry Grier's two accounts of what he saw. He then contrasted Grier's testimony with that of bus passenger Tommy Miller. Garry noted that the police who arrived within minutes of the incident did not mention seeing a bus stopped nearby. He quoted Heanes' testimony that he never saw a gun in Huey Newton's hand. Garry reminded the jury that no paraffin test was done to determine if Newton had recently shot a weapon.

Garry told the jury that the small traces of marijuana found in Huey's pants pocket could have been there before they were resold by Good Will. If not, the police could have planted that evidence. Garry argued that Huey's juvenile record for retaliating against other boys who attacked him should not have been disclosed. He suggested that anyone might have responded similarly under the circumstances. Garry then described Huey's character in glowing terms: "Huey Newton, in my opinion, is a selfless man. . . .A man who is not interested in himself as a person; he is a devoted man; he is a rare man."

Garry then compared Huey to Christ in the Gospel according to Luke, telling his disciples to defend themselves." Walter and Melvin had to appreciate that analogy. Garry reminded the jurors of the findings of the *Kerner Report* on White racism, of Malcolm X, of the White Supremacy embraced in the English language. He gave examples: a white lie versus a black one, of pejoratives like "Blackball" and "Blacklist" as opposed to the benign term "whitewash." He spoke of Dr. Frantz Fanon and Dr. W. E. B. DuBois. Garry wove in reference to the massacre of his own Armenian relatives and the genocide of six million Jews in World War II. Here, he told the jury, Black ghettoes are fighting for the right of survival.

He then exclaimed, "This case is a diabolical attempt to put an innocent man into jail or into the gas chamber."

Garry refocused on bus driver Henry Grier's inconsistencies. He elicited gasps when he called Grier either a deliberate liar or "a psychopath." Garry then demonstrated to the jury that the dark jacket police had confiscated from Newton at the hospital had pockets far too shallow to hold a gun.

Next, Garry focused on key features of Huey Newton's testimony. He had been subjected to a degrading frisk. He had a law book, but no gun in his hand when he was shot. Garry spoke generally about discrimination, racism and ghetto life. He highlighted the actions of Mayor Daley and the Chicago police in the riots that had dominated the news that past week.

Garry had the courtroom spellbound as he ended almost three-and-a-half hours of final argument. Brushing back tears, the emotionally exhausted lawyer embraced Huey's shoulders with one arm and urged the jury to find his client innocent of all charges. Huey looked equally teary-eyed. Judge Friedman appeared moved and offered Garry time to compose himself. Garry thanked him and told the judge he had said "all I have to say."

Jensen jumped up in rebuttal, livid at Garry's accusations of perjured testimony and a police frame-up. Garry had impugned his own integrity as well as that of the state's chief witness. Any discrepancies in Grier's testimony were the product of honest mistakes. With those last words from the prosecutor, the trial itself was over. The jury would be instructed the following day. Outside, under constant surveillance, Black Panthers stood in military formation, waving Party flags.

Anxious Moments Waiting for the Jury Verdicts

ThE NEWTON family hoped and prayed that Huey would be spared. Melvin knew the lawyers had warned the family that might be too much to hope for. Melvin's biggest fear since Huey's arrest was that Huey would be found guilty of premeditated murder and sentenced to die. Melvin could not bear thinking of his parents having to endure the pain if his mother's baby was headed for the gas chamber. It might kill Armelia.

The atmosphere in the courtroom was charged and tense. After forty minutes of instruction on the morning of Thursday, September 5, the jury began its deliberations in a locked jury room on the eighth floor of the courthouse. The window of the room was too high up for anyone from the street to see inside. Meanwhile, Police Chief Charles Gain put twice as many officers on patrol as normal, supplemented by state highway patrolmen and National Guardsmen. All Gain could do then was wait for the jury to announce its verdict.

Anxious reporters, defense lawyers and members of Huey's family moved to the sixth-floor press room and hallway. A few reporters bet against each other on the anticipated verdicts, favoring either first- or second-degree murder. Huey's sister Doris sat on the floor in the hallway with her Bible for solace. She dreaded the potential outcome but still hoped for the best.

That same day in San Francisco, Eldridge Cleaver held a press conference. He ominously declared that "consequences" would be "inflicted" on Whites if Newton were "railroaded," adding: "Then all the strings will be cut." Bobby Seale delivered a similar message on the steps of the Alameda County Courthouse: "The sky's the limit around the world" if Newton were not freed.

Later that day, guards came to Huey's cell to bring him to court again. They had just been alerted that the jury was returning. Melvin's heart sank because Huey's lawyers had warned him that a quick verdict usually meant conviction. But once in session, the judge revealed a signed request from David Harper, as the newly selected foreman of the jury. Harper asked for a copy of Grier's statement to the police and a rereading of Grier's testimony. The request also included a rereading of the testimony of the officer who had arrived first to the scene after the shooting.

The jury wanted to see Huey's wounds again. With the judge's permission, Huey walked to the jury box, removed his jacket and pulled out his shirt. Garry helped him once again display the scars of the entrance and exit wounds. The jury's requests lifted the defense team's spirits.

The news spread quickly that the jury had unexpectedly chosen the one Black among them to be their foreman. Huey's family was elated. The Panthers remained mistrustful of Harper's banking career and his house in the hills filled almost exclusively with middle-class or wealthy Whites. The Panthers thought that meant Harper had to be a bootlicker. Yet Huey's sister Doris and her family also lived in that area of the city.

As a keenly interested observer, civil rights lawyer Thelton Henderson had already been impressed with what the defense achieved. Garry and Stender had succeeded in seating an extraordinary number of women and minorities on the jury. Henderson considered a Black foreman "completely revolutionary." Television reporter Belva Davis reacted the same way: "The selection of the jury foreman was absolutely a surprise, a shock, and of a trial, a high-profile trial like this . . . highly explosive international trial."

The jury continued deliberating all day Friday and through the weekend. They were accompanied by armed bailiffs or sheriff's deputies every time they left for lunch or dinner. They were escorted each night to a different, undisclosed hotel. Most of the reporters remained holed up at the courthouse, afraid they would miss a scoop if they left. Many crammed into the sixth-floor press room, sleeping, eating and playing cards.

Doris continued to camp out in the hall with her Bible. Gilbert Moore, Fay Stender and defense expert Bob Blauner spent some of the time sitting on the hall floor playing chess. By Friday, all of the reporters had taken sides on the outcome. The local police had already prepared for riots.

A tense atmosphere pervaded other U.S. cities and beyond. In London, the week before, an angry demonstration had broken out after a false announcement that Huey Newton had been convicted and sentenced to die. Much more violence was expected in Oakland if the jury found him guilty of first-degree murder.

A group of White radicals called the Berkeley Socialist League announced that it would undertake retaliatory action within two days of an adverse verdict. The Panthers had the same thought.

David Hilliard later said that if Huey got the death penalty, "We're going to come and take him out of the state's hands and we're going . . . to make certain that you don't take his life.... He wasn't going to die in the gas chamber. That was our mandate. That if you kill Huey Newton then, 'The sky is the limit.'" The phrase had become their mantra.

Thousands of National Guardsmen remained on alert, surrounding the city of Oakland, equipped with helicopters. Several hundred police officers were immediately placed on extended duty, augmented by scores of units from the California Highway Patrol. A large contingent was hidden from public view across the street half a block from the courthouse. They were stationed in the basement parking garage of the Oakland Museum which was then under construction.

Inside the courtroom the defense team suddenly realized that when the jury had requested Grier's original statement to the police, what they received was not the original police tape of the bus driver's interview. Instead, the jury saw the transcript that Jensen had produced for trial. At the request of the defense team, Jensen produced the tape itself. The defense lawyers obtained Judge Friedman's permission to check its accuracy.

Fay Stender's husband Marvin and author Ed Keating found an expert who re-transcribed the tape. The expert found that it contained a small but highly significant wording difference. On the tape, the driver had said he "didn't" get a good look at the civilian. The transcript said he "did" get a good look. The defense team considered it a bombshell — evidence the prosecutor had engaged in deliberate deception.

On Saturday afternoon, the jury remained sequestered while the judge heard highly charged arguments on both sides. Judge Friedman then himself listened to the tape and heard the word "didn't." Yet he refused to reopen the trial because he saw no indication that the error in the transcription was purposeful. Jensen had indicated that he was as surprised as everyone else. Yet he considered the issue far less important than Garry did. Newton never denied being at the scene. He had in fact identified himself to Officer Heanes, testified to being shot in the stomach and identified the blood-soaked law book he dropped there. Judge Friedman's solution was to allow the correction of Grier's prior statement to be transmitted without comment to the jury as it continued its deliberations.

Those waiting for the verdict got another false alarm when the jury came back to court Saturday morning for a lengthy rereading of other testimony. That same day the Panthers got out the latest edition of their newspaper. At the top was the usual head shot of Huey in a beret wearing a grim expression on his face. Underneath the photo was the caption "Huey Must Be Set Free" underscored with the image of a rifle. Covering the entire front page below the logo was a photo of three militant Panther Party members on the steps of the Alameda County courthouse. The trio stood at attention in full dress uniform waving "Free Huey" banners emblazoned with the Panther emblem. In bold print above the building were the words "WORLD AWAITS VERDICT" and, ominously below the photo, "FREE HUEY . . . OR THE SKY'S THE LIMIT!"

At a quarter to eight that evening, the jury created another stir when they once more asked to return to court. It turned out they only wanted to have the instructions on the degrees of homicide recited to them again. They also wanted to re-hear the definition of assault. Two of the women jurors looked like they might have been crying. It appeared that their decision was imminent. But the jurors ended that evening with a request that they be escorted to their hotel for the night.

Eldridge Cleaver expected the jury verdict to trigger guerrilla warfare and made plans accordingly. His wife Kathleen could not imagine Huey ultimately being executed. She and the other protesters had pushed too hard for Newton's freedom. "People weren't going to back down." If Huey was headed for the gas chamber, the decision had been made to break him out — or die trying.

On Sunday, the jury returned to court immediately after recommencing deliberations. They sent a message asking the judge to slowly reread the definitions of murder and manslaughter. After Judge Friedman got part way through, foreman David Harper signaled they had heard what they needed to hear. The jurors retired once more to the jury room.

After having all but ruled out first-degree murder on Saturday, the reporters concluded that the jury deliberations had come down to a choice between first- and second-degree murder. That was the same assumption they had when the trial began. Newton's surprisingly effective testimony had lulled a few of them into thinking otherwise. None now believed he would be acquitted.

In his office on the fourth floor of the courthouse, Lowell Jensen noted the eerie calm in the city. It felt like the prelude to a major storm. It amazed Jensen to hear from the police that crime in the city was at an ebb. It seemed that even would-be burglars awaited the jury's verdict. Reporter Belva Davis later recalled her own trepidation at the time: "I think the only thing that those of us who were watching from the sidelines dreaded was a verdict that could act as the flint to ignite a fire of resentment and frustration . . . because of the way our society was structured . . . We feared what could happen. We'd seen people hurt and injured, and none of us wanted to see that again. Nor did we want to see our city going up in smoke."

As head of Oakland's Parks and Recreation Department, Bill Patterson had his pulse on the mood of youth in the flatlands: "Oakland was a powder keg; it could've blown up." Mayor John Reading and other city officials expected violence, too. All of Oakland seemed to grind to a halt awaiting the verdict.

While the nerve-racking weekend wore to a close, Charles Garry and Alex Hoffmann spent Sunday afternoon and evening closeted with Huey at the jail. They were joined by Alex Hoffmann's housemate, KPFA program director Elsa Knight Thompson. She was a strong supporter of the Panthers and long-time friend of Huey's lawyers. Fay Stender, sociologist Bob Blauner and others came in and out during their extended vigil.

Thompson had the surreal experience of having just witnessed firsthand the chaotic Democratic Convention and demonstrations in Chicago. She herself was a veteran World War II BBC radio announcer. It astounded her that in Chicago even television network crews and newspaper photographers had been targeted with Billy clubs. She thought that the misconduct of the Chicago police was helping Yippie leaders Abbie Hoffman and Jerry Rubin galvanize revolutionary fervor among their followers.

Huey enjoyed the distraction of Thompson's travel tales as they awaited the results of the jury deliberations just two floors below. Thompson thought Huey was behaving as if he were entertaining guests in his living room rather than awaiting a life-or-death verdict. Huey even joked: "If they come in with an acquittal, I'm going to ask to poll them individually."

Late Sunday evening a knock on the door alerted them that David Harper had sent a note to the judge that the jury was ready with their verdicts. Only a couple of dozen rumpled and un-showered members of the press still waited on the sixth floor. Their adrenaline flowed as they answered the call to the courtroom. At this hour only a few other spectators joined the exhausted lawyers and Huey's nervous family. There were a large number of empty seats.

Huey arrived dressed in olive drab slacks and a green shirt. He stood tall with a serious, determined expression on his face as he told reporter Rush Greenlee, "No matter how it goes, it's not the end of the road. I've prepared myself." As he had done throughout the trial, Huey kept his volatile temper in check. He had once again summoned the calm resistance he had developed when isolated in that very courthouse back in 1964. He appreciated that this moment of truth called for him to remain deliberate and cautious as he learned his fate. Huey kept himself well-mannered. He was extraordinarily good at projecting different attitudes depending on the situation.

When everyone was inside, Judge Friedman took the bench and announced a new precaution. The doors to the courtroom would be locked, and stay locked, until the verdicts had all been read and the jury dismissed. Sheriff's deputies remained on guard at the building's entrances and in its abandoned hallways. The atmosphere was eerie. Gilbert Moore felt the room seem to shrink "as though we had all been stuffed into some malodorous bottle. The stench of death was everywhere."

When the jurors entered a side door and sat down, they, too, looked bedraggled and exhausted. None looked at Huey as they walked past him. Veteran reporters considered that a sure sign of a murder conviction. Judge Friedman then asked for the verdicts. The tension in the room heightened further as David Harper handed the verdict form to the bailiff to deliver to the judge. The judge reviewed the form silently and then passed it to the clerk, who read it aloud. Newton stood at the defense table, bracing himself for the outcome. First degree murder — not guilty. Sighs of immense relief escaped from the defense team and Huey's family. Second degree murder — not guilty.

Members of the press were astounded. Lowell Jensen was stunned but showed no emotion. He had assumed that if the jury did not come back with first-degree murder, they would have to find Newton guilty of second-degree murder. Voluntary manslaughter — guilty. Jensen sensed a compromise. So did many others. Huey swallowed hard but remained impassive as the reading of the verdicts was completed. Assault upon Officer Heanes — not guilty. Each juror was polled individually on all three counts and affirmed they agreed with the verdict.

Judge Friedman thanked and dismissed the jury for their hard work. He also expressed his appreciation to the alternates for standing by in readiness. The bailiff then led them out by the side door.

The Newton family struggled with conflicting emotions. Most of them looked stunned that Huey was not acquitted of all charges. Huey's sister Doris fainted in shock. When she opened her eyes, she discovered to her delight that she had been saved from falling by the Panthers' handsome young priest, Father Neil. Melvin Newton rejoiced that his mother would not have to face her baby being sent to the gas chamber. Fay Stender squeezed Huey's hand. Charles Garry consoled underground newspaper reporter Karen Wald with a hug and whispered, "This is a victory."

The police were outraged. Jensen concealed as best he could his profound disappointment. Yet above all he had wanted to avoid either a hung jury or the perception of race bias. Those hurdles looked overcome. When word got out, the Panthers who had demonstrated every day were jubilant. Janice Garrett later said: "We were totally shocked. . ... We could not believe it because this was the first time that an armed Black man was in an altercation with the police department and was vindicated." Actually, not totally vindicated. To decide upon voluntary manslaughter, the jury had to have concluded that Newton shot Officer Frey only after he himself was shot. They also had to have decided that Newton acted with diminished capacity. (David Harper would later reveal that was exactly what they decided had happened. They based their reconstruction of the sequence of shootings mostly on the testimony of the State ballistics expert and the jury's courtroom observation of the angle of Huey's wounds.)

The verdicts only got Garry part way to his goal. He pressed onward, immediately filing three motions: for a new trial, for Newton's release on bail, and for the sentencing to be delayed. Judge Friedman set a date for that Thursday, September 12, to take testimony on the bail request. He set the bail hearing for September 27 and then adjourned the proceedings. As bailiffs escorted Huey from the courtroom, Father Neil raised a fist up high with an emphatic "Power to the People." Huey responded in kind.

Bailiffs opened the locks on the seventh-floor stairwell for the first time since the trial had begun almost two months earlier. Reporters rushed for the telephones and for quotes from the lawyers, Huey and the Newton family. Each journalist tried to get a read on which side felt it had won. Some also sought out the jurors before they left the building, but they were protected by armed security guards. That left no opportunity for questions.

Garry spent half an hour with Huey in his cell and reported that Huey believed he had been "sold down the river by a White racist society." But the legal team had in fact buoyed Newton's hopes that the low-level verdict could result in release on bail pending appeal. Otherwise, he faced at least a couple of years in prison. All along, Huey and Melvin had been forewarned that it might take a few years to get him freed.

Huey instructed Garry to tell Bobby Seale to get word out immediately on the street "to keep it cool." He wanted no uprising in response to the verdict that would spoil his chances for release. Bobby Seale agreed and jumped into his car to spread the message. David Hilliard did the same. He understood Huey did not want any of the Panthers "to do anything crazy. . .. Our charge was to make sure that Oakland didn't burn."

Panther Party Field Marshall Donald "DC" Cox was livid. Based on prior instructions from Party leaders, Cox had been all set to assault the jail with his men and liberate Newton. The change of plans rankled long afterwards, causing Cox to side with Eldridge Cleaver when the

Panthers later split. Yet even Cleaver saw merit in holding off revolution in the streets — at least for the time being. So did Seale. Everywhere Seale went, he passed caravans of police and highway patrolmen in riot gear.

Upon hearing the verdict, most members of the defense team were in a celebratory mood. They all knew that the result was far better than it could have been. But Alex Hoffmann, who had spent the most time keeping Huey company in jail, still found the voluntary manslaughter conviction traumatic. The sensitive lawyer may have secretly been in love with Huey, though it would be many years before Hoffmann acknowledged his homosexuality. Fay Stender also remained unsatisfied at anything short of complete exoneration.

Examiner reporters interviewed many Oaklanders for their reactions and found them divided on racial lines. Most Blacks believed Newton "got a raw deal." Most Whites thought he should have no complaints about a result many considered better than he deserved. Veteran trial lawyer Clinton White, who had been the Panthers' top choice for chief defense counsel, was more even-handed. White had anticipated Huey would be acquitted, but thought the jury conscientiously applied the law. He concluded that they "may have believed part of Newton's story and part of bus driver Grier's testimony."

Civil rights lawyer Ann Fagan Ginger, a Lawyers Guild colleague of the defense team, wryly noted: "The concept that the jury could listen to the facts and decide he was innocent of first-degree murder in effect proved that the Black Panthers were wrong in thinking everything was bad. So, it was a kind of a contradictory situation. . . .. The Panther insistence that racism was present every minute couldn't be true. The White community could say we did a fair thing."

Ginger decided that the extraordinary efforts resulting in that historic jury needed to be set down in a handbook. Ginger produced a manual published by the Lawyers Guild the following year: *Minimizing Racism in Jury Trials: The Voir Dire Conducted by Charles R. Garry in People of California v. Huey P. Newton*. It would quickly become a well-thumbed "Bible" for criminal defense lawyers nationwide.

Observing the drama of the 1968 Newton trial was a career-altering experience for *LIFE* reporter Gilbert Moore. When he returned to New York, he brought back 36 notebooks full of the notes he had taken. Howard Bingham, the freelance photographer hired by *LIFE*, had accumulated a staggering 10,000 photos. Bingham later wrote: "We turned in a big fat story. But the great irony is that *LIFE* magazine, after spending all that time and all that dough to get a Panther story, refused to run the submission as written." Moore tried one more draft. He felt "caught in the middle between my editors and the Panthers." He had no intention of becoming "the *LIFE* editors' Negro instrument for chastising the party." He was equally opposed to writing "a Panther puff piece, trying to make them come off like Boy Scouts in leather."

The upshot was that *LIFE* magazine's editors opted to publish nothing at all. Moore left his job to write a book about the deep anger the Panther leaders had stirred inside him: "cursing them for raising ten thousand questions and answering none of them." Huey himself liked to quote James Baldwin's opinion: "To be a Negro in this country and to be relatively conscious is to be in a constant state of rage." Maybe Baldwin's observation influenced the title Gilbert Moore chose for his own book. *A Special Rage*, published in 1971, would be hailed as a classic in African-American literature. Bingham kept his extraordinary photo shoot for future use. He ultimately published the photos in 2009 in his own book, *Black Panthers 1968*.

Innocence Project co-founder Barry Scheck later noted the trial's extraordinary impact:

> "[I]t changed people's approach to jury selection, and the issues of race in jury selection. And it really proved that, even in the most high-profile incendiary kind of political case in the United States, you could get a fair trial. . ... Somebody in Newton's position could take the witness stand and be believed by the jury . . . and that was not self-evident to anyone at the time."

* * *

Lowell Jensen refused to publicly second-guess the jurors out of respect for their efforts. He later said, "The verdict that was rendered shows that this jury was fully capable of listening to the evidence that was introduced and deciding the case on the basis of the evidence, rather than on any racist considerations. As far as I was concerned . . . they were very conscientious . . . [and] should be respected." Privately, he still assumed the jurors had compromised on the result. Even diminished capacity usually reduced premeditated murder to second degree "reckless" murder, not voluntary manslaughter.

Eleven years later in San Francisco, another highly

politicized murder trial ended similarly. The defendant was former Supervisor Dan White, a conservative Republican charged with assassinating San Francisco's Mayor George Moscone and the city's first openly gay Supervisor, Harvey Milk, both liberal Democrats. This time the case involved both a White defendant and White victims. The jury was instructed on what became known as "the Twinkie defense" — impaired judgment from too much junk food. They also came back with a voluntary manslaughter verdict.

Back on September 8, 1968, after the jury verdicts in the Newton case were read, members of the press descended on both Jensen and Garry for their reactions. Jensen deliberately kept his thoughts to himself. Garry postured to the press that the manslaughter verdict was a disappointing, "chicken shit" compromise. After he met with his attorneys, Huey told reporters the same thing. But on Garry's way out of the courthouse, he poked reporter Gilbert Moore in the ribs and whispered, "We got 'em. We got 'em." He shouted to another supporter, "It is a victory, buddy, it's a victory!" The Newton family could now collectively let out their breath. But far more effort was required to get Huey freed.

SUPERIOR COURT OF THE STATE OF CALIFORNIA IN AND FOR THE COUNTY OF ALAMEDA
ABSTRACT OF JUDGMENT
(Commitment to State Prison)

The People of the State of California, Present:
vs.
HUEY P. NEWTON
Defendant

Present:
Hon. MONROE FRIEDMAN
Judge of the Superior Court
D. Lowell Jensen
Asst. District Attorney
Charles R. Garry
Counsel for Defendant

This certifies that on Sept. 8, 1968 judgment of conviction of the above-named defendant was entered as follows:
(1) Case No. 41266 Count No. One of the Indictment.
On his plea of not guilty
he was convicted by verdict of jury of a felony, to wit: voluntary manslaughter, a violation of Section 192, Subdivision 1 of the Penal Code of the State of California, a lesser and included offense within the offense charged in Count One of the Indictment.

with prior felony convictions charged and proved as follows:
Date   County and State   Crime   Disposition

On October 29, 1964, in the Superior Court of the State of California in and for the County of Alameda, defendant was convicted of a felony, to wit: assault with a deadly weapon, a violation of Section 245 of the Penal Code of the State of California under the name of Huey Percy Newton, and pursuant to said conviction, sentence was suspended for three years, during which time he was placed on probation.

(3) IT IS THEREFORE ORDERED, ADJUDGED AND DECREED that the said defendant be punished by imprisonment in state prison of the State of California for the term provided by law and that he be remanded to the Sheriff of the County of Alameda, and by him delivered to the Director of Corrections of the State of California California Medical Facility, Vacaville, California.

FILED
SEP 27 1968
JACK G. BLUE, County Clerk
By K. I. Fagre

(4) To the Sheriff of the County of Alameda and to the Director of Corrections at the California Medical Facility, Vacaville, California
Pursuant to the aforesaid judgment, this is to command you, the said Sheriff, to deliver the above named defendant into the custody of the Director of Corrections at the California Medical Facility, Vacaville, California,
at your earliest convenience.
Witness my hand and seal of said court September 27, 1968.

JACK G. BLUE, Clerk
(SEAL) By K. I. Fagre, Deputy

State of California,
County of Alameda, } ss.

I do hereby certify the foregoing to be a true and correct abstract of the judgment duly made and entered on the minutes of the Superior Court in the above entitled action as provided by Penal Code Section 1213.
Attest my hand and seal of the said Superior Court this

(SEAL) The foregoing instrument is a 27th day of September, 1968
correct copy of the original
on file in this office JACK G. BLUE, County Clerk and ex officio Clerk of the Superior Court of the State of California in and for the County of Alameda.

Monroe Friedman ATTEST SEP 27 1968 By K. I. Fagre, Deputy
Judge of the Superior Court of the State of California in and for the County of Alameda

EXHIBIT A

Source: Department of Special Collections and University Archives, Stanford University Libraries.

IX.

Freeing Huey

Widespread Violence is Avoided

HUEY'S family spent the weeks until his sentencing gathering signatures supporting his release on bond pending appeal. The Panthers had a different realization. His continued incarceration worked as a spectacular recruitment tool for the Party. As long as Huey remained jailed, he represented to his followers all Black men victimized by a racist criminal justice system. He could symbolize all Black men railroaded since colonial days. The cry of "Free Huey!" stood in for freeing all political prisoners — all minorities the Panthers considered unjustly behind bars.

Police Chief Gain was on high alert. He was well aware that the devastating six-day Watts riots three years earlier had escalated from a single incident. A policeman had pulled over an African-American drunk driver and impounded his car in front of hostile neighborhood spectators. Chief Gain realized that after two bloody skirmishes between the Panthers and the police in the last year, Oakland was a tinderbox. The city was so on edge over the Newton trial that the slightest new confrontation could trigger horrendous consequences.

Gain was relieved that calm had prevailed on Sunday night after the verdict issued. On Monday, Emory Douglas and other Panthers working on the newspaper in the Party's headquarters at 4451 Grove Street warily eyed policemen on patrol. The intensity of the officers' hatred was palpable. The staff decided to leave the office early to avoid a confrontation.

When Monday evening ended peacefully as well,

Chief Gain must have gone to bed breathing a sigh of relief. He was awakened before 2 a.m. with most unwelcome news. Around 1:30 a.m., two members of his force had created his worst nightmare. They had driven their squad car past the Panthers' Oakland headquarters and fired a shotgun and a carbine repeatedly at the portrait of Newton in the front window of the empty building. The barrage of bullets struck office furniture, shattered an interior room divider and damaged posters of Eldridge Cleaver and Bobby Hutton that hung on the wall. Three shots struck an adjoining café. One errant shot went through the roof of their own patrol car.

The first shots woke up neighbors, who saw the officers' car make a U-turn and the officers fire a second round. Neighbors wrote down the license number and called the police dispatcher. Gain wasted no time calling for an investigation of Officers Richard Williams and Robert Ferrell. When stopped for questioning, breath and blood tests showed their blood alcohol at .19, well over the generous definition of a person "under the influence of alcohol." If Gain did not act quickly to condemn their conduct, this could be the start of a race war.

Janice Garrett had been working in the headquarters earlier on Monday and came back the next day: "I remember very clearly ... seeing the damage that the policemen had done when they had shot up the office, it was riddled — and we knew then that that was their expression [to] let us know that we are here ... to disrupt and create havoc in your lives." A spokesperson told a reporter this was proof of what they always claimed: "The Oakland Police Department is racist and determined to wipe out the Panthers."

Huey again sent out word to lay low and not give the police an excuse to come down hard on the community. That same day, Mayor Reading issued a press release calling the policemen's behavior "most regrettable and deplorable." Meanwhile, Chief Gain urged locals not to impugn the department as a whole for the shooting spree of two rogue officers. Less than thirty hours after the jury's verdicts, the rogue officers were arrested on felony charges of firing into an occupied dwelling. On Police Chief Gain's recommendation, they were soon fired for gross misconduct.

Anxious to avoid putting themselves at risk, the Oakland Police Officers' Association refused to cover the fired men's legal fees. The organization's president lamented, "I can't think of anything worse they could have done. Policemen long after they're gone are going to have to live with this." Gain was credited with playing a major role in averting riots by taking quick action. The National Guardsmen were sent home as militant Panthers contemplated their next steps. The escalation of tension was not going to help the Newton family and his lawyers in their efforts to get him freed on bail pending appeal.

Huey's Sentencing Hearing

AFTER the verdict was announced, Fay Stender had taken charge of coordinating Huey's family and other volunteers to obtain as many signatures as possible to support Huey's release on bail. By the time of the hearing on September 27, they had amassed 20,000 names of community members to submit to Judge Friedman.

Walter and Armelia Newton both came forward to attest to their youngest son's good character and trustworthiness. For Armelia, this was a true labor of love. Except for her reluctant appearance to make a personal appeal at the February 1968 fund-raiser for Huey, she had spent almost all of the past eleven months in seclusion.

Judge Friedman likely had never seen such an array of support for a prisoner's release as he received that day. It included an association of Black clergy who vouched for Newton as a force for peace in the community. But in view of Newton's record, the judge had to have looked askance at Fay Stender's assertion that Huey did not currently represent "even the mildest aggressive threat to others."

Reverend Earl Neil took the stand and called Newton "the personification of what our American ideals are set up to produce in all of its citizens." He told Judge Friedman that just a week before the verdict was reached Huey had made a tape recording for students at Oakland's predominantly Black McClymonds High School warning them against reacting violently to whatever the jury decided. Duly impressed, Judge Friedman turned toward Huey, who was seated with his lawyers, and commended him for his action.

Huey then took the stand. He told the judge what he had previously told the press. He had advised his own followers in advance of the verdict to "keep cool" no matter what resulted. The judge questioned him at length about his prior record which Jensen contended showed "nothing but contempt for the rules that govern civilized men."

Judge Friedman then rendered his decision which surprised few besides the Newton family and Huey's most devoted advocates. The judge denied the request for release pending appeal. He agreed with Jensen that Huey's record justified imprisonment. In weighing public safety as a factor, the judge could hardly ignore the trial evidence that could have instead convinced the jury to impose a death sentence — as the police still believed had been warranted.

Judge Friedman then ordered Huey to begin serving his sentence immediately. He rejected the argument made by Fay Stender that her client might easily wind up doing two years of prison time before an appellate court decided whether the conviction was valid. Reversal seemed most unlikely. Armelia screamed hysterically. Her baby could not have done what he was accused of. Everyone could now see why Armelia had avoided attending the trial. Huey remained stoic. For now, Stender had to accept a setback. She remained convinced she could win his freedom on appeal.

Moments after the hearing ended, police removed Huey to the Vacaville Medical Facility for evaluation. One reporter assumed that some Panthers believed Huey would have made "a much finer martyr" if he were instead headed for execution. Yet the lesser punishment did not dissipate all racial tension in Oakland or nearby cities. The day after the sentencing, without apparent provocation, a White policeman in San Francisco shot a Black truck driver, who died. At the time of the shooting, the officer was wearing a homemade tie pin —- "Gas Huey." To avoid sparking a riot, the chief of police quickly suspended the officer and arrested him on a charge of using excessive force.

Inside the Men's Colony as All Hell Erupts on the Outside

AS HUEY underwent evaluation at Vacaville, Kathleen Cleaver made local headlines by posing for *Ramparts* magazine with a rifle at her side. She wanted to emphasize she was prepared for armed self-defense. Her message was an echo of the one that got SNCC leader H. Rap Brown prosecuted for inciting riots in Baltimore the summer before: "We have to civilize America... or let it burn."

Meanwhile, San Francisco's and Oakland's Police Chiefs warned their forces that they would have zero tolerance for any rogue cops inciting armed retaliation from the Panthers. It seemed that the Panthers would soon be leaderless in any event. Huey Newton faced up to fifteen years in prison. Plans were already underway in Chicago for Bobby Seale to be among those prosecuted for the recent riots at the Democratic Convention. Eldridge Cleaver had been ordered to return to prison in late November after the Court of Appeal reversed the trial judge's ruling that had freed him in June.

At the beginning of October, prison officials transferred Huey to the Men's Colony in San Luis Obispo, a medium-security facility several hours' drive south. It housed mostly White, nonviolent and gay convicts. Though the prison facilities were better than most, his time behind bars would isolate Huey from Bay Area supporters.

It turned out, much to the warden's dismay, that Huey was also an instant celebrity inside the prison. Inmates at the Men's Colony adopted him as their new hero. News agencies all over the United States inundated the prison with requests for interviews. Few were granted. With rare exceptions, Huey's list of allowable visitors was limited to family and lawyers. No Panther Party members were allowed to visit him except his brother Melvin, who remained the head of the Party's fund-raising efforts on Huey's behalf. When the press renewed their demands for access, exasperated prison officials permitted limited numbers of further interviews.

By the end of the month, Huey launched his own protest. He demanded the minimum wage instead of working in the prison kitchen for "slave wages". That was an apt description of the three cents per hour that the prison offered. The warden put Huey in lock-up for rule violations. As in the Alameda jail, he often paced naked in his poorly ventilated cell. The cell was roughly four-and-a-half feet by six feet like the soul-breaker cell in Alameda.

Melvin got worried when Huey wound up in isolation. He knew his younger brother suffered from periodic bouts of depression. So, Melvin made a practice of driving down for a weekend once a month, sometimes alone, other times with family or a friend. Once he brought his four-year-old son Gregory and Doris's son Ricky. Gregory told the family he was going to "Huey's house."

Melvin tried to get his siblings to schedule regular visits on the weekends when he was not there. That never worked out, but they did come sporadically. His sisters Myrtle and Doris talked their young cousin Eddie Ento into driving them down and back twice in a family Oldsmobile. They traveled one long day in 1969 and again on a day trip in 1970. The round trip took about eight hours of driving, including brief stops for gas and bathroom breaks. That allowed them a two- to three-hour visit with Huey in the prison's large visiting room. Both times, Huey seemed in good spirits considering the circumstances.

In 1970, with his marriage already headed toward divorce, Melvin brought his new girlfriend Barbarette to the Men's Colony. Melvin had met her in the fall of 1969 when she was a part-time student at Oakland City College taking courses from other faculty members. They first started dating in early 1970, much to Barbarette's mother's dismay. The notoriety connected with the Black Panthers made Evelyn Henderson quite leery of its jailed leader's older brother. Barbarette ignored her mother's concerns.

Melvin soon learned that Barbarette had been born in Detroit when her father was stationed there during World War II. She spent her early years in Mobile, Alabama, where her father was from. Her parents had four more children before they divorced. In the 1950s, Barbarette's mother Evelyn moved to San Francisco with her five children, and then to Oakland in 1958 when Barbarette was fifteen. Barbarette graduated from McClymonds High School in 1961, ironically in the same class as Melvin's future wife Joyce.

After graduation, Barbarette had worked at the U.S. Naval Station on nearby Treasure Island. She married Billy Maurice Alcorn when she was just a couple of years out of high school. Their marriage ended in divorce shortly after their son Maurice was born. When Barbarette began dating Melvin, she was older than most students at Merritt College. Her four-year-old son Maurice was just a few months younger than Melvin's son Gregory.

* * *

Melvin with Barbarette Payton Alcorn, who became his second wife

Barbarette was able to join Melvin on his trips to visit Huey because her sister Detta (short for Alfredetta) agreed to take care of Maurice while Barbarette was gone. Detta lived in Oakland, as did Barbarette's mother Evelyn and three younger brothers. Her mother had remarried and had two more children. Altogether, with the remarriages of both parents, Barbarette had thirteen siblings, double the size of Melvin's tribe.

Melvin and Barbarette drove down to San Luis Obispo several times on a Friday night and stayed in a local motel or in King City. The prison allowed open visitation hours all weekend so Melvin and Barbarette would join Huey in a large quad. There, family and friends could visit and eat lunch with their imprisoned relative under the watchful eyes of prison guards. Melvin and Barbarette would visit Huey again on Sunday morning before heading back home to Oakland.

Huey also got regular mail and photos from his family. Huey's lawyers assumed that his mail was opened before he received it, so they kept their posted letters on safe subjects. They only conveyed sensitive reports from the Panthers in person. Of all the visitors, only attorneys were allowed private meetings with Huey. Even then, Stender and Hoffmann whispered or wrote notes for him on their legal pads for him to look at on the assumption their conversations were routinely being eavesdropped upon. Soon, Fay Stender and Alex Hoffman began delivering to Huey personal letters and photos from friends and family they kept hidden from the guards in their briefcases. They would show Huey the letters and photos and pack them back in their briefcases so the guards would not confiscate them.

Meanwhile, the impact of the Panthers emerged front and center in the international arena. In mid-October, Huey was ecstatic to learn what American track stars Tommie Smith and John Carlos had just dared to do at the summer Olympics in Mexico. Both runners were from San Jose State where Mevin had gotten his degree. As was customary, after their race, the two men mounted the podium to accept their gold and bronze medals while a band played the U.S. national anthem. The pair then shocked officials and spectators by lifting their arms in power-to-the-people, fist pumps.

The emphatic gesture prompted their immediate ejection and ban from future Olympics, a reaction that only served to etch a picture of the two Black athletes in the memories of all viewers worldwide. It has since been recognized as one of the most iconic images in Olympic history. (Both men became lifelong human rights advocates, later honored for their courage and venerated with a statue at their alma mater.)

Fay Stender continued working round the clock on Huey's behalf. Besides the tedious job of reviewing the more than 4,000-page trial record to prepare his appeal, she played a key role in expanding his burgeoning number of supporters. Stender recruited celebrities to lend their names, helping galvanize national backing among anti-war activists for the Panthers and the "Free Huey" movement. New Panther branches popped up across the country. That created a far larger market for posters of Huey on the wicker throne. Soon many college students nationwide were pinning them up on their dorm room walls.

In September 1968, Cleaver had been invited to give a series of ten lectures at U.C. Berkeley on urban unrest.

The outraged U.C. Regents canceled the lectures. Cleaver then made an incendiary speech at San Francisco State threatening "If Huey isn't freed, we're going to do it with guns". He called for harnessing "red, yellow, brown and even White power" because "we have to throw this capitalist system into the garbage can of history." Cleaver then encouraged the audience to join him in a chorus of obscenities aimed at Governor Reagan and the U.C. Regents.

In a jailhouse interview, Huey predicted that his trial would become a "springboard that mobilizes the community." He expected the Movement to mushroom to two million members in two years. He told the reporter that he expected "future bloodshed." Provocative rhetoric of this type following two assassinations and the chaotic Democratic Convention in Chicago helped feed into Nixon's "Law and Order" campaign for President.

Nixon appealed to the "Silent Majority" of mostly White voters who did not opt to support the more openly racist "state's rights" platform of Alabaman George Wallace running as the American Independent Party candidate. In 1962, Wallace had been the nearly unanimous choice of White voters for Alabama Governor by urging "segregation now, segregation tomorrow, segregation forever." In 1968, Wallace made separation of the races his national pitch.

Nixon would win a close election over Vice President Humphrey. Yet George Wallace would garner more than 13.5 percent of the vote. For a third-party candidate that could easily be enough to change the result of an election. But in this case, had Wallace not been in the race, his votes from White supremacists would presumably have gone to Nixon, who won anyway.

★ ★ ★

In late October 1968 Cleaver gave *Playboy* magazine an interview at Charles Garry's office in San Francisco. Relishing the limelight, Cleaver hinted darkly that the day of reckoning was coming soon. A few days later, San Francisco police stopped a Panther newspaper delivery truck fleeing from a gas station convenience store robbery. A gunfight then followed in broad daylight near police headquarters at the San Francisco Hall of Justice. Three officers were shot and eight Panthers arrested. Bobby Seale believed the instigator was a provocateur. The Party's central committee refused to bail out the suspected government agent.

Huey soon learned that Cleaver was making plans to barricade himself and supporters inside an Oakland building to precipitate a final bloody confrontation with local police just before Thanksgiving. Cleaver had two goals: to avenge Bobby Hutton's death, and to go down in a blaze of glory. The gun battle he had precipitated back in April had enthralled him with a temporary sense of freedom he longed to feel again.

Outsiders who lumped Cleaver and Newton together as radical firebrands did not appreciate — or understand — the complexity of their relationship. After his arrest in 1967, Huey professed his innocence in court. Yet, much to the Newton family's dismay, Huey had no problem with Cleaver applauding the death of Officer Frey as Huey's bold first step toward revolution.

Huey also gave Cleaver and Cox the green light to have the Panthers storm the courthouse to try to break him out if the jury convicted him of first-degree murder. But the two activists had developed very different strategies by the spring of 1968. Cleaver was thrilled to have instigated a shootout in April with the Oakland police. In doing so, he had defied Newton's orders to stand down and avoid confrontations with the cops. Even as the Panthers publicly accused the police of Bobby Hutton's murder, privately Huey blamed Cleaver for setting in motion the circumstances leading to Hutton's death.

As an immediate strategy, Huey favored strengthening political coalitions and community-building through free breakfasts and health clinics. Cleaver was far more impatient for the revolution to begin. With Governor Reagan and the FBI laser-focused on eradicating the Party, Huey felt that Cleaver was playing right into their hands.

Above all, Huey wished to avoid sacrificing the lives of many more recruits like Bobby Hutton for no good reason. Huey rejected Cleaver's plan to commit suicide by cop and take other Panthers with him. Huey sent orders back via his attorneys for Cleaver to flee the country, head for Cuba, and recruit new international members to the Panther Party. This time, Cleaver did as he was told. He was supposed to give one final lecture at U.C. Berkeley but failed to show up. Much to the embarrassment of his FBI tail, a frantic search came up empty. Disguised as a member of a mime troupe, Cleaver escaped through Canada and turned up in Cuba. Months later he showed up in Algeria, joined there by his very pregnant wife Kathleen.

In November 1968, San Francisco State College erupted in turmoil in what became the first and longest campus strike in American history. Aggressive lobbying for an African-American Studies Department and for the hiring of more Black faculty members had taken a violent turn a year earlier. Some Panther followers physically attacked editors of the campus paper for opposing demands for ethnic studies. Several students were suspended as a result of that confrontation.

In the fall of 1968, renewed protests followed the abrupt suspension of Black Panther Minister of Education George Mason Murray from the adjunct faculty of San Francisco State's English Department. The State College Board of Trustees learned that Murray had stirred up Black students at a rally on another campus with an express call for armed revolt. That resulted in his swift dismissal from the faculty.

Huey grew concerned about state and federal authorities targeting the Panthers. The Panthers also risked violent interactions with a rival organization in Los Angeles,"US" headed by Ron Karenga, who also hailed from Oakland. Fay Stender told Huey on a trip she made to the prison in January of 1969 that two US members had just ambushed and killed Los Angeles Panther branch leaders Bunchy Carter and John Huggins. They were gunned down as they were leaving a meeting with students on the UCLA campus.

Stender rightly suspected the attack was instigated by the FBI. It would later become public that the FBI had secretly instituted a Counterintelligence Program ("COINTELPRO") working hand-in-glove with state special forces. An FBI agent in Los Angeles secretly took credit for prompting the assassinations by sending fake threats to US that purported to come from the Panthers. J. Edgar Hoover promoted the agent for his successful efforts.

While San Francisco State remained in turmoil, similar strikes and sit-ins erupted in 1969 at 300 college campuses across the country. Most of them focused on opposition to the Vietnam War. The escalating student unrest occurred at the same time as unprecedented attempts by the Weathermen and other militants to stop the nation's business as usual by bombing buildings and hijacking airplanes.

In the spring of 1969, Fay Stender likely told Huey about Charles Garry's amazing success defending the Oakland Seven trial that March. The defendants were seven leaders of the mass protest at the Induction Center in mid-October of 1967. Garry was the lead defense attorney, pitted once more against Lowell Jensen.

The judge was George Phillips, the same judge who had issued the landmark ruling declaring a mistrial the summer before because the prosecutor had dismissed all potential Black jurors. Even though all of the Oakland Seven were White, Charlie Garry figured out how to inject race issues into the jury selection. He argued that jurors might be biased against the defendants for opposing a racist draft for the Vietnam War.

When it came time to put on the Oakland Seven's defense, Garry pulled a major surprise on prosecutor Lowell Jensen. Garry called a Stanford University physicist to the stand who admitted he had organized rallies on his campus for the October 1967 Stop the Draft Week. He circulated flyers and coordinated busloads of demonstrators headed for the Oakland Induction Center. The physicist had never been prosecuted or even, to his knowledge, investigated. The defense team then abruptly rested their case without calling any of their clients to the stand. Garry later said that Jensen's jaw dropped. "He looked as if someone had just poured ice water over his head."

While the jury was out, Garry entertained reporters and defense supporters by standing on his head in the courtroom. It was a stunt he often performed at parties.

After three days of deliberation, the jury returned with acquittals of all seven protest leaders. During an interview of Garry by a local reporter, one of his clients asked Garry if he considered himself as good as the fictional Perry Mason. Garry quipped in reply, "I'm *better* than Perry Mason. *All* of his clients are innocent."

Huey had to have heard other news that spring that would have made him wish he was back in Oakland. Students at Oakland City College hosted a national conference aimed at converting the campus into an all-Black college renamed for him. The effort proved unsuccessful, as did student efforts to keep the campus in North Oakland. A long-planned move to a larger site in the Oakland hills went forward with the campus renamed Merritt College.

The relocation made for a difficult commute from North Oakland and caused student involvement in extracurricular activities to plummet. It seemed obvious this was by design. By "resituating the college in a white part of town" administrators hoped it would curtail "some of the social movements, most notably the Black Panther Party, with which Grove Street had close ties." Yet Merritt College did establish the nation's first ethnic studies department with Melvin Newton as its head. (The Black Student Union would later dedicate the campus student center as the Huey P. Newton Student Lounge. It was adorned with a painting of Huey on the wicker throne donated by Melvin, who was then Chair of the Ethnic Studies Department. The school would ultimately adopt the panther as its mascot).

The spring of 1969 quickly grew even more tense. In late May, Huey must have been stunned to hear from Fay

Stender that her hometown of Berkeley had just been placed under martial law. That was Governor Reagan's response after veterans of the Free Speech Movement took possession of university property near Telegraph Avenue on the south side of the campus. The activists planted trees and shrubbery to establish "People's Park." Reagan considered their defiant action a Communist threat. He vowed: "If there has to be a bloodbath, then let's get it over with. No more appeasement."

On May 15, 1969, 250 highway patrol and police officers uprooted the recent plantings and installed a chain-link fence around the property. Thousands of students who had gathered for an unrelated rally that day headed to People's Park to confront the police. A mêlée ensued. The police shot thirty people, killed one, and blinded a bystander. Many others sustained injuries. A large number of activists were arrested and hauled off to jail. That was when Governor Reagan declared martial law in Berkeley, bringing in the National Guard to enforce a curfew. For the next few weeks, helicopters circled the city. Officers were prepared to spray tear gas on any Berkeley residents who assembled.

Historians started describing the situation in 1969 as the worst violence since the Red Summer of 1919. In late June, *TIME* magazine predicted "Guerrilla Summer." The administration feared the role the Panthers could play in that tense environment. President Nixon's new Attorney General, John Mitchell, created a special unit just for Panther prosecutions.

Meanwhile, Huey reassessed the Party's priorities. He wanted to dispel the Panthers' image as "trigger-happy, gun-toting thugs." He directed David Hilliard to focus on expanding community programs. In Oakland and Los Angeles, the Panthers fed thousands of children daily. Assembly Speaker Jesse Unruh (author of the state's pioneering 1959 Civil Rights Act) soon credited the Panthers with serving more meals to needy youngsters than the government was doing. In the process, the Panthers built mainstream political alliances and lured large numbers of new recruits. Some proved to be informants.

J. Edgar Hoover saw the Panther breakfast program as "potentially the greatest threat to efforts by authorities to neutralize the BPP and destroy what it stands for." Hoover encouraged FBI branch offices to interfere with Panther programs any way they could. They ignored concerns about the legality of their actions. Panthers in cities across the country faced more frequent arrests on flimsy charges that were later dismissed. Their office equipment was destroyed; their food supplies were thrown away; their newspapers confiscated and tossed in trash bins.

A commentator for the country's oldest weekly news journal, *The Nation*, condemned the FBI's actions. He wrote: "Panther arrests with charges later dropped, and bail in the millions, constitute an unprecedented national scandal which beggars the fifties." He quoted author and educator Donald Freed: "If what is being perpetrated against the Black Panther Party was being done to any White group, including the Nazi Party, the liberal establishment — from the ACLU to *The New York Times* — would absolutely refuse to tolerate it further."

Several years later, a Senate investigation of "The FBI's Covert Action Program to Destroy the Black Panther Party" would document its extensive misconduct. It chronicled how the FBI had disrupted delivery of

Panther newspapers, trashed the Party's branch offices, spread malicious false rumors, and sent forged letters and anonymous threats to instigate retaliatory killings by rival organizations. (That included the assassination of Bunchy Carter and John Huggins).

The Panthers continued to participate in campus protests against the Vietnam War where "Free Huey" signs and buttons seemed as ubiquitous as "End the War" and "We Won't Go." In the fall of 1969, the center of attention became the Chicago Eight trial where the defense would seek to put the Vietnam War itself on trial. Bobby Seale was the only Black among the eight defendants. Yet Seale had only played a minor role in the protests as a last-minute substitute speaker. When a journalist asked a Department of Justice official what prompted the government to prosecute Seale, the official responded frankly, "The Panthers are a bunch of hoodlums, and we have to get this guy."

Fay Stender kept close tabs on the Chicago prosecution and kept Huey up to speed on its progress. Charles Garry was Seale's lawyer of choice but was scheduled for surgery. After Garry's motion for a short delay of the trial's start was denied, Seale insisted on representing himself.

The Chicago Eight Trial would indeed live up to its reputation as the "most incredible trial in American history" — a symbolic battle between the political establishment and the entire anti-war movement.

Early in the trial the presiding federal judge, Julius Hoffman, lost his temper at Seale, who repeatedly called the judge a "fascist dog," a "pig" and a "blatant racist." To the shock of Liberals and Leftists across the country, Judge Hoffman ordered Seale bound and gagged.

Strapped to his chair with his mouth bound up tight, Seale became an instant symbol of a broken criminal justice system. Seale's case wound up separated from the prosecution of the White activists, who became known thereafter as "the Chicago Seven."

Bobby Seale was extradited to Connecticut on charges of conspiring to murder suspected FBI informant Alex Rackley. His co-defendant was Ericka Huggins. She had become a leader of the New Haven Panthers after the assassination of her husband in Los Angeles. Other local members of the party had confessed to torturing and executing Rackley. Yet charging Seale as a co-conspirator was a stretch. Though New Haven's Police Chief would not say so publicly until much later, he believed the police had "no solid evidence" to link Bobby Seale to Alex Rackley's murder. He was "astonished" when Seale was indicted by prosecutor Arnold Markle. The prosecution of Seale fit FBI Chief Hoover's agenda: to do everything possible to kill off the "Free Huey" movement so there would be no Party left if Huey ever got out of prison.

Meanwhile, through the prison grapevine, Huey heard of a militant maximum-security prisoner at Soledad named George Jackson, who showed interest in joining the Panther Party. Jackson was serving a lengthy indeterminate sentence for participating in a $70 gas station robbery as a teenager. Jackson's application for parole had repeatedly been denied. Huey asked Fay Stender to consider taking Jackson on as a client to seek his release. George Jackson would become Stender's second revolutionary cause célèbre.

As 1969 drew to a close, the nation remained bitterly divided over the Vietnam War. In mid-November hundreds of thousands of protesters gathered in Washington, D.C., to demand that America pull out of Vietnam. A similar rally drew a quarter of a million peaceniks to Golden Gate Park in San Francisco. Panther Chief of Staff David Hilliard was among the speakers. At the time, he was the highest-ranking Panther not in prison or self-imposed exile. Hilliard used the microphone to announce a brazen Panther Party proposal: that Eldridge Cleaver be authorized to negotiate with the Viet Cong for the exchange of POWs for Bobby Seale, Huey Newton and other Panthers.

Hilliard used the podium to lambast American society as fascist. He cursed President Nixon as an evil "motherfucker" who sent his "vicious murderous dogs" out to destroy the Black Panther Party children's breakfast programs. Hilliard boldly announced, "We will kill Richard Nixon." Not surprisingly, that got him arrested for threatening the President's life.

Hoover was far from through in making sure the Party remained leaderless. In early December 1969, he dramatically escalated the government campaign against the Panther Party. In cooperation with the FBI, Chicago police orchestrated a predawn lethal raid on the apartment of Chicago Panther leader Fred Hampton. They had first secured the secret assistance of Hampton's own bodyguard.

The FBI feared Hampton had potential to become the next Black Messiah after the late Reverend Martin Luther King. They murdered Hampton in his bed, killed twenty-two-year-old Panther Mark Clark, and wounded four other Panthers. Four days later, the Los Angeles police conducted another predawn raid on the Panthers' local headquarters and seriously wounded three members.

Charles Garry forestalled a similar raid in Oakland by immediately calling a press conference where he charged that the Panthers were being targeted for annihilation. No public information had as yet leaked about the existence of COINTELPRO. Most Americans could not believe that the FBI Chief and the Nixon administration would go to such extremes. Fay Stender talked San Francisco Lawyers Guild members into spending a couple of nights at Panther Party headquarters in Oakland. No raid followed.

Five thousand people from across the nation attended Fred Hampton's funeral in December 1969 to hear Reverend Jesse Jackson proclaim, "When Fred was shot in Chicago, Black people in particular, and decent people in general, bled everywhere." Worldwide support for the Panthers grew as Party members were increasingly seen as victims of repression.

David Hilliard helped gain Panther admirers by arranging for a new recruit from Los Angeles, singer/songwriter Elaine Brown, to record a Panther-themed album in Motown. Huey played "Seize the Time" over and over in prison but would not meet Elaine Brown until his release. He had to be immensely pleased when an April 1970 poll indicated that a quarter of Blacks held the Black Panthers in high regard, including 43 percent of those under twenty-one.

Between his arrest for the Chicago Conspiracy trial and his trial in New Haven Seale had used much of his time in jail dictating *Seize the Time: The History of the Black Panther Party and Huey Newton*. By then, the Party had been in the headlines for two years. One freelance reporter noted that the Panthers were "deeply revered in colonial and liberated, formerly colonial countries; Eldridge Cleaver is a household word, and the names Huey Newton and Bobby Seale are familiar in homes from coast to coast." *Newsweek* ran a cover story with a picture of Panthers David Hilliard, Elbert "Big Man" Howard and D. C. Cox standing in front of a poster of Bobby Seale. The photo was designed to make them look menacing.

The air of menace had escalated just as Fay Stender arranged to meet inmate George Jackson in late January of 1970. On her arrival, she discovered that Jackson and two other inmates had just been accused of murdering a guard. Instead of seeking Jackson's parole, she found herself taking on another high-profile death penalty case. She teamed up with three other lawyers to defend the Soledad Brothers.

In the lead up to the trial she arranged for the publication of Jackson's edited letters, *Soledad Brother: The Prison Letters of George Jackson*. It became an international bestseller. For the next several months, Stender would have to go back and forth between her intensive pretrial work and publicity campaign for the Soledad Brothers and her ongoing efforts to get Huey out of jail.

Winning Reversal on Appeal

CHARLES GARRY was able to recover from surgery in time to appear with Stender before the Court of Appeal in San Francisco to argue for Huey's freedom. The oral argument took place in mid-February of 1970 preceded by a three-hour "Free Huey" rally at the adjacent Civic Center. Nearly a hundred of the attendees accompanied the lawyers into the appellate courthouse to watch the oral argument. They assumed it would be unsuccessful.

Garry knew that, in general, the chances of reversal were punishingly small — roughly one percent. Yet Stender and Garry emerged surprisingly optimistic after being questioned by a three-judge panel. Yet a week later, a heavily promoted birthday benefit intended to defray the costs of Huey's appeal drew sparse attendance. That was in sharp contrast to the birthday celebrations in February 1969, held in several major cities. Those had drawn large crowds to hear a taped message from Huey that his lawyers smuggled out of prison. By the spring of 1970, Leftists were far more focused on the escalating war than on springing Huey from jail.

On April 30, 1970, President Nixon stunned the nation with the announcement that he had ordered bombing in Cambodia. The news touched off more student strikes and flag-burnings across the country. Nixon's announcement coincided with a large May Day gathering in New Haven, which was carried out in protest of the upcoming Seale/Huggins trial. A large number of civil rights advocates — including future First Lady, Senator and presidential candidate Hillary Rodham — became concerned the Panthers were being systematically deprived of their rights. Rodham helped found the Yale Law School *Review of Law and Social Action,* which devoted an entire issue to constitutional issues raised in cases involving the Panthers.

Just days after the protest at Yale, at Kent State in Ohio, National Guardsmen killed four unarmed White students and wounded nine others. The deadly incident occurred during a campus protest against President Nixon's recent escalation of the Vietnam War. The Kent State massacre galvanized far more campus strikes involving up to eight million students. The shootings at Kent State have since been credited as a turning point in the anti-war movement nationwide. A mere two weeks later, at Jackson State in Mississippi, another lethal police response resulted in the deaths of two Black students and the wounding of twelve others. This further fueled student anger.

The Panthers and other Black activists were particularly incensed because the Kent State massacre of White students in May drew far more national attention than equally shocking police violence in February 1968 in Orangeburg, South Carolina. A group of officers, responding to a protest challenging racial segregation at a local bowling alley, had opened fire on demonstrators. They left three students dead and nearly 30 wounded. This was the first reported case of police gunning down student protestors. As the Black Panthers noted, that tragedy did not receive anything close to the press coverage given to the Ohio State killings. The Panthers realized that was because the Orangeburg victims were all Black. (The State of South Carolina did not issue a formal apology for the Orangeburg Massacre until 2001.)

Perhaps it was because of the escalating protests in the spring of 1970 that the California Court of Appeal took extra care in reviewing all the alleged errors in Huey Newton's trial. Surely, they understood the historic setting of their decision. By late May, word leaked out that the court had written a lengthy opinion that would be released shortly. Fay Stender and Alex Hoffmann sent word to Huey. The two lawyers could not agree on whether a long opinion was cause for concern.

Stender panicked and feared the worst, worrying that a detailed explanation would include rejections of every argument she had made on Huey's behalf. Instead, she was in for a most gratifying surprise. On May 29, 1970, the appellate court issued its unanimous 51-page decision reversing Newton's conviction. This shocking result was one of the supreme highlights in Stender's career as a lawyer. The startling news spread immediately. Reporters tried to contact Huey by telephone for his reaction, but prison officials refused to bring him out of his cell. Still, the jubilation in the cells and corridors of the Men's Colony was palpable. Those in the prison yard erupted in glee, while most of the country reacted with astonishment.

Stender and the defense team prevailed because of three critical errors. One was Judge Friedman's failure to point out to the jury the correction of the taped statement of eyewitness Henry Grier that he "didn't" get a good look at the perpetrator. A second assigned error was that the judge allowed Jensen to read kidnap victim Dell Ross's damaging grand jury testimony in the presence of the jury. Since that testimony was then struck from evidence, the Court of Appeal ruled the jury should not have heard it in the first place.

Most significantly, the Court of Appeal faulted the judge for not giving jurors the option of acquitting Huey. All three appellate justices agreed: "Although the evidence of the fatal affray is both conflicting and confused as to who shot whom and when, some of it supported the inference that the defendant had been shot in the abdomen before he fired any shots himself."

The jury was presented with expert testimony that Newton's grievous injuries might have left him unconscious of his actions. The appellate court reasoned that the judge should have allowed the jurors to consider both the "diminished capacity" and unconsciousness defense.

As a result, Huey was granted a new trial for manslaughter. The stunned prosecution team immediately sought further review by the California Supreme Court, but their request was denied. Huey was then scheduled for release from custody following a bail hearing on August 5, 1970. This announcement was beyond most people's imagination.

In his first interview, Huey credited the reversal in large part to "the pressure the people brought to bear on the case, as well as the work of my attorneys Charles Garry and Fay Stender." In early July of 1970, a month before Huey's scheduled release, Garry and Stender arranged for best-selling author Mark Lane to conduct Huey's last interview in prison. Their goal was to publicize fears for Huey's life at the hands of state or federal agents following his release. They wanted to prevent Huey from sharing the gruesome fate of Chicago Panther leader Fred Hampton.

Huey's family reacted with elation at the reversal of his conviction, but Melvin and his father were among those who worried about what would come afterward. Huey's supporters had succeeded in their mission. Now, Huey's loved ones could only wonder if the Black Panther leader could stay safe from the vengeance of his enemies and his own worst impulses.

Huey Walks Free

HUEY'S attorneys were justified in believing their client's life would be at risk the moment he stepped out of jail. Huey had long since expected to die before he was thirty. At the time of his release, several key Black Panthers leaders were squarely in the sights of law enforcement officers, Huey Newton among them.

Well before dawn on the morning of August 3rd, guards at the Men's Colony turned Huey over to two Alameda County sheriff's deputies. They drove him shackled hand and foot in the back seat of an unmarked car as they proceeded up the coast to the Alameda County jail. Huey's bail hearing was set for 9 a.m. On August 5th two thousand Panther supporters gathered around the Alameda County courthouse early that morning yelling, "We want Huey! Where's Huey? Free Huey!"

This time, Lowell Jensen conceded that Newton had an obvious right to bail since the only pending charge was voluntary manslaughter. Judge Harold Hove set the bail at $50,000. He ordered Huey returned to a 10th floor cell until the money arrived. It only took a few hours. Melvin and Sonny Man joined David Hilliard and his wife Pat, Panther branch leader Elmer "Geronimo" Pratt, and a couple of other Panthers to greet Huey inside the courthouse. They cleared the way for Huey to get past the cameramen and the mass of reporters yelling questions at him.

When the crowd spied their hero exiting the building, they yelled, "Huey's Free! Huey's Free!" Leola, Doris and Myrtle ran up to embrace their youngest brother. Charles Garry stood nearby with Fay Stender and Alex Hoffmann.

The group were swamped with reporters seeking comments from Garry.

Television cameras covered the event so some of the Newton extended family were able to watch the spectacle on TV. Huey's entourage kept the crowd from mobbing him as Huey, David Hilliard and Elmo "Geronimo" Pratt climbed on top of Alex Hoffmann's Volkswagen Beetle. Its roof partially caved in under their weight. Huey shouted, "Right on! Right on! Power to the people!" He punctuated his chant with repeated Panther salutes. Then, to avoid fainting in the heat, he stripped off his khaki shirt. He urged the crowd to support efforts to free the Soledad Brothers and Bobby Seale.

Hilliard was exuberant: "It was one of the greatest days of our life. We were victorious. It was a beautiful day. Two thousand people in the streets of Oakland saying, 'Free Huey or the sky is the limit.' Here this guy comes walking out of the court, the door. A great victory. . . . It was a very powerful moment I will never forget."

Huey wanted to go home but his siblings told him it would be too much of a shock for their father. Recently, Walter had become unable to handle highly emotional situations. Armelia was then in the hospital and had not been told of Huey's release. First, Huey went to Elsa Knight Thompson's home in Berkeley to change out of his prison clothes. He then headed to a press conference at Charles Garry's office in San Francisco, crowded mostly with giddy representatives from the underground press.

Afterward, Huey headed straight to the hospital for a joyous reunion with his mother. Later, he got to see his father, who was deeply moved and wept. Huey was immensely grateful for all of their emotional support for the nearly two years he spent at the Men's Colony. He was deeply aware that his own strength derived from the pride his father had instilled in him and the fierce love of his entire family.

ROOTS OF A REVOLUTIONARY SUICIDE 389

Huey hugging Doris after his release from prison at the Alameda County Courthouse, August 5, 1970

X.

Frayed Relationships

Resuming Life on the Outside

WHILE a growing rift was slowly emerging among Black militants, Huey's star was rising among Leftists. The *San Francisco Examiner* noted that the Left now regarded him as "something of a folk hero." Huey's appeal to the younger generation was obviously quite broad, bolstered by celebrities like singer Harry Belafonte, comedian Dick Gregory, film stars Jane Fonda, Marlon Brando, Donald Sutherland and others who championed civil rights. Many curiosity seekers among the general public viewed Huey as a rock star. His attorneys already had Huey booked to appear on *Face the Nation*. David Hilliard had previously been featured on that program following the government raids on the Chicago and Los Angeles Panther branches.

Fay Stender had already made Huey aware of his celebrity status. He relished his growing political platform. His tone became more confrontational and defiant. At the press conference on the day of his release, Huey threatened unspecified consequences if political prisoners were not freed. When asked for clarification, he did not rule out military action and warned that "the struggle is coming to a final climax."

Yet privately, beneath all the bluster, Huey understood, unlike Eldridge Cleaver, that the timing was not right for insurrection — if it ever would be. Like Bobby Seale, Huey feared that many of the Panthers would be headed for slaughter — suicide by cop — or prison if they did not first build enough community support. Huey took a tour of the new Panther headquarters in West Oakland

and walked his old neighborhood, exchanging salutes with the crowds who turned out to greet him. He now had a major decision to make.

Earlier that summer, the Soledad Brothers had been transferred to maximum security in San Quentin prison in Marin County, awaiting their upcoming murder trial in San Francisco. In an unprecedented victory, Fay Stender and her co-counsel convinced the judge in Monterey County to transfer the death penalty trial from conservative Salinas to San Francisco — the first change of venue for a criminal case ever granted in the county's history.

While Jackson was still in Soledad prison in Monterey County, Huey had welcomed him to the Black Panther Party. Ties had quickly formed between supporters of the Soledad Brothers and the Panthers. Stender's success for the Soledad Brothers following on the heels of the surprising reversal of Huey's conviction rocketed Stender to international fame. She was now regarded as the go-to defense lawyer for radical defendants.

Yet Jackson did not expect to avoid the death penalty even in the more liberal venue of San Francisco. He was proud of killing a guard in retaliation for the recent deaths of radical Black inmates at Soledad at the hands of a sharpshooting guard. Jackson confided in a member of his defense team that he had acted alone in murdering the guard and could not see himself meekly sitting through trial while his lawyers defended his innocence. Instead, Jackson was plotting to escape from San Quentin by arranging for a forced exchange of himself and the other two Soledad Brothers for highly-valued hostages. The plan involved Panther support that had been in the works while Huey was in prison.

When Huey gained his own release in August 1970, he quickly learned that Los Angeles Panthers Geronimo Pratt and his men were intending to meet up with Jackson's younger brother Jonathan at the Marin Civic Center and seize a judge, prosecutor and several jurors as hostages. Pratt had served two tours in Vietnam and emerged highly skilled in military maneuvers. He was a prized asset for the conspirators. The plan also included a second group of Panthers who would head to San Francisco Airport and commandeer a plane to fly the hostages to Algiers so Eldridge Cleaver could barter their lives for the release of the Soledad Brothers.

The night of Huey's release, the Panthers celebrated Huey's freedom with a party. George Jackson's younger brother Jonathan came to seek Huey's support for the hostage-taking planned for August 7th at the Marin County Courthouse where an inmate of San Quentin was on trial. But Huey smelled a set-up and refused to have the Panthers participate. He instructed all the Panthers who had been preparing to join in the scheme to lie low. But Huey's orders did not prevent Jonathan from going ahead anyway to try to save his brother from likely execution.

Packing guns they had smuggled into the Marin County Courthouse, Jonathan and his cohorts took over the shocked courtroom where the trial of the San Quentin inmate was underway. With the help of two other inmates who were waiting to testify, the group tied up and kidnapped the trial judge, prosecutor and three jurors. The kidnappers loaded the hostages in a bright yellow rental van parked in the driveway. They expected to be highly visible as they headed to the airport. They assumed that the value of the lives of their hostages would protect them as they sought to make their getaway.

The conspirators had no idea there were scores of lawmen hiding in the bushes of the courthouse driveway who had no qualms about risking hostage deaths in a gun battle. Moments later, rifle shots blasted into the rented van, cutting down Jackson and two of the other kidnappers. The judge already had a shotgun tied to his body. He also died. Others were wounded, including the prosecutor and one of the jurors.

In the wake of this carnage, mourners held two memorials, showing a stark racial divide. One ceremony was held in Marin County where an overwhelmingly White group of mourners, including officials and community members, crowded into the pews to honor the memory of Judge Harold Haley. Meanwhile, Jonathan Jackson's funeral at St. Augustine's Episcopal Church in Oakland drew a large gathering of Blacks, including militants.

At the Jackson family's request, Huey gave a eulogy honoring the teenager's courage. Not everyone in the crowd was impressed. There were whispers among the Jackson family that Huey was responsible for the bloodbath because he'd called off Panther support for Jonathan's risky plan. Huey at the time was staying temporarily in the two-bedroom home in Berkeley that his lawyer Alex Hoffmann shared with KPFA radio's Elsa Knight Thompson. Everyone came and went under the watchful eyes of plainclothes officers. Obviously phony telephone repairmen perched for four days straight on a pole across the street from the Berkeley apartment, keeping tabs on Huey.

Soon, Huey gave a political speech that the Panthers assumed would contain a fiery call to action. Instead, he took a surprisingly different tack, delivering a lengthy lecture about the steps needed to establish a revolutionary "intercommunal framework" for socialism to thrive.

That speech reflected Huey's persistent concern that the Panthers had developed no actual plan for a successful insurrection. Black activists would have to work to build consensus. Huey envisioned the need for building far more support beyond the United States in all societies across the world where Black people were being oppressed by White power structures. That is why Huey used the term "intercommunalism" to link similar oppressed communities around the globe. He avoided calling for an "international" framework for revolution because that would recognize the legitimacy of racist nations in which most of those oppressed communities lived. But Huey could tell right away that the tone of his preachy talk — a noted departure from his crowd-pleasing revolutionary rhetoric — was not well-received.

The tepid reception did not dampen Huey's ambitions for the Black Panther Party. By prearrangement, he left for the East Coast to visit Bobby Seale in a New Haven jail; to meet Panthers in several new branches that opened while he was imprisoned; to consider relocating the Party's headquarters to New York City or Atlanta; and to promote his new ideas for the Party's future.

While Huey was still in prison he reluctantly allowed David Hilliard and Eldridge Cleaver to initiate plans for a Revolutionary People's Constitutional Convention in Philadelphia that coming December. But Huey quickly decided to put the brakes on their ambitious proposal. Moving from Oakland did not appeal to him, especially since he did not know how many informers would be waiting for him among the branch members. On his return in September, Huey opted to keep his Party's base where it started.

This time, Huey took extra precautions after returning to his hometown. For safety's sake, in October, Huey moved into a penthouse apartment overlooking Oakland's Lake Merritt, paid for by movie producer Bert Schneider. At the time, the FBI kept close track of Hollywood stars who contributed to Huey and the Panthers. The FBI then made the donors targets of COINTELPRO themselves. Among them was actress Jane Fonda, then a leading antiwar activist, whom the Nixon administration dubbed "Hanoi Jane" for openly supporting the Viet Cong.

The sparsely furnished but elegant accommodations on the twenty-fifth floor of 1200 Lakeshore on the south edge of Lake Merritt came with a doorman and space for a car in an enclosed garage. Under the watchful eyes of COINTELPRO, and wary of new recruits who might be government moles, Huey took comfort in the security it offered. Huey began living it up. His drinking, womanizing and drug use worried David Hilliard. Huey's lawyer Fay Stender warned him that many Panther supporters were dismayed by his new lifestyle. The *San Francisco Examiner* soon ran an article describing the luxurious new apartment as a sign of Huey's abandonment of his people. Though the FBI had planted that newspaper story, it was true that he was beginning to alienate followers by moving to a penthouse.

Hilliard wanted Huey to concentrate on completing the revolutionary writings that he started in prison. He introduced Huey to 19-year-old Party member Gwen Fountaine, an attractive young mother with secretarial skills. Soon, Gwen moved in with Huey in the penthouse.

Although Huey was living with Gwen, he soon had another new love interest in Elaine Brown, whose talents as a singer-songwriter had delighted him in prison. Elaine had been one of Eldridge Cleaver's early recruits in the spring of 1968 to the Los Angeles branch of the Party. By the fall of 1970, the Party had already adopted as its anthem a song Elaine had written for Eldridge.

Huey first got the chance to meet Elaine in person in New York a month after his release from the Men's Colony. Elaine had just returned from joining Eldridge and Kathleen Cleaver on a Panther goodwill tour to Communist countries. They had traveled from Paris to Russia, North Korea, North Vietnam, Red China and Cleaver's headquarters in Algiers. After heading back to New York, Elaine moved to Oakland and became one of Huey's closest Panther associates.

At the penthouse, the second bedroom became Huey's office. Gwen's two small children, Ronnie, age five, and his younger sister Jessica, stayed in a house the Panthers had established nearby for raising children of Party members. The children spent a lot of time as well at the penthouse, and on outings with their mother and Huey.

The penthouse, as it turned out, was far from immune from government spying. By November, with the landlord's permission, J. Edgar Hoover had Huey's penthouse bugged. Agents who had taken over an adjacent apartment were able to record what was said. The Panthers already knew that the FBI was wire-tapping their headquarters and other Party members' and supporters' homes. By the fall of 1970, the FBI and state police had many informers infiltrating the Party, some of whom the

Panthers discovered and some they did not. Huey trusted few Panthers he had never met before. Invitees to the penthouse received instructions to take the elevator to the 24th floor, walk up one flight, and use a special knock to be admitted.

Someone gave Huey a high-powered, standing telescope he kept in his living room. He kept it pointed north across Lake Merritt, where Huey focused his gaze at the window of his isolation cell on the tenth floor of the Alameda County Courthouse.

Back in July 1970, on the eve of his release from the Men's Colony, Huey had told author Mark Lane in an interview that people outside of jail were also prisoners, but under minimum instead of maximum security. But now, Huey could not stop looking at the cell he had occupied before his trial. Garry's co-counsel Alex Hoffmann, who had become close to Huey during and after the trial, asked if he missed being isolated. Huey admitted that he was having problems adjusting: life had been so much simpler when he was inside.

Catching Up with Family

WHILE the Panthers were starting to criticize Huey for his lifestyle choices, his family was coping with an especially painful loss. A couple of weeks after Huey was freed, Armelia and her sister Jessie got word that their mother had died back in Monroe. Both of the twins had died years earlier. The news of Mama Stella's death hit Jessie hard and devastated Armelia, who started to scream. The family physician, Dr. Barton, had to give her a sedative to calm her down. Meanwhile, some of Huey's family members in Oakland decided to connect with the relatives they left behind. Now that Newton was free at last he was no longer the center of the family's constant and worried attention. They felt it was time to make travel plans.

It may have been Mama Stella's death that prompted Myrtle's daughter Patricia to look up her other grandmother in Chicago. Patricia was not sure if she met Alice once as a small child. She had no memory of it. Walter had kept in touch with his mother, who was now widowed again, and visited her once in the 1950s. Doris and Glen Godfrey and their three children also took a road trip to Chicago in the early 1950s to visit Alice. Their daughter Debra was only about two or three and recalls how nice Alice was to them. The Godfreys undoubtedly had shared the highlights of that trip with Patricia and Myrtle.

When Patricia planned her trip to Chicago in 1970, she decided not to contact Alice in advance. Instead, she just showed up on her doorstep. Alice was in her eighties by then and still retained her petite figure. As soon as she saw Patricia, Alice grinned with joy and told her granddaughter, "I knew you were coming." Extended family meant as much to her as to Muzz. A year or two later, Melvin's girlfriend Barbarette also made a trip to Chicago and dropped by Alice's house to meet her. That turned out to be shortly before Alice Carter died in February 1973.

Sometime in the fall of 1970, Armelia decided on a trip to Detroit with her sister Jessie to visit Jessie's daughter Ruby Jewel and her son Michael. The impetus for the trip was a different mission that Armelia felt she needed to accomplish. She had learned that David Harper, the foreman of Huey's jury, had quit his job at the Bank of America in San Francisco in 1969 and moved with his wife and family to Detroit. Harper had since become a leader in the local Black community. Inspired by Huey's courtroom lecture, Harper had used his contacts in Washington, D. C., to coordinate creation of a community bank to help Detroit recover from devastating riots in the summer of 1967. For his role in Detroit's recovery, Harper was honored by the city with "David Harper Day."

Maybe it was Ruby Jewel or Walter's stepbrother E.S. Newton who got word back to Armelia and Walter about David Harper's newfound celebrity status. By then, E.S. was living in Detroit with his second wife. Between the two of them they had eleven children.

Armelia talked Leola into coming along to personally thank Harper for saving Huey's life. Leola brought her youngest daughter DeAngela Terrez along on the trip, the first plane ride of the four-year-old's life. Harper was deeply moved by Armelia's gratitude. Harper told her what he told reporter Gilbert Moore when he came to Detroit to interview Harper for Moore's book on the trial. Harper had wanted to achieve justice, and he felt that was exactly what the jury accomplished under his leadership.

***

Huey was eager to reconnect with loved ones now that he was free. Back living in Oakland that fall of 1970, Huey quickly became a favorite of his nieces and nephews. Huey enjoyed inviting Melvin's young son Gregory, who was five in 1970, over to the penthouse to stay for dinner with Gwen's children Ronnie and Jessica. A few times Melvin and Barbarette came with her son Maurice as well. Maurice recalls being impressed with the white, elegantly furnished apartment, and with its amazing view. It was not a place a kid could feel at home, but it made him feel special to visit Uncle Huey there. For Huey, spending time with the young family members may have reminded him of the fun he and Melvin had as young children. Yet Huey remained alert to the fact he was living under constant FBI surveillance. One day his wife Gwen and Doris's daughter Debra actually surprised FBI agents inside the penthouse apartment.

Huey quickly absorbed the extent to which his family had become divided while he was in prison over Melvin's separation from his wife Joyce. Armelia made clear how unhappy this made her. She, like most of the family, was crazy about Joyce. His sisters Myrtle and Doris joined their mother in blaming Melvin and Barbarette for the bitter break-up of his marriage. The family remained unaware that Joyce and Melvin's relationship had become rocky years before he met Barbarette.

When the contested divorce became final, Joyce obtained a house Melvin had bought during their separation on Benvenue Avenue in Berkeley, near the northern border of Oakland. Their two young children, Gregory and Tracy, stayed with Joyce. By design, the area where they lived off College Avenue was almost exclusively occupied by White families. It had originally been kept that way through racially restrictive covenants that the Supreme Court declared illegal in 1948. Melvin only acquired it through the efforts of a sympathetic White realtor. Just one other Black family lived in that neighborhood at the time.

The only Black neighbors the children knew when they were growing up were the family of Judge Henry Ramsey, Jr. who had six children. Gregory often played with two of the boys. (Judge Ramsey, a former professor of criminal law at U.C. Berkeley, was known as a warrior for justice. He later became Dean of Howard University's Law School. His son Ismail ("Izzy") Ramsey served as U.S. Attorney for the Northern District of California from March 2023 to February 2025.

The house on Benvenue was just over two miles from Walter and Armelia's home on 47th Street in North Oakland. Joyce maintained close ties with her parents-in-law and brought Gregory and Tracy along to family gatherings. Joyce, meanwhile, interacted as little as possible with Melvin, who began avoiding family get-togethers to reduce friction. He had moved to Oakland and arranged to take the children every other weekend.

The divorce had been so acrimonious that, for the first few years, Joyce was averse to having Melvin come to her house to pick up Gregory and Tracy. Instead, she dropped the two off at Aunt Jessie's for Melvin to meet them there. At the end of the weekend, he would bring his children back to Aunt Jessie's for Joyce to pick up.

Melvin seemed to his sisters Myrtle and Doris quite changed from the loyal brother they thought they knew.

Jury foreman David Harper and Melvin Newton" meet during the filming of "American Justice on Trial" more than 40 years after Melvin's mother flew to Detroit to thank Harper for his role as the foreman of the jury in the 1968 trial of Huey Newton that spared his life.

But he remained close to his sister Leola, who welcomed Barbarette and her son Maurice for frequent visits. Melvin was then living with Barbarette and Maurice in a small apartment in East Oakland near the Allen Temple Church. Maurice recalls his Uncle Huey stopping by their apartment one evening and leaving as Maurice was headed to bed. Uncle Huey said he was going out to get a nightcap. Little Maurice thought he meant a Panther beret and asked his uncle to bring him one next time he came. Both Huey and Melvin got a chuckle out of that.

To maintain ties with his parents, Melvin brought Barbarette and Maurice to visit with them at their home instead of at family gatherings hosted by one of his sisters. Barbarette did her best to win Armelia over by volunteering to do the dishes whenever they came. Armelia was civil toward Maurice and offered him candy, but she resisted welcoming Barbarette as Melvin's new love. In contrast, his increasingly frail father reassured Melvin: "You'll always be my son." Walter also shared how much he appreciated Barbarette's effect on Melvin's well-being: "Boy, that girl is helpful for you." Melvin greatly valued that show of support.

For Melvin, connecting with Barbarette had indeed brought change. It ushered in the happiest days of his adult life. She enticed him to emerge from his academic cocoon and expand his horizons. She introduced him to a wide array of cuisines beyond the Southern comfort food he grew up on. She challenged him to abandon his sedentary proclivities and to take up running like a couple of her brothers did. Melvin started jogging, found that he enjoyed it, and began running the three-mile circuit around Oakland's Lake Merritt. To his amazement, he wound up easily completing the eight-mile annual Bay to Breakers San Francisco race, which he would enter every year into his sixties.

Barbarette also induced him to indulge his curiosity and embrace the joys of travel. Melvin began to carry wads of cash with him. Like his father, he had developed a habit of squirreling away money for emergencies, a tradition among many African Americans who mistrusted banks. When Walter died, Melvin's sister Leola took him aside. Then she handed him a few hundred dollars Walter had kept at home without Armelia's knowledge.

Over time, Melvin would carry much larger amounts of cash on trips. Sometimes he had up to $5,000 in savings on his person. He and Barbarette would eventually visit together most of the fifty states, as well as Mexico, the Caribbean and England. Walter's observation that Barbarette was good for Melvin had been spot on — through her influence, he flourished.

Melvin's brothers bore no ill will toward him for the separation and divorce. Lee Edward had never even met his own first daughter Esther until she was an adult. He had left a second woman behind in Portland whom his family never knew whether he married or just lived with. He did marry Katherine Johnson in 1950 or 1951. He left her behind when little Armelia was five for a woman named Mildred he stayed with in San Mateo. The infrequent interactions between the two women were quite hostile.

Extended family was important to Melvin's kids. Yet Tracy's earliest memories of her Uncle Huey were not the most pleasant. Whenever he saw her as a toddler, he could not resist grabbing and pinching her cheeks, which was quite painful. But he redeemed himself in 1972 when she was three. She had broken her leg in a car accident and was laid up in bed. Uncle Huey and his bodyguard came over with an armload of toys.

Although Esther had been to many family gatherings in the sixties, by the early 1970s she was too busy to see much of her aunts and uncles. Esther had been working for the Social Security Administration in San Francisco since 1965 while continuing to live with her husband in Berkeley. Esther had her third child, Trasean, in 1968, the year before Tracy was born.

One day in the early fall of 1974 Esther got a call from Trasean's kindergarten teacher, letting her know of a problem that had arisen between him and another classmate. When Esther arrived, she learned that her son had been chasing a shy little girl named Tracy around at recess every day. It was a game Trasean and some of the other boys called Kissy Coot. Being targeted had frightened Tracy so much that she started clinging to the teacher in tears whenever the class went outside at recess. Tracy had cried again when she told her mother that she did not want to go back to school any more. Her mother called the teacher. Tracy was the youngest in her class and had not attended preschool. This bullying needed to stop. The teacher's call to Esther followed.

To Esther's surprise, when she met Tracy she saw that the two children looked like twins. Tracy's last name was Newton. Her mother was Joyce Newton, Esther's aunt by marriage. Esther had not known that Tracy had been sent to the same Berkeley school as her son. She made sure Trasean quit harassing Tracy. When Esther later brought Trasean to a family gathering attended by Sonny Man, he playfully accused her of an affair with Melvin to produce such a lookalike to Tracy.

Ever since Melvin had asked Leola to serve as Gregory's godmother, she took a great interest in all of Gregory's activities. He would grow up to be a bookworm like his Dad and to pursue a similar teaching career. Both also shared a passion for writing poetry.

Meanwhile, "Uncle Black Power" and Melvin were the undisputed favorite uncles of Leola's younger daughter DeAngela, whom most in the family called by her middle name Terrez. Over the next couple of years, about twice a month Melvin and Huey took the kids on outings to parks or playgrounds or, as a special treat, to Marine World in Redwood City.

Huey was also proud to show them landmarks that were most important to him in his life as a revolutionary. Tellingly, Huey took the children to a place of great significance to him at the corner of 82nd and East 14th Street in Oakland. This was the address of the Black Panther Party's newly relocated headquarters which had split off from Eldridge Cleaver's faction in late February of 1971. Since his release, the FBI had stirred suspicions between Huey and Eldridge Cleaver with faked letters from Party members. Their deception helped stoke a growing rift between the two radical leaders.

The feud erupted in public when Huey appeared on a San Francisco talk show on February 28, 1971. By prearrangement, the program hooked Cleaver up by telephone from Algiers. Angry at recent Party expulsions, Cleaver called for the resignation of Panther Chief of Staff David Hilliard, who had only been carrying out Huey's agenda. Furious, Huey immediately expelled Cleaver from the Party. Huey then named Elaine Brown the Panthers'

Minister of Information and editor of the *Panther* paper.

As the Panthers split into two factions, each accused the other of retaliatory killings, most notably the murder in April of 1971 of Sam Napier, which Huey blamed on Cleaver's followers. Napier had been the key distributor of Panther newspapers nationwide, the Party's principal source of revenue. The FBI had also focused on infiltrating the Panthers with informers. That left Panther branches increasingly destabilized. None of this was known to Huey's impressed nieces and nephews. They only knew that wherever their famous Uncle Huey went, he was accompanied by a bodyguard.

Melvin's Dangerous Adventure with Huey

IN the late spring of 1971, Melvin told Huey his plans for the summer teaching break. Melvin was going to join his girlfriend Barbarette on her annual trip to visit her father, Ezra Payton. Barbarette had many other relatives in Mobile, Alabama, including half-siblings from her father's remarriage. Barbarette sometimes brought her son Maurice along. That summer of 1971, Barbarette left Maurice with her sister Detta while she took an extended trip to Mobile. It was important to her to maintain connections with all of her family.

Melvin looked forward to meeting Ezra. Huey asked Melvin if he could fly with Melvin to New Orleans so Huey could visit the local Panther branch. Melvin saw no reason why not, but he soon discovered how much of a headache it was to travel anywhere with the co-founder of the Black Panthers. It turned out to be a harrowing adventure. Melvin did not realize that Huey expected to be tailed by FBI agents everywhere he went. Huey brought along one of his burly bodyguards, Robert Bey. When the three men arrived at the San Francisco airport they were searched for weapons, which was not then a routine security protocol at U.S. airports. That unnerved Melvin but Huey took it in stride.

The plane stopped in Houston. While they were awaiting the next short flight from Houston to New Orleans, a sympathetic reporter approached Melvin and Huey. He happened to be traveling on the same plane and had just received word that Huey and his bodyguard were armed.

Melvin was alarmed. The FBI already knew that Newton and his protector were unarmed. It seemed obvious they were being set up.

Huey noticed that a nearby African-American passenger seemed to be gazing intently at them. Huey assumed the fellow was an FBI agent and began to talk with him. Huey then invited him to sit in an empty seat next to Melvin. That made Melvin even more uncomfortable with Huey's brazenness. Yet no further incident happened on the plane.

When they arrived in New Orleans, Huey and Robert Bey left to visit the Panther office. Most likely, they were being tailed the whole time. Melvin called Barbarette in Mobile from the airport to let her know he had arrived. Her father was excited to meet Huey, so Ezra and his third wife, who was close in age to Barbarette, offered to drive Barbarette to New Orleans. When they got there, Huey was not yet back, so her father left without ever meeting him.

Melvin was now quite fearful of staying overnight at a motel in New Orleans. He worried that the people who were tailing Huey would try to kill him. Melvin thought that his and Barbarette's lives would also be at risk. Huey said that he and Bey intended to take the next plane from New Orleans to Atlanta to meet with Panthers there. Huey asked if Melvin and Barbarette wanted to join them on the flight. They agreed, recognizing that Huey would likely again be tailed but feeling that it would be safer to stay with him than remain in New Orleans.

When Huey and his bodyguard arrived at the Atlanta airport, they found a man waiting for them. He indicated he was sent by Panther members in Atlanta to bring them straight to their headquarters. But Huey suspected him of being a government informant and had a different idea. He told Melvin that David Hilliard had previously suggested a plan for risky situations when traveling. For safety and security, they should stay at the Whitest, swankiest hotel around. Following this strategy, the Newton brothers chose the Hyatt Regency and headed there.

The fellow who had met them on their arrival at the airport had offered to drive them back to the airport when they were ready to return. Huey thought they would likely be ambushed and killed on their way to the airport. Later that night in their hotel room, Barbarette overheard Huey suggesting to Melvin that the men take knives with them from the hotel. Then they would be prepared to kill their driver if they needed to do so to save their own lives.

Barbarette was terrified at the thought of a bloody confrontation between the Newtons and an untrusted driver. She came up with a far better idea. Without telling Huey and Melvin, she called Georgia State Representative Julian Bond, a veteran of SNCC. Melvin and Barbarette had met Bond at a fund-raiser at a mutual friend's home in Berkeley when Bond was running for the Georgia state legislature. In her phone call with Bond, Barbarette explained her concern for their lives and asked if he would take them to the airport. Bond was happy to oblige. Barbarette then shared her escape plan with Melvin and Huey and his bodyguard.

Bond arranged for a caravan, which escorted the foursome back to the Atlanta airport without incident. Melvin and Barbarette then flew on their own to their original second destination to visit her relatives in Cleveland, Ohio. It was a great relief to convert the nightmarish trip with Huey back into the romantic getaway Melvin had originally planned.

Huey Reunites with Bobby Seale as the Party Shrinks

IN the spring of 1971, Charles Garry and his co-counsel wrapped up their defense of the headline New Haven, Connecticut murder trial of Bobby Seale and Ericka Huggins. By then, the Chicago Seven trial was already over. Some of the former defendants had descended on New Haven to help lead demonstrations on Seale's behalf.

The lawyers for Seale and Huggins wound up seating seven women and five men. Five of the women were Black, but none of the men. Garry obtained a hung jury that favored acquittal of both Seale and Huggins by a lopsided margin. The judge dismissed the case, stating that it would have taken "superhuman efforts" to find another impartial jury. After the New Haven trial, both Garry and Seale then returned to the Bay Area, where Huey and Bobby would reunite as free men for the first time in nearly four years.

Their Party was now a shadow of what it was two to three years before. That spring, gory details of the gruesome murder of Alex Rackley by members of the New Haven Panthers had alienated large numbers of former Panther supporters. The Panthers had used boiling water to torture a confession out of Rackley before they killed him on suspicion of being an informant. His assailants later dumped his corpse in the Coginchaug River and fled the scene.

The Panthers also had to contend with unsavory details that emerged in a headline New York trial that ended in acquittals that same month of "the Panther 21." The Panther 21 had faced an array of felony charges for allegedly conspiring to commit numerous bombings of department stores and other landmarks as well as rifle attacks.

Following Fred Hampton's death the year before, the Weather Underground had issued a "Declaration of a State of War" against the Nixon administration and claimed responsibility for several bombing attacks on government buildings. Some Panthers aligned themselves openly with this violent and anarchistic group. In retaliation, Huey expelled them from the Party, just as he had expelled Cleaver and Geronimo Pratt and their followers. What was left of the Panther Party was soon in near complete disarray, with members at each other's throats. As J. Edgar Hoover had hoped, the Panther Party was also broke after defending so many members against prosecutions.

Huey later rejoiced from the fact that his government tormentors faced pressures and unwanted headlines of their own. In the spring of 1976, an outraged Senate select committee headed by Sen. Frank Church would issue a scathing report following a yearlong investigation of U.S. intelligence community abuses. The report detailed facts substantiating Huey's basic claim of government persecution of the Panther Party. Huey would file suit against the government on behalf of the Panthers. His lawyers had obtained records under the Freedom of Information Act detailing the litany of abuses employed against the Panthers. The resulting discovery would ultimately form the basis of his Ph.D. thesis, "War Against the Panthers: A Study of Repression in America."

In the meantime, after Huey's release in 1970, a number of Panthers faced trial on various charges. In the Party's punishing version of musical chairs, at the beginning of

June 1971, it became Chief of Staff David Hilliard's turn to face prosecution for his role in the April 6, 1968 armed confrontation with Oakland police that resulted in Bobby Hutton's death. Panther supporters again filled the courtroom for the high-profile trial of Hilliard. Though he was represented by a veteran defense lawyer, Hilliard had no realistic chance of acquittal.

Other Panthers Hilliard had traveled with that night had already confessed to their roles in planning an ambush of Oakland police to be led by Cleaver. The police had somehow found out and caught the Panthers with an arsenal of weapons in their possession. Hilliard blamed the all-White jury for the verdict that sent him to prison for one to ten years, of which he would serve four. (The federal charge for threatening the President's life had by then been dismissed.)

Now it was Huey's turn again.

The First Retrial for Officer Frey's Death

IN July 1971, Garry defended Huey's retrial, this time without Stender by his side. Huey had distanced himself from her the prior fall. By 1969, Jensen had been elevated to District Attorney. He delegated the second prosecution to a different lawyer in his office, Donald Whyte. With the death penalty no longer an option, much more attention was being paid to the higher stakes Soledad Brothers' murder case gearing up for trial in San Francisco. At least Huey still had the solid support of the underground press.

Shortly before the retrial, *Ramparts* publisher Ed Keating published *Free Huey!*, Keating's account of the 1967 shootout and 1968 trial. The book suggested there was still an unidentified midget on the loose who had fled the scene after murdering Officer Frey. Henry Grier was once again called to testify that he saw a gun in Huey's possession, but the prosecution had never been able to establish the existence of this gun.

In the retrial, Garry managed more courtroom maneuvers, aiming this time to obtain a hung jury. Never good at brief-writing, Garry also privately talked Fay Stender into providing him with needed trial memoranda, for which she took no credit. The proceedings lasted until early August. The panel of ten women and two men included one African-American woman. They deliberated in a heat wave for six days before they announced they were deadlocked eleven-to-one for conviction.

Garry and Huey assumed they had persuaded the

lone African-American woman that the prosecution was part of a genocidal crusade against all Blacks. But she was actually among those who voted for conviction. As it turned out, the one holdout was a Latina. Prosecutor Donald Whyte marched out of the courtroom "tight-lipped and grim" without talking to reporters. Before the afternoon was out, District Attorney Lowell Jensen promised a third manslaughter trial to avenge the death of Officer Frey. Meanwhile, Huey remained free on $50,000 bail.

A Rift Develops with Jackson's Followers

ON August 21, 1971, radio and television stations interrupted their regularly scheduled programs with reports of another Marin County bloodbath. San Quentin Associate Warden Jim Park announced to the press that George Jackson had been killed trying to break out. A total of six men had died and a number of others were gravely injured. The news reported that Jackson had instigated the violence by surprising guards with a gun that had been smuggled in. (Fay Stender had been fired by Jackson months earlier for refusing to bring him a gun.)

Prison officials said Jackson had hidden the gun in his Afro. When he pulled it out, he reportedly declared, "The dragon has come." The statement invoked the memory of his hero, North Vietnamese leader Ho Chi Minh. Jackson overpowered his guards and freed other prisoners. The inmates managed to slit the throats of several guards before the uprising was over. Jackson himself was gunned down in the prison courtyard.

The official account of the uprising raised a number of questions that have never been put to rest. Was it an aborted escape, or a planned massacre by guards, as surviving prisoners contended, or both? Who smuggled a gun to Jackson and how did he get it past his guards? Why was the entire area scrubbed before any outsiders were allowed to visit the crime scene?

British journalist Jo Durden-Smith dug deeply into the events leading up to the death of George Jackson. In his 1976 book *Who Killed George Jackson?* Smith insisted that there was enough blame to assign to both sides. Violence begot violence, he said. Durden-Smith started a tally of related deaths starting from the racial killing of two Black prisoners in the Soledad prison exercise yard in April of 1968. Soledad was known as the "Gladiator School" for its history of racial violence. In response to this latest pair of deaths, the exercise yard was closed for nearly two years. Then, prison officials suddenly opened it up on January 13, 1970 to a mixed-race group of violent felons.

Witnesses later testified that as soon as predictable fist fights started, the sharpshooter in the guard tower opened fire without warning, aiming only at Black inmates. Black prisoners smelled a setup, particularly since one of the three inmates killed was boxer W. I. Nolen. Nolen had dared to become a name plaintiff in a federal lawsuit in 1966 that forced the prison to improve inhumane conditions in lock up. Immediately following the shootings on January 13th, most of the Black inmates went on a hunger strike.

The local district attorney responded to the selective targeting of Black inmates by announcing on the local news just three days later that he saw no reason to prosecute the gun tower guard. Yet prison rules required guards to use tear gas if that was a more reasonable option to break up fights. When using a rifle, tower guards were also required to aim at the prisoners' legs, not their chests. (A later wrongful death suit on the victims' behalf would be successful.) Half an hour after the district attorney's televised news bulletin, in apparent retaliation, a different Soledad guard was found dead by a stairwell on the ground floor of "O" wing in the prison's adjustment center.

George Jackson, who was a close friend and political

disciple of Nolen, had quickly been indicted along with two other Black prisoners. The trio were charged with beating the popular guard and throwing him to his death over the third-floor railing. That was when Stender and her co-counsel became involved and all three "Soledad Brothers" ended up in San Quentin while awaiting trial.

The next 27 months saw multiple related deaths at Soledad, the Marin County Civic Center, and the San Quentin Adjustment Center, ending with George Jackson's best friend, ex-felon Jimmy Carr, being gunned down in San Jose by two hitmen. Durden-Smith figured there were, in addition, "uncounted . . . beatings, stabbings, tear-gassing and consignments to illegal isolation cells," all in the same causal chain.

More than a thousand people attended George Jackson's funeral at St. Augustine's in Oakland. That was the same church where his younger brother Jonathan's funeral had taken place the year before. Tension was once again high between George Jackson's followers and Huey and the Panthers. There was already bitterness over the fact that the Panthers had obtained Jackson's literary rights shortly before his death. When he rewrote his will, Jackson had reassigned the royalties from his two books to the Panthers to help finance weapons for a revolution. Now the Jackson family no longer trusted the Panthers and thought the royalties should have been theirs.

Huey had been socializing at Lake Tahoe with his patron Bert Schneider and the wealthy producer's girlfriend Candice Bergen when he learned of Jackson's death. Huey and Bert had become fast friends, referring to each other as "brother." Furious at Huey for his cushy relationship with these Hollywood types, Jackson's family and supporters believed Huey was trying to exploit Jackson commercially. They thought Huey was using his entertainment industry connections to get a deal for a movie about Jackson's life. So began another major rift. Huey did not realize how long-lasting their anger would be. Georgia Jackson became the matriarch of the Black Guerilla Family prison gang that considered George Jackson their founder. In 1974, they would place Huey Newton prominently on their hit list for execution.

Huey's Bold Visit to Red China

HUEY was more focused at the end of the summer of 1971 on how to prevail in his rivalry with Eldridge Cleaver. At Huey's prompting, Eldridge had used his self-imposed exile from the United States as an opportunity to bolster international support for the Panthers. Huey now felt the need to counter Eldridge's efforts to solidify foreign support for his own following. Huey also wanted to beef up the remaining Panthers' profile as a force to be reckoned with.

A recent federal commission report dismissed the Panthers as a minor threat at most to American society. The dissenting members still embraced the fear mongering promoted by J. Edgar Hoover and the Justice Department. The FBI continued following developments closely as Huey invited to Oakland the remaining Panthers across the country who had won his trust. In the meantime, Huey had modified the Panthers' 10-point program after his split with Cleaver. The program now officially eliminated the call for all Black people to arm themselves for self-defense. In fact, the Party continued to stockpile weapons for an eventual revolution that remained Huey's ultimate goal, as well as that of the Panthers who remained in his camp.

Still eager for the limelight, Huey decided to upstage President Nixon with a dramatic move. The terms of his parole neglected to include travel restrictions. President Nixon was planning an historic visit to mainland China in early 1972 to reestablish diplomatic relations with the Communist country. Huey beat Nixon there. He accepted an invitation from Chairman Mao to make his own trip to China. On his own overseas journey in October 1971, Newton brought two companions: a bodyguard and Elaine Brown as the Panther Party's Minister of Information.

When they arrived in China, Brown's prior experiences accompanying the Cleavers came in extraordinarily handy dealing with Chinese diplomats. Plainclothes agents tailed Huey and his companions the whole circuitous way through Canada to China and back on their ten-day trip.

Meanwhile, the California judicial system was still not through with Huey Newton.

Huey's Second Retrial for Manslaughter

DISTRICT Attorney Jensen authorized yet a third trial of Huey in December 1971, once again only for manslaughter. But that trial also ended in a hung jury, despite prosecutor Whyte's best efforts to learn from the outcome of the second trial. Garry succeeded once more in impaneling a predominantly middle-aged, female jury. This time there were no Black members. As before, Garry's defense included witnesses to Frey's abusive conduct during earlier arrests.

The trial again featured expert testimony on Newton's impaired mental condition after being shot. On December 11, 1971, the jury reported they were deadlocked six to six. At the end of the day, the judge declared another mistrial. All twelve jurors were convinced Newton shot Frey but divided over whether he was conscious of firing the gun. Huey looked tired.

The following Wednesday, twelve television crews set up in the press room as reporters and scores of family members and Panther supporters grabbed seats in the courtroom. Jensen visibly trembled as he rose to speak. He said that, after searching his conscience, he concluded that another trial would be futile. He requested dismissal even though it would be "a frustration of justice." The law contemplated dismissals only "in furtherance of justice," but Judge Hayes granted Jensen's motion. Both knew that public resources would likely be wasted if the District Attorney pursued the case any further.

Walter Cronkite announced the extraordinary result on the CBS national news. At last, Armelia could breathe a real sigh of relief.

The Servant of the People and the Squad

AlTHOUGH Huey avoided further imprisonment for Frey's death, he faced a different threat in 1972. Elaine Brown had told him that Cleaver had placed him on a hit list. For his protection, Huey created two teams of five or six highly trained bodyguards and enforcers. All remained ready on short notice to engage in secret missions from Huey, like Mafia hitmen commanded to assault or assassinate designated targets.

Huey dubbed his two teams Buddha Samurai or "the Squad." They acted under the leadership of Flores Forbes, an early Panther recruit from Southern California. Forbes was known for meting out military discipline to errant Party members as well as providing loyal Party members with weapons. He later revealed that the Squad would do practically anything for the Party leader, even lay down their lives.

The Buddha Samurai modeled themselves after government strategic forces like the Los Angeles CCS Red Squad, which specialized in dangerous and stealthy operations. The Red Squad had orchestrated the ambush of Jonathan Jackson's kidnap attempt at the Marin County Courthouse in August of 1970.

Critics charged that the Panthers began operating like a Mafia protection racket, shaking down businesses to support Party programs. Huey actually did begin modeling the Panthers on *The Godfather* after repeatedly watching the classic 1972 gangster film. He ordered all Party members to view it as well. He himself dressed like a Mafia boss.

"The Servant of the People" now openly scorned Cleaver as a "renegade scab traitor." He ordered the Party purged of Cleaver's followers. Huey rewarded his own Squad members with cocaine, liquor and women. They basked in the aura of "The Supreme Servant of the People." One or another member of the Squad always accompanied Huey on late night forays to nightclubs and bars, most often to the Lamp Post Bar on Telegraph Avenue in Oakland. The Lamp Post was owned and operated by members of the Newton family. Huey had found his comfort zone, surrounded by both his family and his Squad of bodyguards.

The Lamp Post

MELVIN and his cousin Jimmie Ward, his Aunt Ozell's son, had acquired ownership of the license to run the Lamp Post in 1968 from its then owner, whom Melvin knew simply as Angelo. Angelo would retain ownership of the building. With great difficulty, Melvin came up with his half of the money for the bar, but Big Jimmie never raised a penny for his own share. Melvin then followed up on a lead from Huey about a Panther Party member who could help complete the purchase.

After Huey's release from prison in early August of 1970, he asked Melvin to sell him his interest in the bar for $10,000. Huey wanted the bar as a Panther Party operation. Melvin agreed but never received a dime from Huey. Cousin Jimmie became the bartender. His name was the only one they ever put on the license. People who met him there called him Sweet Jimmie or "Sweets." The family called him "Big Jimmie" to differentiate him from Myrtle's son "Little Jimmie" who also worked at the Lamp Post as a dishwasher and busboy.

Leola and Doris helped get the bar ready to open. They both worked as waitresses and Leola spent time in the kitchen cooking for the bar's patrons. (Leola would later work for a food service in San Francisco.) Maurice remembers Melvin and his mother taking him there often for dinner and Shirley Temples before his Uncle Huey took over the Lamp Post for the Panthers. Family parties were held there, too.

Things did not always go smoothly in those early days of the Lamp Post. Myrtle's son, Little Jimmie, often got out of control when he drank too much. One night in 1970, while Huey was still in prison, Little Jimmie punched a customer and was instructed to go home, which he refused to do. Sonny Man happened to be there that night. Little Jimmie tried to lure Sonny Man into a fistfight with him, but Sonny Man stepped back. Melvin then came forward.

Though significantly smaller than his nephew, Melvin was a good boxer. Melvin got in a punch before Little Jimmie got Melvin in a choke hold. Melvin tried to break that hold by jamming his fist down Little Jimmie's throat, but Little Jimmie bit hard on Melvin's hand. Fortunately, Myrtle arrived at that time. Little Jimmie obeyed his mother's order to stop fighting and come home with her. The story would later circulate among other members of the family.

Once Huey took over the Lamp Post for a Panther hangout, Melvin came there less and less. Leola stayed on as a cook and waitress. She sometimes brought her youngest daughter DeAngela Terrez to the bar with her. Gwen's son Ronnie came, too. The two children were both then in elementary school. Ronnie was a year older than Terrez. His sister Jessica was a couple of years younger and came along less often. Until it was time to go home, Ronnie and Terrez would stay in the kitchen or up in the office above the bar, enjoying either a hamburger or fried shrimp and French fries with Shirley Temples.

Myrtle had been working in the cafeteria at the University of California in Berkeley and at the Navy base on Treasure Island. She also came when she could to work at the Lamp Post. Unknown to Melvin, his ex-wife Joyce also worked there in the mid-70s, waitressing and taking the bar's proceeds to the bank. Often, she would bring Tracy and Gregory along to enjoy dinner there.

In the summer of 1974, Huey got into a brawl at the Lamp Post in which several people suffered injuries. Two women customers filed charges against him. Melvin was glad to be sidelined by then, instituting pioneering programs in African-American studies. That was Melvin's effort to revolutionize the teaching of history.

Melvin and Huey around 1971-72

Source: *Revolutionary Suicide, supra,* courtesy of Fredrika Newton, HPN and David Lautaro Newton

Photo of Newton siblings at the Lamp Post. Left to right: Myrtle, Melvin, Doris, Lee Edward, Leola and Huey at a family celebration at the Lamp Post Bar. The only sibling missing from the photo is "Sonny Man"

Melvin Helps Launch African-American Studies

DURING his 1968 trial, Huey Newton took the opportunity to 'school' the judge, the jurors, and everyone else in the courtroom on underreported African American history. His brother Melvin had a similar passion — to fill in the enormous gaps in the historical consciousness about Black life in America. But Melvin chose a more traditional means to get out the message: he became Chairman of the Department of Ethnic Studies at Merritt College.

Melvin soon joined with educators in the Berkeley Unified School District to seek funding from the National Endowment for the Humanities for an ambitious plan to draw more scholarship and instruction on the Black experience in the United States. The group wanted to create curricula from kindergarten through high school and two years of community college focused on African-American studies in the social sciences, history, esthetics, and independent studies. Their aim was to build upon the educators' teaching experience to develop outlines for model programs in each area.

The push for Black studies in Bay Area schools took place in the context of similar efforts elsewhere by other minority groups: the American Indian Movement, which sought to establish a Native American Studies Center by occupying Alcatraz Island; a Chicano Movement; a demand for Asian American studies (which Huey's friend Richard Aoki had been instrumental in initiating); and, more recently, demands for women's studies and courses on gender and sexuality.

Melvin and his colleagues only received enough federal funding for the development of college course outlines for African-American studies. They left it up to other educators to create usable outlines and syllabi for broader programming. But it was a strong start. One proposed introductory college history course started with the preconditions that gave rise to the African slave trade with the Americas. They sought to cover life under slavery and its socioeconomic, political and psychological ramifications. Also included were the varying perspectives of leading nineteenth and twentieth century African-American authors and lecturers. The course extended to the urbanization of Black Americans and the rise of both conventional and radical political groups. It included the Civil Rights Movement, The Nation of Islam, Malcolm X, and the Black Panthers, as well as the progress made by elected Black politicians.

Another proposed course of study focused on the experience of the Black family and Black communities in America. The educators explored how historical African societies influenced the development of African-American family roles and behaviors. They concentrated on how American culture, over time, modified the approach of Black family members to sex roles, child rearing and other behaviors.

The goal of the course was to assess the elements of African heritage that had been underappreciated. They wanted to show its value as a subculture. All of such programming was a bold precursor both to the spread of African American Studies programs and to what would eventually become known as "Critical Race & Ethnic Studies" programs. Such invitation to rethink American history from a multi-ethnic perspective has since engendered a tremendous backlash from traditionalists.

Melvin and his colleagues also proposed courses focusing on African civilizations from prehistoric times; African peoples in the Caribbean and Latin America; and yearlong multi-discipline courses exploring Black music, art, dance, and folklore. The group was bent on institutionalizing what the Afro-American Association had sought to achieve when Huey attended Oakland City College a decade earlier.

Despite his growing estrangement from his brother, Huey had to be especially pleased that writings by and about the Black Panthers were assigned readings in a syllabus covering modern African-American radical politics. At that very time, Huey was bent on driving a wedge between himself and Melvin, as well as expelling co-founders of the Black Panther Party.

Cutting Family Ties and Redefining Party Goals

HUEY struggled with relating to his family while he established his own new self-image. In the first few years after his release from prison, Huey found the challenges he faced as a Panther leader overwhelming. He continued to deal with the fallout from his split with Eldridge Cleaver and his followers. He harbored his own misgivings about plans for the shrinking Panther Party going forward. Often, he struggled with a sense of impending doom. Such feelings were not unfounded. Huey continued to face threats from the FBI and police and from other radicals and gangs like the Black Guerilla Family. He had amassed many enemies.

Huey remained grateful for the strength he acquired from his close-knit family. Yet he found those ties too constraining. He noted in the manuscript for his autobiography: "Even the closest families crumble because outside pressures are so relentless." By the time he had the book ready for publication, Huey identified with the premise of a poem that began "By having no family I inherited the family of humanity."

Drug highs made Huey paranoid and increasingly suspicious even of his longtime friends and colleagues. He had already turned on his lawyer Fay Stender. He did not wish to feel beholden to her for her prodigious efforts to win his freedom. For inexplicable reasons, he even became quite mistrustful of his brother Melvin. Melvin could see that Huey's determination to transform himself into a menacing Godfather-like public persona left no room for

the Huey he grew up with. "The family really had lost their
... little baby brother." His mother also knew she had lost
her devoted youngest child when she asked him to come
clean the kitchen stove like he always used to do for her.
He sent two underlings instead. Huey had found a way to
sever what had seemed an unbreakable bond.

Sometime in 1972, Huey falsely informed one or more
of the Squad that Melvin had pulled a gun on him. Melvin
was shocked and angry when he heard about this dangerous lie from Huey's bodyguard Robert Bey. Yet it did not
make him fearful. Melvin had faced other life-threatening situations. The adrenaline rush just made him more
acutely aware of his surroundings. He did, however, start
to avoid the Lamp Post as much as possible because he
was leery of a violent confrontation with his brother.
Melvin vowed not to interact with Huey again "this side
of glory." The rift lasted for several years.

Huey's increased isolation from family had some
exceptions. His cousin Eddie was arrested and thrown in
jail in 1973 for failure to pay parking tickets. Huey, who
was used to requests for help by jailed Panthers, bailed
Eddie out within eight hours. At his request, Melvin's
girlfriend Barbarette delivered the money. Eddie had
attended a few Panther gatherings when he was at
Merritt College in the late 1960s, but he had never joined
the Party. He was too busy with school and a part-time
job. Huey did not hold that against his cousin.

Bailing Eddie out of his predicament posed no conflict
for the mob boss image Huey was striving to establish.
What did conflict with the Godfather image was anything that reminded Huey of the teasing he got as a child
for looking like a baby. It was hard enough enduring the

taunts of other kids about his high-pitched voice and "baby hair" bangs. Huey also had bitter memories of his loved ones always calling him the baby of the family.

Huey apparently convinced himself that only by distancing himself from his parents and Melvin could he prove himself a true revolutionary leader. That would enable him to claim to represent the entire family of humanity. and he focused on building political power.

Back in 1966, the Panthers had supported Leftist lawyer Bob Treuhaft in his quixotic run for Alameda County District Attorney against Jensen's predecessor, Frank Coakley. In 1968, the Peace and Freedom Party had named Eldridge Cleaver their candidate for President, Kathleen Cleaver their candidate for State Assembly. Huey himself, while in the Alameda County Jail awaiting trial, became their candidate for Congress. (Eldridge could not be listed on the ballot because he was not old enough to qualify). Though the Panthers were considered too radical by the majority of voters, the door then opened for anti-war Berkeleyite Ron Dellums to win a Congressional seat in 1970 (which he occupied until 1998 before ending his career as Oakland's mayor).

On his return to Oakland, Huey had developed a specific goal – to build community support for the Panthers' programs. These not only included free children's breakfasts and sickle cell anemia clinics, but among other programs, bus rides for seniors without their own transportation. But Huey was more intrigued about the prospects of amassing power needed for a revolution. He saw control of Oakland's City Hall as a path to control the Port Authority Board via mayoral appointments. Huey envisioned the Panther Party getting in a position to open an illicit avenue through the Port for international trafficking in contraband. With that improbable goal in mind, he encouraged Bobby Seale to run for mayor and Elaine Brown to run for a city council seat.

Huey himself remained largely sequestered in his penthouse library, dictating additional material for what would turn into two books: *To Die for the People* in 1972 and *Revolutionary Suicide* in 1973. From the summer of 1970 through the early fall of 1971, when Huey and Melvin remained close, Huey had Melvin's help in putting into print the materials Huey dictated. Melvin also converted into standard English the jargon and vernacular J. Herman Blake had written down during prison visits memorializing what Huey had told him about his life.

Meanwhile, Bobby Seale campaigned for mayor in a suit and tie, attracting significant community support. Civil rights leaders, even Martin Luther King's widow Coretta Scott King, endorsed the Panthers' new fourteen-point program. The Panthers gave away truckloads of groceries and shoes as an incentive to voter registration in the flatlands, a practice that has since been outlawed as a perceived attempt to buy votes.

Although his Republican base had shrunk considerably by 1973, Mayor John Reading still enjoyed popularity as the man who built the Coliseum Sports Complex. That was where the Oakland A's had become the reigning World Champions. Seale, however, put in such a strong showing in the election that he forced a runoff which Reading managed to win. Elaine Brown also lost her race.

This foray into mainstream politics would turn out to be one of Huey's most lasting accomplishments. The Panthers soon played a major role in changing the

Oakland City Charter to have city council members elected by district rather than city wide. That made the council members more accountable to neighborhoods. The Panthers also inspired many members to run for office in California and elsewhere, a number of whom won election. On Seale's mayoral campaign staff had been an energetic young political activist named Barbara Lee, who worked in the Panther community programs. She went to work for Congressman Dellums and later, with his endorsement, won his congressional seat when he retired. She would represent her district through 2023 and run for mayor herself and win election in 2025.

Estrangement and Self-Imposed Exile

ONE wonders if Walter Newton ever told his sons the story of the two wolves that represent the ongoing battle between good and evil. Although the tale is often attributed to Native Americans, it more likely originated as a Christian parable. Evangelist Billy Graham was among the religious leaders who incorporated the powerful message into one of his sermons.

To illustrate inner conflicts, a grandfather tells his grandson about a good wolf and an evil wolf wrestling with each other for dominance inside each person. That parable would have resonated deeply with Walter Newton. When asked by his guileless grandson which wolf wins, the grandfather replies: "whichever one you feed."

In 1974, Huey fed the bad wolf. Dependent on drugs and alcohol, he became increasingly violent and paranoid. That spring Huey began expelling old friends from the Party. These included his longtime buddy, Chief of Staff David Hilliard, and other Panthers from its earliest days. In July, Huey provoked an argument with Bobby Seale and then had a member of the Squad beat him.

Hugh Pearson, author of *Shadow of the Panther: Huey Newton and the Price of Black Power in America*, reported that a local doctor patched Seale up. Seale then fled into exile, hiding out on the East coast in fear for his life. Seale later vehemently denied being attacked by Huey, but admitted that he left the Party abruptly that summer. Many years later Seale told a reporter that the big issue dividing the two Party leaders in 1974 was that Newton was trying to "shakedown pimps and drug dealers. As a result, they took out a contract on Newton's life. I was very, very pissed," Seale recalled. "If I stayed around, I probably would have killed Huey myself."

In Seale's stead, Newton elevated Elaine Brown to Party Chair. But soon after Seale's departure, Huey's troubles continued because of his quick temper and lapses in judgment. In addition to the assault charges filed by two woman customers of the Lamp Post, Huey was accused of threatening two plainclothes policemen.

The worst was yet to come. One night in early August 1974, several sex workers were seeking business near a street corner in Oakland when a chauffeur-driven Lincoln Continental came by. One of the young women called out, "Hey, baby." The car turned around and parked. The passenger got out and displayed a revolver. When he began arguing with one of them, the others scattered. They then heard the gun go off. Turning around, at least one of them saw the car speed away. Seventeen-year-old Kathleen Smith lay severely wounded on the sidewalk with a bullet wound through her jaw and spinal cord. She wound up hospitalized in a coma.

Three of the women who witnessed the incident picked Huey Newton out of a photo lineup as the gunman. About a week later, a badly injured tailor named Preston Callins reported to Oakland police that Huey had pistol-whipped him in his penthouse during a fitting. Callins made the bad mistake of calling Huey "baby," a term he often used on friends and family. That set Newton off. He repeatedly bashed the fifty-two-year-old tailor in the head with a pistol, shouting, "Nobody calls me baby." Callins had to be hospitalized.

The police executed a search warrant on the penthouse apartment and found the gun, which led to a separate charge. Ex-felons forfeited the right to possess handguns. Elaine Brown later wrote that she and Gwen Fountaine had made sure to clean off all of Callins' blood from the penthouse walls, ceiling, bathroom and towels by the time the police arrived. The threat of two prosecutions coupled with credible threats on his life from rival gangs prompted Huey to make plans to flee to Cuba with Gwen Fountaine. Huey would leave Elaine Brown in charge of the Party with backup from the Squad.

Huey had something he needed to do first — finally heeding the call of the good wolf.

Daddy and Prodigal Son

BY the time Walter turned 70 in 1973, he had been in declining health for a couple of years. Though his relationship with Huey had become distant and awkward since Huey modeled himself after a Mafia boss, Walter remained the revered patriarch of the family. He enjoyed the respect of the entire clan. The family members were all particularly proud of his calling as a minister, although Walter had stopped telling Bible stories at home to the young ones. Almost everyone in the family still called him "Daddy" and called Armelia "Mother." A doting grandfather, Walter had mellowed to become the gentle voice that interceded when Armelia yelled at the grandchildren or wanted to discipline one of them with a whipping.

Myrtle's daughter Patricia had spent a lot of time with her grandparents when she was young and grew close to her grandfather. Walter would take her to the store with him and ask her what she wanted for a treat. He liked to please her with a chocolate Mountain Bar, which had similar ingredients to Snickers.

Gregory enjoyed spending time with both Mother and Daddy, though he disliked being kissed on the lips when greeted by his grandmother. He remembered that she always kept a full bowl of fruit on a table. He drew the conclusion it was meant for show, not for eating. Armelia did offer Gregory and Tracy snacks of buttered saltines heated in the oven, which Tracy liked much more than her brother did.

Like Patricia, Gregory found his grandfather to be a kindred spirit. Walter owned a recliner that everyone understood he would not allow anyone else to sit in. Yet Walter offered it to Gregory when he visited. Walter also gave Gregory a special gift when Gregory was in elementary school — his prized watch.

Gregory's younger sister Tracy was also a special favorite of Walter's. Born on July 7, 1969, Tracy has indelible memories of her beloved "Daddy", who died when she was five. When no other grandchildren were around, Tracy jumped in the chair and grinned at her grandfather, who could tell she doted on him. He could not resist her impish charm. He told her that she could stay in the chair and that he would let her climb on it again if she did not tell anyone.

The preschooler quickly realized that she should not show off by depositing herself in the recliner in front of her brother and cousins. Only "Mother" and "Daddy" were in on the secret. Melvin never had any idea. Neither did Gregory, who thought he was the only one ever offered that privilege. Tracy later had another secret to keep, a portable radio her grandmother told her that Daddy wanted her to have to remember him by when he passed away.

In early August 1974, it was probably Leola or Doris who told Huey that their father had just entered Kaiser Hospital, possibly near death. Huey realized that once he fled to Cuba, he would likely never see his father again. Worried there might never be an opportunity for reconnection with the family patriarch, Huey headed over to the hospital for a visit: "I needed to tell him I loved him. I never had. We both were crying." But this was one of those cases in which Huey's quick temper would get the better of him. His longing for a tender moment with his father was painful and real — but not enough to overcome his knee jerk reaction to any affront, real or perceived.

The trouble began when a nurse could see that Walter was overwhelmed with emotion at Huey's visit. Apparently believing Huey was bothering her elderly patient, the nurse told him to stop agitating his father. When Huey erupted at her and demanded she leave the room, she called the police. The officers forced Huey out, ending his reconnection with his father on a bitter note.

In spite of the visit's unfortunate conclusion, even a brief talk with his prodigal son had to have meant the world to Walter. He must have known there wasn't much time left. After Huey and his family fled to Mexico, Melvin telephoned Huey to let him know their father's condition was rapidly worsening. Walter was soon transferred to Kaiser Hospital in San Mateo for neurosurgery to remove a suspected brain tumor. He died there on September 1, 1974.

Huey called from Mexico to inquire about his father's condition and heard the sad news. At that point there was no way Huey could return for the funeral. Melvin and Barbarette could tell that FBI agents and police officers were monitoring the funeral service, expecting they might nab Huey. There would be no sign of Huey at the ceremony or at Walter's burial in Rolling Hills Evergreen Cemetery in Richmond.

The necessary absence of Huey, and the watchful eyes of police officers looking for him, must have been cause for concern among some of the mourners. Nevertheless, the funeral was a dignified send-off for a patriarch who retained his importance to his extended family to the end. Lee's daughter Armelia and her half-brother Lawrence, then in their twenties, came to the funeral despite having never been close to either grandparent. Also among the many attendees was Walter's stepbrother E.S., who came out from Detroit to pay his respects.

Seeing E.S. at Walter's funeral prompted efforts to strengthen that family connection. By 1974, E.S. had ascended to the middle class, promoted to the position of foreman of all the custodians at the Ford plant in Detroit. Not long after Walter died, Leola and Doris came out to visit E.S.'s family in their new home in its suburbs. Doris was particularly impressed that E.S. had his own small swimming pool in his backyard. She likely knew no other Black person who owned one. Growing up, Black families where they lived mostly lacked access to community pools and never learned to swim.

Both sisters had to have been even more impressed that E.S.'s pastor was Clarence Franklin, who had led a march with his good friend Martin Luther King, Jr. to end discrimination against Black auto workers in Detroit. Franklin's sermons were still being recorded and nationally distributed in the early 1970s. By 1974, his daughter Aretha was an international sensation. It was seven years since she debuted her rendition of Otis Redding's "RESPECT" – which became her signature song. Respect had always been what Walter Newton demanded and largely achieved.

The Newton Family Divides into Camps

WHILE Huey lay low in Mexico and Cuba in 1974, the lives of his family in California carried on as usual, with all their inherent joys and complications. Melvin was in the process of finalizing his contentious divorce from Joyce. She would retain primary custody of their two children and keep the house on Benvenue Avenue in South Berkeley that Melvin had bought after they separated. The property had a rental house on the same lot, the proceeds of which Joyce was able to use to help cover the mortgage.

With her mother as a willing babysitter, Joyce completed her bachelor's degree and opened up a day care center. All the while, she continued to maintain close ties with her in-laws. She regularly attended family gatherings with Gregory and Tracy and worked part-time at the Lamp Post. Ironically, Joyce was called by the FBI after the divorce to see if she would give the government information they could use against Melvin. She refused. It was actually Joyce, not Melvin, who had more regular interaction with the Panthers who frequented the Lamp Post.

The Lamp Post remained a family business. Before Huey left for Cuba, Doris had already been handling the bar's accounts. She would keep working at the Lamp Post until 1977, co-managing it with Elaine Brown, whom the Newtons considered family, too. In addition to keeping the accounts, Doris supervised non-Panther employees, including her son Ricky who worked at the bar. Elaine oversaw the Panthers employed there.

As petite as Doris was, she was also renowned for her toughness. In fact, she was so calm under pressure and willing to stand up to bullies that her bravery became the stuff of legend. Doris stories lingered in the memory of friends and loved ones nearly fifty years later at her memorial in November 2023. During the ceremony, Elaine Brown shared a hair-raising anecdote, showcasing Doris in a potentially fatal standoff with some thuggish Panthers. It showcased Doris's determination to stand her ground with tough customers at the Lamp Post no matter whom she faced off with. All five-feet and maybe 110 pounds of her were full of the courage of the biblical David that her father had instilled in each of his seven children.

One night in the late summer of 1974, several Black Panthers ordered food and drinks at the bar and declined to pay for them. Doris was having none of it and said so with some choice expletives. One of them threatened to kill her. Elaine reminded him this was Huey's sister, so they should pay up. Elaine promised to ask Huey in his next phone call how to handle similar situations in the future. The Panthers still refused to pay. Doris was not intimidated. She retorted that, if he tried to kill her, she would dispatch the motherfucker. The impasse ended abruptly when someone was heard trying to break into the backdoor of the bar and the Panthers scurried to deal with the intruder.

Melvin was conspicuously absent. By then, he and Barbarette had been together about four years. Her son Maurice lived with them. He saw his birth father occasionally on weekends but was developing a closer bond with Melvin. By the end of that year, Barbarette trusted Melvin so implicitly she let him break the news to Maurice when her ex-husband died. She guessed correctly that

Melvin's recent loss of his own father would help him console Maurice.

Melvin and Barbarette were married on December 19, 1975, at the home of one of her close friends on a trip to Detroit. When they returned from Michigan as a married couple, they felt it important to celebrate the rite again in front of their three children. Leola had already told their kids. Melvin and Barbarette held a small ceremony at Barbarette's mother's home. Maurice was quite excited to have Melvin officially become his father.

Neither Lee Edward nor Sonny Man held Melvin's second marriage against their younger brother. Lee Edward had long since left his wife Katherine to raise their two children, Armelia and Lawrence, by herself. By the time Melvin moved in with Barbarette, Sonny Man had two children of his own by two different girlfriends. (Though he never married, in his sixties Sonny Man would also father two Filipino-Black children, Andre and Valencia Newton, with his newest girlfriend, Veronica Hernandez.)

Sonny Man's first child, Demetrius, born in 1963, was African-American and lived in Los Angeles with his mother, Alice Jackson. His recent girlfriend was a White labor activist in the Bay Area named Sara Frazee. Their daughter Myesha was born in July 1972 and started out living with her mother in Oakland. Until Myesha was seven, Sonny Man visited Myesha mostly on her birthday and at Christmas. He would take custody of her in 1980 when she was eight.

Because of Sonny Man's frequent travel, Myesha would mostly stay with Aunt Leola and her daughter DeAngela Terrez, who was six years older. Leola had by then earned the nickname "Nana". She had four children with her first husband James Carr, of whom fourteen-year-old Terrez was the youngest. Leola had since divorced and remarried Milliard (Mel) Johnson. Both family and church friends routinely brought sick children for Nana to take care of. She was quick to notice if they exhibited signs of feigned illness. Then, Nana would put them to work instead of to bed. Myesha may have been Leola's biggest challenge.

Myesha's mother suffered from mental health issues. The problem was serious enough to cause Myesha to spend several months in foster care before her father obtained custody. She became an angry child, prone to temper tantrums and disobedience, which prompted her aunt to beat her with a switch. Myesha thought that both Aunt Leola and her grandmother Armelia considered her the Black sheep of the family. Nonetheless, Myesha greatly enjoyed family gatherings and listened with awe to tales the aunts and uncles told.

Through most of her adulthood she believed an incredible – and entirely fabricated — secret confided to her by one of her aunts. Myesha was told that Walter Newton's White father was none other than the nation's 28th President, Woodrow Wilson. Not until the summer of 2023 did Myesha learn the truth — that Walter was half Jewish, not fathered by Woodrow Wilson, the scholarly son of a Scottish Presbyterian minister. From 1902 to 1910, Wilson headed Princeton University in New Jersey — more than a thousand miles from teen-ager Alice Hilliard in Uniontown. Myesha realized she had been told a whopping fib.

* * *

Melvin had meanwhile become integrated into Barbarette's family. It was easy for Melvin to adopt Barbarette's family as a surrogate tribe, visiting with her mother and sister and brothers for birthdays and holiday gatherings. Barbarette was so gregarious and organized she became the acknowledged matriarch of her family, hosting Thanksgiving and Christmas and later an "Autumn Fair" every October that no one wanted to miss. She was an excellent, versatile cook and loved to entertain.

In the summer of 1975 Barbarette and Melvin took Maurice on a driving trip from Oakland to Mobile, Alabama and back for a visit to her extended family on the Gulf Coast. That was where she had learned Creole dishes that the Newton clan had not been raised on — jambalaya and crawfish étoufée, among other specialties.

Barbarette was quite fond of Melvin's children. They got along well with her son Maurice, who was just a few months younger than Gregory. Yet it had been difficult for Gregory at first to share a bedroom and toys. Tracy got to know and love Barbarette as a second mother. Gregory remained more devoted to his mother Joyce. Yet both got the benefit of Barbarette's cultural excursions. As they grew older, Tracy and Gregory stayed as much as a month at a time every other summer with Melvin, Barbarette and Maurice. They sometimes all headed off together on family vacations in other parts of California or to explore other states. Barbarette wanted the children to experience plays, opera, and the rodeo. She exposed them to travel to widen their horizons. They had to realize they were getting life experiences far broader than most Black kids they knew.

XI.

Homesickness and Fresh Starts

Huey's Return

LIVING in Castro's Cuba, which he had admired since his late teens, opened Huey's eyes to how much he took for granted in the United States. He missed freedom of speech and listening to rock and roll music on the radio. It was startling for him to see the censorship of artists, and the reality of human rights abuses under an authoritarian Communist regime. The exile also made him more appreciative of family. He kept in touch sporadically by exchanging photos and letters and phone calls initiated by Gwen. The two were now married. Cuba was not the paradise Huey imagined, though he also realized that returning home too soon could put him at risk of being arrested for murder. The teenage sex worker whom he was originally charged with shooting had never recovered from her coma. He awaited a propitious time to come back to Oakland.

During Huey's extended absence, Elaine Brown remained in charge of the Panther Party. She made one trip to visit him in Cuba in 1975 to bring him up to date on their activities. Undoubtedly, one of the subjects was the recent death of former Panther school bookkeeper Betty Van Patter. In December of 1974, months after Huey left for Cuba, the Lamp Post was the last place Van Patter had been seen alive. Shortly before she disappeared, she had been seeking information to respond to an IRS inquiry into potential misuse by the Panthers of federal funds intended for the school. Elaine Brown had then fired her.

In January of 1975, Van Patter's battered body washed up on the other shore of the San Francisco Bay. Suspicion fell on the Squad, sent to prevent Van Patter from becoming a witness in the pending IRS investigation. But the murder was never solved. Huey's former advisor David Horowitz never got over his guilt for recommending Van Patter as a bookkeeper for the Panther school. He had wanted to write a book about revolutionaries when he first met Huey while Huey was still incarcerated in the California Men's Colony. In Horowitz's zeal to develop a close relationship with Huey, he had turned a blind eye to the Panther Party's violence. Horowitz assumed Huey had ordered the murder, which Huey denied when confronted about it after his return from Cuba. The IRS continued to pursue its own investigation of misuse of government grant money and ultimately got Huey to plead guilty to embezzlement of school funds.

Meanwhile, Huey had followed with interest President Nixon's impeachment, resignation and September 1974 pardon by new President Ford. Coverage of the Watergate scandal revealed Nixon's complicity with the FBI and CIA in the "Huston Plan." The Huston plan was a secret 43-page report that President Nixon implemented by executive order. It purported to suspend the constitutional rights of its targets for reasons of national security.

The Panthers topped the list of Huston Plan targets. The FBI's and CIA's overreaching and illegal persecution of targets formed the basis of one of the articles of impeachment that prompted Nixon to resign. Several reports were prepared that would shock the public with details of international assassination plots by the CIA and illegal domestic spying by the FBI.

Those bombshell discoveries came to light in April of 1976 when Senator Frank Church's Senate Select

Committee published its alarming findings in "The FBI's Covert Action Program to Destroy the Black Panther Party." These included inciting members of United Slaves (US) to murder Los Angeles Panther leaders John Huggins and "Bunchy" Carter as they left a meeting on the UCLA campus; playing a role in the Newton/Cleaver rift; spreading feces and foul odors on Panther newspapers to make them unsalable; destroying food pantries and equipment at Panther offices; and conspiring with the Chicago police to murder Chicago Panther leader Fred Hampton.

Fred Hampton's death was already the subject of a 1971 documentary, *The Murder of Fred Hampton*. The details were further exposed in a 1973 reinvestigation of his killing by the Commission of Inquiry into the Black Panthers and the Police, headed by NAACP executive director Roy Wilkins and former Attorney General Ramsey Clark. The Wilkins/Clark Commission issued a scathing report that detailed a prior state and federal cover-up.

None of the perpetrators ever got prosecuted for Hampton's murder but Hampton's family brought suit for his wrongful death. That gave the Panthers' lawyers the incentive to file their own suit against the FBI, CIA and local police alleging $100 million in damages. The Panthers' lawsuit ended in dismissal. Not until 1983, after more than a decade of legal wrangling, did Hampton's family receive an historic $1.85 million from the City of Chicago in compensation.

Meanwhile, Huey was still angling to find a way home. By the spring of 1977, the political landscape had changed sufficiently that Huey began to believe that getting back to the United States might be feasible after all. He soon began to call relatives, letting them know his plans to get resettled in Oakland.

When Maurice found out Uncle Huey was returning, he was quite excited. Maurice knew how extraordinarily famous his uncle was. He went down to Panther headquarters in East Oakland and used his allowance to buy a "Free Huey" t-shirt. He was surprised when his parents did not react well. His impression of Huey was far removed from the radical leader's "street tough" reputation.

Maurice knew there were folks who now viewed his uncle in a bad light. In his mind, Huey was an admirable man and an asset to his community. From what Maurice knew as a young teen, his uncle had been instrumental in establishing breakfast programs for children in the projects, sickle cell anemia clinics and shoe giveaways for needy kids. Lee Edward's daughter Armelia most appreciated the food giveaways, which helped her mother put meals on the table, but she and her mother were not comfortable around the Black Panthers.

Meanwhile, Huey continued to exercise political influence in California, despite his temporary exile. Huey was friends with Judge Lionel Wilson's son. With Huey's enthusiastic backing while still in Cuba, Elaine Brown helped orchestrate Wilson's successful 1977 campaign to become the city's first Black mayor.

Wilson would become only the second African-American mayor of a major city on the Pacific Coast (after Tom Bradley of Los Angeles). Huey considered the liberal Democrat a modern-day Dr. Sun Yat-Sen, the revolutionary doctor venerated by both the Communist Chinese and Nationalists in Taiwan for establishing China as a republic.

Wilson would serve three terms, ushering in a new era in city politics that the *New York Times* dubbed "a racial, cultural, economic and political revolution." With the support of the Panthers among other community activists, Wilson instituted a pioneering Citizens Police Review Board. Wilson got Parks and Recreation head Bill Patterson appointed as the first African-American foreman of the Alameda County Grand Jury. Wilson filled many other city positions with Black applicants and steered contracts to Black-owned businesses. He also worked closely with both Governor Jerry Brown and Republican businessmen to rejuvenate downtown Oakland with a building boom of new high rises. As an integral part of the plan, Wilson oversaw the creation of 10,000 new jobs and hundreds of low-income housing units for West Oaklanders.

* * *

Within days of Wilson taking office in the summer of 1977, Huey returned from three years of exile in Cuba. He and Gwen and her two children moved into a ranch house purchased for them by Hollywood producer Bert Schneider just off Snake Road in the Oakland hills. But it was hardly a peaceful homecoming. Almost immediately after returning home, Huey would have to stand trial yet again. This time he faced amended charges stemming from when he fled the country in August 1974. Seventeen-year-old Kathleen Smith's death now resulted in a homicide charge against Huey.

Undaunted by what his client faced, Charles Garry scheduled a press conference at the San Francisco airport. There, Huey announced that the Panthers would undertake as their new goal ridding Oakland of the menace of drug dealers. Huey had an ulterior motive for such a plan — to target rival gangs that had grown powerful in his absence. At the same time, the Panthers had shrunk in power. Some no longer felt the same commitment to Huey reassuming leadership of the Party.

To David Horowitz, who had greatly admired Huey in the early 1970s, Huey's new professed desire to cleanse Oakland of crime lords constituted the epitome of chutzpah. Horowitz began speaking privately with freelance reporter Kate Coleman about what he knew of the Panthers' own violent history and his suspicions regarding Betty Van Patter's murder. It would result in a July 1978 article "The Party's Over: How Huey Newton Created a Street Gang at the Center of the Black Panther Party." It was a shocking exposé of the Squad's ruthless enforcement techniques and shakedowns of Black business owners both before Huey fled to Cuba and during his absence. It included reasons to point to the Squad for the unsolved murder of Betty Van Patter. In the meantime, in contrast to the mixed response from Panther Party members and former supporters, Huey enjoyed a warm welcome back from most members of his family.

Family Reunions and Dust-ups

HAVING corresponded with family from Cuba, Huey felt comfortable returning to the bosom of his family. He did not seem to reflect much on the strain he had put his mother and Melvin through before he left. At the first family gathering, Huey took the opportunity to go soak in a bathtub. Melvin was still so angry with his younger brother he could not contain himself. He found Huey relaxing in his bath. Melvin confronted him with the false threat Huey had communicated to the Squad five years before that had put Melvin's life at risk. Melvin had lived with boiling resentment ever since. Huey confessed to having had a mental breakdown back then. Melvin never said another word to Huey about the issue.

Other family members, including Melvin's stepson Maurice, were thrilled that Huey was back in town. Maurice was awestruck that his uncle was recognized everywhere he went. On one of the kids' excursions with Uncle Huey, he took them to Great America amusement park in Santa Clara. They all piled into his car: Uncle Huey and Gwen, Jessica and Ronnie, Gregory, Maurice and one of Huey's bodyguards. Throughout the park, people stopped and stared as they recognized the Panther Party founder.

What Tracy remembered was the lesson she got from her uncle, demonstrating the difference between a boy raised in poverty and the next generation born into the middle class. Shortly after they arrived in the amusement park, Huey spotted a penny on the ground and pointed it out to the kids. None of them moved to take it. He was quite surprised and asked "Isn't anyone going to pick up that penny? "Tracy then bent to get it. Her Uncle Huey then asked, "If you have 98 cents and pick up a penny, how much is that? Tracy said. "99 cents." Huey said, "That's right!" He added, "and if you get another penny what do you have? Tracy shouted out "a dollar." Huey said, "Tracy is the only one who gets anything in the park because she respects a penny." Uncle Huey kept returning to the subject of the penny all afternoon. "Tracy, if you have $1.99 and pick up a penny, what do you have?" Tracy gleefully responded, "Two dollars!"

Tracy and Gregory recall another outing with Uncle Huey and Gwen to the movies. They traveled with his bodyguard in Uncle Huey's Lincoln Continental. The kids greatly admired the car's "suicide doors." They were hinged at the rear instead of the front like horse-drawn buggies used to be. (When originally marketed, the car did not come equipped with seatbelts, so if the back door opened while the car was moving a passenger might fall out trying to close the door, giving rise to the deadly nickname.)

When the group was close to the Shattuck movie theater in Berkeley where they were headed, a police car slowed down, and the officers stared at them as they went by. Once inside, there were multiple movies to choose from. The group split up and rejoined each other when the films ended. The family members and Huey's bodyguard Robert Bey came out to find that someone had egged the car and stuck matchsticks in the key holes of the doors. The same patrol car rolled slowly by with the officers now laughing at the scene.

Tracy and Maurice recall their uncle finding the malicious mischief amusing. It did not faze him. But Tracy had a sense of unease. She believed she had a sixth sense inherited from her grandfather. She felt a strong premonition that her uncle would not be around much longer.

Gregory would later have a premonition of his own much closer to Huey's death.

Huey's New Trials

CHARLES GARRY had appeared by Huey's side at the airport when Huey returned from Cuba. But by that time, Garry's courtroom victories were behind him. That same year Garry would publish his co-authored autobiography, *Streetfighter in the Courtroom: The People's Advocate*. Garry was now representing People's Temple leader, Reverend Jim Jones. Jones had visited Huey in Havana in early 1977. Huey hired a different veteran defense counsel to represent him at his pending criminal trials.

The hard-hitting article by Kate Coleman and Paul Avery showed up in newsstands in early July, 1978. It created shock waves as Bay Area residents absorbed details of the Panthers' savage underbelly. The fact that two veteran Lefties authored the exposé based on inside information greatly diminished the remaining support of White Leftists in the East Bay for the Panthers. Both Coleman and Avery received death threats sending them into hiding for months to avoid retaliation by Huey Newton or other Panthers.

That fall of 1978, Garry would have his own personal nightmare to deal with — the worst American massacre before September 11, 2001. Garry barely escaped with his life in November of that year during the mass murder/suicide of U.S. citizens in Jonestown, Guyana, orchestrated by Reverend Jones. Over nine hundred people died at Jonestown, including Congressman Leo Ryan. Ryan had arrived to investigate the strange cult at the urging of worried family members in his district — and was gunned down as he was leaving.

***

The political context of Huey's 1977 and 1978 trials was much different from Huey's original Movement trial in 1968. With much less fanfare, Huey's new defense lawyers won dismissal of the pistol-whipping charge after the tailor, Preston Collins, refused to testify. Instead, Collins spent twelve days in jail for contempt of court. In Huey's trial for the murder of Kathleen Smith, the jury consisted of mostly middle-aged suburbanites (nine women and three men). The gun used in that murder had never been found. A key eyewitness recanted prior testimony. Huey took the stand to swear he was at home at the time of the shooting. The jury deadlocked ten to two in favor of acquittal.

After consulting with District Attorney Lowell Jensen, prosecutor Tom Orloff decided to retry Huey in 1978. Huey's oldest sister Myrtle faithfully attended that trial together with her 10-year-old granddaughter Kim. Myrtle had to keep poking Kim to keep her from falling asleep. The second re-trial before a jury panel of four men and eight women hung eleven to one for acquittal. Frustrated, Orloff then dismissed the case.

As Huey rejoiced, an *Oakland Tribune* reporter noted how few Panthers attended this last trial. Elaine Brown departed the state in the fall of 1977. Reportedly Elaine fled after Huey, in one of his recurrent fits of rage, assaulted Ericka Huggins, who then headed the Oakland Community School. The scathing article by Coleman and Avery on the history of the Panthers published in *New Times* in July of 1978 contributed to the Panthers' loss of Leftist support amid the Party's downward spiral.

The Oakland Community School

THE Panther Party's 10-Point program included as a key tenet the need to teach Black people their true history. The Party started out by insisting on ethnic studies programs and inclusion of Black faculty in colleges. For years, Huey wanted to expand on that, especially as Panther members had their own children. The enrollees included Gwen's two children, Barbarette's son Maurice, and other elementary school-aged nieces and nephews.

Less than six months after Huey's release in the summer of 1970, Elaine Brown and others in the Party had created the Huey P. Newton Youth Institute. After Sam Napier's murder in 1971, the school was renamed the Samuel L. Napier Intercommunal Youth Institute. It was designed as an alternative to public education primarily for impoverished Black students in Oakland's flatlands.

The students were originally housed together and fed three meals a day as they focused on becoming young revolutionaries. Gregory remembers visiting his cousin Ronnie there overnight, likely in the summer. For Gregory, it was uncomfortable to be a stranger among all the students in uniform. He had not realized that Ronnie lived apart from his parents in the Panther Party bunkroom where Gregory spent the night.

In addition to math, science and language skills, the students studied the history of the Black Panther Party and received political education. When they went on field trips to places like San Quentin prison, they wore their Panther uniforms and berets as they did in class. Sometimes they were given the task of distributing Party literature. That was one assignment Gregory remembered participating in.

Among their class projects was writing letters to the numerous incarcerated Panther Party members. Ericka Huggins had started teaching at the institute when she returned West from New Haven in the summer of 1971, after dismissal of murder charges against her and Bobby Seale. Ultimately, she became IYI's Director. Gregory had her as a teacher in summer school.

By 1973, IYI had outgrown its space. The Panthers then opened an alternative learning center featuring IYI. It soon evolved into the Oakland Community School, with its new home in the Fruitvale District of Oakland. The establishment of the Community School was spearheaded by Huey's new Leftist admirer David Horowitz, a former editor of the now-defunct *Ramparts* magazine. The school's motto was: "The World is a Child's Classroom." In order to be self-sustaining, it required accreditation and federal funding. Obtaining government funding necessitated accepting a broader range of students. It also involved dropping residency requirements and uniforms as they broadened their curriculum from Panther-focused teachings. Some of the federal funds wound up being embezzled, for which Huey would later plead guilty. Yet the school itself thrived under Huggins' leadership.

Huggins focused on teaching critical thinking. The school drew inspirational visits from national megastars. Among the guest speakers were civil rights icon Rosa Parks, authors and poets James Baldwin and Maya Angelou, and pioneering farm labor organizer Cesar Chavez. In 1977, the school would earn a commendation from the California legislature for reaching "the highest level of scholastic achievement in elementary education and for having concretely defied the myth of the uneducable child." The school drew television cameras to an assembly. Maurice was puzzled to see his uncle wearing makeup. His parents explained that it was common for speakers being prepared for the glare of television cameras.

Gregory and Tracy remember an event on August 17,1978 when reporters and cameramen again flocked to the school. Both Gregory, age 13 and Tracy, age 9 were enrolled in the summer program. On the stage with Huey and more than 20 schoolchildren was Huey's former tailor, Preston Callins. The children were taught to sing a song written for them which praised "Mr. Preston" as a hero for retracting his accusation of pistol-whipping by Newton in 1974. Tracy still remembers the lyrics:

> Mr. Preston is the hero of the day.
> He tells the truth in every way.
> He set our leader free,
> Stop the oppression of the DA.
> Mr. Preston is the hero of the day.

Regaining Close Ties With Nieces and Nephews

When Maurice was old enough to attend high school, he and his parents lived in the Rockridge District of North Oakland. That was too far away to qualify for admission to his preferred choice of Skyline High in the Oakland hills. His Uncle Huey let Maurice use his address instead, so Maurice was able to attend Skyline High in the same class as Huey's stepson Ronnie. Gwen's daughter Jessica was two years behind them. During these years, Maurice spent a lot of time with his cousin Ronnie and Uncle Huey. Tracy grew close to Ronnie's sister Jessica, often staying at each other's home overnight.

Maurice discovered Uncle Huey to be as accessible as Sonny Man and Brother. Despite his celebrity status, Huey put on no airs. Maurice found him both charismatic and passionate about subjects that intrigued him. He also gave Maurice advice on movies, girls and other topics the teenager was interested in. He even encouraged Maurice when he said he wanted to attend the Air Force Academy after graduation. (Of course, military service was what taught Bobby Seale to be an excellent marksman, which also prepared him for the Panther Party.)

To the delight of Huey's niece Terrez, she was also able to use the address of her "Uncle Black Power" to attend Skyline High School. It was top-ranked academically among public high schools in Oakland. Most memorably, Huey and Gwen let their teenaged relatives host parties at the house. More than once parties ended with the Oakland Police busting in to follow up on a neighbor's noise complaint. Huey absolutely loved that ranch house. He was proud of his ability to offer it to Fredrika as a place to raise her son, and to make it a place his nieces and nephews considered their second home.

Meanwhile, Huey achieved the pinnacle of his formal education. He earned a college degree and PhD. at the University of California at Santa Cruz, much to the astonishment of the national press.

Dr. Huey P. Newton

THE danger Huey once again faced on Oakland's streets and the dim prospects for a strong Panther Party comeback likely played major roles in his decision to re-enroll in college to pursue his bachelor's degree. Melvin was then Assistant Dean of Merritt College in charge of ethnic studies, business and social science curricula. He assigned psychology instructor McKinley Williams to supervise Huey in student teaching at Merritt College for credit toward his college degree. Huey completed his college degree at U.C. Santa Cruz and was accepted into a new Ph.D. program, the History of Consciousness.

Huey commuted back and forth from Oakland where he still faced criminal proceedings. He cut quite a figure on the UC Santa Cruz campus. Because of his unique circumstances, the department chair let Huey's bodyguards accompany him to classes. The university also accommodated Huey's schedule when he had to spend weeks at a time staying in Oakland for his felony trials. But Huey still battled with addiction while enrolled at the university. The professors drew the line at letting him attend classes when obviously high on drugs.

By 1979, Huey had long since ceased contact with his former lawyer Fay Stender. They were no longer on speaking terms. Fay had progressed from representing revolutionary clients to launching the nation's largest prisoners' rights program. She had filed class actions and recruited volunteers from mainstream law firms to champion prisoners' constitutional claims. Her ambitious project ran out of funding in 1973 but spawned far more such efforts going forward by pro bono lawyers, criminal law professors and law school students. More recently, she had focused on women's issues and promoting Lesbian adoption rights. Yet her past association with Huey Newton and George Jackson still left her despised by the Black Guerilla Family. Like Newton, her name wound up in 1974 along with Charles Garry's on the Black Guerilla Family's hit list.

In Berkeley, on Memorial Day weekend 1979, Stender was shot execution-style in her kitchen by a late-night home invader. The gunman accused her of betraying George Jackson. She was the latest in the chain of related violence that started in Soledad in 1968. Indeed, there were already more names to add to the 64 deaths British journalist Jo Durden-Smith had counted as related to the death of George Jackson at San Quentin in 1971. Eleven hostages and 32 inmates died in September of 1971 at Attica when the prisoners erupted in response to George Jackson's death. Stender became yet another casualty.

Stender's assailant, Edward Brooks, turned out to be affiliated with the Black Guerilla Family. Stender barely survived that attack, which permanently cost her the use of her legs. Wheel-chair bound, Stender became the star witness for the prosecution, under 24-hour police guard in a secret location in San Francisco prior to the headline Oakland trial. After the jury convicted Brooks in February 1980, the police protection ended, and Stender secretly fled to Hong Kong for her continued safety.

A year after the shooting, Stender remained in constant pain and still feared for her life if she returned. Seeing no option for a safe homecoming, she committed suicide. Her son, who had also been a threatened state witness at Brooks' trial, was then living in China. He braved the trip back to San Francisco with her body. There, following her wishes, she was remembered at an elaborate funeral at the Temple Emanu-el Congregation. Over 300 friends, colleagues and relatives attended, including California's Chief Justice Rose Bird, who knew Stender as a co-founder of California Women Lawyers.

At Stender's funeral some took ironic notice that the attendees were almost exclusively White. Neither Huey, nor the many other former Black Panthers she had worked with, joined those paying their respects. Though Huey stayed focused on getting his Ph.D., Fay Stender's death must have reminded him how much his own life remained at risk. By the time of Fay's funeral, Huey was about to turn in his thesis, "War Against the Panthers: A Study of Repression in America." A friend asked him how long he had been working on it. Huey facetiously replied: "Thirteen years — since the Party was founded." Actually, it echoed key parts of his lecture from the witness stand in the summer of 1968, so it did reflect years of historical study and contemplation.

Huey's thesis also drew on discovery in two recent Panther Party lawsuits against government officials and the FBI. The dissertation placed covert FBI and COINTELPRO operations against the Party in the context of historical repression of political dissidents dating back to the violent confrontation between militant laborers and police in the infamous 1886 Chicago Hay Market Square May Day incident.

Huey actually went further back in time to the founding of the country, tracing the genesis of the war against the Panthers to two key original problems with the

Constitution that persisted ever since: "class and racial cleavages ... and the inherent and longstanding distrust held by the American ruling class of ... the mass population." He asserted that both had kept "the very fabric of American society in rather constant peril."

The dissertation noted that the wealthy landowners who created the Constitution restricted democracy to privileged people like themselves, leaving out "sizable sectors: African Americans, Native Americans, and, to a lesser extent, women." Huey considered this exclusion "the original wellspring of dissent in America" because "democracy is a dynamic and infectious idea ... which inspires the hope of universal inclusion." He contended that "the arbitrary, capricious, and sinister exclusion of large sectors of the American population ... predisposed the population to varying but continuous levels of warfare ...." Still unremedied nearly two centuries later, that polarization inspired resort to "force of arms, and resolve to face death before capitulation."

Huey stated that the "scruples-free premise of American ruling class authority from the society's inception to the present" perpetuated their "initial socioeconomic advantage, begotten by chattel slavery." He linked slavery in later times to "political repression, peonage (debt slavery), wage slavery, chicanery, and the like ... always accompanied by the actual or threatened ... violence."

With this background, Huey's aim was to chronicle "the rise in the 1960s of control tactics heavily reliant upon infiltration, deliberate misinformation, selective harassment, and the use of the legal system" to destroy the Panther Party. A direct link was made to the appeal of the Panthers' 10-point program. Huey attributed the

FBI's motivation to quash "the Party's . . . potential for organizing a sizable group of the country's population . . . historically denied equal opportunity in employment, education, housing, and other recognized basic needs." The thesis then focused upon measures undertaken by the government summarized by the FBI itself: to "expose, disrupt, misdirect, discredit or otherwise neutralize" the Black Panther Party.

Two principal sources of information for the thesis were FBI records obtained under the Freedom of Information Act and material recently made public by the Senate Church Committee. That Committee revealed shocking details of the secret executive order signed by President Nixon. "The Huston Plan", named for the White House aide who prepared the original report, had given the CIA and FBI Nixon's purported authorization to engage in burglary, illegal wiretapping and interception of mail of a list of targets. In the case of the Panthers, the committee report noted that the FBI took it upon itself to physically destroy office equipment in Panther offices across the country. It also sabotaged the Panthers' hugely successful free breakfast program for school children in ghettoized neighborhoods and sales of Panther papers, the Panthers' main source of revenue. Most shockingly, the report revealed that the CIA and FBI also framed key Panther targets for murder, relentlessly hounded a prominent actress who ultimately committed suicide; and themselves committed other violent crimes, including murder.

Walter would have been as proud as Armelia and other family members in Huey's achievement in chronicling the FBI's history of outrageous misconduct toward the Panther Party. Armelia delighted in the chance to see her son awarded a PhD. Melvin and Barbarette brought her down to Santa Cruz to witness the ceremonies along with their teenaged son Maurice and toddler son David Lautaro. Maurice knew this was a higher achievement than college, but he wasn't sure quite what it signified. Huey jested that, from then on in Oakland, those who treated him with racist derision would now have to call him "Dr. Nigger."

Huey with his toddler nephew David Lautaro Newton at the ceremony where Huey was awarded his Ph.D. at U.C. Santa Cruz in June of 1980

Source: Huey Newton and Herman Blake, *Revolutionary Suicide* (New York, Harcourt, Brace & Jovanovich (1973),

DéjàVu

IN December 1982, Huey totaled his car while driving under the influence. He almost killed himself and Ronnie and Jessica, who were riding with him. His wife Gwen took custody of her teenagers. Ronnie was in his senior year at Skyline. He graduated that spring as Gwen was preparing to leave the state and file for divorce.

One night in late 1983, a recent graduate of the Oakland Police Academy was patrolling alone on the graveyard shift in West Oakland. Sometime after 2 a.m., Officer Timothy Sanchez was headed East on 10th Street, approaching its intersection with Willow Street. So far, the rookie's shift had remained unexciting. Then he saw a dark Mercedes Benz whiz by on Willow, traveling south at a rate far in excess of the 25 mile per hour speed limit. Officer Sanchez switched on his lights and siren and gave chase.

The patrol car was within half a block of the Mercedes as its driver neared 8th Street, still headed south. The car then ran the stop sign at 7th and Willow. It started to turn right and then veered left, heading east on 7th. The maneuver slowed the vehicle down enough for Officer Sanchez to catch up and to notice there was at least one passenger in the car. At that point, the driver yielded to the siren and pulled over in front of the main post office. When Officer Sanchez started to exit his patrol car, he saw the driver's door open. The driver jumped out and began to walk back toward him.

As an Oakland native, Sanchez immediately recognized the man coming toward him was none other than Huey Newton. The passenger also got out — a huge bodyguard.

Sanchez froze. He knew that his good friend Cliff Heanes had been wounded at that very location in the infamous 1967 predawn confrontation with the Black Panther leader that left officer John Frey dead. It flashed on Sanchez that he could easily meet the same fate.

Yet Huey quickly threw his hands up and assured Sanchez that "everything's ok." Sanchez took a close look at Huey's eyes. They looked like saucers, which he assumed his own eyes did, too. Sanchez thought Huey was just as terrified as he was. But Huey's widely dilated pupils might have instead indicated he was once again driving high on cocaine.

Both men then handled themselves quite politely. Huey produced his driver's license and Sanchez started writing up a ticket. There was no way to clock the excessive speed of the Mercedes Benz, so Sanchez simply charged Huey with running the stop sign. Sanchez handed the ticket to Huey, who drove off with his bodyguard without further incident.

Armelia's Last Years

ARMELIA continued as long as she could living alone in the house she and Walter had purchased on 47th Street in North Oakland. For entertainment, she still loved daytime soap operas. But ill health impelled her to begin to stay alternately with one of her three daughters, mostly with Leola. Armelia rented out her own house. She probably realized that Myrtle's apartment was bad for her health, since Myrtle was a chronic smoker despite her asthma.

Some of the time that Armelia lived with Leola, Leola was also raising Sonny Man's daughter Myesha with mixed results. The only aunts and uncles Myesha responded well to were Uncle Huey and Aunt Gwen and Uncle Melvin and Aunt Barbarette. They were sympathetic and patient with her anger management problems. Huey and Gwen took her to the park and on long walks. Myesha recalled them also taking her to San Francisco to ride on a cable car and tour Fisherman's Wharf.

For Terrez, Armelia's stay had both pluses and minuses. On the one hand, Terrez, like Myesha, experienced her grandmother's ire when Terrez did not do her bidding. On the other hand, Armelia almost always presented her grandchildren with a brown paper bag containing candy. Sometimes, there were only three wrapped pieces of butterscotch or peppermint. Armelia must have recalled how popular her mother-in-law Alice was with Armelia's children when Alice brought them treats.

Even in her later years, Armelia was not always attentive to her health. She had a habit of using snuff, which not everyone in the family knew about. Her children refused to buy it for her. The tobacco product was a bad health risk for diabetics. Her doctor may have warned Armelia against smoking or using snuff because of its known tendency to exacerbate diabetes and dangerously lower the user's blood sugar.

Armelia, however, was not dissuaded. She turned to a couple of Black Panthers, and her older grandchildren, Terrez among them, to buy snuff for her. Armelia also was partial to sherry, which is generally lower in sugar than most other wines. Her doctor may have actually suggested sipping sherry when taking blood sugar medications to make the medicine more palatable. Yet Armelia must have been drinking far more sherry than was good for her. She kept running out and often sent her granddaughter Terrez out to buy more while Armelia was living out her last years with Leola.

Barbarette, meanwhile, had continued her efforts to ingratiate herself with Armelia. Finally, as Armelia approached the end of her life, those efforts seemed to be paying off. For about two decades, Armelia had been in and out of hospitals several times. She entered the hospital for the last time in the spring of 1985. Lautaro recalls visiting her in that final stay. He was six-and-a-half when she died that June, surrounded by close family. Her funeral at the Paradise Baptist Church drew a full house of grievers.

This time Huey was able to attend his parent's funeral. The prior fall, he had remarried. His second wife was Fredrika Slaughter, the daughter of Panther realtor Arlene Slaughter. Huey had dated Fredrika on and off since 1970 when she was a college student. Fredrika had a child of her own, Keiron Slaughter, who lived with them. In her last months, Armelia had to hope that her adored youngest son was in a stable situation that might last. She had worried about Huey so much since he was a teen.

Among the mourners was Armelia's namesake. Lee Edward's daughter Armelia had little contact with her grandmother, or her father for that matter, after she had started elementary school. Yet she fondly remembered the movies her father took her and her brother Lawrence to at the Fox Theater in Oakland and the dollhouse and tricycle he bought her. Later, they had little or no interaction while her mother barely made ends meet as a domestic worker raising two children in West Oakland on her own.

Armelia the younger only began having regular contact with the Newton family in the 1980s, when she was in her 30s and had sons of her own. Her father would invite her and his two grandsons to come with him when he joined Sonny Man at Doris's house to watch football games.

Doris soon began inviting Armelia and her family to attend Thanksgiving and Christmas dinners at her home. Because of Melvin's long estrangement from Doris and Myrtle, he had little contact with Armelia until his brother Lee's funeral and later the services for his sisters. It was likely no coincidence that Doris's outreach to Lee Edward's daughter came after the family matriarch had died. Mother never took a liking to her namesake.

* * *

Soon after the funeral for their mother, the siblings met up at Melvin's home to divide up Armelia's personal effects. A decision was also made to sell Armelia's home to cousin "Big Jimmie" Ward, who would soon remodel it and rent it to Esther and her family. Myrtle had hoped the property would be gifted to her since she owned no home, instead of simply splitting the proceeds among all of the siblings. Maybe that was on her mind when she took out a cigarette.

Melvin had adopted a rule in his home about smoking because Barbarette was allergic to smoke. Visitors could only light cigarettes in their family room on the bottom floor. Myrtle took offense at the way he spoke to her about not smoking upstairs and believed Melvin was telling her she had to leave his house. She quickly departed. Other issues had arisen between them. She was determined never to speak to Melvin again.

Myrtle's anger was likely fueled in part by Melvin's avoidance, since the summer of 1970, of her family parties where Joyce generally made an appearance. But Myrtle's rift with Melvin did not affect her daughter Patricia's fondness for Melvin and Barbarette. Patricia would often come to babysit their son Lautaro and his baby sister, Brianna, who was born in January 1986.

Despite the unresolved issues between them, Melvin did come to visit Myrtle once or twice after 1985 at her home. In December 2012, when Myrtle was about to celebrate her 87th birthday with family at the nursing home where she spent her last days, Myrtle asked after Melvin, apparently hoping they could celebrate their mutual birthday together once more. Unfortunately, he was not in town.

Winning the Heart of Another Nephew

IN 1988, Huey had a major falling out with Fredrika over his recurrent drug use and violent behavior. She had previously persuaded him to enter rehabilitation programs for his drug problem, but he could not shake his addiction. She later reflected that Huey exhibited extreme mood swings indicative of undiagnosed bipolar disorder. The pair were broke. After he lost his Oakland hills home to foreclosure by the IRS, they had moved to the house in Berkeley she inherited from her mother. When Fredrika kicked him out, he asked Melvin and Barbarette if he could stay with them in their house on Redwood Road in Oakland. They welcomed him to use their renovated ground floor.

By then, Melvin and Barbarette's youngest son, David Lautaro Newton, was nine years old. Their baby daughter, Brianna, was just a toddler. Gregory, Tracy and Maurice were all grown. Gregory had pursued a teaching career; Tracy had become a corporate trainer; and Maurice went to the Air Force Academy and became a pilot.

At school, David went by his first name. The family all called him by his middle name, Lautaro, which means "swift hawk" in the native language of the Chilean hero they named their son for. Lautaro was a sixteenth century warrior. As the son of a chieftain, he led the Mapuche tribe against Spanish invaders when the conquistadors sought to enslave his people. He died in battle at age 23. Huey had to be especially proud to call his little nephew Lautaro.

For his part, Lautaro was thrilled to have Uncle Huey

come live with them. Lautaro had already enjoyed visiting Uncle Huey and Aunt Fredrika in Berkeley and had gone on a number of local outings with his favorite uncle. Huey offered to babysit when Melvin and Barbarette went out. Then Uncle Huey would let Lautaro stay up to watch his favorite movies and music videos with him.

Top of the list was Emilio Estevez's debut as a director, "Wisdom," released in 1986. Huey could easily relate to the movie's hero, John Wisdom, played by Estevez. Wisdom's girlfriend, Karen Simmons, was played by Demi Moore. The film depicts Wisdom engaging in a drunken spree the night he graduated high school that ended with his arrest and conviction for auto theft. The felony record prevented him from obtaining a good job following college, so he opted instead to turn to crime to benefit poor farmers and other low-wage workers as a modern Robin Hood.

One could understand why the film appealed so much to Huey. Instead of taking money, the pair deleted loan records, which delayed the farmers' debt collectors. When the couple were pursued by the FBI, a sheriff recognized them. Karen panicked and killed him. Soon, Karen was shot, and John Wisdom proceeded alone, only to die unarmed in a hail of gunfire from police and FBI men. When the film ended, the entire saga turned out to have been a bad daydream. Wisdom was actually on his way to a job interview. Huey and Lautaro watched it twice.

Once while babysitting, Huey decided to teach Lautaro to drive. This was something Huey had previously offered to other teenage relatives. Myrtle's granddaughter Kim relished the secret driving adventure Great Uncle Huey took her on around 1980, when she was 11 or 12. Lautaro was ten in 1988 when Uncle Huey gave him his own private driving lesson. Melvin's youngest son was still too short to reach the car's foot pedals, so Huey sat as close as he could to Lautaro. Huey then put his own feet on the brake and gas pedals while Lautaro steered.

Melvin and Barbarette had no idea about this excursion until they headed home and saw Huey in his car coming down Redwood Road near their house with a small child behind the wheel. They suddenly recognized their son Lautaro. For Lautaro, it was a memorable adventure. For his parents, it was an unpleasant reminder that they had left their son with a babysitter who recognized no behavioral guardrails.

Trying to Make Amends

DURING the time Huey stayed with Melvin and Barbarette, he was once again on probation — this time from his conviction for embezzling funds from the Panther school. That meant periodic visits from a parole officer to check Huey's urine. Huey had to know that he would fail the test, as he had started using drugs again. Yet he took drugs anyway. which Melvin could see from the glazed look in Huey's eyes. Lautaro sometimes heard his uncle pacing the downstairs floor at night, like Huey used to do in jail. When drugs were found in his urine, Huey wound up once again in San Quentin. Perhaps that parole violation was purposeful. There was something he wanted to do there.

Huey must have known that Geronimo Pratt was still at San Quentin. Geronimo was serving his sixteenth year in prison following his conviction in 1972 for a 1968 murder in Southern California. Since then, Pratt had changed his last name and now went by Geronimo Ji Jaga. Huey knew that Ji Jaga had not committed the murder of a schoolteacher and wounding of her husband during an armed robbery at a Santa Monica tennis court on the evening of December 18, 1968. Huey was aware that Geronimo had been wrongly picked out of a lineup two years later by the victim's husband. The FBI also knew that Geronimo was misidentified as the perpetrator. Geronimo had been framed by one of their informants who claimed that Geronimo had confessed to him.

Huey had good reason to know the truth as well as the FBI did. On the very day of the murder, the FBI had tailed Geronimo to Oakland where he was observed attending a Panther Central Committee meeting with both Bobby Seale and David Hilliard. At his 1972 murder trial, Geronimo had insisted he was 350 miles from Santa Monica on the evening of the armed robbery. But the FBI suppressed confirmation of that alibi. So did the Panthers under Huey's leadership. Back in 1971, Pratt had opted to side with Eldridge Cleaver in his split with Huey. In retaliation, Huey had given Seale and Hilliard strict orders not to come to Pratt's defense at the 1972 trial. But that was then, and the injustice now weighed on Huey's mind.

The day scheduled for Huey's release from his parole violation, Melvin drove to San Quentin with street clothes for Huey to wear on their ride back to Oakland. Melvin waited for a while but left when told that Huey was refusing to leave prison unless they freed Geronimo as well. Prison officials then locked Huey up in the Adjustment Center. Word got out quickly among the prisoners, including both Geronimo JiJaga and former Panther Rudolph Mitchell in a nearby cell. The two asked a guard if they could get permission to go talk to Huey and convince him to accept his release.

The unusual request was granted. Mitchell and JiJaga were escorted to Huey's cell and convinced him that there was no way that JiJaga would be released in response to Huey's protest. Huey would be of far greater service to them on the outside. Huey then decided to cooperate with the prison administration and accept his immediate release.

Later that day, Huey showed up at Melvin's front door, still in his prison garb. Melvin had no idea how his brother managed to get back to Melvin's house. It was hard to imagine anyone wanting to pick up a hitchhiker outside San Quentin still wearing jailhouse clothing. Huey then remained at Melvin's home in Oakland until he reconciled with Fredrika.

It took another decade for Ji Jaga to win his freedom, with help from Kathleen Cleaver as one of his appellate lawyers. (Kathleen had divorced Eldridge and pursued a Yale law degree and career on the Yale and Emory University faculties.) Meanwhile Ji Jaga had attracted considerable international attention to his claim of political persecution. After the charges were dismissed, Ji Jaga sued the City of Los Angeles and the federal government for false imprisonment and obtained a $4.5 million settlement.

XII.

Death and Rebirth Larger Than Life

Irony in Death

AFTER several months living with Melvin, Huey was invited back home by Fredrika. He stayed sober for months. That summer of 1989, he and Fredrika were expecting news any day confirming that he would be the subject of a film biography. Huey had faith that the project would be his savior even after his longtime Hollywood buddy and patron Bert Schneider stopped supporting him. Meanwhile, to eke out a living, Fredrika was taking in young foster children. A condition of their placement with Fredrika required her to keep Huey out of the house due to his felony record. She relented when she saw how kind and caring he was toward the preschoolers. Fredrika knew how volatile he would have quickly become if he were then back on drugs.

On Monday, August 21, Huey was surprised to learn that the film deal had fallen through. The news left him inconsolable. Its timing could not have been worse. The phone call came just before a social worker was about to pay a visit. Fredrika shooed him out of the house with instructions to collect her son Kieron from the day camp he attended. Fredrika regretfully never saw Huey alive again.

Looking back, she believed Huey must have had a premonition of his impending death. Despite their desperate finances, he had recently urged her to buy a life insurance policy on him. He had also begun giving away his suits. He gave one to Sonny Man and to his eldest brother Lee, with whom in those days he rarely interacted. Huey also arranged with Fredrika to sell Panther memorabilia they had kept in her basement. That sale never happened.

Fredrika soon learned that Huey did not pick up her son at daycare. It appeared he was off on another binge. She was right. He headed for a crack house on Center Street in West Oakland. It was in the same neighborhood where the early morning shootout with officers Frey and Heanes had happened almost 22 years before. As of late, Huey had been a frequent visitor to that drug den, where he lectured anyone who cared to listen to his political philosophy. Huey had once established social programs in that same building. Down and out, he was now once again looking to buy drugs.

Huey understood the risk of going out alone at night unarmed. That was why he had spent years surrounded by bodyguards. Perhaps he felt safe heading back to his old haunts in West Oakland. Or perhaps his fatalism and depression got the better of him. Huey had envisioned his own death many times throughout the course of his short life. He'd often talked about "fighting to the death" among his comrades. But the abrupt end of Huey's life would have nothing in common with courageous confrontation of adversaries at the risk of life and limb.

It happened when he'd returned to the notorious Lower Bottoms community in search of a fix. His body was discovered at 5 a.m. on August 22, 1989 just outside the crack house on Center Street. An assailant left him lying on a sidewalk with three gunshot wounds to the head. Huey was 47, the same age as Fay Stender when she was shot execution style.

In an ironic twist, one of the two Berkeley police officers who testified for the prosecution in Huey's 1968 trial had since become both the Alameda County Sheriff and Coroner. In his role as Coroner, Charlie Plummer made a personal visit to the morgue to see for himself that the victim really was Huey Newton.

The news appeared so quickly on television that the cameras caught the firemen hosing Huey's blood off the pavement of Center Street. Melvin got a call early that morning and woke up his son Lautaro to tell him the shocking news: "They've killed Huey." He then called other family members and David Hilliard to break the news: "Huey's dead." It took some repetition for Hilliard to absorb that Huey had been shot and left to die in West Oakland's streets.

Melvin had no idea at the time which of Huey's many enemies might have taken his life. Melvin confided to David: "We always knew this was gonna happen. We just didn't know when." Hilliard realized that he had also felt for more than a decade that Huey was living on borrowed time. After coming back from Cuba, Huey's enemies multiplied: "police from Party days, gangsters and dealers from the days after." Hilliard also figured that Huey's drug habit could have played a part. Hilliard also attributed Huey's death to cockiness in assuming he could always outmaneuver his antagonists. Hilliard himself had recently completed a rehab program. He wanted to be careful not to trigger any retaliation if he started asking around to find out who killed Huey and why.

***

The intense media coverage left the entire Newton family with no privacy to absorb the devastating blow. They were only grateful that both of their parents had died before Huey. Their pain would have been even more unbearable. It would take years for Myrtle to adjust to the loss of her beloved baby brother. Like Melvin and David Hilliard, she and others in the family had worried for a long time about something happening to Huey, given all the enemies he had made. But all that unease did not prepare them for the actuality of Huey's death.

The next day, the *Oakland Tribune* ran a three-page spread on the life and death of Huey Newton. The coverage was far more balanced than if the Knowland family had still owned the paper. For the preceding decade, the *Tribune* had been edited by acclaimed African-American journalist Robert Maynard, who became its owner in 1984. The extensive coverage included an article captioned: "Friends and foes remember Newton: 'visionary,' 'thug,'." Among others with diametrically opposed views, it quoted Charles Garry and prosecutor Thomas Orloff. Garry said that his long-time client "should be remembered as a tremendous contributor to the quality of [life for] Black Americans." Orloff bluntly disagreed: "The Newton I dealt with in the '70s was basically a gangster. There was nothing political about him."

Melvin had a new mission. He had to find out what happened to Huey both for Melvin's own sake and for his family. The murderer of his brother needed to be held accountable. He would do what he could to make sure his brother's death did not remain an unsolved crime.

Melvin and David Hillard paired up to seek out potential witnesses just as they had done back in the fall of 1967. Hilliard had already put out word that he was looking for information. He quickly learned from the autopsy that Huey had been banged on the head with a gun. Three bullets struck him in the face from someone standing close to him with a nine-millimeter gun. No gun was found with Huey's body. The police determined he was unarmed.

Huey's corpse was found with his head in the rose bushes and his body on the street near the corner of Center and Ninth Streets. When told the details, both Melvin and David thought the job sounded like that of a hitman, but this was no "drive-by." The bullets had been fired within six inches of Huey's head. They assumed Huey had to have been meeting this fellow by prearrangement. Fredrika mentioned that he was extremely depressed at the time she last saw him the afternoon before he died. It seemed most likely that it was a drug purchase gone awry.

The pair visited the site of the killing more than once over the next week. At first, there were just two police officers and a handful of television crews. Soon, people left bouquets of flowers and cards expressing their sorrow. It only took a week for the police to zero in on a young drug dealer who had boasted of the killing to several friends. It was not someone who Melvin would have expected.

Twenty-five-year-old Tyrone Robinson had participated as a child in a Panther free-breakfast program when his family lived in a West Oakland housing project. Robinson's father had gone to elementary school with Melvin. Huey knew his uncles, too. Robinson had since become a small-time crack cocaine dealer who had been in and out of prison since 1983 when he was convicted of robbing a fifteen-year-old. The stocky street hustler's nickname was "Double R." He had just been released again on parole in June of 1989.

Huey may not have known that in prison Robinson had become a member of the Black Guerilla Family, the gang founded at San Quentin by George Jackson. The members of the BGF were sworn to secrecy — their own Mafia-like omertà. Robinson believed that nearly twenty years after Jackson's death, the BGF still prioritized killing Huey. That belief had likewise propelled BGF wannabe Edward Brooks to avenge the presumed 1971 betrayal of George Jackson by shooting Fay Stender in 1979.

Robinson made the mistake of bragging to a couple of friends about killing Newton to gain street cred with the BGF. Two of them were interviewed on tape by the police three days after the shooting. One quoted Robinson saying: "I'm going to move up in the ranks because I killed Huey Newton." When arrested, Robinson told the police he acted in self-defense after Huey drew a gun in an attempt to rob him. Further investigation would convince the District Attorney's office that was a lie.

Yet Robinson had committed a cardinal sin. Once word got out about his boast, reporters heard that the gang responded by issuing a new death sentence. This time it was against Robinson himself, for violating their code of silence. Robinson must have counted himself lucky that he remained in prison awaiting trial.

Shortly after Huey's murder, Tyrone's father Lee Aiken came to Melvin's house and saw the press had converged there. Lee spotted Melvin's daughter Tracy outside the house and took her aside to convey his heartfelt apology for Huey's death at Tyrone's hands. He said, "Huey was my friend." Then he left without seeing Melvin.

A Funeral for the Ages

A CARAVAN of limousines accompanied the hearse carrying Huey Newton's flower-bedecked wooden casket. Television cameras and a flock of reporters covered the funeral procession. Reporter Brenda Payton called Huey "the face of Black defiance." She included herself among his admirers for his brash show of militancy, though she ultimately considered his approach immature.

The entourage passed through blocks of buildings whose walls were newly covered with Panther slogans and graffiti silhouettes of Huey. The caravan then pulled up to the Allen Temple Baptist Church, Oakland's largest Black congregation. Huey had become a member of Allen Tempe in his last years. The church was festooned with Pan-African flags, Panther posters and an enormous banner proclaiming "Huey Lives."

Ironically, Huey's death echoed that of the populist Southern governor for whom he was named. Huey Long had also made deadly enemies and was ultimately murdered. Yet more than 200,000 people had attended the Kingfish's funeral. Close to two thousand people attended Huey's service. About 1300 of them crowded into the pews. Hundreds more gathered to listen to the loudspeakers outside. Most of the crowd were Black but some Whites and Latinos were also present.

Maurice Newton wore his full-dress uniform as a Lieutenant in the Air Force as he joined his grieving parents and siblings. The size of the crowd stunned younger members of the family, including Lucy Newton Robinson, E.S's daughter, who came from Detroit to pay her respects to her cousin. Huey had made an indelible impression on Lucy on her first trip to California to meet her Uncle Walter's family in the summer of 1984. The first place her Aunt Leola took Lucy to was a bar called "Sweet Jimmy's." Jimmy Ward ran that bar after leaving the Lamp Post. It was there that Lucy met her famous cousin Huey. He invited her to come with Leola to dinner the next night at his own house in the Oakland hills where they were joined by his new fiancée, Fredrika. Huey fixed a simple steak and salad for the four of them — one of the very few meals he tended to prepare — and told stories from his three years in Cuba.

Lucy found Huey fascinating. A day or two later, he took her on a driving tour of Oakland, pointing out where the family had lived, and locations of sites associated with the Black Panthers. It left Lucy feeling a special connection to Huey. There was no way she would miss paying her respects at his funeral. Lucy stayed with Doris, who made sure to keep her cousin close by as they navigated the swarming crowds, the likes of which Lucy had never seen before.

From the vehicles emerged Huey's widow Fredrika and her son Kieron as well as a Who's Who of former Panther stars: Bobby Seale, Elaine Brown, Angela Davis, David Hilliard and H. Rap Brown (now calling himself Imam Jamal Abdulla Al-Amin as head of an Islamic community in Atlanta). Though two Black City Council members showed up at the service, noticeably absent was Oakland's Mayor, Lionel Wilson, then ending his third term, and gearing up to run unsuccessfully for a fourth. (His successor, Elihu Harris, was also African-American).

Upon learning how many ex-Panthers would be

attending the funeral, city officials feared an outbreak of violence. It was something of a surprise to see Bobby Seale back in Oakland after fifteen years' absence. Following his precipitous departure from the Party in the summer of 1974, Seale had never again crossed paths with Huey. But there was no reason to consider him a threat to anyone's safety. The surviving Party co-founder had become best known near the end of his long absence from Oakland for his popular 1988 cookbook, *Barbeque'n with Bobby, Down-Home Barbeque Recipes by Bobby Seale*. He dedicated the proceeds to charity.

To no one's surprise, Eldridge Cleaver did not show up. It had been over eighteen years since Huey had expelled him from the Panther Party. By the time the Cleavers returned to the United States from Algeria in 1975 with their two children, Eldridge was totally disillusioned with the Left. He announced that he had undergone a religious epiphany and was now a born-again Christian who embraced capitalism.

Before Eldridge arrived in California, his lawyers had already arranged a plea bargain for his 1968 parole violation. He pleaded guilty to assaulting police officers back in April of that year, and, in exchange, was promised no jail time. The Panthers suspected that part of the deal involved Cleaver turning government informant. After he split with Kathleen, Eldridge was baptized into the Mormon Church, registered Republican, and endorsed his old nemesis Ronald Reagan for President.

Inside the capacious church, the Servant of the People lay in an open casket with his beard shaved off, dressed in a gray suit, shirt and red tie. His legs were festooned with roses and carnations in a well-designed, heavy wooden casket — not the simple pine box Huey had once envisioned. The flowers only partially masked the odor of death. The family had not been happy that the police took so long to release Huey's body so the medical examiner could complete his autopsy.

Seale donned a trademark Panther Black beret to lead the eulogies in the three-hour service as if there had been no love lost between them. KPFA public radio in Berkeley covered the orations live. With a clenched fist salute to his co-founder, Seale recounted the major community programs the Panthers instituted. He told his audience that they tested more people for sickle cell anemia than all state and federal programs combined.

Congressman Ron Dellums told the audience that he first met Newton as a student at Merritt College when they were in a study group together (the Afro-American Association). Dellums pointed out that "the very same streets that [Huey] tried to make safe for the children are the streets that took his life." David Hilliard challenged the audience to deal with drug and alcohol dependency before it brought down their whole race. Elaine Brown remembered him as "a hero who sparked a dream of freedom in all of us runaway slaves."

Dr. Donn Granville Davis counted himself among the large number of attendees who revered Huey as a man who moved mountains. Dr. Davis focused on Huey's contradictions: "as despised by some as much as he was loved by others. His life . . . was an unparalleled series of highs and lows; a huge, jagged mountain of peaks and valleys that only he could traverse . . . .. Passionate and fearless determination were perhaps the most memorable aspects of Huey's undaunted personality . . . .." Yet he noted: "Those looking for such shortcomings found many in Huey, for he was quintessentially human."

Father Earl Neil lambasted the mainstream press for focusing only on Huey's misdeeds. Neil urged his listeners to see the most famous member of the congregation as he did — a brilliant visionary and courageous prophet. Father Neil called Huey "our Moses" battling modern day pharaohs. One elderly woman reportedly shook her head in disbelief at all the lavish praise for a "plain old thug." All these fools are trying to make him into a saint, but he was a real-life sinner. Comparing him to Dr. King or Malcolm [X] is downright blasphemy."

Reverend Smith ended the eulogies by asking the congregation to repeat the old familiar chant from 1968: "Free Huey, Free Huey" and then added, "Well, let me tell you, he's free!! He's free!!!"

Within days of the funeral, poet Carolyn Baxter sought to capture both the strengths and weaknesses of "The Servant of the People" in "Huey P. Newton — The Frailty's and Flaws of a Man":

> Genius of an Innovator.
> Heart of a Black Panther.
> Spoken about on the News like a Criminal,
> mentioning Drug use.
> So much blood, from his head,
> they said covered almost 15 feet in diameter
> around his body,
> as Huey lay [in] eternal sleep on Concrete . . .
> Who killed Huey, Yo!?
> The same people he set out to feed, educate and free.

The very size of the funeral crowd belied Baxter's assumption that Huey died at the hands of the same people "he set out to feed, educate and free." Tyrone Robinson did not represent most Blacks in the flatlands. Most residents there admired the way "The Servant of the People" encouraged them to stand tall. It was mostly their small donations that funded Huey's elaborate funeral.

The turnout for his funeral demonstrated that the Black community as a whole valued Huey's overall aim and accomplishments. They were forgiving of his personal flaws. As Melvin Newton later pointed out, it was Huey's decision to put America on trial in 1968 with his own life on the line that launched the Panther Party and its platform as an international phenomenon. Otherwise, they would likely have disappeared within a year:

> "These were very young people. If you were twenty-six years old in the Panther Party, you were an elder. These were people who were in their teens and early twenties, and they went about the business of sacrificing themselves and they didn't necessarily expect to come out of it alive, and some of them didn't. I believe Huey was idealistic . . . he saw himself planting the seed. . . .. [It is] the people who see things a little bit differently than everyone else that foster change and often make for a better society. . ... The people who hear another drum . . . are very, very important to all of us."

The Tyrone Robinson Murder Trial Becomes a Retrial of Huey Newton

BY 1986, Lowell Jensen had been appointed to the federal bench after serving as Assistant Attorney General in the Reagan administration. The latest Alameda County District Attorney, Jack Meehan, would oversee the prosecution of Robinson to get justice for Huey's death. As a Deputy District Attorney, Meehan had once prosecuted Huey. But the policy of the office was to seek justice for all perceived homicide victims, including Huey Newton. Even so, many in the DA's office still harbored great frustration from their inability in the 1970s to convict him for the death of Officer John Frey.

For the police, Frey was not a forgotten victim. His killing was commemorated annually at a ceremony in front of a memorial wall inside police headquarters. Plaques on the wall honored officers who died in the line of duty. Frey's daughter, who was just three when her father died, was invited each year to attend the ceremony after she reached adulthood.

When the police were notified of Newton's violent death, they knew all eyes were on them to handle the investigation professionally. The arrest of Tyrone Robinson marked a significant step forward, but investigators continued to gather evidence to build a strong murder case against him. They uncovered an eyewitness, Brian Walton, another cocaine dealer who had been with Robinson in the crack house on Center Street earlier that night, before Huey's body was found on the street corner.

In exchange for immunity, Walton testified at a preliminary hearing that he and Tyrone had just emerged from the crack house when Huey came up to them and demanded drugs. Walton said that Huey appeared high and was acting crazy. Walton offered to take Huey to another house where he had a stash of cocaine he was willing to share. As Huey started to walk away, he yelled to Walton that Robinson had just struck him. Apparently, Robinson had intended to shoot Huey, but his gun jammed. So, Robinson bashed Huey in the head with the gun instead. Robinson quickly borrowed Walton's 9-millimeter gun and shot Huey three times. The first bullet hit Huey in the jaw, knocking him down. The next two hit him in the forehead. Robinson then told Walton that he shot Huey in order to claim bragging rights with the Black Guerilla Family for Huey's' execution. Robinson wanted to position himself to "get me some stripes."

The trial did not get scheduled until two years after Huey died. In the meantime, Robinson remained jailed. Oddly, earlier that year Melvin and Barbarette had attended the 30th reunion of her graduating class at McClymond's High School. Melvin's ex-wife Joyce, Tyrone's aunt and two of his uncles also attended the ceremony.

Melvin had no interest in attending this trial. The single eyewitness, Brian Walton, had been killed committing a robbery in December 1990. Some of the delay involved pretrial litigation by a television station seeking court permission to film the sensational murder trial. Its motion was denied. The defense subpoenaed a reporter, Ken Kelley, to establish admissions Newton made to Kelley about past crimes. Tyrone's lawyer wanted to show that he was justified in fearing for his life when they met that August. Kelley was a former associate of Huey Newton's to whom Huey had apparently let down his guard. Kelley sued to prevent disclosure of his notes and his testimony about that interview. He lost, too.

The jury was comprised of five men and seven women and lasted more than a month. The friends to whom Robinson had bragged of the crime suddenly had fuzzy memories or denied ever informing on Robinson. Instead, police officers took the stand to read the witnesses' taped interviews into the record. The prosecutor had colleagues reenact Brian Walton's pretrial testimony, which both implicated Robinson under the prosecutor's questioning and retreated from some of Walton's earlier bold statements during the defense's cross-examination. Most convincing was the medical examiner, who came to court with gruesome photos of Huey's head wounds. (An amazing job had been done at the mortuary to get his face ready for his open casket funeral just a few days after he was shot.)

Robinson testified on his own behalf, but he had little credibility. He was an ex-felon drug dealer, who admitted using a gun illegally to kill someone. He insisted that Huey drew a gun on him first and that he feared for his life. Robinson cited previous incidents where Huey had brandished a weapon toward him during multiple clashes over cocaine. His defense attorney, Alfons Wagner, used tactics similar to those of Charles Garry. Wagner called a series of witnesses who testified about Newton's history of violence. That tactic had worked better for Garry in vilifying Officer Frey, blaming him as the instigator of the violent confrontation with Huey in 1967.

Among the witnesses was Ken Kelley, the subpoenaed

reporter who unwillingly revealed that Huey had confessed to him several serious crimes. These included the murder of a prostitute (for which Huey had faced two hung juries in the 1970s) and the pistol-whipping of a tailor (who had dropped charges). The reporter also testified that Huey had admitted to ordering the murder of a Black Panther Party bookkeeper. By 1989, when Huey died, the 1974 murder of Betty Van Patter remained unsolved, though Huey was suspected of having ordered it while he was in self-imposed exile in Cuba.

Prosecutor Kenneth Burr told the jury in his closing argument that Huey Newton's propensity for violence was not the issue: "The most violent man who walks the Earth does not deserve to be executed without the protection of the law." As proof of first degree murder, Burr referred to the wounds to Newton's body. Three shots to the head from inches away was not self-defense. After four-and-a-half days of deliberation, the jury came back with a verdict of first-degree murder. The next month, the judge sentenced Tyrone Robinson to 32 years to life in prison.

Only in retrospect, in 2024, did Melvin connect Huey's death at Robinson's hands to the long chain of causally-related deaths that went back to George Jackson's killing in August of 1971. Jackson's death itself could be traced back to retaliation for the death of his mentor Nolen and, even further, to the killing of two Black prisoners in the Soledad "Gladiator School" in 1968.

In November of 2023, 32 years after the sentence was handed down, Robinson received a parole hearing. Huey's widow Fredrika was permitted to attend via Zoom and read a moving statement as the victim's widow. In 2015, Tyrone had killed a cellmate, so his chances of release were slim to begin with. So, it was no surprise when parole was denied, but one of the officials made a point of complimenting Fredrika on her eloquence on behalf of her late husband. Tyrone Robinson, the killer of Huey P. Newton, is not eligible again for parole until 2028.

Up Jumps the Monkey

AMONG Huey's nieces and nephews, Gregory may have been the most affected by his famous uncle's dramatic life and death. As Gregory grew up, he was told by some family members that he shared some of his Uncle Huey's traits. Gregory tilted his head the same way and had a similar voice. He even pronounced some words the same idiosyncratic way that Huey did. If a family member closed his or her eyes Gregory might be mistaken for his uncle.

For Gregory, a sixth sense reinforced a feeling of an extraordinary bond between himself and his Uncle Huey. Hearing speakers at his uncle's funeral eulogize the iconic Servant of the People prompted Gregory to regret he did not engage in more dialogues with Uncle Huey when opportunities had presented themselves.

More than a decade passed after the funeral before Gregory embarked on his master's degree in liberal arts at Saint Mary's College in Moraga, California. Saint Mary's is located just under ten miles East of Merritt College. Gregory must have ruminated for years before he emerged with the idea for his ambitious thesis. In 2004, Gregory completed a draft of a three-act play he called "Up Jumps the Monkey from Obscurity to Fame (A Revolutionary's Tale)."

The proposed drama drew on Huey's key role in founding the Black Panthers; his battles with depression, alcohol and drug use; and his inspirations, goals and impact. Gregory made the ghost of his uncle the protagonist directing a documentary about himself. The play featured real life figures — Gregory and his parents among them — interacting with invented characters, including the personification of Death.

The storyline incorporated both actual events and imaginary conversations, starting with Huey at his own graveyard honoring revolutionaries who died before him. Gregory was fascinated to learn as much as he could about the influences on his uncle's life. Huey was an ardent student of African American history — and in particular the 1822 revolt planned in Charleston, South Carolina by a Black pastor named Denmark Vesey. A former slave trained as a carpenter, Vesey had purchased his freedom. Over the first two decades of the 19th century, Vesey laid the groundwork for a major slave rebellion and escape to Haiti. Betrayed to the authorities by two uneasy slaves, Vesey was tried and hanged along with many of his co-conspirators. What inspired Huey when he learned about Vesey was that he risked his life to free slaves long after he had become a free man himself.

Huey also studied Nat Turner's Rebellion in Virginia in 1831 which ended as unsuccessfully as Vesey's ambitious plot. After Turner was caught, his body was mutilated, and his body parts distributed as souvenirs — a gruesome warning to others. Backlash followed. The very next year Alabama passed a law requiring that any service by a Black preacher be attended by "five respectable slaveholders."

The project kept returning Gregory to his desk after numerous interviews with family members. Gregory gleaned all he could from Huey's writings and other biographical sources. He included in the play confrontations Huey had with police officers and FBI agents, as well as Huey's death scene outside a crack house at the hands of a young man raised in the projects, who had benefitted from the Panthers' community outreach.

Gregory cited Walter Newton as Huey's role model for self-respect; Huey's oldest brother, Lee Edward, as his first instructor on self-defense; Gregory's father, Melvin, as the inspiration for Huey's thirst for knowledge; and Armelia's teachings as the wellspring for Huey's instincts to help others in need.

The proposed play featured Seale's speech at Huey's funeral describing his pride in the 10-point program they developed together for the Panther Party. Gregory highlighted Seale's apparent forgiveness of Huey for expelling him from the Party in 1974. When asked to justify that expulsion, Gregory's character, Director Huey, recognized in retrospect he did not have a good reason. The character's explanation: "The monkey always rises to the occasion. Right or wrong." Up jumps the monkey.

Huey's character then broke the fourth wall by explaining to the anticipated audience that he collaborated with Gregory on this project to help his nephew complete his thesis. A key point in the play occurred when Gregory had Huey mention a letter he had addressed to Melvin and Joyce on learning they were expecting their first-born. The play ended with Gregory finding the long-misplaced letter in his mother's basement.

Huey had penned that letter in January of 1965, more than a year and a half before co-founding the Panther Party. Huey sent the typewritten letter to his brother and sister-in-law from the Santa Rita jail in mid-January 1965. The letter was intended to be read to the child upon reaching an age of awareness of life's absurdity.

In the letter, Huey analogized the dysfunctional state of the world they occupied to an injured man needing to heal. He told his future nephew: "You must love this world and all the painful things . . . therein. . . .. Your purpose in this life should be to make the world a better place. . . .. I love you because you are my brother's and sister's child. You are bones of my bones, and blood of my blood . . . you are part of me. The people of the world are part of you . . . your brothers and sisters."

Melvin Newton with his grown children. Left to right: David Lautaro Newton, Melvin, his daughter Tracy, his son Maurice, and his son Gregory.

Myth Trumps Reality

A PERSISTENT rumor arose over time that Huey Newton's last words were, "You can kill my body, and you can take my life, but you can never kill my soul. My soul will live forever!" That quote has been repeated in numerous books, essays and articles about Newton, and replicated on Huey P. Newton t-shirts. It shows up on ChatGPT and even appears on a digital online page of the National Archives.

Those words, while inspiring, did not match Robinson's 1991 murder trial record and should, in any event, have been cause for skepticism. What person — even a revolutionary leader — would have the presence of mind to utter such a statement while high on cocaine pursuing his next drug purchase? It also assumes Huey had time to utter anything before his assailant pulled the trigger. In fact, the shooter and his companion Brian Walton were the only witnesses to the circumstances of Huey's predawn death on a street corner in West Oakland. That was not how Walton described what happened after he was given immunity.

The claimed last words of Huey Newton can be traced back to David Hilliard's 1993 book, *This Side of Glory: The Autobiography of David Hilliard and the Story of the Black Panther Party*, in which Hilliard fantasizes about Huey, uttering a nearly identical phrase of defiance.

David Hilliard had long since become familiar with Huey's efforts throughout his life to differentiate what Huey called reactionary suicide from revolutionary suicide. As David later wrote about Huey: "His definition of reactionary suicide was when someone's life is taken by a set of reactionary conditions, where it's by crime in the community, getting involved in drugs, or committing suicide out of depression . . . a set of reactionary conditions that drove a person to self-murder." In contrast, Huey considered himself to be living as a revolutionary suicide — someone who faced certain death for a cause that was sacred to him, like a Kamikaze pilot, or, as he told his father, just like Jesus.

David instead envisioned Huey on his last day behaving like a reactionary suicide, giving in to his depression and going straight to West Oakland to get high on crack with the money Fredrika gave him. David figured that maybe Huey visited a girlfriend before returning to the crack house on Center Street around 5 a.m. where he saw two street hustlers by a parked car. He recognized one of them, Tyrone Robinson, the son of a family friend from the neighborhood. Huey was desperate — "Alone. No wife, girlfriend, running partners." He hit Tyrone up for more dope but got into a heated argument when Huey had no money left to pay for it. Huey kept getting more belligerent until Tyrone hit him on the head with his gun.

David then pictured Huey's despair and surprise as he staggered from the blow: "Man, why'd you do that?" Then Huey summoned his inner "intrepid rebel," the Huey who was quintessentially "bold, angry, intractable." At that point, David saw Huey recovered enough from the pistol-whipping to take charge of his own destiny. Huey challenges Robinson to kill him: "Go on, nigger, make history." In David's mind, it was "just as he did with the cops: 'Kill me, motherfucker! I'm not afraid of death!' Huey stands facing Tyrone, legs planted, and arms outstretched, taunting Tyrone to pull the trigger: "You can kill the body, but not the spirit, motherfucker! Go on." Tyrone obliged.

Yet David's vision of Huey's last moments were tempered by his own barely survived battle with addiction. He was also well aware of the ignominious fate of too many inner-city men. David considered the name of Huey's killer unimportant: "He was killed by the insanity of the drug culture." In David Hilliard's 2006 biography, *Huey: Spirit of the Panther*, he again noted the irony of Huey's death on the streets at the hands of a drug dealer: "Huey's own life became such a degrading, painful, and out-of-control situation that he himself met the kind of reactionary suicide that he talked about so often."

But that was not to be how Huey would be remembered.

A World-Changing True Story

AS NOTED in 2007 by scholar Jayne Rhodes in her book, Framing *the Black Panthers: The Spectacular Rise of a Black Power Icon*, the Black Panthers established an indelible image in American history:

> "The passage of time has not eroded the strength of their] symbols and rhetoric — the gun, the snarling panther, the raised fist, and slogans such as "All power to the people" and "Off the pig." Today, representations of the Black Panthers linger in diverse arenas of commodity culture, from news stories to reality television to feature films and hip-hop, as they function as America's dominant icons of Black Nationalism."

Six years later, two African-American authors, Joshua Blook and Waldo Martin, collaborated on the tome, *Black against Empire: The History and Politics of the Black Panther Party*. The book was acknowledged by a critic as the first comprehensive effort to treat the Black Panthers "as the serious political and cultural force they were." Walter Newton would have enjoyed the book's title. It evoked the David v. Goliath imagery that he and his son embraced.

In 2016, during halftime at Super Bowl L (50), more than 110 million viewers witnessed megastar Beyoncé's dance troupe perform a raised-fist tribute to the Black Panthers. The Panthers own fiftieth anniversary year coincided with that of the Super Bowl. Beyoncé paired that tribute with the release of a new video, "Formation," which paid homage to the Black Lives Matter movement, whose members Kathleen Cleaver has called the grandchildren of the Black Panthers.

For generation after generation, the most iconic figure representing the Panthers has been Huey Newton. That includes places like *The Boondocks* syndicated comic strip and television cartoon series, whose central character Huey Freeman was named for him. In 2001, Spike Lee directed an acclaimed 2001 movie remake of the 1996 one-man show *A Huey P. Newton Story*.

The title of Huey's biography, co-authored by former Panther Chief of Staff David Hilliard, underscores his centrality to their cause — *Huey: Spirit of the Panther*. Rap artists like Paris, Public Enemy and the Fugitives have sung of the life and death of Huey Newton the way Irish immigrants in Australia lionized the 19th century outlaw Ned Kelly. It is thus not surprising that Huey Newton's name came to appear among the "Black People Who Changed the World" on a British Black History month website.

Newton and Seale's alma mater has featured since 2001 the Huey P. Newton Lounge honoring the pair's pioneering roles in organizing Black students on campus. That capacious lounge is also where more than 300 mourners gathered in January 2015 for memorial ceremonies for Melvin's wife, Barbarette, who died in November 2014 after a hard-fought battle with cancer.

Barbarette had distinguished herself for decades through her own extensive community involvement and outreach to family, friends and neighbors. More than two hundred of them relished attending the annual October "Autumn Fair" she and Melvin had hosted in their back yard for roughly fifteen years.

The outpouring of emotional tributes at Barbarette's service attested to her extraordinary impact not just on Melvin. He shared two soulful poems to "the love of my life." Many others lauded her for reaching out with a helping hand, comfort in their time of need, or both. Barbarette's unique focus and skill set were summed up by her son Lautaro: "When I think of my mother the first things that come to mind are family, love, class, strength, dedication, beauty and multi-tasking at the highest level." Her son Maurice added: "She was someone who donated a lot of her time to everyone else."

* * *

In 2006, to celebrate the 40th anniversary of the Party's creation, San Francisco's Yerba Buena's Center for the Arts mounted a "Black Panther Rank and File" show that drew crowds for several months. The Oakland Museum of California permanently features a bronze replica of Newton's empty wicker throne, which it invites all visitors to try out for themselves. In 2016-17, OMCA hosted its most highly attended exhibit in the museum's history, celebrating the 50th anniversary of the Panther Party's founding.

In *No There, There, Race, Class and Political Community in Oakland,* author Chris Rhomberg recognized how much Huey Newton and the symbolism he and Bobby Seale popularized radically altered the inner-city battles over racial inequality:

> What had begun to occur elsewhere as spontaneous rioting or disorder took the form of an organized political actor . . . [The Panthers'] armed refusal to accept the boundaries of a racialized civil order gave voice to deeply held grievances in the

Black community, while their dramatic presence brought the issue of racial inequality of power forcibly into the public sphere."

Professor Jane Rhodes was right. The Black Panther Party for Self-Defense and its leaders had become "lasting fixtures in mass culture and popular memory." In 2015, millions watched Stanley Nelson's film *The Black Panthers: Vanguard of the Revolution* in theaters or on public television. In 2018, the blockbuster film "Black Panther", a Marvel comic heroic African king, included a cousin of the king, who lived in Oakland and was loosely based on Huey Newton. The most lasting tribute, arranged by Huey's widow Frederika, was yet to come.

Public Memorials to Huey's Historic Impact

A LARGE crowd gathered in the strong winds and pouring rain on Sunday, October 24, 2021, at the corner of Mandela Parkway and Huey P. Newton Way in West Oakland. That section of Ninth Street had been renamed in his honor on Huey's birthday in February of that year. The location of the fall dedication ceremonies was less than a mile from DeFremery Park, known unofficially since 1968 as Li'l Bobby Hutton Park. In October 2016, the Oakland City Council had formally dedicated a grove in that park to Bobby Hutton.

Those gathered to honor Huey's memory on October 24, 2021, braved the elements to cap off a month of festivities celebrating the 55th anniversary of the founding of the Black Panther Party. The series of events were instigated by his widow, Frederika Newton, as President of the Dr. Huey P. Newton Foundation, a nonprofit Fredrika founded with David Hilliard a quarter of a century earlier to preserve the legacy of the Black Panther Party and of Huey as its co-founder.

Huey's bust was placed about a half mile from the October 1967 pre-dawn shooting at Seventh and Willow Streets, and just a block from the sidewalk in front of 1456 Center Street where Huey met his death at the hands of drug dealer Tyrone Robinson.

At the ceremonies on October 24, 83-year-old Melvin Newton joined Huey's widow and other invited speakers, including Congresswoman Barbara Lee, the late Fred Hampton's son, Fred Hampton Jr., and Oakland Mayor

Libby Schaaf. Members of younger generations of the Newton family stood proudly in the umbrella-wielding crowd. Many attendees sensed Huey's presence at the celebration. The emcee was the daughter of singer and civil rights champion, Harry Belafonte, who had been a major backer of the Panthers.

Channeling her father, Gina Belafonte proclaimed: "You are all here today to witness history." The unveiling represented official recognition of Huey Newton's positive impact on the city as a co-founder of the Black Panthers. Fredrika Newton and sculptor Dana King were congratulated for bringing the project to fruition. Grammy-award-winner Fantastic Negrito observed that the weather matched the occasion: "The rain is very symbolic of the struggle and the obstacles that become our fuel." (Negrito was only an infant when Huey faced the death penalty in the summer of 1968.)

The speakers also paid tribute to artist Rachel Wolf-Goldsmith who, not long before, had completed a mural that honors key Panther women for the success of the Party's community programs, particularly the breakfasts for children in the flatlands and the free clinics. The tribute was painted on the outside wall of a nearby house that had been transformed into a museum for the Black Panther Party.

The predominantly Black audience had a mixed reaction to Mayor Schaaf's remarks, but she had been good friends in high school with Huey's late stepson, Ronnie Newton. After high school, Huey paid for Ronnie to attend hairdressing school in Paris where he became so accomplished that on his return he developed a celebrity clientele at the Central West Salon on Lakeshore

Avenue in Oakland. Ronnie had sadly died by suicide in 1990. Schaaf's decision to embrace the dedication as a city-sponsored event was not without controversy, especially among the members of the Oakland Police Department who still honor the late John Frey each year as an officer killed in the line of duty.

The unveiling of the bust was filmed for a 20-minute short documentary "For Love and Legacy" featuring Fredrika and sculptor Dana King. The two had collaborated on the bust's creation. When the covering was removed, King explained that she had taken great pains to capture Huey's look: "I felt compelled to create him as authentically as I could . . . and as detailed as I could because I want people to look at him. I want them to look into his eyes and I want them to question where that came from to co-create the Panthers."

Unstated, but obvious, was the decision to make the bust inspirational. It did not reflect any of Huey's torment over the conflict between his idealistic goals and his personal demons. It did not suggest the various internal and external forces that ultimately brought him down. Huey himself had written in his PhD dissertation his concern that too much emphasis was often placed on any one participant in a movement: "Individuals, with all their strengths and weaknesses, make significant differences in the outcome of political struggles; however, their roles are too often romanticized, clouding an understanding of the political forces propelling them into struggle."

In addition to its subject's penetrating eyes, the bust features the nose inherited from his White grandfather that made Huey self-conscious. His facial features reflected the genes of his "crazy nigger" bi-racial father,

Bust of Huey Newton by Dana King in West Oakland

whom Huey believed to have been conceived in violence. In fact, Huey could have claimed persecuted ancestors both Black and White, African-Americans and Jews.

When Melvin took his turn at the podium, he spoke from the heart about his younger brother, just like his mother had spoken in February 1968 at the Oakland Auditorium fundraiser for Huey's defense. All of Melvin's mixed feelings were swept aside in celebrating the symbol Huey had become of African-American dignity and self-respect. "Huey was maybe the only man I've ever known that was a truly free man. He was universal. He felt that no one could be on his back if he stood up. And he always stood ramrod straight."

Walter and Armelia Newton would have been bursting with pride. What a contribution their two youngest sons had made since their arrival in the mid-1940s in the segregated community of West Oakland.

At the ceremony's end, reporter Brenda Callins observed the "attendees continued to dance, sing, and converse in the rain. The bust unveiling festivities were about the need for continued progress, equity, and community being able to weather the storms of change."

Melvin himself would be honored later that day at a ceremony in Oakland's Brooklyn Basin arranged by the Black Panther Party Alumni Legacy Network. Melvin received the First Annual Lumpen Award for his scholarly work as the original head of the ethnic studies department at Merritt College and his activities supporting the Black Panther Party in the late 1960s when Huey risked his life to put the American justice system on trial.

Like Monroe-born pioneering reporter Belva Davis, all three men — Walter, Melvin and Huey — did not let their hardscrabble beginnings in sharecropper shacks keep them down. The success of acclaimed African-American academic Ruth Simmons also provides insights into the Newtons' motivation. Born three years after Huey, Simmons was the twelfth and last child of a Texas sharecropper. Her ancestors on both sides were slaves. Raised through early childhood in a two-bedroom shack, Simmons applied herself in school, excelled in comparative literature, and rose in the administration of various universities to become President of Smith College in 1995 and then Brown University in 2001. She was the first of her race to serve as university president in any Ivy League school. She is now advising Harvard University on how to strengthen its relationship with historically Black universities.

Though Melvin was the only one in his family to become a pioneering academic, both he and Huey internalized their father's determination to follow his dreams to make a difference. Regardless of how vilified Huey remains among his detractors, he unquestionably made a positive impact on the treatment of Black citizens in this country.

Huey Newton enhanced the political power of Black Americans. That is the same quality *New York Times* columnist Pamela Paul admires in role models like Simmons: "It's not, their stories tell us, the circumstances into which we are born that bind us; it's how we allow, or refuse to allow, them to define us that makes us who we are." Or, as Walter Newton preached: "He who can make the rhyme repeat itself can also rewrite it."

* * *

On April 22, 2022, "For Love and Legacy" premiered at the San Francisco International Film Festival. It was paired with the debut of the award-winning documentary "American Justice on Trial" based on this author's 2016 book of the same title. Co-directors Andy Abrahams' and Herb Ferrette's 40-minute film about Huey's revolutionary 1968 trial won multiple awards at a number of film festivals and wound up short-listed for an Oscar. In 2025 it was featured by PBS across the country during Black History month.

Neither Armelia nor Walter Newton could have anticipated how the heart-wrenching death penalty trial of their youngest son would lead the way to greater diversity in American jury panels — a legacy that is still generating national repercussions. One example is the composition of the jury that rendered the second-degree murder verdict in 2021 against Officer Derek Chauvin for the death of George Floyd. When a majority of women and minorities was seated to decide the outcome of Chauvin's criminal trial, the diversity of the panel was no longer considered radical. Instead, it was accepted as a "jury of one's peers."

Today, across the country, economic hardship still leaves too many minorities out of the pivotal decision-making role in criminal trials that the Panthers made a key goal of their platform. Who gets to sit in judgment of the accused? Even one minority on a jury panel has been found to change the dynamics of deliberations. Much more progress needs to be made, but it was Huey and his lawyers and the Panther Party that jump-started the effort to minimize racism in jury selection.

Looking back, Bill Patterson, the first Black foreman of the Alameda County grand jury, called Huey's 1968

Melvin Newton posing with Co-Directors Herb Ferrette (left) and Andrew Abrahams (right) at the premier of "American Justice on Trial" at the San Francisco International Film Festival on April 22, 2022. (The film was re-released by Open Eye Pictures in June 2025 under the title In The Crosshairs.*)*

trial — with his life at risk — one of the greatest trials in history. But it took half a century to achieve widespread public recognition of its singular impact. Melvin has a short answer: "Huey was a threat . . . His actions were so raw and so challenging ... his desire to be an agent for social change. . .. Huey is someone that proper authorities would like to forget."

The installation of the bronze bust of Huey was as gratifying to Melvin as it was to Fredrika and sculptor Dana King. The larger-than-life, weatherproof bust made it impossible for the government to ignore his brother's achievements in his truncated, turbulent life. Both Melvin and Fredrika had experienced some of the most troubled parts and the ignominy of his reactionary suicide death and nonetheless remembered him lovingly. Now he would be remembered as a revolutionary suicide, a man who lived most of his adult life dedicated to a cause. Like other historical giants, he would be the subject of selective memory, his heroic qualities eclipsing, for those who admired him, his many serious flaws.

But the bust was not to be the pinnacle of Huey's legacy. The Dr. Huey P. Newton Foundation led by Huey's widow Fredrika fund-raised to create the Black Panther Party Museum, featuring a major contribution from the State of California through the efforts of local Assemblymember Mia Bonta. The museum opened in January 2024, a block from Oakland's City Hall in downtown Oakland. It displays artwork and historical photographs. Researchers can also access the world's most extensive archival collection of materials documenting the Party's history and that of its community programs. Staff conduct educational seminars and tours to local historic sites — an extraordinary tribute to the Party Huey and Bobby Seale launched, and the impact the Party's achievements will continue to have through this museum.

Fredrika Newton has an even bigger goal in mind: securing national monument status for several sites in Oakland that mark the birthplace and historical significance of the Black Panther Party. She and her colleagues at the Huey P. Newton Foundation recognize that this designation would allow the federal government to have the final say on how the Party and her late husband are represented in plaques and official descriptions of the Black Panthers. Currently, Fredrika's goal faces huge obstacles. Whether she ultimately succeds remains to be seen.

***

Huey never expected to live to old age. He did see himself molded not only by his own experiences, but by what came before him. As he wrote in *Revolutionary Suicide*: "Life does not always begin at birth. My life was forged in the lives of my parents before I was born, and even earlier in the history of all Black people."

Endnotes

Abbreviations Used in the Notes
BB *The Berkeley Barb*
BP *The Black Panther* newspaper
HPN Dr. Huey P. Newton Foundation, Inc. Collection, 1968–1994, M864, Green Library Special Collections, Stanford University, Series
LAT *The Los Angeles Times*
NYT *The New York Times*
OP *The Oakland Post*
OT *The Oakland Tribune*
SFC *The San Francisco Chronicle*
SFE *The San Francisco Examiner*

Introduction

David Hilliard quote: David Hillard interview for the film "American Justice on Trial." All quotes in this book that are not specifically sourced in these endnotes are from interviews for the documentary "American Justice on Trial" by the film director and the author or interviews conducted by the author specifically for this book.

"The younger Whites": Excerpt from Huey Newton's trial testimony, *People v. Newton*, August 22, 1968, Appendix C to Appellant's Brief on Appeal, private collection of Melvin Newton.

David Hilliard quote: Hilliard film interview, *supra*.

"in furtherance of justice": Cal. Penal Code section 1385.

"To my mother and father": Huey P. Newton with assistance of J. Herman Blake, Introduction by Fredrika Newton. *Revolutionary Suicide*, (New York: Penguin Books, 2009) Kindle ed., location 47.

I. WALTER NEWTON'S HERITAGE

Starting Out

"Life does not always begin at birth": *Revolutionary Suicide, supra*, 9.

The African Roots of the Newtons

"slavery has been practiced": Jill Lepore, *These Truths: A History of the United States* (Kindle ed., 2018) 16-17.

The Legacy of Slavery

"Almost all of those Blacks were considered to be property": The few free Blacks in Alabama during the early 19th century faced many of the same restrictions as those imposed against slaves. They generally could not gather on their own in groups, go to the community's schools or establish their own. They also could not legally own guns. But, unlike slaves, they could marry and own property.

Gag rule: Heather Cox Richardson "August 12, 2023" *Letters from an American* (newsletter), Substack, Aug 12, 2023, https://heathercoxrichardson.substack.com; The "gag rule" resolution was renewed for the next eight years over opposition led by John Quincy Adams.

Southern students and readers: Donald Yacavone, *Teaching White Supremacy: America's Democratic Ordeal and the Forging of our National Identity* (New York: Pantheon Books, 2022), 143.

Quote re Gov. Ron DeSantos: Jamelle Bouie, "There is a Reason Ron De Santis Wants History Told a Certain Way," *NYT*, May 20, 2023, Opinion page.,

"ensign of abolitionism": David Yacavone, *Teaching White Supremacy: America's Democratic Ordeal and the Forging of our National Identity*, (New York: Pantheon Books, 2022), 143-44.

"slaves loved the people of the plantation": Bouie, *NYT* Opinion page, *supra*, n. 6, citing David W. Blight, *Race and Reunion: The Civil War in American Memory*, (Cambridge, MA: Belknap Press of Harvard University Press, 2001).

"positive good": Bouie, *NYT* Opinion page, *supra*, n. 6.

"contacts with civilized life": Blight, *Race and Reunion:supra*, 361.

"a segregated society": Blight, *Race and Reunion, supra, 361*.

"until the mid-1960s": Yacavone, *Teaching White Supremacy, supra*, 310.

"We want education": Toni Morrison (Ed.) *To Die for the People: The Writings of Huey P. Newton*, (San Francisco: City Lights Books, 2009), 4.

"cotton, rice": Edward Ball, *Slaves in the Family* (New York: Farrar, Straus and Giroux, 1998), 7.

Growing Up Outside Constitutional Protection

"Southern Horrors": Ida B. Wells, "*Southern Horrors: Lynch Law in All Its Phases*" (1892); reprinted in The Project Gutenberg eBook of

Southern Horrors: Lynch Law In All Its Phases, (Feb. 8, 2005) https://www.gutenberg.org/files/14975/14975-h/14975-h.htm

"used it in self-defense": Thaddeus Russell, "How 'Crazy Negroes' with Guns Helped Kill Jim Crow," reason.com. July 22, 2014. https://reason.com/2014/07/22/how-crazy-negroes-with-guns-he/. Russell's article is a review of Charles E. Cobb, Jr.'s book, *This Nonviolent Stuff'll Get You Killed: How Guns Made the Civil Rights Movement Possible,* (Philadelphia, Pennsylvania: Basic Books, 2014).

Clemsen University quote: Jacob Sullum, "A New Study Suggests That Black Southerners' Access to Firearms Reduced Lynchings," September 8, 2022. A New Study Suggests That Black Southerners' Access to Guns Reduced Lynchings Reason.com, https://reason.com/2022/09/08/a-new-study-suggests-that-Black-southerners-access-to-guns-reduced-lynchings/

Frederick Douglass quoted in Russell, "How 'Crazy Negroes' with Guns Helped Kill Jim Crow," *supra*.

"a rat in a trap": Ida B. Wells Biography, Ida B. Wells - Quotes, Facts & Children Biography.com; https://www.biography.com/authors-writers/ida-b-wells

Walter's White Father

"Maternal death rates": Tanisha Bhat, "High Maternity Morbidity Rate Remains a Deep Concern for Black Women," *The Bay Street Banner*, August 2023, www.baystatebanner.com/2023/08/02/high-maternal-morbidity-rate-remains-a-deep-concern-for-Black-women/

History of the Simon family: This is the information the Newtons were provided by a descendant of Elias Simon: "Elias Simon along with his wife Caroline and several children arrived in Baltimore from Germany on 30 Sept 1845. They were from Hesse-Darmstadt, Germany [today, part of the Frankfurt metropolitan region]. They were Jewish. They show up in the 1850, 1860 and 1870 Federal Census. Elias died on 21 June 1871 and is buried at the Hebrew Friendship Cemetery in Baltimore. Most of Elias's children lived in Baltimore or Philadelphia. I think you will be interested in [the family of] his youngest son Joseph Simon, born 10 May 1853 in Baltimore. He is shown in the 1880 Federal Census as married and living in Prairieville, Alabama.

According to family stories Joseph was a mule trader. . . . . Joseph was married to Mary Kaufman on 31 March 1878 in Baltimore and soon after they moved to Prairieville . . . At some point they moved into Demopolis, which was only a few miles away. In the 1900 Census they are living in Demopolis with 8 children. Joseph died on 12 August 1904 and is buried in the B'nai Jeshurun Jewish Cemetery in Demopolis."

Jews in the early days of the rural South: Lee Shai Weissbach, *Jewish Life in Small-Town America: A History*. (New Haven, Connecticut: Yale University Press, 2005).

"Judenordnung": "Hesse," Jewish Virtual Library, 2023, www.jewishvirtuallibrary.org/hesse

The Move to Southern Arkansas

The Great Migration: Great Migration from Alabama, Encyclopedia of Alabama. https://encyclopediaofalabama.org/

"reason offered for Willams' murder": John Steelman, *A Study of Mob Action in the South* (Chapel Hill, North Carolina: University of North Carolina, 1928), 178, archive.org https://archive.org/details/studyofmobaction00stee/page/n9/mode/2up

"barbarous criminal": Hayes, *A Colony in a Nation*, (New York: W. W. Norton Co., 2017), 68-69.

Lessons in Courage

"a poor boy": Rev. Kelly Brown Douglas, Foreword to the 2022 Edition of Howard Thurman's *Jesus and the Disinherited*, (Boston: Beacon Press 2022), Kindle edition, xi.

Goliath against David: Historian Robert Dohrenwend as quoted in Malcom Gladwell, *David and Goliath: Underdogs, Misfits, and the Art of Battling Giants,* (New York: Little Brown Hachette Book Group, 2013) Introduction, part 3 and note 2.

Lt. General Polk: "Leonidas Polk" American Battlefield Trust, www.battlefields.org/learn/biographies/leonidas-polk. In June of 2025, President Trump announced he was renaming several forts, including Fort Johnson, to revert to their prior names, but to honor different servicemen with the same last name (to avoid the Congressional ban on naming forts for Confederate rebels). Fort Johnson will be renamed Fort Polk after World War II General James H. Polk.

II. ARMELIA JOHNSON'S BACKGROUND

Armelia's Ancestry

"Armelia was the first": Estella's birth year was listed as 1885 in both the 1900 and 1950 censuses and 1888 according to the 1920 census. But according to the headstone on her grave in the tiny town of Oakwood, Texas, in Leon County, Estella was born on March 20, 1884.

Ouachita Parish: At least one historian has concluded that the name was originally two words -- "owa chito" -- a Choctaw phrase that meant "good hunting grounds." Others believe it to be derived from a phrase meaning "silver water."

Isaac Burnett and his wife Annie: Records show Isaac had previously been living in an unincorporated area of Leon County, Texas less than 30 miles southwest of the county seat of Centerville, when he married Annie Fennell on November 14, 1903. Centerville is about 80 miles southeast of Waco.

"*Unforgiveable Blackness*" Ken Burns, *Unforgivable Blackness: The Fight of the Century*, PBS, www.pbs.org/unforgivableBlackness/fight/

Jack London quote: Michael Walsh, "Great Expectations," *Smithsonian*, June 2010,54.

"Jubilant Blacks took to the streets": Unforgivable Blackness: The Lingering Legacy of Jack Johnson | Public i Contact (ucimc.org)

Movie banned: Colin Linneweber, "The Black Boxer No White Could Beat Fairly," Bleacher Report, April 7, 2009, http://bleacherreport.com/articles/152523-the-Black-boxer-no-white-could beat-fairly.

Jessie Mae's birth: Jessie told her son she was born in Arkansas, but no records have been found to substantiate that.

The Infamous Lynching History of Monroe

"He signed his name with an X.": *Monroe News-Star*, April 29, 1919, 1.

Bolden's lynching: Aiello, *The Kings of Casino Park*: Black Baseball in the Lost Season of 1932 (University of Alabama Press: Tuscaloosa, 2011) 8-9.

"the lynch law capital": *New Orleans Times-Picayune*, May 12, 1919, 5; *New Orleans Item*, May 6, 1919, cited in Aiello, *The Kings of Casino Park*, 2, 4.

Parish lynching record: Kaleb Causey, "Ouachita Parish's bloody past appears in lynching study," Feb. 24, 2015, *The News Star* [kcausey@thenewstar.com].

Ida Wells-Barnett investigation: Ida B. Wells-Bennett, "The Arkansas Race Riot" (Chicago: 1920) via archive.org https://archive.org/details/TheArkansasRaceRiot/page/n61/mode/2up

Racism today in Monroe: McHenry, *The Monroeians*, 38.

III. ARKANSAS

The Move to Southern Arkansas

The Winston Pounds lynching: Steelman, *A Study of Mob Action in the South, supra.*

Walter and Armelia Meet and Marry

The Union Saw Mill railroad: Union Saw-Mill Company at Huttig, Arkansas in 1907, excerpts from American Lumberman magazine. Texas Transportation Archive Historical Notes, March 30, 1907, ttarchive.com/library/Articles/Union-Saw-Mill_1907-03-30-American-Lumberman.html

IV. BACK TO LOUISIANA

The Johnsons Return to Monroe

Source of details re Stella and John Johnson: author interview of Doris Newton Godfrey

The Newtons Move to West Monroe

Pleas of self-defense: "When people in the U.S. said, 'A man's home is his castle,' what they actually meant was, "A White, property-owning man's home is his castle." Caroline Light, interview re her book, "Stand Your Ground: A History of America's Love Affair with Lethal Self-Defense," news.harvard.edu/gazette/story/2017/03/the-loaded-history-of-self-defense/

43 per cent had no jobs: Fifteenth Census of the United States, 1930. Vol.3, part 1, Alabama-Missouri (Wash D.C. 1932) 982, 990, 999, 1003; Aiello, *The Kings of Casino Park, supra* 21 and n. 21.

25 per cent of Whites: Aiello, *The Kings of Casino Park, supra,* 21.

When it hit the white man"; Aiello, *The Kings of Casino Park, supra,* 21.

Life Under the Kingfish

"among registered voters": Lepore, *These Truths, supra,* Kindle edition, 457.

The Freedman's Hospital: LibGuides: Black History Month: A Medical Perspective: Hospitals guides.mclibrary.duke, edu/Blackhistorymonth/hospitals.

"well-equipped": *Journal of the National Medical Association,* 53(5):439-446; Sept. 1961.

"overbreeding": "21 Quotes by Margaret Sanger That Will Probably Make You Sick," TFP Student Action, https://tfpstudentaction.org/blog/margaret-sanger-quotes

"the extermination of the Negro population": "21 Quotes by Margaret Sanger That Will Probably Make You Sick," *supra*, Letter to Dr. Clarence J. Gamble, December 10, 1939, p. 2.

outlawing compulsory sterilization: *Skinner v. State of Oklahoma Ex rel. Williamson*, 316 U.S. 533 (1942).

Black hospitals: Black History Month: A Medical Perspective Hospitals - Black History Month: A Medical Perspective - LibGuides at Duke University Medical Center citing Health, Hospitals and the Negro *Modern Hospital*, Eugene H. Bradley, August, 1945).

Medicare funding: D. Mark Anderson, Kerwin Kofi Charles, and Daniel I. Rees, "The Federal Effort to Desegregate Southern Hospitals and the Black-White Infant Mortality Gap", March 17, 2021; The Federal Effort to Desegregate Southern Hospitals and the Black-White Infant Mortality Gap | Cato Institute.

The Move to Bastrop

Sources of Walter Newton standing his ground: Melvin Newton interview by author and Newton with Blake, *Revolutionary Suicide*, 29.

White officer for Black units: John D. Winters, *The Civil War in Louisiana* (Baton Rouge, Louisiana: Louisiana State University Press, 1991).

"Heaviest blow yet dealt": The quote is from a letter from Abraham Lincoln to his old friend James C. Conkling dated August 26, 1863, intended to be read at a Union rally in Springfield, Illinois in September 1863 on Lincoln's behalf. He was unable to attend in person. Abraham Lincoln's Letter to James Conkling (abrahamlincolnonline.org)

The paper mill: "International Paper Louisiana and Bastrop Mills", International Paper Louisiana and Bastrop Mills - Nemeroff Law

"If you hit me a lick": Quoted in Newton with Blake, *Revolutionary Suicide*, 30.

Monroe in the 1930s

The flood of the century: Belva Davis and Vicki Haddock, *Never in My Wildest Dreams: A Black Woman's Life in Journalism* (San Francisco: Berrett-Koehler Publishers, Kindle Ed., 2010), 12.

"fearing a Negro uprising": Davis and Haddock, *Never in My Wildest Dreams, supra*, 12.

No indoor plumbing: *The Monroeians, supra*, interview of Jacquelyn Cliffortene Hilton-Dawson-Simmons, 548-580.

Union Carbide: The corporate name was simplified to Union Carbide in 1957 and is now a wholly owned subsidiary of Dow Chemical. During World War II, it ran the government's secret Manhattan project for development of the atom bomb at the Oak Ridge National Laboratory in Tennessee, which is still the nation's largest scientific research center.]

"Black Star" cars: werehistory.org-the-new-orleans-streetcar-protests-of-1867/

Black patrons in the balcony of the Paramount: Isabel Wilkerson, *The Warmth of Other Suns, supra*, 105-07.

Zion Travel Baptist Church Survives its Own Civil War

"disturbing pubic worship": Aiello, *The Kings of Casino Park, supra*, 72 and notes 31-32.

"shoot up the church": Thomas Aiello, "Calumny in the House of the Lord: The 1932 Zion Traveler Church Shooting," Thomas Aiello - Academia.edu

"a concealed weapon": Aiello, *The Kings of Casino Park*, 135.

The Monroe Monarchs — a Glimmer of Integration

"or say 'we'": Aiello, *The Kings of Casino Park, supra*, 4.

"the team's winning ways": Ian Robinson, "Monroe Monarchs baseball team made history in the Negro Leagues, bridged racial divide," *Monroe News-Star*, February 20, 2022, www.thenewsstar.com/story/news/2022/02/20/how-monroe-monarchs-negro-leagues-baseball-team-made-history-casino-park-racial-divide/9245416002/

'all the way to Jackson": "A Look Back: Monroe Monarchs", www.myarklamiss.com/news/hidden-history/a-look-back-monroe-monarchs; quoting Paul Letlow, 'Ballparks', *Negro League Baseball Players Association*.

Bastrop in the Late 1930s

The Mississippi Blues Trail: Our Story – 100 Men Hall, www.100MenHall.com/pages/our-story

Cliffortene Hilton: *The Monroeians, supra, 551*.

"The White man weighed 200 pounds": Newton with Blake, *Revolutionary Suicide, supra*, 31.

Sharecropping in Oak Grove

Inspiration for *Uncle Tom's Cabin*: "History of Little Eva Plantation", https://www.natchitochespecans.com/history-of-little-eva/

Five races of men: George W. Hunter, *A Civic Biology Presented in Problems* (New York: American Book Co., 1914).

Summer for the Gods: Edward J. Larson, *Summer for the Gods: The Scopes Trial and America's Continuing Debate Over Science and Religion* (New York: Basic Books Penguin Book Group, 1997), 265.

"a 'low-life White man'": *Newton and Blake, Revolutionary Suicide*, supra, 31.

Huey's "Outdooring Ceremony"

History of the ritual: www.adesawyer.com/the-outdooring-dedication-and-naming-of-an-african-child-a-ceremony-of-the-gadangme-people-of-southeastern-ghana-ganyobi-kpojiemc-vol-1-book-review-by-gyau-kumi-adu/?share=linkedin#_ftn2

"kpojiemo ": E.A. Ammah, *Kings, Priests, and Kinsmen: Essays on Ga culture and Society*, ed. Marion Kilson (Accra: Sub-Saharan Publishers, 2016), 225.

"The outdooring ceremony": Oxford Dictionaries "Outdooring – Definition of Outdooring in English", http://en.oxforddictionaries.com/definition/outdooring

"the unseen world": Ernest Tetteh, *The Outdooring Dedication and Naming of an African Child: A Ceremony of the GaDangme People of Southeastern Ghana* (London: Ophelia Vanderpuye On-line Publishing, 2016), vii., ix.

"family identity": Gyau Kumi Adu, www.adesawyerr.com/the-outdooring-dedication-and-naming-of-an-african-child-a-ceremony-of-the-gadangme-people-of-southeastern-ghana-ganyobi-kpojiem□-vol-1-book-review-by-gyau-kumi-adu/?

"ears pierced": Mensah, Joseph Nii Abekar. *Traditions and Customs of Gadangmes of Ghana: Descendants of Authentic Biblical Hebrew Israelites*. Strategic Book Publishing, 2013.

"he took me outside": Newton with Blake, *Revolutionary Suicide*, supra, 12.

Lee Edward and the Simmons Family

Principal source: Esther Smith White interview

Life in Monroe with Muzz

Principal sources: interviews of Eddy Ento, Doris Newton Godfrey and Patricia Johnson

V. WESTWARD BOUND

Walter Decides to Join the Exodus

"When the people kept leaving": Isabel Wilkerson, *The Warmth of Other Suns: The Epic Story of America's Great Migration* (New York: Vintage Books, 2011) 220-222.

"banned from testifying against Whites": See, e.g., *People v Hall*, 4 Cal. 399 (1854). The 394th section of the Act Concerning Civil Cases provides: "no Indian or Negro shall be allowed to testify as a witness in any action or proceeding in which a White person is a party." The 14th section of the Act of April 16th, 1850, regulating Criminal Proceedings, provides that "No Black or mulatto person, or Indian, shall be allowed to give evidence in favor of, or against a White man."

The Closet Slave State of California

"involuntary servitude": Jean Pfaelzer, *California: The Slave State,* (New Haven: Yale University Press, 2023) Kindle ed), 31-32.

"the hydra": Pfaelzer, *California: The Slave State, supra*, 28.

"White gold miners": Platt, *The Scandal of Cal, supra*, 41.

"unpaid apprentices": Pfaelzer, *California: The Slave State, supra*, 43, 168.

"the misery of the Indians": Platt, *The Scandal of Cal, supra, 42.*

Chief Justice Murray: *People v. Hall*, 4 Cal.399 (1854) 400-01.

"offensive racial rhetoric": Michael Traynor, "The Infamous Case of People v. Hall (1854), *California Supreme Court Historical Society Newsletter* (Spring/Summer 2017) 2.

"sold into slavery": "Narrative of the Seizure and Recovery of Solomon Northrup," NYT, January 20,1853 reprinted in Documenting the American South, "THE KIDNAPPING CASE. Narrative of the Seizure and Recovery of Solomon Northrup. INTERESTING DISCLOSURES FROM NYT" 20 Jan. 1853.   https://docsouth.unc.edu/fpn/northup/support1.html

The underground railroad: Pfaelzer, *California: A Slave State, supra, 174.*

"The Sunday system": Pfaelzer, *California: A Slave State, supra,* 191.

California Black Codes: Platt, *The Scandal of Cal, supra,* 42.

"black face": Platt, *The Scandal of Cal, supra,* 162-63.

"ghetto in West Oakland": Jesse Barber, "Redlining: The history of Berkeley's segregated neighborhoods," *Berkeleyside,* Sept.20, 2018, www.Berkeleyside.org

Starting Out Again in California

Train travel: Mia Bay, *Traveling Black: A Story of Race and Resistance* (Cambridge, Massachusetts: Belknap Press, 2021) 4.

The Jim Crow car: Gunnar Myrdal, *An American Dilemma, vol.2: The Negro Problem and Modern Democracy* (New York: Harper and Brothers, 1944 (New Brunswick, New Jersey: Transaction, 1996), 635.

16th Street station: Don Hausler, unpublished manuscript, Blacks in Oakland 1852-1987, Vol. 3, 113, 116, Oakland Public Library History Room.

White residents feared integration: Gary Kamiya, "When WWII brought Blacks to the East Bay, Whites fought for segregation," *SFC,* Nov. 23, 2018, sfchronicle.com

"chicken coops": Kamiya, *supra,* citing Marilynn S. Johnson, *The Second Gold Rush: Oakland and the East Bay in World War II,* (Berkeley: University of California Press, 1944).

Oakland unemployment: Kamiya, *supra,* citing Marilynn S. Johnson, *The Second Gold Rush: Oakland and the East Bay in World War II,* (Berkeley: University of California Press (1944)).

Harry Truman's unpredicted victory: Lepore, *These Truths, supra,* 542.

Riot on 12th Street: Hausler, unpublished manuscript, *supra.*

Oakland's History

"KKK membership swelled" : Liam O'Donoghue, "The Sinister, Evil KKK In Oakland Once Ruled City Hall. The Klan's incompetent regime started crumbling right away." February 21, 2017, The Sinister, Evil KKK In Oakland Once Ruled City Hall | East Bay Express | Oakland, Berkeley & Alameda

KKK in Oakland: Chris Rhomberg, *No There There: Race, Class and Political Community in Oakland* (Berkeley: Univ. of California Press, 2004).

The KKK burned crosses: O'Donoghue, "The Sinister, Evil KKK In

Oakland Once Ruled City", *supra*.

Black unemployment in Oakland: Douzet, Frédérick, *The Color of Power Racial Coalitions and Political Power in Oakland*. (Charlottesville, Virginia: University of Virginia Press, 2012); M. *Johnson*. The Second Gold Rush, *supra*.

"you get stopped": William Patterson film interview for "American Justice on Trial."

See *Douzet, (2012). The Color of Power Racial Coalitions and Political Power in Oakland supra;* M. Johnson. *The Second Gold Rush, supra.*

"Raincoat Jones": Thomas C. Fleming, History "Raincoat" Jones, Black businessman extraordinaire, *March 17, 1967*"SLIM JENKINS, OAKLAND'S PIONEER BLACK ENTERTAINMENT ENTREPRENEUR (1890-1967)", GEOFFREY'S INNER CIRCLE (geoffreyslive.com)

West Coast Blues: "The Music They Played on 7th Street," www.bayareabluessociety.net/The_Music_They_Played_On_7th_Street_Project.html

Walter's Family Takes the Train West

"spat tobacco juice": Mia Bay, *Traveling Back, supra,* 1.

VI. THE PUSH AND PULL OF FAMILY

The Family Settles in Oakland

Grove Street: See "Martin Luther King Jr. Way", Oakland - LocalWiki; https:localwiki.org/Oakland/Martin_Luther_King_Jr._Way

The Central Role of Religion in the Newtons' Family Life

Principal sources Melvin Newton and Doris Godfrey interviews

In Oakland to Stay

The housing shortage: Eikeme. "Black History Month: How War Transformed Island's Population." *Alameda Sun*, Feb 20, 2019, alamedasun.com/news/Black-history-month-how-war-transformed-island%E2%80%99s-population

Officers would beat them: Jessica Mitford, *A Fine Old Conflict*, 108.

"Tow trucks moved in": An account by Stan Weir, Libcom, Nov 22, 2005 "1946: The Oakland General Strike - Stan Weir." libcom.org, libcom.org/article/1946-oakland-general-strike-stan-weir; http://socialistworker.org/2011/12.

Maintaining Close Ties Through Daddy and Mother

Sources: Multiple family interviews

"races tend to bury their own": Kim Severson, "Helpful Hands-on Life's last Segregated Journey," *NYT*, June 23, 2012.https://funerals-remain-a-segregated-business-in-the south.html

Keeping Up with Extended Family

Bernice and E.S's family: In 1947, Bernice and E. S. had a daughter they named Lucy in honor of E.S.'s deceased mother. The family left Arkansas in 1950 to live in Frisco City, Alabama where Bernice was from. While there, they had another daughter Betty in 1949 and four years later, a son they named E. S. Jr.in 1953, but called "Earl" — the same name as his oldest half-brother Earl Newton in Bastrop, Louisiana. Six weeks after E.S. Jr. was born, the family moved to Detroit, Michigan, where E.S. had obtained work as a janitor in the Ford Motors plant. He would spend the rest of his working life there, rising to supervise all the janitors at the Ford plant. In his leisure time, E.S. was a lifelong baseball fan and raised his children to love the sport as well. E.S. Jr. became a star ballplayer in his youth, acquiring the nickname Jake when his skills as a second baseman were likened to Detroit Tigers second baseman Jacob "Jake" Wood. E.S. Jr. officially still went by the name Earl but invited family to start calling him Jake. That made for far less confusion than having two cousins both named Earl Newton.

"the million-dollar voice": Clarence LaVaughn Franklin | Detroit Historical Society. detroithistorical.org/learn/encyclopedia-of-detroit/franklin-clarence-lavaughn

The Move to a Mixed Neighborhood

Clifford Rishell: https://localwiki.org/oakland/Clifford_E._Rishell. In 1982, the Raiders moved to Los Angeles, where the team stayed through 1994. It then returned to Oakland until 2019 when it left to play thereafter in Las Vegas).

Black home ownership: Tim Henderson, "Black Families Fall Further Behind on Home Ownership", *Stateline*, October 13, 2022, stateline.org.

Message for Morrie Turner's White co-worker: film interview of Morrie Turner.

Huey and Melvin Follow Different Paths

sources: Melvin Newton interview; Newton with Blake, *Revolutionary Suicide*.

The Impact of Emmett Till's Murder

Beastly lynching": "Erica L. Green, "Biden Dedicates Monument to Emmett Till and His Mother", *NYT*, July 26, 2023, A14.

Double jeopardy: The woman who accused Emmett Till of molesting her, Carolyn Bryant Donham, died on April 27, 2023. She published her memoir in 2022, *I Am More than a Wolf Whistle: The Story of Carolyn Bryant Donham*.

Huey Reaches a Turning Point in Junior High

"*it will not come again*": *Rubaiyat of Omar Khayyam,* trans. Edward Fitzgerald w. Illust. by Edmund Dulac [Garden City, NY: Garden City Publishing, 1937] via project guttenberg, guttenberg.org

The Hammer Incident

Source: Melvin Newton interview

Huey Takes Lessons from Melvin

Sources: Melvin Newton interview; Newton and Blakeley, *Revolutionary Suicide*

Huey's Beatnik Phase

Sources: Melvin Newton interview; Newton and Blakeley, *Revolutionary Suicide*

Life-changing Tests of Fraternal Loyalty

Source: Melvin Newton interview

The Afro-American Society

Quote from Judge Henderson: Judge Thelton Henderson interview for "American Justice on Trial."

"Inhumanity and fear": James Baldwin "A Letter to My Nephew," *Progressive Magazine*, December 1, 1962, https://progressive.org/magazine/letter-nephew.

The Violent Clash with Odell Lee

Source: Melvin Newton interview. This conversation was also retold by Melvin to David Hilliard as one that Huey told Melvin. It appears in David Hillard and Lewis Cole, *This Side of Glory: The Autobiography of David Hilliard and the story of the Black Panther Party* ((Boston: Little, Brown & Company, 1993), 71.

Thomas Broome quote: Stanford University, HPN, Box 14, Folder 11, Probation Report, 9. Letter of Deputy Probation Officer Thomas Broome.

Reconnecting with Esther Lee

Fair Housing Act: "Anti-Fair Housing Kit Floods Area," *Los Angeles Sentinel*, June 11, 1964.

Proposition 14: Proposition 14 on the November 1964 California ballot amended the state constitution to nullify the 1963 Rumford Fair Housing Act. Supported by nearly two-thirds of all state voters, it permitted property sellers, landlords and their agents once again to discriminate on racial and ethnic grounds when selling or renting property — just as they had been free to do before the Rumford Fair Housing Act went into effect in 1963. In 1966, Proposition 14 was declared unconstitutional by the California Supreme Court for denial of equal protection under the Fourteenth Amendment to the United State Constitution. That decision was affirmed by the 1967 decision of the United States Supreme Court in *Reitman v. Mulkey*, 387 U.S. 369 (1967).

Family Ties Bolster Endurance

Sources: Multiple family interviews

VII: A NEW ERA

Survival Lessons from Solitary Confinement

Sources: Melvin Newton interview and *Revolutionary Suicide, supra*.

The Birth of the Black Panther Party for Self-Defense

"a cleansing force": Frantz Fanon, *The Wretched of the Earth* (New York: Grove Press, 1963) English translation by Constance Farrington, chapter one "On Violence." [Originally published in French under the title, *Les Damnés de la Terre*, 1961].

"The ballot or the bullet": "Malcolm X, "The Ballot or the Bullet," April 12, 1964", Bill of Rights Institute.

Right to counsel: *Miranda v. Arizona*, 384 U.S. 436, (1966)

The Sacramento World Stage Debut

The trip to the State Capitol: This historic trip to Sacramento is described in detail in Pearlman, *American Justice on Trial*, supra, 97-100.

"Shock-a-buku": David Hilliard and Lewis Cole, *This Side of Glory*, supra, 123.

Front-page stories: P.S. Foner, *The Black Panthers Speak* (Cambridge, Massachusetts: DaCapo Press, 1970),5-6.

"I would not have done it": Melvin Newton film interview.

National Race Riots and Local Anti-War Protests

"Better education": Belva Davis film interview.

"ground zero": Belva Davis and Vicki Haddock, *Never In My Wildest Dreams*, [Oakland, CA: Berrett-Koehler Publishers] Kindle Ed., loc 1848.

The Predawn Shootout and Huey's Arrest for Murder

"bring a gurney": David Hilliard film interview.

Drawing Parallels to the Landmark Scottsboro Boys' Cases

"to send them to the chair": James Goodman, *Stories of Scottsboro* (New York: Pantheon Books, 1994), 16.

Dead Man Walking

"What choice did I have?": "1967: Aaron Mitchell, Ronald Reagan's first and only execution" April 12, 2011, http:// www.executedtoday.com/2011/04/12/1967-aaronmitchell-ronald-reagan.

The Family Rallies to Huey's Side

LaVerne Williams' interview: Taped interview by British journalist of Huey's sister Leola and Huey's fiancée Laverne Williams at the Alameda County Courthouse, March 6, 1968, www.youtube.com/watch?v=yE39MFcyyUs.

"The Sky is the Limit": Janice Garrett-Forte film interview.

"We all had weapons": Garrett-Forte film interview, *supra*.

Assassinations Inflame the Community

Kerner Report: The National Advisory Commission on Civil Disorders (1968) known as "The Kerner Report", (Washington, D.C.: United States Government Printing Office, 1968), 322.

President Johnson's vow: "'King's Dream is Not Dead'— LBJ", *SFE*, April 5, 1968, 4.

"White men ran to buy guns": Pearlman, *American Justice on Trial, supra*, 168 quoting John Burris.

Tribute to Li'l Bobby reprinted in Newton and Blake, *Revolutionary Suicide, supra*, Kindle loc. 231-236.

VIII. THE TRIAL

The Internationally Watched Trial Begins

"a signal to declare open war": Gilbert Moore, "The Black Panthers" essay in Howard Bingham, *The Black Panthers: 1968*,(Los Angeles: Ammo Book, 2009) 76.

"besieged fortress": OT, July 16, 1968, 1.

"warning messages": See Pearlman, *American Justice on Trial, supra,* 203 n. 27.

"a chance in Hell": "Bombs and Bombast," *OP,* Vol. 5, No. 11, July 17, 1968, 1.

The Battle to Select a Jury of Peers

Proposition 14 struck down: See *Reitman v. Mulkey,* 387 U.S. 369 (1967).

"window dressing": Irving Stone, *Clarence Darrow for the Defense* (New York: Signet Books,1941, 1969), 538.

"a taste for oranges": Moore, *A Special Rage,* [New York: Harper and Row, 1971], 139.

'absolutely pioneering": Karen Jo Koonan film interview.

"Garry remained dissatisfied": Ann Ginger, *Minimizing Racism in Jury Trials* (Berkeley: National Lawyers Guild 1969) xxi.

"blinded by the crumbs": Newton with Blake, *Revolutionary Suicide, supra,* 292.

Opening Statements

"A damn fool question": Rush Greenlee, "Newton's Dad: Guilty? That is a Fool Question" *SFE*, August 6, 1968, 6.

"Revenge is ours": Moore, *A Special Rage*, [New York: Harper and Row, 1971] 154.

The Prosecution Puts on Its Case

"The gentleman in the gray coat": Pearlman, *American Justice on Trial, supra*, 259 quoting trial witness Officer Herbert "Cliff" Heanes.

"Huey remained motionless": Jeff Morgan, "Re-enactment of Officer's Murder, "*OT*, August 7, 1968, 7.

Trying to gut Grier's testimony: Jeff Morgan, "Defense in Newton Trial Fires Back," *OT*, August 7, 1968, 7.

"Send me to jail then!": "Threatened Deadlock in Newton Trial Broken: 'See No Evil, Tell None 'Try' Fails' ", O*P* August 14, 1968, 4.

"like a rat in a trap": "Threatened Deadlock in Newton Trial Broken," *supra*, 4.

The Defense Takes Its Turn

"I am the Gestapo": Keating, Edward M., *Free Huey!* (Berkeley: Ramparts Press, 1971). 120-30.

"by chance or otherwise": Garry and Goldberg, *Streetfighter in the Courtroom, supra*, ix.

Huey's Historic Testimony

"When a defendant chooses to testify": Barry Scheck film interview.

On line for 400 years: Gilbert Moore, *A Special Rage*, [New York: Harper and Row, 1971] *supra*, 191.

"weed in the car": Hilliard and Cole, *This Side of Glory, supra*, 130.

Excerpt from Testimony of Huey Newton reprinted as an exhibit to the appellant's brief on appeal in *People v. Newton*.

"not all judges would do": Scheck, film interview, *supra*.

"a rare ruling": Judge Thelton Henderson film interview.

"talking directly to the jury": Hilliard film interview, *supra*.

"Off the pigs": Almena Lomax, "Newton Talks Peace as Panthers Shout Defiance," *OP*, Aug. 28, 1968, 3.

"trying to liberate his people": "Stokely at Newton Trial—'Political,'" *SFE*, Aug. 22, 1968, 8.Fn 12

"Excuse me": Sam Blumenfeld and Rush Greenlee, "D.A. Ends Newton Grilling," *SFE*, Aug. 26, 1968, 1.

"like hot soup": "Huey Relates His Story of Shooting," *OT*, Aug. 23, 1968, 1, 9.

"approach to resistance": P. S. Foner, *The Black Panthers Speak*, (Cambridge, Massachusetts: Da Capo Press, 1970), 41–42.

"The Courage to Kill": Anthony, *Spitting in the Wind: The True Story Behind the Violent Legacy of the Black Panther Party* (Malibu: Roundtable, 1990), 23.

"Huey is our Jesus": Eldridge Cleaver, "Newton On Trial," *Ramparts*, Fall 1968, 23

Dr. Blake's letter to Huey: HPN Series 1, Box 11, File 9 [letter, dated Aug. 28, 1968, from J. Herman Blake to Huey Newton].

"not willing to take it any longer": Gilbert Moore, *A Special Rage*, *supra*, 204.

Dr. Diamond's testimony: Greenlee, "Newton Casts a Long Shadow," *SFE*, Aug. 27, 1968, 16.

The Jury Hears from an Expert on Diminished Capacity

Abdominal gunshot wound: HPN Box 19, folder 1, transcript direct examination of Dr. Diamond, 3397 at 3405-3407.

Dueling Rebuttal Witnesses

"Kill the pigs!": Garrett-Forte film interview, *supra*.

Reinterpreting graphic phrases: "Defense Winds Up Case in Newton Murder Trial" OT August 27, 1968, 3.

"Gestapo tactics": Ribicoff Protests "Gestapo Tactics" at 1968 Chicago Convention, History Channel, https://www.history.com/speeches/ribicoff-protests-gestapo-tactics-at-1968-chicago-convention.

"close to the breaking point": Daryl E. Lembke, "Newton Case Strains Nerves of Police," *the Vallejo Times Herald*, Sept. 25, 1968, HPN, Series 1, Box 23 [publicity clipping]

Closing Arguments: Villain or Victim?

"a forgotten man": Huey Newton Trial Enters Final Phase," *OT,* Sept. 3, 1968, 1.

"actions speak louder than words": Huey Newton Trial Enters Final Phase," *supra.*

"a clear view of his face": "Newton Case to Jury," *OT,* Sept. 3, 1968.

"moment of truth": Jeff Morgan, "Jury Given Newton Murder Case: Jurors Select Negro Foreman," *OT,* Sept. 5, 1968, 1.

"Jury selects Negro foreman": "Huey Newton Trial Enters Final Phase," *OT,* Sept. 3, 1968, 5.

"the noose tightens": Gilbert Moore, *A Special Rage,* (New York: Harper and Row, 1971) 211.

Excerpts from Garry's summation: Ginger, ed., *Minimizing Racism in Jury Trials, supra,* 204, 216.

"a psychopath": Blumenfeld, "Newton Attorney: Witness a Liar — Or Psychopath," *SFE,* Sept. 3, 1968, 1.

"all I have to say": Blumenfeld and Greenlee, "Newton Jury Hears Closing Arguments," *SFE,* Sept. 4, 1968, 1.

Anxious Moments Waiting for the Jury Verdicts

Eldridge Cleaver speech: Blumenfeld and Greenlee, "Newton Fate Up To Jury," *SFE,* Sept. 5, 1968, 1, 4. At the Barristers Club, Cleaver had told the audience of White liberals that he loved the handful who supported him. But as for the rest, he said, "Fuck you, all of you. I hope a nigger gets you on a dark street and kills you, takes your fat wallets and your credit cards and cuts your throats." Quoted in Bingham, *The Black Panthers 1968, supra,* Moore, "The Black Panthers," 73.

"completely revolutionary": Henderson film interview, *supra.*

"highly explosive international trial": Belva Davis, film interview.

"If you kill Huey Newton": David Hilliard film interview.

Grier's prior statement: Greenlee, "Row on Newton Evidence: Judge Refuses Defense Plea," *SFE,* Sept. 6, 1968, 1, 4.

"People weren't going to back down": Cleaver, Kathleen, film interview.

"going up in smoke": Davis, film interview, *supra.*

"Oakland was a powder keg": William Patterson, film interview.

Abbie Hoffman and Jerry Rubin: Anderson, *The Movement and the Sixties*, *supra*, 225 and n. 32, quoting one gleeful Yippie calling the Chicago debacle "a revolutionary wet dream come true."

"poll them individually": Blauner, Robert, unpublished manuscript, Chapter Two, 10.

"I've prepared myself": Greenlee, "How the Jury Decided; Puzzling Newton Verdict," *SFE*, Sept. 9, 1968.

"the stench of death": Moore, *Rage*, *supra*, 229.

"This is a victory!": Karen Wald, film interview.

"We could not believe it": Garrett-Forte, film interview, *supra*.

"sold down the river": Montgomery, "Newton Is Guilty Of Manslaughter," *OT*, Sept. 9, 1968, 1. fn. 24.

"Keep it cool": "Huey Says He Ordered 'Keep Cool'," *OT*, Sept. 12, 1968, 7.

"make sure that Oakland didn't burn": Hilliard film interview, *supra*.

Cox later sided with Eldridge Cleaver: Curtis Austin, *Up Against the Wall*, (Fayetteville: University of Arkansas Press, 2006) 115 and fn., citing Cox's unpublished manuscript.

Reactions divided on racial lines: Sam Blumenfeld and Rush Lee, "Oakland Reaction Parallels Race," *SFE*, Editorial, "The 'Free Huey' Demonstrations, *SFE*, Sept. 10, 1968, 32.

Clinton White's comment: Blumenfeld and Lee, "Oakland Reaction Parallels Race," *supra*, 6.

"a contradictory situation": Anne Fagan Ginger film interview

"a big fat story": Howard Bingham, *The Black Panthers* 1968, (Los Angeles: Ammo Booka, 2009), 20.

"caught in the middle": Bingham, *The Black Panthers 1968*, *supra*, 79 {essay by Gilbert Moore).

"ten thousand questions": Moore, *A Special Rage*, *supra*, 268.

"a constant state of rage": James Baldwin quotes, https://quotefancy.com/james-baldwin-quotes

It changed jury selection: Scheck film interview, *supra*.

"they were very conscientious": Jensen, D. Lowell, film interview

"We got 'em!": Moore, *Rage*, *supra*, 231.

"It's a victory!": Montgomery, "Newton Is Guilty of Manslaughter," *supra*, 1.

IX. FREEING HUEY

Widespread Violence is Avoided

"create havoc in our lives": Garrett-Forte film interview, *supra*.

Fay Stender's assessment of Huey: Terry A. Reim, "Cops' Panther Shoot Blows 1000-year Cover," *BB*, Sept. 19, 1968, 1.

"Panther HQ Shot Up: 2 Police Fired," *SFE*, Sept. 10, 1968.

Huey's Sentencing Hearing

HPN, Box 11, Folder 5, Probation Report, M864, letter of support for Huey Newton from Fay Stender.

"Keep cool no matter what": "Huey Says He Ordered 'Keep Cool'," *OT*, September 12, 1968, 7.

"nothing but contempt": HPN Probation Report, *supra*, M864.

"a much finer martyr": "Tensions, Martyrdom and Where Causes Lie, "*San Rafael Independent Journal* editorial, HPN, Series 1, Box 23, Folder 1 [clipping].

Inside the Men's Colony as All Hell Erupts on the Outside

"We have to civilize America": Terry Ryan, "Mrs. Cleaver criticizes white men," *The Redwood City Gazette*, Oct. 2, 1968; HPN Box 23, Folder 1 [clipping].

Cleaver's speech at San Francisco State: "At State: That Old Cleaver Rhythm," *BB*, October 17, 1968, HPN, Box 23, Folder 1.

"future bloodshed": "Newton Predicts Bloodshed," *The Redwood City Tribune*, Oct. 25, 1968, HPN Box 23, Folder 1 [clipping].

Impact on Nixon's campaign: Greenberg, David, "Civil Rights: Let 'Em Wiretap!" History News Network, October 22, 2001.

"State's rights" platform: "The 1963 Inaugural Address of Governor George C. Wallace," Alabama Department of Archives and History. https://digital.archives.al

"poured ice water over his head": Charles Garry and Arthur Goldberg, *Streetfighter in the Courtroom: ThePeople's Advocate* (New York: E. P. Dutton, 1977), 178.

"I'm better than Parry Mason": Garry and Goldberg, *Streetfighter in the Courtroom, supra.*

Merritt College move: Robin Buller, "Controversial move had lasting effects on Oakland," *SFC*, August 23, 2023, 1,A9.

"No more appeasement": "Bloodbath 'Figure of Speech'," *OT*, April 8, 1970, 1.

"gun-toting thugs": Hilliard, *Huey: Spirit of the Panther, supra,* 126.

J. Edgar Hoover's view of the Panther breakfast program: J. Ward Churchill and Jim Vander Wall, *Agents of Repression: The FBI's Secret Wars Against the Black Panther Party and the American Indian Movement* (Boston: South End Press, 1988, 1990), 175.

"an unprecedented national scandal": L.F. Palmer, "Out to Get the Panthers," *The Nation,* July 28, 1969, 80.

"we have to get this guy": Palmer, "Out to Get the Panthers," *supra,* 78.

"a symbolic battle": Mark Levine, George McNamee, Daniel Greenberg, *The Tales of Hoffman* (New York: Bantam Books, 1970), quote from the cover.

"blatant racist": Levine et al., *The Tales of Hoffman, supra,* 55-57, 62, 68-69.

New Haven Police Chief's reaction to Seale's prosecution: Associated Press, "Chief 'Was Astonished' by Indictment of Seale,", *SFC*, April 4, 1972.

"We will kill Richard Nixon": Hilliard and Cole, *This Side of Glory, supra,* 264-65.

Jesse Jackson quote: Fred Hampton 1948-1969, http://www.hartford-hwp.com archives/45a/715.html; see also, "Today in Counterculture History, The Murder of Fred Hampton," https:/www.shroomery.org/forums/sjhowflat.php/Number/13580978.

April 1970 poll: Churchill and Vander Wall, *Agents of Repression, supra,* 63, quoting Noam Chomsky and a June 1970 special report to President Nixon.

Panthers "deeply revered" in colonial and liberated African countries: Levinson, "Huey is My Brother, Too," *Black Panther Newsletter*, February 28, 1970, 2.

Winning Reversal on Appeal

The Kent State shooting: Kent State Shooting - Causes, Facts & Aftermath | HISTORY, https://nationaltoday.com/kent-state-shootings-remembrance/

Appellate court opinion: *People v. Newton* (1970) 8 Cal. A 3d. 359, 375.

Huey's first interview: "Huey: 'BPP Will Go to UN'," *SFC*, June 5-11, 1970, 4.

Huey Walks Free!

"We want Huey!": Richard Branning, "Newton Warns Establishment: Free Political Captives," *SFE*, August 6, 1970, 1.

"It was a beautiful day!": David Hilliard, film interview, *supra*.

X. FRAYED RELATIONSHIPS

Resuming Life on the Outside

"a folk hero": Branning, "Newton Warns Establishment: Free 'Political Captives,'" *SFE,* Aug. 6, 1970, 1.

"the struggle is coming to a final climax": Branning, *supra*.

Catching Up with Family

Sources: multiple interviews with family members

Melvin's Dangerous Adventure with Huey

Principal source: interviews with Melvin Newton

Huey Reunites with Bobby Seale as the Panther Party Shrinks

Seale and Huggins New Haven trial verdict: Garry and Goldberg, *Streetfighter in the Courtroom, supra* , 216. Donald Freed published a book on the New Haven trial the following year, *Agony at New Haven: The Trial of Bobby Seale and Ericka Huggins* (New York: Simon & Schuster, 1973).

The First Retrial For Officer Frey's Death

"tight-lipped and grim": "Jury Hopelessly Deadlocked in Newton's Trial," *SFC*, August 9, 1971, 1.

A Rift Develops with Jackson's Followers

"The dragon has come": Jo Durden-Smith, *Who Killed George Jackson? Fantasies, Paranoia and the Revolution* (New York: Alfred A. Knopf, 1976), 142-144; Paul Liberatore, *The Road to Hell: The True Story of George Jackson, Stephen Bingham, and the San Quentin Massacre* (New York: The Atlantic Monthly Press, 1996), 93-94.

Federal lawsuit: *Jordan v. Fitzharris*, 257 F. Supp. 674 (N.D. Cal. 1966)

"the same causal chain": Durden-Smith, *Who Killed George Jackson?*, supra.

Huey and Bert Schneider became fast friends: Hilliard, *Spirit of the Panther, supra,* 279.

Huey's Bold Visit to Red China

Federal commission report: "House Probers Split on Panther Study," *OT*, Aug 24, 1971, 36 E.

Huey's Second Retrial for Voluntary Manslaughter

Mistrial declared: Drew McKillips, "Huey Newton Free — Case Dismissed," *SFC*, Dec. 16, 1971, 1.

The Servant of the People and the Squad

The squad: Kate Coleman with Paul Avery, "The Party's Over: How Huey Newton created a street gang at the center of the Black Panther Party," *New Times,* July 10, 1978, 29–30. See also Flores Forbes, *Will You Die with Me? My Life in the Black Panther Party* (New York: Washington Square Press, Simon & Schuster, 2006).

The Lamp Post

Sources: multiple family interviews

Melvin Helps Launch African-American Studies

The push in the 1970s for ethnic and women's studies: LePore, *These Truths, supra,* 634.

Cutting Family Ties and Redefining Party Goals

"Outside pressures": Newton with Blake, *Revolutionary Suicide, supra,* 42.

"I inherited the family of humanity": Newton with Blake, *Revolutionary Suicide, supra,* kindle loc. 242.

"The family had lost their little brother": Melvin Newton, film interview.

Authorship of *Revolutionary Suicide*: Professor J. Herman Blake, who had testified on ghetto slang at Newton's 1968 death penalty trial, had originally assisted Huey in writing *Revolutionary Suicide*. But Blake used wording that did not match Huey's style, so Huey enlisted Melvin's aid in rewriting the book. Blake would, however, get credit as a co-author.

Estrangement and Self-Imposed Exile

Seale fled into exile: Hugh Pearson, *The Shadow of the Panther: Huey Newton and the Price of Black Power in America* (Reading, Mass: Addison-Wesley Publishing Company, 1994) 264.

Seale's reason for leaving the state: Flynn, "Panther Leader Seale Confesses," *Front Page*, Front Page magazine.com, April 23, 2002, http://archive.frontpagemag.com/read Article.aspx?ARTID-24216.

Pistol whipping of tailor: "Nobody calls me baby": Coleman with Avery, "The Party's Over," *supra*, 35.

Cleaning the blood off the walls: Elaine Brown, *A Taste of Power: A Black Woman's Story (*New York: Anchor Books, Doubleday, 1992), 356.

Daddy and Prodigal Son

Principal sources: multiple family member interviews

"We both were crying": Hilliard, *Huey: Spirit of the Panther*, *supra*, 225-226.

The Newton Family Divides into Camp

Principal sources: multiple family interviews

XI. HOMESICKNESS AND FRESH STARTS

Huey's Return

See discussion in Pearlman, *American Justice on Trial, supra*, 408-410.

Family Reunions and Dust-ups

Sources: multiple family interviews

Huey's New Trials

See discussion in Lise Pearlman, *The Sky's the Limit: People v. Newton, The REAL Trial of the 20th Century?* (Berkeley: Regent Press, 2012) 633-638 and related endnotes.

The Oakland Community School

Principal interview sources: Tracy Newton, Gregory Newton, Maurice Newton, and DeAngela Terrez Carr.

The Oakland Community School: See "The Black Panthers' Education Revolution," revolution.berkeley.edu/projects/Black-panthers-education-revolution. The school was declared by a state official "a model" for other inner city schools, Cassidy Rosenblum, *Oakland North,* December 15, 2016, "At historic Black Panthers school, Black teachers were key to student success," Oakland North.net; Ida Mohadad, "Black Panthers ran a first of its kind Oakland School," sfstandard.com

Regaining Close Ties with Nieces and Nephews

Principal sources: Tracy Newton, Gregory Newton, Maurice Newton, DeAngela Terrez Carr.

Dr. Huey P. Newton

The shooting of Fay Stender. For Fay Stender's biography and tragic death, see Lise Pearlman, *Call Me Phaedra, The Life and Times of Movement Lawyer Fay Stender* (Berkeley: Regent Press, 2018)

Newton, PhD. dissertation, "War Against the Panthers: A Study of Repression in America," Santa Clara University, June 1980.

FBI efforts to neutralize the Black Panther Party: Newton, PhD. dissertation, *supra,* p. 7, citing Robert Woodward and Carl Bernstein, *The Final Days* (New York: Simon & Schuster, 1976). See also "Submission of Recorded Presidential Conversations to the Committee on the Judiciary of the House of Representatives by President Richard M. Nixon: April 30, 1974" (Washington, D.C.: Government Printing Office, 1974), 1308.

"Dr. Nigger": Hugh Pearson, *The Shadow of the Panther* (New York: Perseus Books, 1995), 286, 288.

Déjà vu

Principal sources: Hilliard, D., *Huey: Spirit of the Panther* (New York: Thunder's Mouth Press, 2006), interviews of retired Officer Timothy Sanchez, Melvin and Tracy Newton

Armelia's Last Years

Principal sources: interviews of Melvin Newton, Tracy Newton, DeAngela Terrez Carr, Kim Johnson and Gregory Newton

Winning the Heart of Another Nephew

Principal sources: interviews of Melvin Newton and David Lautaro Newton

Trying to Make Amends

Principal sources re Huey's release from San Quentin: Interviews of Melivn Newton and former San Quentin inmate Black Panther Rudolph Mitchell

Geronimo Ji Jaga Pratt wins his freedom: See *In re Pratt,* 82 Cal. Rptr.2d 260 (Cal.App. 2 Dist.1999);

Wrongful conviction: Jack Olsen, "*Last Man Standing: The Tragedy and Triumph of Geronimo Pratt*", Last Man Standing: The Tragedy and Triumph of Geronimo ji-Jaga Pratt | Democracy Now! October 5, 2000.

XII. DEATH AND REBIRTH LARGER THAN LIFE

Irony in Death

"Huey's enemies multiplied": Hillard and Cole, *This Side of Glory, supra,* 2.

Reactions to Huey's death: William Brand and Larry Spears, "Friends and foes remember Newton 'visionary,' 'thug,'" *OT*, August 23, 1980, 2.

Tyrone Robinson boast: Craig Staats, "Prosecutor Testifies to Critical Interview; Suspect Bragged About Killing Newton, DA Says," *OT*, August 29, 1991, 3; Kelly Gust, "Newton Jury hears incriminating tape," *OT*, August 30,1991, 10.

Gang threatens to kill Robinson: *UPI*, "Gang 'Death Sentence for Accused Killer of Newton," August 27, 1989,Gang 'death sentence' for accused killer of Newton - UPI Archives.

A Funeral for the Ages

Principle sources: Newton family and David Hilliard interviews; Hilliard and Carter, *This Side of Glory, supra.* Hilliard with Keith and Kent Zimmerman, *Huey: Spirit of the Panther, supra.*

Quotes of speakers at the funeral are from the unpublished memorial brochure for Huey Newton, August 29, 1989 private collection of Melvin Newton and from Pacifica radio KPFA, Huey P. Newton funeral transcripts, http://www.lib.berkeley.edu /MRC/netwonfuneraltranscripts.html.

"downright blasphemy": Pearson, *The Shadow of the Panther, supra,* 322–324.

"The Frailty's and Flaws of a Man": Bill Snyder and Michael Collier, "Newton laid to rest: Many former Black Panthers attend rites," *OT*, Aug. 29, 1989, 1. "Frailty's" was the spelling in the poem' title.

"These were very young people": Melvin Newton film interview, *supra*.

The Tyrone Robinson Murder Trial Becomes A Retrial of Huey Newton

"get me some stripes": Will Jones, "Dead man's testimony heard in Newton case," *OT*, Sept. 4, 1991, p. 5

Prosecutor's closing argument: Peter Fimrite, "Murder Conviction is Handed Up in Murder Case," *SFC*, October 10, 1991, p. A19.

Up Jumps the Monkey

"five respectable slaveholders": Fallin, *Uplifting the People, supra,* 26.

"Right or wrong": Gregory Newton, Dissertation. "Up Jumps the Monkey--A Revolutionary's Tale, Acts I and II." Saint Mary's College of California (June 2004) 226.

Letter to his future nephew: G. Newton, Dissertation, *supra.* 306-07.

Myth Trumps Reality

Huey's definition of reactionary suicide: David Hilliard, *Huey: Spirit of the Panther, supra,*

"out-of-control situation": Hilliard and Cole, *This Side of Glory: The Autobiography of David Hillard and the Story of the Black Panther Party* (Boston: Little, Brown & Company, 1993), 9-10.

A World-Changing True Story

"*Framing the Black Panthers*": Jane Rhodes, *Framing the Black Panthers: The Spectacular Rise of a Black Power Icon* (New York: The New Press, 2007), 3.

"*Black Against Empire*": Hector Tobar, "Black Against Empire tells the history of Black Panthers." *Los Angeles Times*, January 24, 2013.

Quotes re Barbarette Newton: Barbarette Newton memorial pamphlet, private collection of Melvin Newton.

"*No There There*" : Chris Rhomberg, *No There There, supra,*155.

"lasting fixtures in popular culture": Rhodes, *Framing the Black Panthers, supra*, 3.

Public Memorials to Huey's Historic Impact

The Dr. Huey P. Newton Foundation: Dr. Huey P. Newton Foundation, https://hueypnewtonfoundation.org/

"The rain is very symbolic": Brandy Callins, "Huey P. Newton bust unveiled in West Oakland," Oakland Side, Arts & Community, October 25, 2021, oaklandside.org/2021/10/25/huey-p-newton-bust-unveiled-in-west-oakland, *supra*.

Quote from sculptor Dana King: "Huey P. Newton bust unveiled in West Oakland," *supra*.

Individuals' roles are often romanticized: Huey P. Newton, "War Against the Panthers: A Study in Repression," *supra*, 2. Quote from Melvin Newton at unveiling: Huey P. Newton Honored With Statue Commemorating the 55th Anniversary of the Black Panther Party | 92Q WQQK-FM (92qnashville.com); see also https://abc7news.com/huey-p-newton-statue-oakland-Black-panther-party-bronze-bust-55th-anniversary/11153103/ Huey P. Newton bust unveiled in West Oakland

Ruth Simmons: Pamela Paul, "Some Words of Wisdom from the Top of the Ivy League" *NYT,* Opinion Section, Sept. 23, 2023, Opinion | The Parallel Memoirs of Ruth Simmons and Drew Gilpin Faust — The NYT (nytimes.com).

Melvin Newton film interview, *supra*.

Newton with Blake, *Revolutionary Suicide, supra*, Kindle, 9.

Sources

Individuals

Many people graciously gave of their time for interviews and background information for this book on the Newton family history and for my prior works related to the 1968 death penalty trial of Huey Newton. These interviews were conducted in person, by telephone and via e-mail over the course of more than 20 years starting with *The Sky's The Limit: People v. Newton, The Real Trial of the 20th Century?* [Regent Press, 2012]; followed by *American Justice on Trial: People v. Newton* (Regent Press 2016) and the award-winning 2022 film project of the same name which I co-produced and participated in conducting numerous interviews, "American Justice on Trial: People v. Newton" (2022), www.justicemovie.com (recently retitled "In the Crosshairs").

The sources I interviewed include: Robert Blauner, Thomas Broome, Allan Brotsky, Malcolm Burnstein, DeAngela Terrez Carr, Debra Chase, Kathleen Cleaver, Kate Coleman, Penny Cooper, Joan De La Sceaux, Eddie Ento, Debra Godfrey Gatling, Doris Newton Godfrey, Peter Franck, Gordon Gaines, Ann Fagan Ginger, Anwar Hasan, Hon. Thelton Henderson, David Hilliard, Alex Hoffmann, David Horowitz, Howard Janssen, Hon. D. Lowell Jensen, Kim Johnson, Patricia Johnson, Sandra Levinson, Rudolph Mitchell, Armelia Newton (Lee Edward's daughter), David Lautaro Newton, Earl ("Jake") Newton, Gregory Newton, Maurice Newton, Melvin David Newton, Myesha Newton, Tracy Newton, William B. Patterson, Charles Plummer, Lucy Newton Robinson, Jon Sager, Timothy Sanchez, Bobby Seale, Harry Simon, Marvin Stender, Morrie Turner, Karen Lee Wald, Doron Weinberg, Esther Smith White and Jayne Williams. If I left someone out, my apologies.

Special Collections

Black Panther Collection, archives of the African American Museum and Library, Oakland, California. Department of Justice FBI FOIA Files: The Black Panther Party, Huey Newton, Fay Stender, Student Nonviolent Coordinating Committee. Don Hausler, unpublished manuscript, *Blacks in Oakland 1852–1987*,

Vol. 3, 113, 116. Dr. Huey P. Newton Foundation, Inc. Collection 1968–1994, M864. California: Green Library Special Collections, Stanford University.

U.C. Berkeley Bancroft Library: Meiklejohn Civil Liberties Archives; Elsa Knight Thompson papers. Oakland Public Library History Room. Open Eye Pictures, film archives for "American Justice on Trial" and the former archives of Arc of Justice Productions, Inc.," for "American Justice on Trial."

Included in the text are quotes from interviews of Newton trial participants and observers and of experts on criminal law, jury and civil rights by the original film Director Robert Richter and myself as Co-Director for the Arc of Justice Productions, Inc. film project *American Justice on Trial: People v. Newton* and two further interviews by Director Andy Abrahams of Open Eye Pictures. These interviews were conducted from July 2013 through August 2018 mostly in California, with a few taking place in New York, one in St. Louis, Missouri, and one in Atlanta, Georgia.

All direct quotations from the following individuals included in this book are from either these interviews or interviews I conducted specifically for this book unless otherwise indicated: Louis Armmond, Robert Blauner, James Brosnahan, John Burris, Kathleen Cleaver, Penny Cooper, Belva Davis, Leo Dorado, Emory Douglas, Janice Garrett Forte, Ann Fagan Ginger, David Harper, Anwar Hasan Hon. Thelton Henderson, David Hilliard, Thomas Hofmann, D. Lowell Jensen, Karen Jo Koonan, Melvin Newton, Nancy O'Malley, Bill Patterson Barry Scheck, Bryan Stevenson, Morrie Turner and Doron Weinberg.

Private Collections

Trial notes of Prof. Robert Blauner from *People v. Newton*, 1968; David Lautaro Newton — photographs; Melvin Newton — memorabilia, family papers and photographs, "A Proposal for A Model African-American Studies program for Community Colleges, African-American Studies Curriculum Project, Merritt College, 1972; "Up Jumps the Monkey from Obscurity to Fame," a play in three acts presented by Gregory Newton in partial fulfillment of the requirement of Master of Arts, June 2004, St. Mary's College of California Graduate Liberal Studies Program; Maurice Newton, family photograph; Tracy Newton, family photographs; Armelia Newton, Lee Edward Newton memorial.

Principal Newspaper and Periodical Sources

Berkeley Barb, Black Panther Newspaper, The Chicago Defender, The Guardian, Los Angeles Times, Newsweek, New York Times, Oakland Post, Oakland Tribune, Ramparts, San Francisco Chronicle, San Francisco Examiner, TIME, Wall Street Journal.

Books

Acker, James R., *Scottsboro and Its Legacy* (Westport, Connecticut: Praeger, 2008).

Aiello, Thomas, *The Kings of Casino Park: Black Baseball in The Lost Season of 1932* (Tuscaloosa: The University of Alabama Press, 2011)

Alexander, M., *The New Jim Crow: Mass Incarceration in the Age of Color Blindness* (New York: New Press, 2010).

Anderson, T., *The Movement and the Sixties: Protest in America from Greensboro to Wounded Knee* (New York: Oxford Univ. Press, 1995).

Anthony, Earl, *Picking Up the Gun: A Report on the Black Panthers* (New York: The Dial Press, 1970).

_____, *Spitting in the Wind: The True Story Behind the Violent Legacy of the Black Panther Party* (Malibu, California: Roundtable, 1990).

Armstrong, Gregory, *The Dragon Has Come* (New York: Harper & Row, 1974).

Austin, Curtis, J., *Up Against the Wall* (Fayetteville: Univ. of Arkansas Press, 2006).

Avrich, Paul, *Sacco and Vanzetti: The Anarchist Background* (Princeton: Princeton Univ. Press, 1991).

Ball, Edward, *Slaves in the Family,* (New York: Farrar Strauss and Giraaux, 1998).

Bay, Mia, *Traveling Black: A Story of Race and Resistance* (Cambridge: The Belknap Press of Harvard University Press, 2021).

Bingham, Clara, *Witness to the Revolution: Radicals, Resistors, Vets, Hippies and the Year America Lost Its Mind and Found Its Soul* (New York: Random House, 2016).

Bingham, Howard, *Black Panthers 1968* (Los Angeles: Ammo Books, 2009).

Bloom, Joshua, and Martin, Jr., Waldo, *Black Against Empire: The History and Politics of the Black Panther Party* (Berkeley: University of California Press, 2013).

Bradford, Amory, *Oakland's Not for Burning* (New York: David McKay, 1968).

Breard, Sylvester Quinn, *Early History of Monroe* (Gretna: Pelican Publishing Company, 2012)

Broussard, A. S., *Black San Francisco: The Struggle for Racial Equality in the West, 1900–1954* (Lawrence, Kansas: University of Kansas Press, 1993).

Brown, Elaine, *A Taste of Power: A Black Woman's Story* (New York: Anchor Books, 1992).

Burris, John, *Blue v. Black: Let's End the Conflict Between Cops and Minorities* (New York: St. Martin's Press, 1997).

Carr, James, *Bad: The Autobiography of James Carr* (Oakland, California: Nabat/AK Press, 2000).

Carroll, P. N., and Noble, D. W., *The Free and the Unfree: A Progressive History of the United States*, 3d rev. ed. (New York: Penguin Books, 2001).

Carson, C., Garrow, D. J., Gill, G., Harding, V., and Hine, D. C., *The Eyes on the Prize Civil Rights Reader* (New York: Penguin Books, 1991).

Carson, Clayborne, *In Struggle: SNCC and the Black Awakening of the 1960s* (Cambridge, Massachusetts: Harvard Univ. Press, 1981, 1995).

Churchill, W., and Vanderwall, J., *Agents of Repression: The FBI's Secret Wars Against the Black Panther Party and the American Indian Movement* (Boston: South End Press, 1988, 1990).

The COINTELPRO Papers: Documents from the FBI's Secret War Against Dissidents (Boston: South End Press, 1980).

Cleaver, Eldridge, *Target Zero: A Life in Writing* (New York: Palgrave Macmillan, 2006).

Collier, Peter, and Horowitz, David, *Destructive Generation: A Second Look at the Sixties* (New York: Summit Books, 1989).

Darrow, Clarence, *The Story of My Life* (New York: Da Capo, 1996

Davies, David R. (ed.), *The Press and Race* (Jackson, Mississippi: University Press of Mississippi, 2001).

Davis, Belva, and Haddock, Vicki, *Never In My Wildest Dreams: A Black Woman's Life in Journalism* (San Francisco; Berrett-Koehler Publishers, Kindle Ed., 2010).

Dellums, R. V., and Halterman, H. L., *Lying Down with the Lions* (Boston: Beacon Press, 2000).

Diouf, Sylviane A., *Slavery's Exiles: The Story of the American Maroons,* (New York: NYU Press, 2014).

Dudziak, M. L., *Cold War Civil Rights* (Princeton, New Jersey: Princeton Univ. Press, 2000).

Durden-Smith, Jo, *Who Killed George Jackson? Fantasies, Paranoia and the Revolution* (New York: Alfred A. Knopf, 1976).

Fallin, Wilson, Jr., *Uplifting the People: Three Centuries of Black Baptists in Alabama* (Tuscaloosa: University of Alabama Press, 2007).

Fanon, Frantz, *The Wretched of the Earth* (English translation: Constance Farrington), New York: Grove Press, 1963).

Foner, P. S., *The Black Panthers Speak* (Cambridge, Massachusetts: Da Capo Press, 1970).

Forbes, Flores, *Will You Die With Me? My Life in the Black Panther Party* (New York: Washington Square Press, 2006).

Garry, Charles, and Goldberg, Arthur, *Streetfighter in the Courtroom: The People's Advocate* (New York: E. P. Dutton, 1977).

Geis, Gilbert, and Beinen, Leigh, *Crimes of the Century* (Boston: Northeastern Univ. Press, 1998).

Ginger, Ann Fagan, *Landmark Cases Left Out of Your Textbooks* (Berkeley: Meiklejohn Civil Liberties Institute, 2006).

_____, *Minimizing Racism in Jury Trials* (New York: National Lawyers Guild, 1969).

_____, *The Relevant Lawyers: Conversations out of court on their clients, their practice, their politics, their life style* (New York: Simon & Schuster, 1973).

Goodman, James, *Stories of Scottsboro* (New York: Pantheon Books, 1994).

Grant, Robert, and Katz, Joseph, *The Great Trials of the Twenties: The Watershed Decade in America's Courtrooms* (New York: Sarpedon, 1998).

Hilliard, D., *Huey: Spirit of the Panther* (New York: Thunder's Mouth Press, 2006).

Hilliard, D., and Cole, L., *This Side of Glory* (New York: Little, Brown & Co, 1993).

Horowitz, David, *Hating Whitey and Other Progressive Causes* (Dallas, Texas: Spence Publishing, 1999).

_____, *Left Illusions: An Intellectual Odyssey* (Dallas, Texas: Spence Publishing, 2003).

_____, *Radical Son: A Generational Odyssey* (New York: Touchstone, 1997).

Jackson, George, *Blood in My Eye* (Baltimore: Black Classic Press, 1990).

Soledad Brother: The Prison Letters of George Jackson (Chicago: Lawrence Hill Books, 1994).

Jones, Charles E. (ed.), *The Black Panther Party* [Reconsidered] (Baltimore, Maryland: Black Classic Press, 1998).

Keating, Edward M., *Free Huey!* (Palo Alto, California: Ramparts Press, 1971).

Knappman, E. W., *Great American Trials From Salem Witchcraft to Rodney King* (Detroit, Michigan: Visible Ink Press, 1994).

Lanahan, D. J., *Justice For All: Legendary Trials of the Twentieth Century* (Bloomington, Indiana: Author House, 2006).

Lepore, Jill, *These Truths: A History of the United States,* (New York: W.W. Norton & Company, 2018).

Levine, M., McNamee, G., and Greenberg, D., *The Tales of Hoffman* (New York: Bantam Books, 1970).

Liberatore, Paul, *The Road to Hell: The True Story of George Jackson, Stephen Bingham, and the San Quentin Massacre* (New York: The Atlantic Monthly Press, 1996).

McHenry, James O., *The Monroeians, The Pine Street Blues Collective*, (Bloomington: Archway Publishing, 2015).

Mitford, Jessica, *A Fine Old Conflict* (New York: Vintage Books, 1956, 1977).

Moore, Gilbert, *Rage* (New York: Carroll & Graf, 1993).

_____, *A Special Rage* (New York: Harper & Row, 1971).

Newton, H., and Blake, J. H., *Revolutionary Suicide* (New York: Harcourt, Brace, Jovanovich, 1973).

Newton, Huey, *To Die For the People* (New York: Random House, 1972; City Lights Books, 2009).

Ogletree, Charles J., Jr., and Sarat, Austin (eds.), *From Lynch Mobs to the Killing State: Race and the Death Penalty in America* (New York: New York Univ. Press, 2006).

Pearlman, Lise, *The Sky's the Limit: People v. Newton, The REAL Trial of the 20th Century?* (Berkeley: Regent Press, 2012).

_____, *American Justice on Trial: People v. Newton* (Berkeley: Regent Press, 2016).

_____, *With Justice for Some: Politically Charged Criminal Trials of the Early 20th Century that Helped Shape Today's America* (Berkeley: Regent Press, 2017).

_____, *Call Me Phaedra: The Life and Times of Movement Lawyer Fay Stender* (Berkeley: Regent Press, 2018).

Pearson, Hugh, *The Shadow of the Panther* (New York: Perseus Books, 1995).

Penningroth, Dylan C., *Before the Movement: The Hidden History of Black Civil Rights* (Kindle Edition, Liveright Publishing Corporation, a Division of W.W. Norton & Company, 2023).

Pfaelzer, Jean, *California: A Slave State,* (New Haven: Yale University Press, 2023).

Raiford, Leigh, *Imprisoned in a Luminous Glare: Photography and the African-American Freedom Struggle* (Chapel Hill: Univ. of North Carolina Press, 2011).

Rhodes, Jayne, *Framing the Black Panthers: The Spectacular Rise of a Black Power Icon* (New York: The New Press, 2008).

Rhomberg, Chris, *No There There: Race, Class, and Political Community in Oakland* (Berkeley: Univ. of California Press, 2004).

Rosenfeld, Seth, *Subversives: The FBI's War on Student Radicals and Reagan's Rise to Power* (New York: Farrar, Straus & Giroux, 2012).

Russell, F., *Sacco and Vanzetti: The Case Resolved* (New York: Harper & Row, 1986).

Seale, Bobby, *Seize the Time: The Story of the Black Panther Party and Huey P. Newton* (New York: Black Classic Press, 1970, 1991).

Stone, Irving, *Clarence Darrow for the Defense* (New York: Signet Books, 1941, 1969).

Tackwood, Louis., and The Citizens Research and Investigation Committee, *The Glasshouse Tapes, The Story of an Agent-Provocateur and the New Police-Intelligence Complex* (New York: Avon, 1973) 114.

Temkin, Moshik, *The Sacco-Vanzetti Affair* (New Haven, Connecticut: Yale University Press, 2009).

The Whole World's Watching: Peace and Social Justice Movements of the 1960s & 1970s (Berkeley: Berkeley Art Center Association, 2001).

Wilkerson, Isaabel, *The Warmth of Other Suns, The Epic Story of America's Great Migration,* New York: Vintage Books, a division of Random House, Inc., 2010).

Yacavone, Donald, *Teaching White Supremacy: America's Democratic Ordeal and the Forging of the National Identity,* (New York: Pantheon Books, a division of Penguin Random House, 2022).

Web Sources

Alameda County Sheriff's Office, https://www.alamedacountysheriff.org.

Alexander, Bass, Jack, "Documenting the Orangeburg Massacre," Nieman Report. niemanreports.org/articles/documenting-theorangeburg-massacre.

"Biography of Richard Aoki, The Asian-American Black Panther," http://racerelations.about.com/od/trailblazers/a/Biography-Of-Richard-Aoki-The-Asian-American-Black-Panther.htm.

Burris, John L., Blue vs. Black, http://www.johnburrislaw.com.

Coleman, Kate, "Elmer 'Geronimo' Pratt: The Untold Story of the Black Panther Leader, Dead At 63," *The New Republic,* June 27, 2011, https://newrepublic.com/article/90735/Black-panther-geronimo-pratt-murder-conviction-prison-huey-newton.

"The Party's Over, " Center for Investigative Reporting, http://cironline.org/reports/partys-over-1276.

Crime Magazine, "The Scottsboro Boys: Jim Crow on Trial," http://crimemagazine.comscottsboro-boys-jim-crow-trial.

Crouch, Stanley. "The Joy of Goetz." New York http://nymag.

com/nymetro/news/anniversary/35th/n_8601/.

FBI, "COINTELPRO." What Really Happened, http://www.whatreallyhappened.com/RANCHO/POLITICS/COINTELPRO/COINTELRPO-FBI.docs.html.

Flynn, Dan, "Panther Leader Seale Confesses," *Front Page*, April 23, 2002, http://archive.front-pagemag.com/read Article.aspx?ARTID=24216.

Freeman, Jo, "Social Protest in the Sixties," http://www.jofreeman.com/sixtiesprotest/ sixties.htm.

Frontline, "Two Nations of Black America," PBS, Frontline http://www.pbs.org/PBS, "Two Nations of Black America," http://wwww.pbs.org/wgbh/pages/frotnline/shows. Race. interviews/ecleaver.htmlwgbh/pages/frontline/shows/race/interviews/ecleaver.html.

Griffey, Trevor, "When celebrated activist turns out to be informant:making sense of Richard Aoki's FBI file," May 5, 2012, http://www.truth-out.org/news/item/12555-when-celebrated-activistturns-out-to-be-informant-making-sense-of-richard-aokis-fbi-file.

"The History Makers," The HistoryMakers.com – African American history archive, www.thehistorymakers.com.

Hoffman, Abbie, "Conspiracy in the Streets" Haymarket Books,http://www.haymarketbooks.org/product_info.php?products_id=1187.

Huey P. Newton Foundation https://hueypnewtonfoundation.org

"Impeachment: Richard Nixon." The History Place. http://www.historyplace.com/unitedstates/impeachments/nixon.htm.

Kahn, Jeffery, "Ronald Reagan launched political career using the Berkeley campus as a political target," University of California, Berkeley, http://www.berkeley.edu./news/media/releases/2004/06/08_reagan.shtml.

King, Jr., Martin Luther, "Beyond Vietnam: A Time To Break Silence," April 4, 1967. [Full speech www.youtube.com/watch?v=OC1Ru2p8OfU].

Linder, Douglas O., "Famous Trials" School of Law University of Missouri–Kansas City, http://law2.umkc.edu/faculty/projects/FTrials/ftrials.htm.

McMullins, Curtis, "Ruchell Cinque Magee – Political

Prisoner" It's About Time – Black Panther Party Legacy & Alumni 45th Year Reunion http://www.itsabouttimebcom/ Political_Prisoners/Release_Ruchell_Cinque_Magee.html.

The Negro in Chicago: A Study of Race Relations and A Race Riot, Chicago Commission on Race Relations, Chicago, Illinois: University of Chicago Press, 1922); ebook.

Nittle, Nadra Karim, "Biography of Richard Aoki, The Asian-American Black Panther," January 8, 2016, http://racerelations.about.com/od/trailblazers/a/Biography-Of-Richard-Aoki-The-Asian-American-Black-Panther.htm.

Report of the Select Committee to Study Governmental Operations with Respect to Intelligence Activities, United States Senate ("The Church Committee Report"), https://acrchyive.org/details/finalreportofse101unit.

Rosenfeld, Seth, "Richard Aoki, Man Who Armed Black Panthers, was FBI Informant" (video) August 20, 2012, updated October 20, 2012, http://www.huffingtonpost.com/2012/08/20/richardaoki_ n_1812167.html.

Rosenmann, Alexandra, "Gun Rights, Police Brutality and the Case of the Century," AlterNet, July 7, 2016, http://within-www.alternet.org/civil-liberties/gun-rights-police-brutality-and-case-centuryvideo.

"The San Francisco State College Strike Collection," J.Paul Leonard Library, http://library.sfsu.edu/sf-state-strikecollection.

Thomas, Robert McGill, Jr., "Lionel Wilson, 82, A Mayor of Oakland for Three Terms," *NYT*, Jan. 31, 1998. http://www.nytimes.com/1998/01/31/us/ lionel-wilson-82-a-mayor-of-oakland-for-three-terms.html.

TIME, "The Nation: Odyssey of Huey Newton", Nov. 13, 1978, http://content.time.com/time/magazine/article/0,9171,946144,00.html.

"Truman Library Desegregation of the Armed Forces Online Research File," Harry S. Truman Library and Museum, http://www.trumanlibrary.org/whistlestop /study_collections/desegregation/large/index.php?action=chronology. (Univ. of Washington Press 1982).

Weir, Stan, "Oakland: The Last General Strike," November 5, 2005, http:// libcom.org/library/oakland-general-strike-stan-weir; http:// socialistworker.org/2011/12/12/the-last-oaklandgeneral-strike.

Wing, Nick, "Here's How The Nation Responded When A Black Militia Group Occupied A Government Building," *Huffington Post*, January 6, 2016 (updated Jan. 9, 2016), http://www.huffingtonpost.com/entry/Black-panthers-california-1967_us_568accfce4b014efe0db2f40.

Zirin, Dave, "Dave Zirin: An Interview with John Carlos" *Counter-Punch*: http://www.counter- punch.org/2003/11/01/an-interview-with-john-carlos/.

Zuru, Deena, "Beyoncé gets political at Super Bowl, pays tribute to 'Black Lives Matter'," CNN, http://www.cnn.com/2016/02/08/politics/beyonce-super-bowl-Black-lives-matter/index.htm."America: 1968-2015; What has changed, what hasn't?" *TIME* cover story, May 11, 2015.

Journal Articles and Pamphlets

Cleaver, Eldridge, "Newton On Trial" *Ramparts*, Fall 1968.

Frankfurter, Felix, "The Case of Sacco and Vanzetti," *The Atlantic Monthly*, March 1927.

Palmer, L. F., "Out to Get the Panthers" *The Nation*, July 28, 1969.

"Report from Black America." *Newsweek*, June–July 1969.

Rosebury, Celia, "Black Liberation on Trial: The Case of Huey Newton," *The People's World*, Summer 1968. Reprint by the Bay Area Committee to Defend Political Freedom, Berkeley, California, 1968, from articles originally appearing during the summer of 1968 in *The People's World*. Archives of the Oakland, California African-American Museum and Library, Black Panther Collection.

Stern, Sol, "The Call of the Black Panthers," *NYT Magazine*, August 6, 1967, 11.

Wald, Karen, "Jury is selected for Newton trial," *The Guardian*, August 3, 1968.

Index

The names of members of the Newton family tree are **bolded**

A

Abbott, Robert *28* (see also *The Chicago Defender*)
A Colony in a Nation 29
Abrahams, Andrew 526
Aiello, Thomas 95-96
Alameda County Central Labor Council 172
Aiken, Lee 495
Alameda County Courthouse vii, xviii,1-5, 268-69, VIII *passim*, 269-352, 389, 399
Alameda County District Attorney 1, 147, 149, 243, 438, 502 (see also Frank Coakley, Lowell Jensen, Jack Meehan)
Alameda County Grand Jury 458, 526
Alameda County Jail x, 230, 234, 271, 386, 437
Alameda County Sheriff 32, 260, 386, 491
Alcorn, Barbarette Payton xvi, 364-66, 410-12 (see also **Barbarette Newton**)
Alcorn, Billy Maurice 365
Alcorn, Maurice xv, 364, 366, 402, 405, 410, 448-49 (see also **Maurice Newton**)
Ali, Muhammad 40, 239-40, 253 (see also Cassius Clay)
Allen Temple Baptist Church 496
American Anti-Slavery Society of New York 14
American Communist Party 258
American Constitution 4, 11, 19, 41, 69, 72, 132, 135, 227, 235, 272, 290, 316, 473 (see also Bill of Rights,13th Amendment, 14th Amendment)
American Dilemma, The 137
American Justice on Trial 525-26
American Nazi Party 228
Angelou, Maya 466
Antioch Missionary Baptist Church 153-54
Aoki, Richard 238, 239, 241, 432
Armmond, Louis 237, 249
Ashley, Chester 53-54
Ashley County, Arkansas 52-59
A Special Rage (see also *Rage*) 351
Avery, Paul 463
Axelrod, Beverly 246-47, 264

B

Baldwin, James 214, 350-51, 466
Ball, Edward 17
Bastrop, Louisiana 74-82, 86, 97-102, 106, 182
Baxter, Carolyn 500-01
Beach, Herbert 173, 184
Belafonte, Gina 520
Belafonte, Harry 520
Berkeley Barb, The 240
Bey, Robert 410, 461, 477
Beyoncé 515
Bible, The 30-31, 64, 338; Adam and Eve 108; David and Goliath ix,448, 514, 30-31; Gospel 166, 183, 336; Jesus 30-31, 119, 216, 250, 326,336, 513 ; Job ix; Luke 336; Moses 30, 64, 500; Prodigal Son 266, 445-46; Samson 30; Solomon 30; Ten Commandments 64; Walter with his Bible 167 (photo)
Bill of Rights Fifth Amendment 305, 310, 313; Sixth Amendment 264
Bingham, Howard 350-51
Birth of a Nation 135
Black Against Empire 515
Black Lives Matter 515
Black Panther 518
Black Panther newspaper 259, 272, 309, 323-24, 333, 369, 376, 409
Black Panther Party vii,1-3; 16-18; 232-528 *passim*; FBI targeting for extinction 455-56; formation 235-245; Sacramento debut 246-250; Ten Point Program 17, 242, 252, 465, 509 (see also Huey Newton, Bobby Seale)
Black Panther Party Alumni Legacy Network 523
Black Panther Party for Self-Defense 242 (See Black Panther Party)

Black Panther Party Museum 527
Black Panther Party of Northern California 241
The Black Panthers: Vanguard of the Revolution 518
Black Power 241, 290, 317, 408, 440, 468, 515
Black Star street cars 86
Blake, Herman 5, 326, 329-30, 438, 476
Blauner, Robert 326, 340, 344
Blight, David 16
Blook, Joshua 515
Bolden, George 44-46, 49, 52
Boondocks, The 516
Bouie, Jamelle 16
Bradley, Tom 457
Brando, Marlon 279-80, 392
Brooks, Edward 471-72, 495
Broome, Thomas 218, 220
Brotherhood of Sleeping Car Porters 127, 236
Brown, Elaine campaign for Oakland City Council 438 ; Huey's funeral 497, 499; in charge of BPP 441-42, 454; joining BPP 379; Lamp Post 448, 457; meeting Huey 398; BPP; Minister of Information 408-09, 423-25; Oakland Community School 464-65; Red China trips 398, 423-24
Brown, H. Rap 274, 362, 497 (see also Imam Jamal Abdullah Al-Amin)
Brown, Jerry Brown 458
Brown, Willie 252
Bryan, William Jennings 108
Buck v. Bell 71
Buddha Samurai 424-25 (see also the Squad)
Burnett, Annie ("Sissie") xi, 38, 41, 55-56, 83, 93
Burnett, Isaac xi, 34, 38, 41-43 (with photo), 45, 56, 62-63, 83, 88-89, 93, 99, 119,182
Burnett, Jordan xi-xii, 35
Burnett, Martha xi-xii, 35
Burns, Ken 39
Burris, John 286

C

California Men's Colony 5, 362-80, 399, 455
Callins, Brenda 523
Callins, Preston 442, 467
Carlos, John 367
Carmichael, Stokely 240-41, 321 (see also Kwame Ture, SNCC)
Carpetbaggers 21
Carr, De Angela Terrez xiv, 178, 401, 408, 428, 449-51, 468-69, 479-80
Carr, James xiv, 177, 450
Carr Leola Newton xiv, IV, VI *passim;* visit with David Harper 401; Newton trial 271; and Barbarette Newton 405; godson Gregory Newton 408; and Myesha Newton 449-50 (see also **Leola Johnson, Leola Newton**))
Carter, Alice x, 401 (see also Alice Hilliard, Alice Newton)
Carter, Alprentice "Bunchy" 371, 376, 456
Casey, Delores 266
Casino Park 93-96
Chauvin, Derek 525
Chavez, Cesar 466
Chicago Conspiracy Trial 379
Chicago Defender, The 28, 45, 90, 109, 196
Chitlin Circuit 98-99
Church, Frank 414, 455
Clark, Ramsey 456
Clay, Cassius 239 (see also Muhammad Ali)
Cleaver, Eldridge Algeria 394, 498; author 246-47, 325; Axelrod and 246-47; and Elaine Brown; candidate for President 437; Communist countries tour 380, 398, 422; and Kathleen Neal Cleaver 266, 498; and Bobby Hutton police confrontation 278, 357, 369; joining BPP 246; Newton jury verdict prediction 338, 343; Newton pretrial speech 285; order to return to prison 362; split with Newton 348-49, 408, 435, 487; parole violation 285; *Ramparts 325*; Republican Party 498; revolution 392, 396

Cleaver, Kathleen Algerian exile 498; on Black Lives Matter 516 candidate for State Assembly 437; BPP Communications Director 24; Communist countries tour with husband Eldridge 398; divorce 488, 498; Bobby Hutton's death 279; Huey Newton trial 285-86, 294, 343; marriage Ramparts magazine 362; law degree 488; teaching career 488 (See also Kathleen Neal)
Clinton, Bill 141
Coakley, Frank 438
COINTELPRO 371, 379, 397, 472
Cole, Nat King 152
Coleman, Kate 459, 463
Columbus, Christopher 13
Communist Manifesto, The 239
Communist Party 258, 263 (see also American Communist Party)
Compromise of 1850 132

D

Daley, Richard 331-32, 337
Darrow, Clarence 108, 291-92
Darwin, Charles 108
Davis, Belva Melton childhood in Monroe 72-73, 84-85; 523; on BPP platform 252; on David Harper 340; on Huey Newton; on Newton jury 343-44; on Stop the Draft Week 254; Uncle Ezra's lawsuit 123-25
Davis, Donn Granville 499-500
DeFremery Park 251, 269, 279, 284, 285, 519
Dellums, Ron 213, 252, 274, 437, 439, 499
Depression, The Great 67- 69, 74, 83, 93, 125, 147, 149, 261, 363, 491, 513
De Santos, Ron 15
Diamond, Bernard 328
Dixie League 92
Dohrenwend, Robert 31
Douglas, Emory 254, 270, 356
Douglass, Frederick 19, 131-32
Dowell, Denzil 246-47
Dreyfus, Barney 294
DuBois, W. E. B. 336

Durden-Smith, Jo 418-20, 471
Dymally, Melvin 252

E

Edwards v. California 128
Eisenhower, Dwight David 197
Engels, Friedrich 239
Ento, Eddie James xii, 128, 131
Ento, Eddie Jr. xii, 63, 176, 181,188-89, 227, 363, 436-37
Ento, Jessie Johnson xii, 128, 137, 139, 176, 181, 188, 190, 225, 400-01; 403; (see also Jessie Johnson; Jessie Mae Smith)
Equal Justice Initiative 49
Executive Order 8802 127, 140

F

Fair Housing Act of 1963 227-28
Fanon, Frantz 237, 239, 284, 336
Federal Bureau of Investigation (FBI) assassination of Carter and Huggins 371; assassination of Fred Hampton 378-79, bugging Newton's penthouse 298-402; Chicago Eight 376-77; Cleaver focus 370; Cleaver-Newton split 408-11; Huey in Red China 423; Huston Plan 436,455-56, 472; infiltration of BPP 398, 402; 1968 trial 2, 287; Oakland Auditorium BPP fundraiser 272; San Francisco State 370-71;; *Up Jumps the Monkey* 508; Pratt 486-87; Walter Newton focus 168-69; Walter Newton's funeral 448; "*Wisdom*" 484 (see also J. Edgar Hoover, COINTELPRO)
Ferrette, Herb 526
Five Points 39, 62, 85
Flatlands, The 53, 55 139, 147-48, 172, 293-94, 344, 438, 464, 501, 520
Floyd, George 525
Fonda, Jane 392, 397
For Love and Legacy 525
Forbes, Flores 425
Forte, Janice Garrett 273, 544, 547, 549-50, 560
Foster, Leland 94
Foster, Madison 89-91

Fountaine, Gwen xiii, xvi, 397-98, 402, 428, 442 (see also Gwen Newton)
Framing the Black Panthers 515
Franklin, Aretha 183, 446
Franklin, Clarence 183
Frazee, Sara xv, 450 "Free Huey" Movement 277, 279, 284, 342, 368, 376-77, 381, 446, 457
Free Huey! 417 (see also Ed Keating)
Free Speech Movement (FSM) 233, 237, 374
Freed, Donald 375
Freedom Riders 241
Frey, John 1-5, 256, 274, 299-300, 334, 478, 501-02 521 (see also *People v. Newton*)
Friedman, Monroe 2, 3, VIII *passim*, 359-60, 383
Fugitive Slave Law 134

G

Gain, Charles 332, 338, 356-57
Garry, Charles 273, VIII, *passim*; 381-85, 504
Gatling, Debra Godfrey xiii, (see Debra Godfrey)
George, John 265
Gibson, Josh
Ginger, Ann Fagan 349-50 (see also *Minimizing Racism in Jury Trials*)
Gingrich, Newt 433
Godfrey, Debra xiii, 190-91; 400
Godfrey, Doris Newton xiii, 6, 175-76, 400 and Stella and Armelia; funeral 177-78; and the Lamp Post 447-48; at Martin Luther King speech 216-17, photo 389, 431 (see also **Doris Newton**)
Godfrey, Glen xiii, 175-76, 178-79, 400
Godfrey, Glen ("Ricky") xiii, 188
Godfrey, Kathy xiii, 190-91, 400
Goodlett, Carlton 258, 264
Grapes of Wrath, The 125
Great Migration, The 27, 122, 126, 142, 146
Green Book, The 124, 126
Greenlee, Rush 300, 326-27, 345, 546-49
Gregory, Dick 392

Grier, Henry 298, 303, 309, 314, 331, 335-42, 349, 383, 416
Griot, Griotte 178-80
Grove Street Orators 236
Guevara, Ernesto "Che" 210

H

Haley, Harold 395
Hampton, Fred 456, 378-79
Harmony Club 89-91
Harper, David 22, 94, 295-96, 312, 317, 325, 339, 343, 345-347, 401 (photos 296, 404) (see also Newton jury)
Hasan, Anwar 232=33
Hayes, Chris 29
Heanes, Herbert "Cliff" 1, 3- 4, 298-303, 331, 334-36, 342, 346, 478, 491
Henderson, Thelton 213, 319, 339
Hernandez, Veronica xv, 450
Hill, Warner Washington 88-91
Hilliard, Alice x, 13-14, 22, 451 (see also **Alice Newton, Alice Carter**}
Hilliard, David *passim Introduction, VI, VIII, IX, XII;* Cleaver-Newton split 408; co-creating Huey P. Newton Foundation 519 ; effect of Emmett Till's murder 197 ; expulsion from BPP 440; on *Face the Naton* 392; FBI protection strategy 412; Huey's release from jail 382, 397; Huey's biography 516; Huey's funeral 497; myth re Huey 512-14; investigation of Huey's death 492-95; marriage 222-23; meeting Huey 200 ; plans for Revolutionary People's Constitutional Convention 396-97; threat to President Nixon 415
Hilliard, Walter x, 14 (see also **Walter Newton**)
Hilton, Jacqueline Cliffortene 80, 99
Hoffman, Abbie 344
Hoffmann, Alex 271, 304, 344, 349, 366, 383, 386-87, 395, 399
Holiday, Billie 99,152
Hoover, J. Edgar 371, 375, 377-78, 398, 414, 422
Horowitz, David 455, 459, 466
Hove, Harold 386

Huggins, Ericka 377, 381, 413, 456, 464, 466
Huey P. Newton Foundation 18, 519-28
Huey P. Newton Story, A 516
Huey P. Newton Youth Institute 465
Huey: Spirit of the Panther 516
Huggins, John 371, 376, 456
Hughes, Langston 170
Hunter, Clementine, 103-06
Huston Plan, The 455, 474
Hutton, Bobby 242, 278-80, 284, 357, 369-70, 415, 519

I

International Labor Defense Committee (ILD) 263
In the Crosshairs (see *American Justice on Trial*) 526

J

Jackson, Alice xv, 450
Jackson, Andrew 14
Jackson, George 377, 380, 393-95, 418-21, 471, 495, 505
Jackson, Jonathan 394-95, 420, 425
Jenkins, Harold "Slim" 151-52
Jensen, D. Lowell VIII *passim*; District Attorney 417-18, 425, 464; Federal Judge 502; Newton sentencing hearing 360; Newton release on bond 386; Newton appeal 381-83; Oakland Seven case 372
Jim Crow 21, 37, 49, 86, 135
Johnson, Armelia xii, ancestry 33-35; childhood 38, 49, 52; meeting Walter Newton 32 (see also **Armelia Newton**)
Johnson, Estella xii, ("Mama Stella", "Muzz") II *passi*m; in Arkansas 52 ; 62-63; and brother Isaac; death 400; laundry work 84; marriage of Armelia and Walter 56; and grandchildren 83, 118-19, 155, 357, 401; death 400; photo 117; visit to California 176 (see also **Estella O'Neal**)
Johnson, Jack 39-41
Johnson, John xii, 33, 35 ,37-51, 52-59, 62-63, 92
Johnson, Jessie Mae xii-xiii, 41, 9, 63, 66, 118, 128 (see also **Jessie Ento, Jessie Smith**)
Johnson, Kim xiv, 463
Johnson, Leola xiv, (see also **Leola Carr, Leola Newton**)
Johnson, Lyndon 72, 252, 277-78, 332, 545
Johnson, Orell xiii, 41, 49, 226-27 (see also **Orell Woods**)
Johnson Ozell xiii, 41, 49, 226-27 (see also **Ozell Ward**)
Johnson, Patricia xiv, (see also Patricia Seymour) 243, 400-01
Johnson, Steve xvi, 243
Jones, Charles "Raincoat" 151-52
Judenordnung 25
Juneteenth Day 251-52

K

Kamiya' Gary 139
Kammerknechte 25
Kansas City Monarchs 92
Karenga, Maulana Ron 371
Keating, Ed 291, 341, 417
Kelley, Ken 504-05
Kennedy, Robert 280
Kerner Report, The 55, 276-77, 290, 336
King, Coretta Scott 438
King, Dana 520-22
King, Martin Luther Jr. 162, 215, 238, 240, 276, 446
Knowland, William 149-50, 152, 173, 493
Koonan, Karen Jo 293
Korean War 200
KPFA 344, 395, 498
Ku Klux Klan (KKK) 21, 25, 46, 72, 84, 146-49

L

Lamp Post 427-29, 431-32, 442, 448-49, 454, 497
Lane, Mark 384, 399
Lawson, Ruby Jewel xiii, 66, 118, 154, 181, 188, 401
Lee, Barbara 439, 519
Lee, Odell 217, -20, 230, 311, 325
Lee, Spike 516
Lee, Zeke 80, 99
Lepore, Jill 12-13

LIFE magazine 198, 285-86, 292, 300, 350
Little Black Sambo 169-70
Long, Huey Pierce ('The Kingfish") 69-72, 496
Lovejoy, Elijah Parish 15
Lumpenproletariat 239
Lyceum Theater 39, 86

M

March Against Fear 241
Mandela, Nelson 94, 518
Mann Act 41,
Marshall, Thurgood 140-41
Martin, Waldo 515
Marx, Karl 239
McCarthy Era 265
McKinney, Gene 254, 256, 310, 313, 322
Meehan, Jack 502
Meese, Ed 235
Melton, John 73, 123-24
Merritt College (see also Oakland City College) 209, 364, 373, 432-34 436, 470, 499, 507, 516, 523
Minimizing Racism in Jury Trials 350
Miranda v. Arizona 544
Miranda rights 243
Mississippi Flood of 1927 57,83
Mitchell, Rudolph 487
Monroe, Louisiana 33-52, 83-96
Monroe Colored High School 83, 89, 115, 222
Monroe Monarchs 92-96
Monroe Twins 92
Moore, Gilbert 285-86, 292, 300, 312, 335, 340, 346, 350-52, 401, 484
Mount Nebo Missionary Babtist Church 41
Mount Nebo Church School 99
Mule trade 25-27
Murray, George Mason 371
Myrdal, Gunner 136

N

Napier, Sam 409, 465
Nation, The 375
National Guardsmen 262, 277, 285, 332, 338, 341, 358, 382
National Lawyers Guild 350; S.F. Branch 264, 305, 349, 379

National States Rights Party 228
Nation of Islam 238-41, 253, 433
Neal, Kathleen 266, 269
Negrito, Fantastic 520
Neil, Earl 287, 297, 347-48, 359, 500
Nelson, Stanley vii, 518
New Left 465
Newton, Alice x, 22-23, 56, 59, 113, 115, 400-01, 452, 479 (see also **Alice Hilliard, Alice Carter**)
Newton, Andre xv, 449
Newton, Antoine xiv
Newton, Armelia Johnson xii, *passim* Introduction, II-XI; Arkansas 52-59, and Barbarette 480; in Bastrop 74-82, and extended family 183, 223, 405, 479-80 ; Huey's arrest and trial 255-58, 271; Huey distancing 436-37; ; at Huey's sentencing hearing 359-61; last years 479-82; matriarch 175-76, 227; meeting and marriage to Walter Newton 55-56; move to Oakland, California; in Oak Grove, Oakland Auditorium speech 273; photos 167, 275; post-trial visit with David Harper 401; in West Monroe 65. (See also **Armelia Johnson**)
Newton, Armelia (Lee Edward's daughter) xiv, 188-89, 445, 449, 457, 481
Newton, Barbarette Alcorn xv, 363, 436, 451, 479, 516-17, background 363; and her children 451, 516; community involvement 516; death and memorial 516-17; death of ex-husband 449-50; and extended family 479; and Armelia Newton 405, 475, 480; and Huey Newton 402, 405-06, 410-12, 437,436, 483-85; marriage to Melvin 98, 450-51, 483-86; meeting Melvin 364-66; Walter Newton 405, 446; photo 365; 30th high school reunion 503; visit with Alice Carter 401(see also **Billy Maurice Alcorn, Maurice Newton and Melvin Newton**)
Newton, Ben x, 22-23
Newton, Benjamin x, 23
Newton, Brianna, xv, 482-83

Newton, David Lautaro xv, at Aunt Doris's funeral 178-79; ; childhood 476, 483-85; DNA test 23; last visit with grandmother Armelia 480; and mother Barbarette Newton 451, 516; photos 476, 511; with Uncle Huey 476, 483-85

Newton, Demetrius xv, 449

Newton, Doris xiii, birth 75, 77; childhood 55-57,62-63,97-100; Bastrop; Oak Grove109 and the Simmons family 113, 115; high school 169; staying with Muzz 118,19; move to California 128-29, 176. (see also **Doris Godfrey**)

Newton, Earl xv, 97

Newton, Earl xv, ("Jake") 541

Newton, E.S. x, 23, 65-66, 86, 96, 401, 447

Newton, Fredrika Slaughter xiii, xvi background 480-81; and Huey P. Newton Foundation 513, 519-21, 527-28 ; marriage to Huey 469, 480-84; 488, 490-91, 494; Huey's funeral 497; Revolutionary Suicide (2009) 6 ; Robinson's parole hearing 505-06 (see also **Fredrika Slaughter**)

Newton, Gregory xiii, grandparents 177, 224, and grandparents 443-44; 447, 451; childhood 242, 363-64, 402-03, and Godmother Aunt Leola 408, 429; ; and Oakland Community School 465-66, 467; Uncle Huey 461-62; Oakland Community School 465-66, 467; 483; photo 511; *Up Jumps the Monkey* 507-09 (see also **Barbarette Newton, Joyce Newton and Melvin Newton**)

Newton, Gwen Fountaine xiii, xvi, 454, 458, 460-61, 465, 468, 477, 479 (see also **Gwen Fountaine**)

Newton, Huey xiii, *passim*; Beatnik phase 209-10; birth and outdooring ceremony 110-12; BPP newspaper; BPP Sacramento debut 246-50; bust unveiling 520-23 (photo); Cuban exile 442,454; death 491; on death row 268-69; Denzil Dowell shooting 246-47; funeral 496-501; hammer incident 202-04; Bobby Hutton 242, 279-80; impact 515-18 international reputation 380; Odell Lee incident 217-21; marriage to Fredrika 469, 480-84, 488, 490-91, 494; lessons from Melvin 205-07; marriage to Gwen 454, 458; Merritt College; myth 512-14; Oakland Community School 465-67; Peace and Freedom Party candidate for Congress 437; PhD.470-76,521; photos x, 158, 208, 389, 430, 476; prodigal son 444-445; Red China visit 422-23; relationships with nieces and nephews 468-69, 476 ; release from prison 386-89; retrials for Frey's death 416-17; sentencing hearing 359-61; solitary confinement 230-34,363-64; the Squad 425-26; and Esther Smith White 222-24; threatening Melvin 435-36; train to California 155-59; writings 1-6, 323-24, 439, 470-76, 521

Newton, Jessica xiii, 460, 468-69, 477

Newton, Joyce xv-xvi, and the BPP 242, 428-29; and her children 402-03, 447, 451, 509 ; Huey's letter on news Joyce and Melvin were expecting 509; Huey's murder arrest 255, 266; and the Lamp Post 428-29 , 447; marriage to Melvin 222-24; separation and divorce from Melvin 364, 402-03, 447; meeting Esther White and her son Trasean 407; relationship with Newton Family 482. 3oth high school reunion 503 (see also **Joyce Thomas**)

Newton jury (1968) VIII *passim*, deliberations 338-44; pivotal moments 2-5, selection of 290-95; verdict 345-53; (see also David Harper)

Newton, Lamont xiv 188; 445

Newton, Lee Edward, "Brotha") xiv, III, IV *passim;* with Richard Aoki 238; birth 59; and daughter Esther Lee Smith 115-16, 182, 222; Cleaster Simmons and the Simmons family 113-16; job

115; move to San Mateo County 211; and Huey's parting gift 490; Melvin's job help 211; at family gatherings 191, 227; photos 102, 114, 431; siblings' self-defense instructor 107, 509
Newton, Leola xiv, III –IV *passim*; birth 65, living with Muzz 155; work stories 177; at the Lamp Post ; the 1968 trial 265; photo 431; visiting Huey in jail 232
Newton, Lucie 21-22
Newton, Maurice xv, 451, 457, 460-61, 465, 467-68, 475, 483, 496; photo 511, 517 (see also Maurice Alcorn)
Newton, Melvin David, vi, ix, xv, *passim;* African roots 12; asthma source 100; birth 76; Bastrop 76-82; BPP 10 point program creation 242; book dedication vi; falling out with Huey 435-36; and FBI; falling out with Myrtle 482; foreword ix; ; fund-raising for Huey's defense; growing up in Oakland 163-163; Huey's funeral; Bobby Hutton eulogy 279-80; Huey's impact 501; inspiration for Huey 509; Lamp Post 427-29, 436, 448; marriage to Barbarette Alcorn 405-06, 449-51; marriage to Joyce Thomas 222-23; Merritt College 432-34; move to Oakland 155-59; photos 159, 365, 404, 430-31, 511, 526; search for Huey's killer; Southern adventure with Huey 410-12; 424; split in family 447-51; testifying at Huey's trial 329; unveiling of Huey's bust 519-23; visiting Huey in jail 232, 268, 362-66; on West Oakland ghetto 150
Newton, Melvin Lee x, 23, 59
Newton, Myesha xv, 449, 479 (see also Sara Frazee)
Newton, Myrtle xiv, III, IV *passim;* birth 59; , move to California 155-59; childhood 64-65, mother's helper 100 and the Simmons family 113, 115; settling in Oakland 162-63; photo 431(see also Myrtle Seymour)

Newton, Ronnie xiii, 460, 477, 520-21
Newton, Sonny Man xv, (see Walter Newton, Jr.)
Newton, Tracy xv, and Aunt Doris 178; 429, and grandparents 443-44, and father Melvin Newton 402; and Barbarette Newton 451; and mother Joyce Newton 402-03, 447, 451; photo 511; and Uncle Huey 460-62; 467-68, 483, 495; and Trasean White 406-08; (see also **Barbarette Newton, Joyce Newton, Gregory Newton, Melvin Newton**)
Newton, Valencia xv, 449
Newton, Walter x-xi, *passim* I, III-VI, birth 22, father 22-28 ; hobo days 29-31; Huey's arrest 255-58; meeting Armelia 55-56; life under the Kingfish 69-72; move to CA 136-44; photos 102, 145, 167; prodigal son 266, 445-46 ; patriarch 175-76, 227; on Barbarette 405; funeral 445-46; role model for Huey 509
Newton, Walter, Jr. ("Sonny Man") xv, IV *passim*; Richard Aoki friendship 238; birth 65-66; Huey's outdooring ceremony 110-12; living with Muzz 115; living with Uncle Issac 155; Oakland Tech 169; purchase of Newton home 185-86; at family gatherings 193, 226, 407, 481; Lamp Post 428; children 449, 479; Newton trial 287-88, 291; photo 186; Huey's parting gift 490.
Nixon, Richard 368, 374, 378-82, 397, 414, 423, 455, 474
Northrup, Solomon 134

O

Oakland City College 202, 205, 209, 224, 235, 238, 315, 364, 373, 434 (see also Merritt College)
Oakland Museum of California 517
Oakland NAACP 173-74
Oakland 1943 Race Riot 143-44
Oakland 1946 Walkout 172

Oakland Police Department (OPD) 185, 357, 521
Oakland Police Officers Association 358
Oakland Post, The 306
Oakland Seven 372
Oakland Tribune 149-50, 173, 285, 464, 493
Om Lovers 210
O'Neal, Estella Johnson xii (see Estella Johnson)
100 Men Hall Blues Club 98-99
Origin of the Species, The 108
Orloff, Thomas 464, 493
Ouachita Parish 64
Outdooring Ceremony 110-12

P

Panther Bill 251
Panthers (see Black Panther Party)
Paramount Theater 86-87
Parkdale, Arkansas 28, 55-59, 152
Patterson, William 258, 260, 262-65 (American Communist Party)
Patterson, William "Bill" 344, 458, 525 (Oakland NAACP leader)
Paul, Pamela 524
Payton, Brenda 497
Peace and Freedom Party 437
People v. Hall 133
People v. Newton 283-352
People's Park 374
Phi Beta Sigma
Pinchback, P.B.S. 37
Pfaelzer, Jean *131*
Plato's Republic 206-07
Platt, Tony 132-33
Plummer, Charlie 491
Poitier, Sidney 278
Port Chicago 140-41
Portland, Arkansas 58
Pratt, Elmer "Geronimo" Ji Jaga 386, 387, 394, 414, 487-88
Price, Victoria 261
Proposition 14 228, 290
Pullman, George 127
Pullman Porters 147-48, 151-52

Q

R

Ramparts magazine *246-47, 291, 325, 362, 417, 466*
RAM (Revolutionary Action Movement) 236
Randolph, A. Philip 127
Reading, John 344, 438
Reagan, Ronald 235, 252, 269, 368, 370, 374, 498, 502
Reconstruction Era 11, 19, 25, 37, 54, 92
Red Scare 47
Red Squad 425
Red Summer of 1919 45-48, 374
Revolutionary People's Constitutional Convention 392
Revolutionary Suicide 1, 5, 528
Rhodes, Jayne 515, 518
Rhomberg, Chris 517-18
Rishell, Clifford 184
Robinson, Lucy Newton xvi, 496
Robinson, Tyrone 494-95, 501-06, 513, 519
Roosevelt, Franklin 69, 127, 128, 140, 152
Ross, Dell 298, 305, 310, 383
Rubin, Jerry 344, 549
Rumford, William Byron 137, 139, 142, 227-28

S

Sacco, Nicola 263, 264
Saint Augustine's Episcopal Church 287, 395, 420
Sanchez, Timothy 477-78
San Francisco Lawyers Guild (see Nat'l Lawyers Guild)
San Francisco State College 370
Sanger, Margaret 71
San Francisco Sun Reporter 258 (see also Carlton Goodlett)
San Quentin 268-69, 393-94, 418, 420, 465, 471, 486-88, 495
Schaaf, Libby 520-21
Scheck, Barry 311, 319, 351, 346
Schneider, Bert 397, 420, 458, 490
Scopes "Monkey" trial 108
Scottsboro Boys 28, 259-64
Seale, Bobby *passim* VII-IX; 16-17 background 235-36; international reputation 380; military expe-

rience 235; falling out with Huey Newton; exile; Merritt College; Sacramento debut 246-50; re-uniting with Huey 1971 413—14; candidate for Oakland Mayor 438; Huey's funeral 497-99,509; Chicago Eight 331, 376-77
Seale, Thelma (Bobby Seale's mother) 46
Seymour, James xiv,176, 181
Seymour, "Little Jimmie" xiv, 428-29
Seymour, Myrtle Newton xiv, 181, 187-90, 202, 204, 209, 226, 257, 263, 386, 400-03
Seymour, Patricia xiv, 176, 187, 444, 482 (see also **Patricia Johnson**)
Sharp, Joseph 67
Simmons, Cleaster xiv,113-16
Simmons, Ruth 523-24
Simon, Elias 25
Simon, Joseph 23-27
Simon, Solomon xi, 25-28, 521
Slaughter, Arlene 480
Slaughter, Fredrika xiii, xvi, 497(see also Fredrika Slaughter Newton)
Slaughter, Kieron xiii, 490, 497
Slaves in the Family 17
Smith, Arthur 80
Smith, Bertha 80
Smith, Esther Lee xiv-xv, 115-16 (see also **Esther White**)
Smith, Jessie xii, (See **Jessie Mae Johnson, Jessie Mae Ento**)
Smith, Kathleen 441, 458, 464
Smith, Tommie 367
SNCC (Student Nonviolent Coordinating Committee) 240-41, 272-74, 285, 321, 363, 412
Soledad Brother: The Prison Letters of George Jackson 380
Soledad Brothers 380, 387, 393-94, 416, 420
Song of the South 170
Soul on Ice 246-47
Soul Students Advisory Council 237
Southern Christian Leadership Conference *240*
Southern Horrors: Lynch Law in all its Phases 19
Spanish Flu 52

Squad, The 425-26, 460 (see also Buddha Samurai)
Steelman, John 54
Steinbeck, John 125
Steinem, Gloria 17
Stender, Fay VIII, IX passim; assailant Edward Brooks 471-72, 495; distancing by Huey 397, 416, 435, 470; firing by George Jackson 418 470; international fame 393; meeting Huey 268, Soledad Brothers 380, 387, 393-94, 416, 420; suicide 471; targeted by Black Guerilla Family (BGF) 471-72, 491, 495 (see also Charles Garry, George Jackson)
Stop the Draft Week 253, 372
Stoval, Fred 94-96
Student Nonviolent Coordinating Committee (See SNCC)
Sutherland, Donald 392

T

Testimony Exclusion Laws of 1850 132-33
13th Amendment 11,19, 135
Thomas, Joyce xv- xvi, 222 (see Joyce Newton)
Thomas, J.L. 153
Thompson, Elsa Knight 344-45, 387, 395
Thorne, Richard (William Brumfield) 210-11
Till, Emmett 196-99
To Die for the People 438
Treuhaft, Robert 265, 437
Truman, Harry 54, 142, 168,
Tse-Tung, Mao 423
Ture, Kwame (see Stokely Carmichael)
Turner, Morrie 148, 185
Turner, Nat 508
Twelve Years a Slave 134

U

Uncle Remus 170
Uniontown Alabama 9-11, 22, 25, 28, 451
Unruh Act 375
Up Jumps the Monkey 507-10

US 371 (see also Maulana Ron Karenga)

V

Van Patter, Betty Louise 454-55, 459, 505
Vanzetti, Bartolomeo 263-64 (see also Nicola Sacco)
Vesey, Denmark 508
Vietnam War 216-17, 237, 253, 323, 332, 371-72, 376-77, 382

W

Wagner, Alfons 504
Wallace, George 368
Walton, Brian 503
War Against the Panthers 414, 472
Ward, Annie Mae xiii
Ward, "Big Jimmie" xiii, xv, 428, 482, 497
Ward, Jack xiii
Ward, Opal Mae xiii
Ward, Ozell xv, (see **Ozell Johnson**)
Warden, Donald 213, 218
Warren, Earl 243, 293
Wells, Ida B. 19-20, 47
Wells, James 19
West Monroe 64-66
White Citizens Councils 228
White, Clinton 265, 361
White, Esther Smith xiv-xv, 222-225, 227, 243, 406=07, 482 (see also **Esther Smith**)
White, Lennon xv-xvi, 222, 224-25, 243-44
White, Tony xv, 222
White, Tonja xv, 222
White, Trasean xv, 407-08
Whyte, Donald 416-17, 424
Wilkins, Roy 456
Williams, LaVerne 242, 265, 287, 302
Williams, Robert 236
Wilson, Lionel 240, 457-58, 497
Wilson, Woodrow 31, 450
Witherspoon v. Illinois 293
Wolf-Goldsmith, Rachel 520
Woods, Jake Jr. xiii, 226
Woods, Jake Sr. xiii
Woods, Berniece xiii
Woods, Clyde xiii
Woods, Edward Lee xiii
Woods, Estella xiii
Woods, Glinda xiii
Woods, John xiii
Woods, Linda xiii
Woods, Orell xiii (See **Orell Johnson**)
Woods, Roy Lee xiii
Woods, Shirley xiii
Woodville, Alabama 14, 25 (see Uniontown)
World War I 30, 151-52
World War II 16, 122, 127-28, 139-40, 148-49, 168, 171, 238, 254, 276, 336, 344, 364
Wretched of the Earth, The (see also Frantz Fanon) 237, 239

X

X, Malcolm 238

Y

Yacovone, Donald 15-16
Yat-sen, Sun 457
Yippies 344 (see also Abbie Hoffman, Jerry Rubin)

Z

Zion Travel Baptist Church 88-91
Zoot Suit Riot 143

Acknowledgments

Most of all, I want to thank Melvin, David Lautaro and Tracy Newton for inviting me to undertake this book and providing me with their recollections and family photos. My deep appreciation also to Gregory and Maurice Newton for sharing their memories and providing me with materials, to the late Doris Newton Godfrey for having shared her own colorful memories of her childhood and all the others in the Newton family who gave of their time as sources for this book. Thanks also to David Hilliard for sharing his memories as a close friend of the family. Tremendous appreciation to Harry Simon and Jon Simon Sager for their insights about the history of the Simon family. Special thanks to my extraordinary editor Dan White (author of *The Cactus Eaters: How I Lost My Mind and Almost Found Myself on the Pacific Coast Trail*, and *Under the Stars: How America Fell in Love with Camping*), to Mark Weiman of Regent Press and to Emily Burch Wollenweber for her work on the book's covers. Thanks as well to Andrew Abrahams and Open Eye Pictures, Inc. for allowing me to use excerpts from transcripts of filmed interviews and a photo of Melvin Newton from the documentary *American Justice on Trial: People v. Newton* [recently reissued under the title In the Crosshairs, www.justicemovie.com]. Thanks again — always — to my daughter Jamie Benvenutti for her amazing research assistance and accompanying me on a memorable day trip for background research in Monroe,

Louisiana, to my daughter Mali Benvenutti for her invaluable technical assistance, my sister Leslie Pearlman for her proofreading skills and editing suggestions, to Melvin Newton for all of his editing and proofreading diligence on top of everything else he contributed, and my husband Peter Benvenutti, for his editorial prowess and for being a constant source of excellent advice and support as I launched and completed this project.

www.ingramcontent.com/pod-product-compliance
Lightning Source LLC
Chambersburg PA
CBHW030507080526
44586CB00011B/97